THE
TWILIGHT
BEFORE
THE STORM

ADVANCE PRAISE

"Viktor Shvets's new book is a must read for those trying to understand the rapidly developing change in the relationships between labor, capital, and the state. What role for markets in this new world of state activism? What are the consequences for politics, societies, and economies? Viktor asks all the right questions in this book, and he provides answers based upon a deep understanding of financial and economic history that enlighten, educate, and frighten in perhaps equal measure."

RUSSELL NAPIER, Independent Investment Strategist and author of *Anatomy of The Bear: Lessons From Wall Street's Four Great Bottoms* and *The Asian Financial Crisis 1995-1998: Birth of the Age of Debt*

FROM THE FRACTURED 1930s
TO TODAY'S CRISIS CULTURE

THE
TWILIGHT
BEFORE
THE STORM

How to Avoid a World on Fire

VIKTOR SHVETS

Boyle
&
Dalton

Book design and production by Boyle & Dalton
www.BoyleandDalton.com

Paperback ISBN: 978-1-63337-825-4
Hardcover ISBN: 978-1-63337-826-1
E-book ISBN: 978-1-63337-827-8

Manufactured and printed in the United States of America

CONTENTS

PROLOGUE

"Twilight—a time of pause when nature changes her mind. All living things would fade and die from too much light or too much dark, if twilight were not."
Howard Thurman[1]

On April 30, 1939, the New York World's Fair was officially opened. Following in the footsteps of the highly successful Chicago Fair of 1933–34, it aimed high in every respect, from the quality of exhibits and upbeat futuristic message to outrageously high costs and innovative financing. Ironically, it was the communist Joseph Stalin who was the first to pay (four million dollars) for a prime location at the fair, with organizers then convincing Benito Mussolini to also profile fascism by spending five million dollars for another prime spot.[2] Eventually more than sixty countries were willing to pay for the privilege to be at the fair, investing around $30 million. This was in addition to many corporations, from General Motors and General Electric to DuPont and Westinghouse. While today, there is nothing unusual about soliciting funds and sponsors, at that time, the New York World's Fair approach was unique. Even with such extensive sponsorships, investors barely recovered 50 cents in a dollar. Although high operating costs played a role, organizers also encountered unique challenges that were not present at the Chicago Fair, not the least of which was the onset of the Second World War. By the time the fair closed in October 1940, more than a dozen countries had disappeared from the map.

While organizers aimed to look toward the future with the theme "The World of Tomorrow," history intervened in most unexpected and disruptive ways. Many exhibiting nations that were swallowed and/or partitioned by Nazi Germany and the Soviet Union, never left the fair.

Some of the best French chefs from their country's pavilion stayed behind, and today's Le Pavilion restaurant in New York is the transplant from the French pavilion at the fair. The Polish pavilion remained defiantly open, though its buildings were draped in black. Ultimately the Polish government-in-exile sold it to Chicago, where it survives as the Polish Museum of America, and the statue of the medieval Polish-Lithuanian King Jagiełło continues to grace New York's Central Park. Other exhibits were sold to cities and university campuses across the country.[3] The fair was also rocked by terror threats, reflecting the violence that was starting to engulf the world, as well as numerous other issues that were destined to become far more prominent in decades ahead, such as anti-colonialism and the future of the Middle East. For instance, the Palestinian exhibit— for the first time—attempted to articulate what the future of the Jewish homeland might look like.

At the heart of the fair were two futuristic structures: Trylon and Perisphere. The Perisphere was a giant 180-foot sphere connected to the 610-foot spire-shaped Trylon by the world's longest escalator. Inside the sphere, visitors were transported by a moving sidewalk, marveling at a slideshow projected onto the dome of the sphere that depicted the city of the future. Just behind the Trylon and the Perisphere lay a free space called the "Court of Peace." It was originally designed to showcase different cultures, cuisines, and costumes, with Fiorello La Guardia, New York's mayor, opening it by releasing 500 white doves of peace. Unfortunately, as global tensions escalated, the Court of Peace morphed into a place of clashes, political debates, and protests. Albert Einstein was a frequent visitor, warning that "much blood will yet have to be spilled."[4]

Despite the specter of war, today the fair is mostly remembered for its uncannily accurate predictions of the future. The exhibits profiled a range of new technologies, with some having their first ever public debut. The entire fair was lit up with fluorescent lighting of many colors supplied by General Electric and Westinghouse—lighting that had only been invented a year before the fair. DuPont had an amazing chemistry exhibition, most memorably introducing nylon, including nylon stockings. Dishwashers and air conditioners were introduced by General Electric, while Packard debuted air conditioners for cars. RCA unveiled the first ever fax machine (not commercialized until the mid-1960s), while Kodak introduced color photography (not commercialized until the late 1950s). Television was a popular feature at the fair, with FDR being the first president to use television for the opening address. Unfortunately, at that time, there were only a few hundred television sets in New York, with none working terribly well. It was not until the early 1950s that television truly proliferated across the country. However, the most popular exhibition was one by General Motors called "Futurama." Laid out on a one-acre site, it presented the future of American cities and transportation, including mockups of modern housing with new appliances, suburbia, and interstate highways connecting the country from Atlantic to Pacific—something that did not become reality until the late 1950s to the early 1960s.

The fair conveyed a hopeful message that the future would be brighter and better, and that the turmoil of the 1930s would fade into history. Indeed, cohorts born between the early 1900s and early 1940s (conventionally labeled as "Silent" and the tail end of "GI" generations) were destined to build that brighter and better world through the 1950s and 1960s.

But all of that lay in the future. In 1939, the world was being reshaped and convulsed by those deeply traumatized by the Great Depression, the Dust Bowl, and the poisonous legacy of the unresolved Great War. A young American man who was interviewed in the dark days of 1932–33, perfectly captured the zeitgeist of the troubled 1930s when he said, "If someone came along with a line of stuff in which I could really believe, I would follow him pretty much anywhere."[5] That poor young man was ready to accept almost anything. These were times that shook to the core the foundations upon which people depended to define themselves and their societies, with deeply cherished and widely held views mercilessly crushed in a matter of months. These included many quintessential American values: the belief that ambition, hard work, and loyalty is bound to bring personal success; that college graduates could pretty much get any job they wanted; that banks and corporations could be trusted to do the right thing; that outside of a few distressed communities, poverty was mostly due to incompetence, laziness, or misfortune; that the role of the government was not to directly help people, but rather to foster and protect free spirit to enable capitalism to navigate intermittent bumps in the road. As described by Philipp Blom, people started to ask a question: "How do I live in a world with values and ideas that have suddenly become discredited."[6] The Depression, followed by the Dust Bowl, changed everything, from social manners and skirt hemlines to working conditions and the role of the government, and what societies expected from the state.

The defeated President Herbert Hoover (1929–1933) could barely comprehend the seismic shifts suddenly remaking his country. To the end he believed that "Economic depression cannot be cured by legislative action or executive pronouncement. Economic wounds must be healed by the action of the cells of the economic body—the producers and consumers themselves." Although far from economically illiterate or ignorant, he continued to hold on to the traditional liberal ideas of self-help and initiative rather than what he perceived to be "soul destroying" government handouts. Hence, he was always willing to help farmers feed their animals but not their starving children, who, in his view, needed to be encouraged to be self-reliant, or at extreme, to be supported by the charity and the goodwill of fellow Americans, but not the government. Although Hoover launched a number of programs that were later formalized and expanded by the next administration, he never fully accepted that the private sector could be wrong or that free markets are just as susceptible as the government to inefficiencies and misallocation of resources.[7] He also never accepted that laissez-faire policies might fatally destabilize societies. In 1933, FDR's New Deal ushered in a new chapter, and the roaring 1920s were suddenly replaced by a deep loss of almost everything that most people held dear. The inevitable disorientation created such deep tissue scarring that it profoundly transformed societal consensus, casting a long shadow well into the 1950s and 1960s.

Dislocations caused by the Great Depression were even deeper and more disruptive outside of the US, especially in France, Germany, and

Austria, where rapid rise in unemployment and re-emergence of extreme poverty were greatly magnified by the demographic, emotional, and national honor legacy of the Great War. The disappearance of an entire generation of men (killed or maimed during the meat grinder stalemate of 1915–1918[8]); psychological and emotional traumas; upending of the traditional social class hierarchy; collapse in fertility rates; hyperinflations and deflations; lack of resolution of issues that led to the Great War; injury to the national honor in Germany; and the collapse of the Austrian-Hungarian empire created a highly polarized and disorienting environment. While the situation in Bolshevik Russia was radically different, Stalin's reign of terror, debilitating collectivization of the early 1930s, accompanied by widespread hunger, and forced inhuman industrialization had equally brutalized the Soviet society.

The 1930s was a time when people were willing to entertain extreme views and accept what in the past would have been considered unacceptable answers to their mounting problems. This was a period when Hitler, Mussolini, Stalin, and Franco had either come to power or significantly strengthened their rule. It was also a decade that witnessed militarization of Japan, collapse of liberal experiments in China, and the beginning of Mao's long and bloody march to power. Even in established democracies, such as France, the political climate became almost ungovernable, with waves of labor protests and strikes driving rapid shifts between left- and right-wing governments. In the US, it was the time of populists and demagogues. From Huey Long and Father Charles Coughlin to Upton Sinclair and the KKK. Even Communists and Fascist veterans found fertile ground, threatening to upend social and economic order. Indeed, if it was not for FDR's New Deal and occasional luck (e.g. Huey Long's assassination in 1935), they might have succeeded.

As in Van Gogh's twilight paintings, the 1930s could be best thought of as a time when nature changed its mind, germinating a new order. The searing experience of the 1930s led not only to the destruction, death, and the "world on fire" of the 1940s, but also to the beatniks, hippies, yippies, and yuppies of the 1950s–70s; sexual, gender, social, and racial revolutions that altered our societies through the 1960s–80s; and ultimately even to the finance and the Information Age revolutions that have been reshaping our lives over the last three decades.

My objective is to examine positive and negative consequences of these decades, and most importantly, argue that similar disorientation and polarization that afflicted societies in the 1930s–40s are today once again convulsing almost every country on earth, driven by similar underlying forces. The question this book addresses is: What are those forces, and can we master them better than our ancestors could?

The anthem "Dawn of a New Day" (the last piece of music composed by George Gershwin) was played across most places at the Fair.[9] However, instead of a new day, almost 45 million visitors who thronged to the New York Fair were staring at an unimaginable abyss. Within years, the futuristic Trylon and Perisphere that overlooked the Court of Peace were razed, their metal used to fight the war. Today, we stand in a place not so different from those who visited the fair almost ninety years ago. Will we be able to avoid their terrible fate?

• • •

A recent opinion piece in the *Atlantic* magazine asked, "Why America Abandoned the Greatest Economy in History."[10] The article referred to the miracle of the 1950s and 1960s, which in the US and most other western nations is invariably described as the glorious decades. It was a time when the word miracle was casually used to describe the economic progress and rapid, near-miraculous rebuilding of politics and societies destroyed over the course of the Second World War. There were German and Italian miracles, France's glorious decades, and the best economy ever in the US. This period featured the fastest ever productivity growth, the creation of the greatest ever middle class, steep declines in income and wealth inequalities, nearly unimaginable improvements in healthcare and life expectancy, and an equally dramatic change in lifestyle and educational opportunities. While nowhere near as good, even in the Communist controlled East, these were the best of times.

This is not to say that there were no challenges—from racial and gender inequality to liberation wars and an ever-present specter of nuclear holocaust. These decades were also far from economically and socially liberal. However, generations who suffered so much through the 1930s and '40s were willing to make compromises, sacrificing some of their freedoms by agreeing to stricter societal and moral rules and consenting to tighter curbs on capitalism. They viewed governments as the only meaningful guardrail against chaos, which they were afraid could at any time engulf their lives once again. A great deal of emphasis in this era was placed not only on conformity and the stabilizing role of the state, but also on a popular demand that corporations, banks, and the private sector act for the benefit of broader societies, not just profits.

This consensus that had emerged in the late 1940s remained largely undisturbed until the late 1960s and early 1970s. My book, therefore, starts with these glorious decades (Chapter One), describing key themes while also shining light on crevasses and ravines that were deepening and broadening underneath what appeared to be placid and content societies. By the late 1960s, these contradictions could no longer be contained or bridged, breaking out in violent protests (e.g., student, anti-war, race, and gender) while also powering the next revolution—the rise of the Baby Boomer generation (Chapters Two and Three). Although each cohort is different and rebels against prior generations, I argue that the gap between young Baby Boomers and their parents and grandparents was significantly wider and deeper than usual.

By the early 1980s, this new generation radically altered every aspect of Western politics, societies, and economies, ushering in a world that in George Packer's perceptive formulation[11] was more entrepreneurial and less equal, far more tolerant but less fair. The new consensus also set institutions of state and democracy on a long-term decline (from parliaments and regulators to policymakers, and from public libraries to media) as Boomers' desire for freedom of choice without guaranteeing outcomes, personal responsibility, and free markets clashed with constraints that prior generations imposed through strict societal norms and the expansive role of the state. The transition was not an easy one, and the late 1960s to early 1980s (or what became known as the "extended bad '70s") was a period of turmoil as societies struggled to forge a new consensus.

However, depending on a country, by the early to mid-1980s, Baby Boomers achieved both adult and electoral power. This was then followed by three decades during which the role of the public sector and the state was not just denigrated but progressively dismantled, with a neoliberal theoretical framework (Chapter Four) becoming dominant in almost every Western nation. The mantra that the public sector is inherently inefficient and unjust while the private sector knows best, and free markets are capable of fixing most problems if only the government stops interfering, solidified through the 1980s–90s as the single most powerful driving force across countries ruled by both right- and left-wing parties. At the time, it did not really matter whether it was Republican or Democratic administrations in the US, Labor or Conservatives in the UK, Social Democrats or Christian Democrats in Germany, Labor or Liberals in Australia. In the 1980s–90s and into early 2000s, societies had embraced neoliberal ideas, and politics naturally followed the popular lead, reversing the 1950s–60s consensus when both right- and left-wing parties accepted the logic of FDR's New Deal and supported a pervasively expansionary state role. However, freedom of choice without concern for the outcomes had its price, and following the Global Financial Crisis (2010), the check had arrived. The book discusses both economic and social consequences of the neoliberal world (Chapters Five and Six).

Since then, we have been struggling to formulate the new consensus, and this time, demand for change is driven by the young Millennials and Gen Z, who unlike their parents and grandparents witnessed the negative side of neoliberalism—pursuit of growth and wealth creation without regard for externalities (e.g., wealth inequalities, denigration of public services, disruptive globalization, systemic inequities, and environmental degradation); disconnect between corporate and societal objectives; inability of democratic politics to solve problems; and extreme polarization. These younger cohorts have also been exposed to the winds of the

Information Age, as it started to disintermediate both labor and capital, with an atrophy of jobs, professions, and career paths. As the Ancient Greeks recognized, no society or polity can survive unless there is a countervailing force that minimizes inequities and uncertainties against the natural tendency toward the opposite (i.e., greater concentration of power and wealth, and hard to control risks).

I argue that these negative outcomes bequeathed by the neoliberal world were the inevitable and predictable consequences of sidelining the state (the only actor with sufficient power and legitimacy to redress many of these issues) while embracing philosophy that only works in an "ivory tower" where economists still insist on equilibrating global market systems, availability of near perfect information and price competitive markets, despite ample evidence that this is not how either economies or societies actually work. As the likes of Karl Polanyi and John Maynard Keynes highlighted as far back as the 1940s–50s, the idea that economies and markets can be separated from a society and that pricing and monetary signals are the only thing that matter, is not just faulty but dangerous, as it ultimately risks discrediting liberal norms in the eyes of the electorate, prompting a search for more extreme answers—from dictatorships to communism and fascism. In Chapter Four, I extensively discuss the origins, tenets, and impact of neoliberal theories, including examples of places and countries where neoliberals claim their ideas were shown to work.

Ronald Inglehart,[12] an American sociologist, illustrated in his groundbreaking study (Chapter Six) that at times of rising economic and physical *insecurity*, people revert to "circling the wagons," becoming far more insular, xenophobic, and unwilling to accept new ideas, while insisting on strict interpretation of *their* in-group morality. As a result, the scope for discussion and compromise dramatically narrows, as the other side is no longer viewed as fellow citizens but rather as immoral and debased heretics who are not only wrong, but unpatriotic and profoundly opposed to what is perceived to be the natural order. As Lilianna Mason argued, the two sides start to resemble fans of football teams, with the single objective of winning, even if everyone is ultimately worse off.[13] These times also tend to trigger what Inglehart described as an "authoritarian reflex" or desire to reach out to a strongman whom they hope will solve their mounting problems, creating an opening for populists and demagogues who benefit from and exploit these concerns. One can best describe them as "grievance merchants," who despite their strong image and promise of salvation, make countries more brittle and ultimately weaker.

In Chapter Six, I show the extent and the depth of polarization in the US and Europe, which over the last decade, has gone far beyond mere policy disagreements, and has become exceptionally personal, determining where one lives and shops, what news one listens to, and whether or not one is comfortable having a member of an alternative party joining one's family. Such extreme polarization is present whenever societies disagree on what constitutes the "right" political, economic, and social model. This was the case in the 1930s and again in the late 1960s to early 1980s. It is also true today, at least since the Global Financial Crisis (2010), which marked the breakdown of the consensus that dominated our world for the three preceding decades.

•   •   •

The above does not explain, however, why such extreme polarization becomes at times the dominant feature of the political and economic landscape, while at other times, disagreements and schisms are much more navigable. Whenever headlines talk about dysfunctional Washington, London, or Paris, it seems clear that it is not so much politics that are dysfunctional but rather people who are dysfunctional, confused, and scared, and politics simply reflect this popular disorientation. It is only when a broadly accepted societal consensus exists that politics revert to being consensual institutions that strive to solve problems as most parliamentary democracies did in the 1950s–60s or 1980s–90s. However, when people do not agree, politics can't agree either. The same applies to corporations and their goals, as they are nothing more than extensions of societies. A considerable part of this book is dedicated to the question of what causes extreme polarization. Is it culture, economics, technology, finance, personalities, or just a random walk?

It is not random. In Chapter Seven, I argue that in most cases it is the fusion of technology and finance that drives these ruptures (what I describe as the Fujiwara effect, or a merger of several powerful hurricanes), which are either aggravated or helped by climate, healthcare, and demographic trends. Whenever a highly disruptive technology reaches the escape velocity (whether it was the first or second Industrial Revolution or today's Information Age), it disrupts most societal and economic relations. It is no coincidence that Karl Marx penned his *Communist Manifesto* at the peak of the first Industrial Revolution in 1848. Similarly, the "Long War" (i.e., the Great War and Second World War) was in many ways an aftershock of the second Industrial Revolution, while today's polarization is a direct outcome of the disruptive power of the Information Age. As I described in my first book,[14] we can date the beginning of the Information Age to the early 1970s. However, the impact was rather muted until the early 1990s and had only become disruptive toward the end of the 1990s and the early 2000s. As past waves have shown, it usually takes several generations for societies to adjust to a new technological backdrop, and in the meantime, chaos rules supreme, with its intensity rising markedly toward the peak of disruption. In an economic jargon, the Information Age alters the nature and functioning of both capital and labor, while in political and social terms, it drastically changes almost all social relations—from political systems to the way in which contribution of different cohorts is measured and rewarded, from the private sphere to morality, and from education to entertainment.

It is not just about ChatGPT and AI, but the "supercluster" of innovation[15] that is accelerating at a speed that neither regulators nor societies can match. The best way to look at AI is as the highly disruptive general-purpose technology that is reaching escape velocity and starting to propagate across numerous other applications (from robotics and automation to biotech). In the process it disintermediates labor (over the next decade, at least 60 percent of the global labor force will likely lose at a minimum of 30–50 percent of their functionality—increasingly in more cognitive, rather than routine, functions); capital (i.e., the role of tangible when compared to intangible capital, the purpose of money, and banks); and social relations (i.e., the role of the state and nation, ownership of new technologies, and the structuring of rewards and regulatory settings). At the same time, the Information Age is driving the marginal cost of almost everything toward zero. Neither economies nor businesses have an answer to zero. As in the case of the Industrial Revolutions, the Information Age initially causes a considerable spike in wealth inequalities while depressing aggregate productivity, despite a popular belief that technology raises productivity, which is only true over long periods of time. Indeed, the Information Revolution is far broader, deeper, and more dislocating than the Industrial Revolutions were, with the McKinsey Global Institute[16] estimating that its power and impact might be 3,000 times greater, or as Kevin Drum described it, the Industrial Revolution changed the world, and all it did was replace human muscle power.

Although innovation is a human spirit, the speed at which it propagates critically depends on the availability of capital and its cost. What I describe as the most intense ever Financialization of the global economy (Chapter Five) has now reached the stage that capital, for the first time in human history, exceeds real demand by at least five-to-ten times, whereas in the 1950s–80s, it was broadly in line with GDP. Ironically, this represents another side effect of Boomers' desire for unlimited growth. Such a dramatic capital expansion can best be described as the equivalent of pouring kerosene on the bonfire of the Information Age. Ample availability of capital and its depressed cost (as financialization requires ever more liquidity to be created beyond current needs in order to control volatilities and bad debts), has been accelerating technological evolution at a pace that societies are finding hard to accept. In turn, the Information Age is re-accelerating Financialization by creating a never-ending stream of new financial instruments and products and new ways of leveraging real or financial assets ad infinitum.

It is this mutually reinforcing fusion of the highly disruptive Information Age and deep Financialization which is at the heart of the

Fujiwara effect. The net impact is that over time, people from different localities, and of different ages, racial, and ethnic backgrounds start moving at different speeds and in different directions (depending on their proximity to the key drivers of technology and finance), causing and/or aggravating domestic inequality and heightening polarization issues. At the same time, countries also find themselves moving in different directions and at different speeds (depending on their location and the structure of their economies), opening uncomfortable performance gaps and, as a result, causing and/or aggravating preexisting geopolitical and historical tensions.

During such ruptures, demographics play a crucial role, as it is people who ultimately shape human institutions. As I discuss in Chapter Eleven, personal experiences are the backbone of generational analysis[17] which in turn are shaped by the prevailing economic and technological backdrop: the greater the volatility and the disparity of outcomes, the greater the differences in intergenerational views and outlook. This explains why GI and Silent generations[18] generally saw the world pretty much the same, while the gap between these early 20th century cohorts and Baby Boomers was an unbridgeable ravine. Then again, differences between Boomers and the following Generation X were relatively minor.

I suggest that there is another rupture that is emerging, and this time, between the ageing Baby Boomers and Generation X, and the younger Millennials and Generation Z (anyone born after early 1980s, and especially those post mid-1990s). In the same way as Baby Boomers had fundamentally and radically reshaped the world, starting from the late 1960s to early 1970s with the peak of transition in the early to mid-1980s, today's younger cohorts are already reshaping our world, with the impact peaking in the late 2020s to mid-2030s and continuing through the 2040s, at which time these younger cohorts will become the dominant adult and electoral cohort across all mature economies. I examine (Chapter Eleven) what these younger cohorts think and what social, political, and economic structures they prefer. The conclusion is that they are far closer to their great-grandparents (i.e., GI and Silent generations) than to their parents and grandparents. Neil Howe has arguably provided the best summation of what makes these younger cohorts tick: "Millennials seek no risk, but security. Not spontaneity, but planning. Not a free-for-all marketplace, but a rule-bound community of equals."[19] In other words, Millennials and Generation Z look toward the government and community for support and guidance, rejecting the free-for-all world of the Baby Boomers. On a darker note, just like their great-grandparents, these younger cohorts are willing to sacrifice some of their rights and freedoms to ensure that chaos is kept at bay. They want guardrails and equality rather than the Boomers' freedom, free markets, and personal responsibility. They are reverting to the views from the 1950s–60s of the private sector and its responsibilities to society and the community. Throughout this book, I discuss various surveys that profile these extreme intergenerational differences, and how they are already changing government policies, societies, culture, and the behavior of the corporate sector. Millennials and Generation Z are also our only hope of avoiding the 1940s' "world on fire."

•   •   •

Why do I compare our current times to the 1930s rather than a more conventional comparison to the 1970s, which in the wake of the COVID-19 pandemic, has dominated discussion in popular and financial press? While no cross-time review is ever totally consistent with prevailing evidence, there are just far too many commonalities between our environment and the 1930s to be an accident.

In Chapter Eight, I outline the reasons why I firmly believe that the 1930s is the most appropriate parallel to our times. In an eerie replay, it includes almost everything—from financial crises and recessions to extreme inequalities; "secular stagnation" or the inability to grow without monetary and fiscal supports; technological disintermediation to demographics; deep societal polarization, insecurities, and culture wars to the division of the world into competing camps with radically different political and economic systems; and collapse in the credibility of international institutions. As Philipp Blom argued: "Both the interwar period and the first decades of the twenty-first century have been marked by a pervasive sense of insecurity, and in both periods the reasons and possible remedies for this insecurity have been the subject of intensive debates."[20] The 1930s marked a dramatic shift from Anatole Kaletsky[21] "Capitalism 1.0" to "Capitalism 2.0"—or the transition from the classical liberal world of the 19th and early 20th centuries to one far more dominated by the state and public sectors. Ever since the Global Financial Crisis, we have been similarly dismantling the neoliberal version of the original liberalism, with the state and public sector tentacles growing and spreading at an unprecedented pace.

Although there are parallels with the 1970s as well, the differences are far greater. For example, the 1970s was a time of one of the historically most equal income and wealth distributions as opposed to today's Gilded Age-like inequalities. The 1970s was also a time when neither technological nor financial disruptions were as acute. There were also no alternative governing and social systems on offer in the 1970s, with communism already visibly fading in attractiveness and vigor and democratic principles not questioned but modified. This is in stark contrast to a direct and disruptive competition today, as indeed it was in the 1930s.

The heart of the book is found in Sections Two and Three (Chapters Seven to Twelve), where I discuss two interrelated issues. First, how much are our societies and economies likely to change in the wake of the Fujiwara effect? And second, what policies do we need to put in place to lower tensions and enable us to transition to a new world with as little violence and damage as possible? The key phrase is found in the subtitle of this book, "how we can avoid a world on fire," and the terrible fate of those who lived through disasters of the 1930s only to experience the even greater horrors of the 1940s.

First, I maintain the view expressed in my first book four years ago that whatever is coming down the pike is highly unlikely to look anything like conventional capitalism or even remotely close to its prior iterations. The fusion of the Information Age and Financialization is likely to dismantle all key ingredients of the capitalist system. In economic terms, neither labor, capital, nor money will look the same, and indeed, some of their functions are likely to disappear entirely. This includes everything that makes today's capitalism work—redefinition of conventional employee-employer relations; radically different ways of rewarding and valuing human contribution; changes in functioning of and the need for corporations and the role and nature of money and capital. The late 20th century's ideas of monetarily valued human capital will disappear to be reinvented in a very different form. The ideas of investment cycles and discounted cashflows that have become so deeply imbedded over the last six to seven decades will also become largely redundant, at least in their current form. Whenever people suggest that this is too extreme and too far out into the future, I disagree. The outlines of the New World have already been emerging for years, and the pace of change is likely to accelerate rapidly through the 2020s–30s.

Second, given the highly disruptive nature of these changes, how long would it take for a new global consensus on the "correct" economic and social model to emerge? This is hard to answer, other than saying that it is still a decade or two into the future, at least. In the meantime, chaos is likely to become more intense, and this book examines whether these dislocations could break out into openly hostile and destructive conflicts and civil wars (Chapter Eight and Nine), and what can be done to reduce these tensions and frictions, including reversion to Cold War policies of containment and dusting off what have been perceived over the last three decades as discredited concepts of *détente*.[22] In particular, I believe that attention should be paid to several potential conflicts: China and its economic and geopolitical positioning; the future of the remnants of the Russian Empire; the evolution of acute domestic polarization in the US; and finally, climate change and the need to manage unprecedented migratory waves. Each of these fault lines is capable of converting our world into an equivalent of the 1940s rather than into a far more preferable and moderate transition of the 1950s–60s.

As in the 1930s, a lack of a global consensus implies that today there are alternative political and social models on offer with what appears to be almost equal legitimacy and the right to propagate. Carl L. Becker, a pre-scient American historian who was writing in the middle of the upheav-als of the late 1930s to early 1940s, asked a key question that was as pertinent as it is today: how can "possessors be sufficiently dispossessed and the dispossessed be sufficiently reinstated without resort to violence, revolution and the temporary or permanent dictatorship?"[23] In order to keep democratic norms, economies need to grow with relatively fair dis-tribution of rewards while minimizing inequalities (wealth, civic, educa-tional). Mariana Mazzucato[24] of UCL recently described this dilemma, as recognizing which sectors in the economy actually create value as opposed to those that are mostly involved in rentier and value capture activities, and what policies can help promote value creators while placing obstacles in the path of those who simply capture someone else's value. This is a heretical line of thought, as economics stopped measuring value in the 19th century, with David Ricardo and Karl Marx being the last giants to pay attention to value, as the profession focused instead on marginal pricing. In economics today, the finance industry is deemed to create value, but most of the government's activities cannot be measured and hence, are regarded as either worthless or at least something that cannot be counted. Is finance a value-generating activity while the government's role in research, law and order, education, etc. is not? It won't be easy to resolve this. However, what seems clear is that the neoliberal world of Baby Boomers, though offering more freedom, has led to an unacceptable level of inequality, stagnating productivity and growth as well as deeper and far more toxic polarization. This transformed the original Boomers' idea of freedom and individual responsibility as the key to prosperity and social stability into a Frankenstein monster of dependence on the state to maintain an economic and social model predicated on rising asset prices, leverage, and financialization.

China and, to a much lesser extent, Russia are today advocating an alternative state-driven model that radically redefines the relationship between the state and non-state actors, society and individuals, while promising more efficient outcomes and ultimately a better and fairer share of national wealth. Unlike the West, there is no pretense that the state is anything other than firmly in the driver's seat (no Western hypocrisy here), and China in particular, believes that technological innovations can be better marshalled under a more authoritarian structure. This extends even as far as resurrecting the "socialist calculation debate"[25] of the 1920s–40s that asked whether centrally controlled capital allocation and pricing could be more efficient than the "invisible hand" of the market. Was Nikolai Bukharin (Bolshevik leader who in the 1920s established the Soviet planning agency *Gosplan*) right after all, and was he just ahead of his time, lacking appropriate computational tools? It is indicative of the confusion that is currently convulsing our societies that this debate, which most people had assumed was already won as far back as the 1950s (in favor of markets), is making a comeback in the 2020s. Everything is up for grabs: from the role of the market and the importance of the free flow of capital, goods, and people to who (or what) decides how capital is allocated and wealth shared. The 1930s was the last time the world experienced a similar state of flux, with nations, policy makers, and economists staking out extreme and irreconcilable positions.

But as in the 1930s, the West and democracies have considerable inbuilt strengths which theoretically should allow them to survive, succeed, and avoid extremes.

However, for this to happen, there is an urgent need to start implementing wide-ranging economic, social, and geopolitical reforms. In Chapter Ten, I spend time discussing what I believe to be the most critical policies: (a) the urgent need to consider implementation of some version of the Universal Basic Income (UBI), coupled with reforms of public finances, including reassessment of central banks and other tools, such as Modern Monetary Theory (MMT) as well as taxation policies; (b) the redefinition of state involvement in basic research which is needed to replenish the pool of inventiveness while also launching coherent industrial policies, something that over the last five decades has been treated as a heresy; (c) changes in the functioning and role of educational and skill-based institutions; (d) the redesign of regulatory and competitive rules of ownership and sharing of technology; and finally, (e) a globally coordi-nated "Marshall Plan" for the less developed economies to minimize what promises to be the historically most disruptive migratory wave while also reducing geopolitical tensions and climate and healthcare risks.

•   •   •

The genius of FDR was to understand that perfect outcomes are not pos-sible. The choice in 1933 was not between freedom and slavery, but rather how much freedom needed to be sacrificed, eroded, and corralled, in order to avoid far worse outcomes. Despite criticisms that he was building an equivalent of a fascist or communist state in America, FDR had actually managed what, at the time, must have looked like an impossible feat of keeping as much of freedom and private space as he could while reducing polarization and defanging the extremes. Without the New Deal, the US could have turned either fascist or communist, which would have resulted in a complete elimination of freedoms and political discourse as well as either total elimination of property rights (communism) or the private sector being subjected to an absolute diktat of the state (fascism). This is what Carl Becker was discussing in 1941—there are no perfect solutions, rather experiments, and anyone who ever claimed to have perfect answers (whether religious zealots, fascists, or communists) always spawned sys-tems that were far worse than the disease. Experimentation was and still remains the name of the game, hopefully leading to better, more accept-able, and humane compromises.

Today, as in the 1930s, there is a great deal of discussion of the benefits of having a "strongman" and authoritarian systems (especially on the right side of politics) while disparaging frailties and fault lines of democratic systems. Whether it is Viktor Orbán, Donald Trump, Jair Bolsonaro, Recep Erdoğan, Geert Wilders, or Marine Le Pen, the last decade witnessed an avalanche of leaders who either captured or came close to capturing levers of power with an explicit objective of weaken-ing institutions of state and democracy, and in many cases establishing the single-man rule. This could never have occurred if people were not disoriented and prepared to entertain any option to ease their pain and revenge the perceived wrongdoings (*à la* the young man in 1932–33 who was willing to follow almost anyone).

If Polybius, a Roman-Greek historian, were alive today, I doubt that he would have much difficulty in characterizing the current state of political life in the US and most other developed states as being an "Ochlocracy," which is a rule by the masses at a time when healthy democracy has degenerated to a stage in which disoriented and angry masses fall prey to opportunistic dictators, populists, and demagogues. According to Polybius's scheme of perpetual cycles, this stage should be followed by a monarchy, or a rule by one individual. He would undoubtedly shrug off our disbelief and argue that people who live in history do not know that they are already inside one of his cycles. Similarly, Oswald Spengler, who in 1918 was anticipating a period of Caesarism, might feel, if he were still alive, (finally) vindicated. However, it should be kept in mind that history is not deterministic, and Spengler turned out to be only partially right (with the rise of dictatorships in the 1920s–30s) but terribly wrong over the longer term. Polybius himself believed that there is a way of breaking out of the perpetual cycles that rotate between democracy (rule by masses), aristocracy (rule by few) and monarchy (rule by one). In his view, it is all about balancing individual elements in order to reduce the impact of greed and corruption, or what we in the modern world would call "managing inequalities and inequities." Unfortunately, as he penned *The Histories*, praising exactly such balance which he saw in the Roman Republic, he was unaware that it was already on its last leg, soon to be replaced by an Empire that ruled the Mediterranean world for another five centuries.

Therefore, anything is possible. However, as I discuss in Chapter Nine, the West has incredible strengths. As a broadly (and admittedly imperfectly) defined category, it controls over 55 percent of the global economy (even though it is home to only 13 percent of the world's population). It is responsible for 70 percent of global research and development (R&D) and largely "owns" the global intellectual capital while completely dominating capital markets and financial intermediation. The West also remains the world's most formidable armed force, with the most advanced integrated military tactics. Unlike Russia, which remains largely a kleptocratic nuclear petrostate, and unlike China, which faces significant economic headwinds (including a possibility of Japan-style multidecade stagnation), the West also has more vibrant economies. Although there is a great deal of discussion about China and Russia offering different and more appealing economic and social models and their desire to lead what is known as the Global South, there is no evidence that this could become a viable grouping, just as the Non-Alignment movement of the 1950s–70s had never achieved much. Only the West itself can defeat the West by allowing domestic social polarization to undermine the key pillars that have made the West unique and successful, and by not responding to real challenges that the Fujiwara effect presents, with a coherent set of economic and social policies that reduce pressures and defang extremes.

The state is the only actor with the strength and legitimacy to maintain societal cohesion while steering economies and ensuring fairer distribution. It is therefore inevitable that the role of the state will continue to grow in years to come (*à la* 1930s–60s), and while there will be frequent calls to rein in state power, it is unlikely that the Millennial and Generation Z cohorts would agree, and as they become the electoral majority, it will be their view that will count. In 1937, Lewis Mumford, an American sociologist, encapsulated the dilemma: "The question that confronts us today is not *if* we shall plan [as opposed to theology of free market orthodoxy], but *how* we shall plan."[26] This perfectly describes our own dilemma—it is no longer a question *whether* the state involvement will grow but the *method* and *how far* it should be allowed to expand. The danger, of course, is that as in the 1970s, the state might overreach (and indeed, it is likely to do so). However, as Carl Becker and Arthur Schlesinger[27] highlighted, there are no perfect answers, and few optimum outcomes exist at the intersection of history, politics, and economics. Instead of perfection, it is all about complex and imperfect compromises. Both labor and capital are already undergoing a radical transformation that cannot be stopped or reversed, and whatever system ultimately emerges, it is unlikely to look anything like conventional capitalism. The front runners are either a modern iteration of despotic feudalism or an enlightened version of communism (defined in its original sense, as societies of such high productivity that they dispense with the need to toil to earn a living while maintaining most, but not all, personal and economic freedoms). I hope the latter will be the right answer, and in Chapters Eleven and Twelve, I discuss how such a system might emerge under the guidance of younger cohorts.

•　　•　　•

In his first book, Polybius wonderfully described the importance of history: "The soundest education and training for a life of active politics is the study of History, and the surest and indeed the only method of learning how to bear bravely the vicissitudes of fortune, is to recall the calamities of others."[28] The question facing today's leaders and their societies: Have we learned lessons of the 1930s–40s, and are we prepared to tackle the grave challenges ahead with as much foresight and fortitude as FDR did, or will sound advice be ignored in the maelstrom of anger, disorientation, and populism?

The Twilight Before the Storm is structured as part history, part political science, part economics, part technology and futurology. It traverses centuries, decades, nations, geographies, and economic and political systems, learning from the past while projecting into the future. The book is structured in three sections: "What Went Wrong?"—which examines the legacy of the 1950s–60s and the consequences of neoliberal and Baby Boomers' revolutions; "Staring into the Abyss"—which reviews key challenges facing the world, including the possibility of global and civil conflicts; and finally "Building a Bridge from Today to Tomorrow"—which discusses policies that might help avoid the worst outcomes and the role that Millennials and Generation Z are likely to play in this transition.

Given that policy choices would undoubtedly be hotly contested with decisions lagging the intensifying pace of change, we might not be able to avoid the 1940s "world on fire." The best that can be argued is that we have options, and one hopes that we will not wait too long to exercise them, and that the verdict about us by the future generations will be kinder than our verdict of the disastrous choices made by those who lived in the 1930s. I finish with a similar prediction as the one I had in my first book: "Darkness before dawn, with a several decades-long protracted birth of the new world."[29]

WHAT WENT WRONG?

"Success has many fathers, but failure is an orphan."

—John F. Kennedy

Chapter 1

FROM BLACK AND WHITE TO COLOR

"Moloch! Solitude! Filth! Ugliness! Ashcans and unobtainable dollars!
Children screaming under the stairways! Boys screaming in the armies! Old
men weeping in the parks! Moloch! Moloch the loveless! Mental Moloch!
Moloch the heavy judger of men! Moloch the incomprehensible prison!
Moloch the stunned governments! Robot apartments! Invisible suburbs!
Blind capitalists! Demonic industries!"
Allen Ginsberg's poem "Howl"

On the evening of October 13, 1955, a young and visibly nervous Allen Ginsberg made his way to the lectern at the Six Gallery in San Francisco to read what eventually became the classic poem "Howl." The poem painted a depressing and threatening picture of a 1950s American society that was intolerant and hostile not just to Ginsberg (who was Jewish and homosexual) but to anyone who deviated from what were, at the time, perceived to be the "right" societal norms.[1] Due in part to clumsy attempts by the San Francisco Police Department to ban distribution of the poem, Ginsberg and the Beats, by the late 1950s, had moved from the periphery into the mainstream of American culture.

The Beats (or Beatniks) was the first movement to reject what they perceived to be a conformist and stifling postwar society. They could be best described as misfits in what was otherwise one of the happiest and most cohesive periods in US history, spanning almost two decades from the late 1940s until the mid- to late 1960s. Beats simply refused to obey and conform. They believed that the American system had become so irredeemably corrupt and controlled by the mighty dollar and corporations that it was beyond redemption, and thus any attempts to reform it were bound to fail. Instead, Beats focused on alternative lifestyles. They rejected security, careers, and respectability, and "searched for ecstasy, mystical experience, sexual release, and emotional honesty."[2] They mingled in places like Greenwich Village in New York and North Beach in San Francisco, and their life was the opposite of conformity. Beats wore simple clothes (often black), grew beards, and sported long hair (in the days when crew cuts with "men wearing suits, ties and—when outdoor—hats, and women with their hair in modified pageboys, pert and upbeat"[3] were the norm). Beats developed their own hip language, hitchhiked across the nation while smoking marijuana, reading poetry, and practicing orgies and free sex. "They desired to commit civil disobedience against a national dress code which required trimmed minds to match trimmed lawns."[4]

Beatniks had a strong impact on the generation growing up in the 1950s and 1960s, and apart from the onset of rock and roll and a number of increasingly disturbed Hollywood movies (such as *Man in the Gray Flannel Suit*, *The Power Elite*, and *Rebel Without a Cause*), they were the key guidepost for the next restless generation that ultimately built the modern world of the 1990s–2000s with all its benefits, shortcomings, and inconsistencies. Beatniks presaged the student, gender, and civil rights movements as well as hippies and yippies, and were at least a decade ahead of their time.

However, during their own time, they were a tiny minority,[5] largely ignored by society at large. As David Halberstam, one of the best-known chronologists of the 1950s, described: "The Fifties were captured in black and white by still photographers; by contrast, the decade that followed was, more often than not, caught in living color on tape or film. Not surprisingly, in retrospect the pace of the fifties seemed slower, almost languid… Young people seemed, more than anything, 'square' and largely accepting of the given social covenants."[6]

•   •   •

Following the Great Depression and World War II, a strong societal consensus formed that emphasized the government as the key guardrail to ensure stability and keep the anarchy these generations had become intimately familiar with at bay. These generations had also accepted that tight societal norms were the only way to cage the forces of darkness that could at any time overwhelm their lives. What were later called the GI and Silent generations (born between the early 1900s and the first half of the 1940s) lived through such terrible times that sacrificing some personal freedom was regarded by most as a small price to pay for stability, security, and good jobs.

And they got all three. Despite occasional mild recessions, the two decades after World War II was the longest ever period of economic expansion, not only in the US but across most Western and even Communists nations. Propelled by postwar reconstruction and rising productivity, it was an era of unprecedented inventiveness and growth, with governments playing a major role in guiding and shaping both societies and economies. In the US it included everything from the GI Bill to interstate highways, from NASA, space exploration, and Bell Labs to the Great Society, while in Europe it featured Marshall Plan, free milk, healthcare, and comprehensive safety nets that were all highly effective tonics and societal healing instruments.[7]

Between 1950 and 1973, the US average income per capita rose at a compound rate of 2.5 percent per annum, compared to 1.5 percent between 1880 and 1913. In other countries, improvement was even stronger. In Japan per capita income increased at a blistering 8 percent per annum (compared to 1.5 percent prior to the Great War). The pace was closer to 5 percent in West Germany and Italy and around 4 percent in France. The income gap between Western nations had dramatically shrunk. West Germany, which in 1946 had a standard of living that was only 25 percent of the US, rose to 72 percent by early 1970s, while in France the average income increased from 42 percent to 77 percent of the US, and in Japan from less than 20 percent to 69 percent. Even in the Soviet Union, the standard of living is likely to have risen to as high as 35 percent of the US.

This rapid growth was achieved while global inflation remained relatively low, and almost everyone who wanted a job could get one. As a result, inequalities within countries had also meaningfully declined. It was the age when the productivity growth was sufficiently robust to enable a fairer sharing of spoils, with a greater portion flowing to labor, even as growth rates were maintained at a pace strong enough to encourage investment without excessive financial speculation or rent seeking. Corporations mostly preferred negotiations to strikes, and whether it was the groundbreaking GM agreement in 1949, or an emergence of collective bargaining and worker-management participation in Germany, through the 1950s and for bulk of the 1960s, most societies pulled together.

Why would one challenge a system that, on the whole, seemed to be working so well, with most social indicators improving beyond people's wildest dreams? Automobile ownership in the US increased from 200 cars per 1,000 people at the end of World War II to almost 500 by the early 1970s (or in other words, almost every family had at least one car) while ownership of TV sets rose from 9 percent to over 95 percent, and by the late 1960s, almost every American household had at least one refrigerator. The same applied to telephones, with 65 lines per one hundred people when compared to 26 in the late 1940s. In Japan, prewar car ownership was barely one car per thousand people. However, by the early 1970s it increased to over 130, and the penetration was above 250 per thousand in West Germany, France, and Italy. By the late 1960s more than half of French households already had TV sets, and in the UK that ratio exceeded two-thirds.

Figure 1. GDP Per Capita Growth (%), 1880–1910 vs. 1950–1973

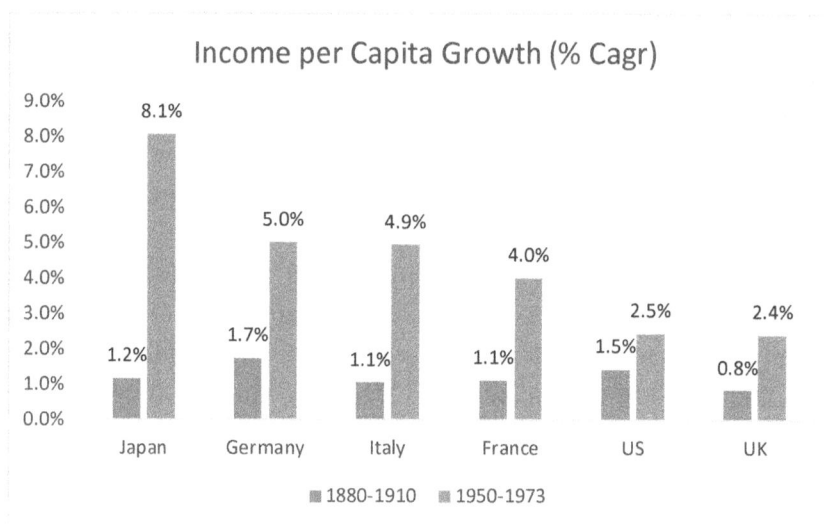

Income per Capita Growth (% Cagr)

Country	1880-1910	1950-1973
Japan	1.2%	8.1%
Germany	1.7%	5.0%
Italy	1.1%	4.9%
France	1.1%	4.0%
US	1.5%	2.5%
UK	0.8%	2.4%

Source: Maddison Project Database, 2020

Figure 2. Relative GDP per Capita (US=100%), 1880–1973

	UK	Netherlands	France	Austria	Germany	Italy	Japan	Russia/USSR
1880	95.9%	74.6%	54.0%	53.0%	50.7%	44.7%	27.6%	22.0%
1900	94.5%	66.0%	57.0%	57.2%	59.2%	40.6%	26.4%	23.7%
1913	81.2%	63.9%	55.0%	54.6%	57.5%	40.1%	24.0%	22.3%
1920	69.1%	66.3%	50.7%	37.9%	43.9%	37.3%	29.3%	9.0%
1929	73.4%	75.9%	62.8%	49.3%	54.0%	40.9%	30.7%	18.5%
1939	89.4%	79.1%	68.4%	58.4%	77.1%	47.0%	43.0%	31.9%
1946	72.5%	47.9%	41.5%	21.0%	23.8%	25.7%	18.7%	20.6%
1950	72.6%	62.7%	54.2%	38.8%	40.6%	36.6%	20.1%	29.7%
1955	72.2%	67.2%	56.9%	46.4%	53.2%	42.9%	25.4%	30.4%
1960	76.3%	73.2%	65.3%	57.5%	68.0%	52.2%	35.2%	34.8%
1965	72.7%	73.0%	68.3%	57.6%	68.5%	56.6%	44.2%	34.5%
1970	71.6%	79.6%	75.9%	64.9%	72.1%	64.7%	64.6%	37.1%
1973	72.1%	78.4%	76.8%	67.3%	71.7%	63.7%	68.5%	36.3%

Source: Maddison Project Database, 2020

Figure 3. Motor Vehicle Ownership (per 1000 people), 1937–1973

	US	Canada	France	UK	Germany	Italy	Japan
1937	196.1	97.3	48.2	38.8	16.3	6.3	0.5
1948	226.6	113.6	36.9	40.4	6.1	4.7	0.4
1955	314.2	182.9	68.2	69.7	32.6	18.1	1.7
1960	340.0	224.7	119.1	105.8	81.2	39.7	4.5
1965	385.5	263.0	192.8	166.1	158.6	105.2	22.1
1970	433.3	303.5	248.5	209.7	230.2	189.7	84.1
1973	476.6	348.7	264.4	243.3	269.4	245.0	133.1

Source: UN Statistical Yearbook, various editions

Figure 4. US Television Penetration (%), 1950–1965

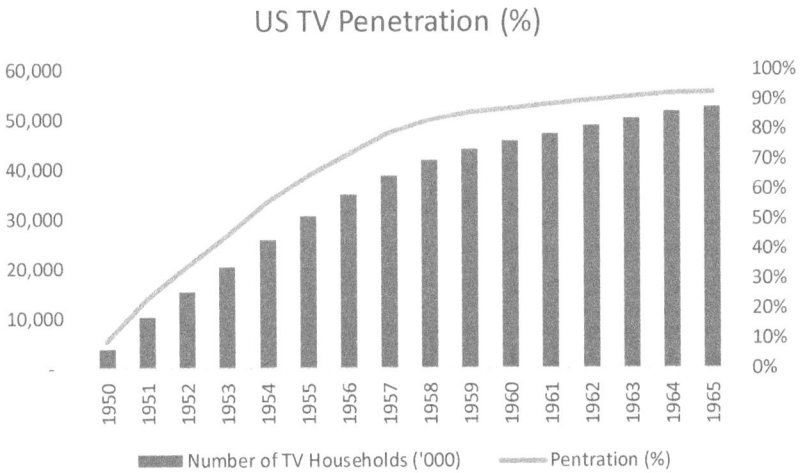

US TV Penetration (%)

Source: The American Century, "The Number of TV Sets in America," accessed December 11, 2022

Todd Gitlin, an American sociologist who is closely associated with the spirit of the age, described these decades as a period when "affluence was assumed to be a national condition, not just personal standing."[8] Despite the fact that most economists and businessmen expected a severe recession, even a highly skeptical *Fortune Magazine* conceded that, "We would seem to have it in our power a standard of living far beyond anything in recorded history."[9] While there were pockets of extreme poverty (decried by John Kenneth Galbraith[10]), most people were undoubtedly far better off than their parents and, more importantly, than they themselves had been only two decades prior. This cross-time (rather than inequalities) comparison was the salient one, with most people, including 20–25 percent of households who still lived in abject poverty, expecting that progress would ultimately help all Americans.

The same trends were visible across most other Western societies, explaining the unprecedented baby boom that started in the US in 1946, and in Europe slightly later, and which did not abate until the 1970s. More babies were born in the US in 1948–53 than in the previous sixty years.[11] The US fertility rate which was barely above replacement levels prewar (2.1 children per woman), skyrocketed to 3.7 by 1960, doubling the number of families with three children and tripling those with four children or more. One of the US's more popular sitcoms, *Cheaper by the Dozen*, advocated large families, and most people agreed. One Harvard business major remarked in the late 1950s, "I would like to have six kids. I don't know why I said that—it just sounds like a minimum production goal."[12] In Germany, the postwar fertility rate of 1.9 rose to 2.5 by 1965, and in France, it increased from 2.1 in the aftermath of the war to almost 2.9.

Having a family and a growing brood of kids was the whole point of and rationale for the prosperity and growth that societies enjoyed in these two decades, especially after the nightmares of the 1930s–40s.

Figure 5. US Fertility Rates (children per woman), 1920–1973

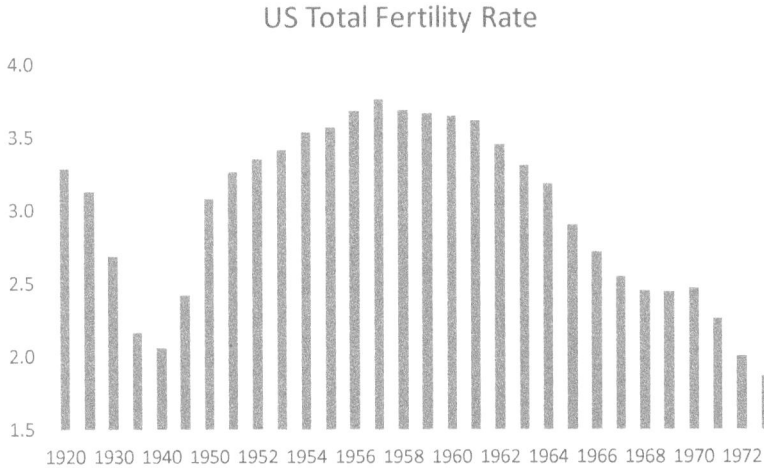

US Total Fertility Rate

Source: United Nations, World Fertility Data, 2019

This new optimism was not just confined to the bedroom. It had an unprecedented ripple effect on all aspects of life.

One of the first to realize the profound changes the American economy was undergoing was Bill Levitt. Borrowing from his wartime Navy experience as well as from Ford assembly-line techniques, Levitt was the first to grasp that after marrying and buying a car, the next thing returning GIs would want to do would be to buy their own home. As described by David Halberstam, an American academic and author, "After World War II, most Americans had a vision of a better life ahead. At the core of it was owning one's own house."[13] The combination of the Great Depression and the war had slashed new housing starts[14] to a point that by 1946, the country was conservatively short at least 5–6 million homes. As in many other instances in the 1950s–60s, the government stepped in by rushing through the Federal Housing Bill that contained ironclad federal insurance to protect builders through federal mortgage guarantees (i.e., the Veterans Administration and the Federal Housing Administration).

With the number of marriages skyrocketing (up from 1.4 million in 1944 to 2.3 million in 1946 and staying at close to 2 million in 1947–48), the housing situation was dire, with most newlyweds having no choice but to squeeze into small inner-city flats with their parents and sometimes grandparents as well. It was a national emergency, and Levitt had the answer: "suburbia" constructed on farmlands adjoining major cities and built on an assembly line akin to Ford cars. In 1946, Levitt bought 1,200 acres of land on Long Island and adopted his assembly line technique, with specialist teams moving rapidly and efficiently from one house to the next. Within a matter of months, he completed 17,000 homes, providing accommodation for more than 80,000 people. By July 1948, Levitt was building 180 houses per week, a huge leap compared to two to five houses per annum an average builder constructed in the 1930s.[15] The signs went up: "This is Levittown! All yours for $58. You are a lucky fellow, Mr. Veteran. Uncle Sam and the world's largest builder have made it possible for you to live in a charming house in a delightful community without having to pay for them with your eye teeth."[16]

Many others imitated Levitt, and the pent-up energy was released in a massive explosion. In 1946, new starts increased from 100,000 to over 900,000, exceeding 1.7 million in 1950 and remaining between 1.5 and 2.5 million through the rest of the 1950s and 1960s, with construction teams bulldozing a million acres per annum (or larger than Rhode Island)[17] to create new suburbia. By the early 1960s, more people lived in suburbs than cities, with 62 percent of American families owning their own home, compared to 43 percent in 1945. While keen observers of this revolution such as Lewis Mumford despaired at the "multitude of uniform roads, in a treeless command waste, witnessing the same television performances, eating the same tasteless prefabricated foods, from the same freezers,"[18] with sameness of the suburbs also brutally satirized in movies like *The Invasion of the Body Snatchers*, Levitt regarded these views as snobbish, and he was confident that the overwhelming majority of people supported expansion of the suburbia.

However, suburbia would never have captured the hearts and minds of returning GIs if it were not for an equally impressive expansion of transit and highway systems. Once again, as local governments were connecting suburbs to inner cities, the federal government stepped in with the Federal Aid Highway Act of 1956, which authorized 41 thousand miles of interstate roads. This was one of the few bills that ever passed Congress without specific costing—it was simply expected to continue until all of the mile requirements were satisfied. Indeed, it did, with construction continuing into the 1970s.

The same was true of the GI Bill, passed in 1944, which offered previously unattainable educational opportunities to all GIs returning from World War II. By the end of the original GI bill, nearly 8 million veterans attended colleges or other training institutions, massively boosting the stock of national human capital. Soon, for the first time in history, America had more students than farmers. As the bulge of babies born post 1945 had grown up and started en masse enrolling in colleges, it was once again the government that underwrote an unprecedented expansion of educational spending, with funding for public institutions of higher education rising from $742 million in 1945 to $6.9 billion in 1965.[19] As a result, the number of degrees granted more than doubled between 1956 and 1968. It was a perfect case study of the bottom-up demand for education matching the Cold War and technology-inspired top-down needs.

There were many other changes that proactive government policies and the demographic bulge brought about. For example, it was Kemmons Wilson, one of the more successful Memphis builders (in the mold of Levitt) who in 1951 realized that Americans having bought a car and a house would next want to travel to see the country. He started Holiday Inn, launching a motel revolution. Similarly, the McDonald Brothers understood that as more people commute and travel, they would prefer to eat quickly and in a pleasant environment. The brothers (Dick and Mac) also realized the importance of a rising tide of young children and positioned their roadside restaurants to be as child friendly as possible. After all, children came equipped with paying parents.

Suburbanization and the proliferation of TV sets beyond major cities was another major revolution. In 1949, out of 1 million TV sets, almost half were in New York and most of the remaining in major cities, like Philadelphia, Chicago, and Los Angeles. However, by 1951, the number of TV households expanded to over 10 million, exceeding 50 million by 1960, with most spread across smaller towns, suburbia, and the countryside. This radically altered the nature and the power of television, as a cultural, social, and political medium, as Nixon discovered in the first televised presidential debate against Kennedy, in which radio listeners thought that Nixon had won, but those viewing it on television believed that the fresh-faced Kennedy had won decisively. Television replaced the more cerebral and somewhat darker depression-era radio programming that required a certain cynicism as well as imagination with much blander but more upbeat and visually appealing offerings. Typical examples were the replacement of *The Fred Allen* radio show with the *Stop the Music* game show or the wildly popular *I Love Lucy* sitcom. Americans no longer wanted dark humor; they wanted to participate in the country's success and wanted to be entertained, and programmers delivered the type of entertainment that confirmed the popular belief that everything was good and tomorrow would be even better.

While stifling, conformist and irredeemably bland, the 1950s and the first half of 1960s was a time of plenty for many, with a majority believing that there were technocratic solutions to any problem, and most expected their representatives and the government to be honest. This period boasted the highest ever trust ratings for every institution, from the Administration to Congress and Judiciary, media and corporations. As Todd Gitlin observed: "When the majority of Americans called themselves middle class, they meant at least they were on their way...with the long-sought and long-feared American wilderness...trimmed back and made habitable. The prairie became the lawn; the ranch, the ranch house; the saloon, the Formica bar."[20]

The changes in Europe were even more pronounced. Unlike the US, most of Europe was devastated by the war. It is estimated that almost 37 million Europeans[21] died between 1939 and 1945 from war-related causes. This is equivalent to losing the prewar population of France. Indeed, even this astronomic number ignores people who died indirectly from the war (from hunger, pandemics, and disease) and the number of children who would have been born if there had been no war. These statistics also ignore the mental anguish that people of Europe had to endure not just during the war but also for years afterward.[22] Unlike the Great War—which left civilians and local populations largely alone, even as borders shifted—the aftermath of World War II was accompanied by one of the greatest ever ethnic cleansings and resettlements, even as borders (with the notable exceptions of Germany and Poland) remained largely unchanged. It is what Tony Judt described as a "tidier and more ethnically homogeneous" Europe emerging from the ruins. In Poland and Czechoslovakia, the doctrine of a collective German guilt and punishment was the official policy, with pillage and expropriation rife,[23] while as many as 15 million, including survivors of concentration camps and slave labor, were caught for years in displacement camps that did not fully close until 1957.[24] These included more than 2 million French, 1.6 million Poles, over 700,000 Italians, 350,000 Czechs, and many others.[25]

The degree of economic and property destruction was equally unprecedented. In 1945, Austria's GDP plummeted to its lowest level since 1886. France's economy shrank to a size roughly equivalent to that of 1891. Similarly, Italian, German, and Dutch postwar GDP regressed to levels not seen since 1910.[26] The destruction of property was of unimaginable proportions. In Budapest, 84 percent of the buildings were damaged, and 30 percent were uninhabitable. About 80 percent of the city of Minsk in Belarus was destroyed while Berlin lost 50 percent of its habitable premises, and in Cologne, the ratio was closer to 70 percent. Almost 20 million Germans were rendered homeless—more than the prewar population of Holland and Belgium combined. Across France almost 2.5 million buildings were either destroyed or severely damaged. Holland lost 60 percent of its road, rail, and canal transport, and up to one-third of Italy's road network was destroyed and 13,000 bridges had either collapsed or were severely damaged. Yugoslavia lost around one-third of its entire industrial wealth and 60 percent of its livestock. In the Soviet Union, as many as 1,700 towns and cities had simply vanished.[27] Europe had essentially reverted to the medieval age, or as one American journalist described it, living was "surrounded by the broken-down machinery of the twentieth century."[28]

In this context, the recovery, both in its speed and breadth, of the western portion of the European continent was nothing short of breathtaking.

Between 1950 and 1973, the German and Austrian GDP per capita more than tripled in real terms, and the French real income level almost doubled. German prewar industrial output was regained by 1950, and by 1960, the industrial output was more than double. By 1965, it was triple that of 1938. The same was true for France, with its economy recapturing its highest prewar level by 1950, while the progress in Italy and Austria was even more spectacular. Unemployment, the bugbear of 1930s Europe, had been largely eliminated. The unemployment rate in Germany and the Netherlands in the first half of the 1960s, averaged less than 1 percent, while in Italy and Austria it was around 3 percent, compared to 9–11 percent prior to the war.[29] Electricity consumption per capita—an all-encompassing measure of economic activity—increased everywhere. In Germany, France, and Italy, energy intensity in 1965 was four times its level in 1937–38, and more than five times in the UK.

As mentioned above, in 1965, the number of cars per a thousand people in Germany was 17 times prewar levels and in Italy it was 40 times greater. As a curiosity, in 1950, West German retailers sold 900,000 pairs of ladies' nylon stockings (a luxury tradeable postwar product), but by 1953, the same retailers sold 58 million pairs.[30] Supermarkets started to proliferate from the late 1950s (and especially in the 1960s) and by 1970, more than half of European households had access to television, replacing the radio sets that were still dominant through the 1950s, and more than 80 percent of Europeans had a fridge.

What were the key drivers of such a dramatic turnaround? As most complex phenomena, the European economic and political miracle of the 1950s–60s was an outcome of many interconnected, and sometimes contradictory, forces.

First and foremost, Americans played a key role in stabilizing and repositioning Europe. Notwithstanding the disdain that European highbrow intellectuals felt (and still feel) for Americans—in the words of Jean-Paul Sartre, "America is a land of hysterical puritans, given over to technology, standardization and conformism, bereft of originality of thought"[31]—people at large embraced a broad range of American values and products, from Levi's jeans to music and consumerism. At the same time, the US government was a critical component of recovery, especially in its early years. Most of the investment in the late 1940s and early 1950s originated from the US Marshall Plan, which was designed to help Europeans help themselves. In the years of its operation, the US government sponsored investments equivalent to almost $200 billion in today's US dollars, with the greatest impact felt in Germany. Most academics agree that the Marshall Plan kick-started the European miracle by helping to revive trade and restore production while controlling inflation. Although economists continue to debate its nature and purpose, it seems indisputable that without the Marshall Plan, recovery would have been far more hazardous and volatile. It is true that a growing antagonism between the US and the Soviet Union played a role, but almost all evidence points to America's understanding that even in the absence of the communist threat, European recovery was in its own best interests.

Another less tangible impact of the Marshall Plan was institutional in nature. In order to secure funds, countries needed to make certain undertakings to support the evolution of the private sector. There is a healthy debate about the extent to which European institutional settings had actually changed, and certainly, if judged by the criteria of 1990s–2000s, all economies were tightly regulated and controlled. Governments everywhere played a significant role—either directly in the UK (through nationalizations) or indirectly (through corporations and unions) in Germany. France adopted a top-down approach of "picking the winners" and guiding private investment, and the government's role was crucial in Italy, especially in the country's south. Nevertheless, when compared to the fascist or socialist economies of the 1930s, there was undoubtedly a far greater free space for the private sector to grow throughout the 1950s–60s. Most crucially, in most European countries a series of formal and informal agreements between governments, employers, and employees struck the right balance of constraining wage demands while increasing fixed asset investment and ensuring the stability of inflation rates and currencies. Only in the 1970s, did these arrangements, which were so critical to containing costs while offering a greater macro stability, fall apart.

The US also played a key role in the creation of the European Economic Community (EEC), which later evolved into today's EU. Although even before the Treaty of Rome in 1958, a large portion of European trade was already intra-regional (e.g., in the mid-1950s, around 30 percent of German trade was going to France, Italy, and Benelux), the creation of EEC anchored Europe and allowed for better scale and competitive advantages to flow to individual member states. Even today, the project is still a work in progress (with squabbles around issues like qualified majority votes or functioning of the European Central Bank), but there is no doubt that on balance, whether it is through dedicated investment programs or ensuring that weaker and poorer members gradually catch-up, the EU has been one of the greater success stories economically, socially, politically, and geopolitically.

The other major driver of accelerating growth was the change in the structure of economies. Whereas prior to the war, Europe (except Britain) was still largely agrarian, this started to change at a rapid clip. In Italy, agriculture as a percentage of economy dropped from almost 28 percent in 1949 to 13 percent by 1960, while employment in agriculture declined to around 16 percent by the early 1970s. In France and Austria, agricultural employment more than halved to approximately 10 percent. Unlike Britain (which abolished agricultural protections in the 19th century), Germany had kept its agricultural sector largely unchanged, dominated by small unproductive family farms, all the way until the end of the war. As a result, in 1950, more than 22 percent of German employment was agriculture based. This dropped to only 7 percent by 1970.[32] As labor relocated from lower to higher productivity occupations, the overall productivity across Europe had significantly increased. Total Factor Productivity (TFP) grew at a blistering pace of more than 3.5 percent per annum in both France and Germany, and in Italy, the growth trajectory was in excess of 4 percent.[33]

Demographics was the final nudge. While at a slightly later stage than the US, European marriage and birth rates noticeably picked up from the mid-1950s through the late 1960s, while life expectancy significantly increased. These improvements were due to both higher birth and survival rates. Mortality rates plummeted across Europe, not only because of peace but also due to significantly strengthened medical care and better social safety nets (including cash subsidies and free milk). For example, in Italy infant mortality dropped from almost 106 per 1,000 live births in 1950 to less than 30 by 1970, while the French infant mortality collapsed from 63 to 15, and in Belgium it was down from 53 to 21.[34] By comparison, US infant mortality dropped from around 30 in 1950 to 20 by 1970. The logical outcome of more births and less death was that in the 1960s as much as 30 percent of the population of countries like the Netherlands, Finland, and France were under the age of 15, creating a demographic dividend that supported European growth all the way into the 1970s.

However, none of this would have been possible without strong and consensual support from the state. In the era before neoliberalism had come to dominate politics and the policy debate, the view of the government as an indispensable guardrail and a guiding force in both social and economic spheres was embraced by societies. As a result, this was a bipartisan position (whether Democrats and Republicans in the US or Social Democrats and Christian Democrats in Europe) with objections viewed as a relic of the pre-Keynesian era, propagated by those who had not learned the lessons of the Great Depression and World War II. The anti-state views remained marginal until the late 1970s. In the US, the share of GDP attributable to the state increased from around 13 percent in 1950 to almost 33 percent by 1973, while in Germany the state share had gone up from 30 percent to 43 percent, and in the Netherlands the state's spending increased from 24 percent of GDP to 45 percent, and Italy's share had more than doubled from 17 percent to 35 percent.[35] An overwhelming bulk of the increase went into spending on insurance, healthcare, pensions, education, and housing. In the US it also turned into a cold-war-driven research and development expenditure through universities and bodies like NASA and Bell Labs, which fueled a wave of inventiveness and later innovation in the 1970s–90s (from wireless telephony to internet, from space flights to new materials).

On balance, one has to agree with Bradford DeLong[36] that this was one of the best ever periods, at least for Western nations, as long as one was not black or an indigenous citizen or an immigrant worker in Europe. It's no wonder Paul Krugman (Nobel Prize winner in economics) and Robert Reich (President Clinton's labor secretary) have fond memories of that golden age and why the French described this period as *Les Trente Glorieuses*.

The belief that the world had finally left the turbulence and uncertainties of the preceding decades was so entrenched that some even suggested that we had attained a state of blessed equilibrium in which ideological battles became largely defunct. Daniel Bell and Seymour Lipset, American sociologists, openly declared the end of ideology as the driving force, replaced by technocratic and professional solutions to occasional and discrete problems that from time-to-time affected interactions.[37] Nothing was out of reach for what were perceived to be modern techniques for resolving disagreements that were no longer rooted in enduring and irreconcilable schisms of class, ethnicity, or privilege. Economic growth was expected to ultimately create equal opportunities for everyone while technology and technocratic solutions were assumed to be capable of resolving most other issues, without resorting to the violence and rupture that characterized prior periods.

Raymond Aron, one of the best minds of postwar European liberalism, also hailed the end of violence and the near-miraculous arrival of a strong societal consensus that left behind the hot debates and infighting of the 1920s and 1930s. Although Aron never suffered from illusions of the nature and limitations of the formalized European democracy, like Daniel Bell, he had by the end of the 1950s declared the end of the age of ideology.[38] This was not dissimilar to a much later proclamation by Francis Fukuyama of the end of history following the fall of the Berlin Wall in 1990.[39]

Despite threats of communism and nuclear war, as they entered 1960s, most people on both shores of the Atlantic Ocean agreed with William Atwood's survey published in *Look* magazine on January 5, 1960,[40] that the coming decade would bring some of the best times ever—with citizens expecting to "go enjoying their peaceful existence, right through the sixties and may be forever."

•   •   •

However, all was not well in this Garden of Eden. As Czeslaw Milosz, a Polish American Nobel Prize winner in poetry, said, "In a room where people unanimously maintain a conspiracy of silence, one word of truth sounds like a pistol shot." Lurking beneath the surface of an apparent tranquility and relief that the horrors of the preceding era had ended were unprecedented crosscurrents of discontent that touched on a multitude of discontinuities, failed expectations, and disappointments that had not just persisted through this glorious era but were rapidly escalating.

First, there was a ravine between the world of plenty and the dark shadow of the past, accompanied by a rising discomfort with the "constrained" present. In the words of Todd Gitlin, "The affluent society was awash with fear of the uncontrollable…the middle class furnished its islands of affluence, but around it the waters kept rising."[41] The fear that bad times would come back was ever present, and uneasiness grew as to whether or not the price that society required everyone to pay as a ticket to this world of plenty was worth it.

Ben Stein, an American economist and comedian, once remarked, "My parents, products of the Great Depression, were successful people, but lived in a state of constant fear that my sister and I, and they, would sink into the kind of insecurity that their generation knew so well." A deep ravine started to emerge between parents and their children, with the younger generation insisting that their life experiences were so historically unprecedented that the older generations simply could not understand what motivated them or the rules of the new world. As one of the teenagers of that age described it: "Parents could never convey how they were haunted by the Depression and relieved by the arrival of affluence; the young could never quite convey how tired they were of being reminded how bad things had once been, and therefore how graced and grateful they should feel to live normally."[42]

If there were one word that encapsulated the societal consensus of the 1950s and the early to mid-1960s, it was *conformity*. Bruce Springsteen, growing up in the new suburbs, recalled that parents and officials were "very intent on maintaining the status quo; everything was looked upon as a threat."[43] High schools across the US enforced dress codes, with officials frequently banning jeans or ducktail haircuts because they perceived a direct connection between undisciplined dress and bad behavior. "Thus, teens looked remarkably like their parents. Girls wore hair that resembled mom's perma press head and... dad cropped his son's hair in a World War II crew cut."[44] The same conformity spread to college campuses, especially in the wake of McCarthyism. As one student said, responding to a professor's concern that there was not enough vibrancy and debate: "Why should we go out on a limb about anything? We know what happened to those that did."[45] It was an era when colleges and universities had higher admission requirements for women and female quotas at graduate schools. Colleges were regarded mainly as places where women could learn how to sing French songs to their children, and these institutions were meant to function as marriage supermarkets, with coeds who were not engaged before their senior year suffering from "senior panic."[46] In most states cohabitation among unmarried couples was illegal, and in some (like Alabama) extramarital sexual intercourse was a felony, and most surveys highlighted overwhelming popular support for the idea of virginity before marriage.

Although female employment had increased (between 1948 and

1958, the number of employed women with children under the age of eighteen rose from 4.1 million to 7.5 million[47]), social roles were tightly segregated. *Life* magazine declared in 1956 that "of all accomplishments of the American woman, the one she brings off with the most spectacular success is having babies."[48] The pressure to maintain home and happy children while also frequently working, and at the same time maintaining an obligatory sunny disposition and remaining sexually desirable, was placing an enormous burden on women. It is not surprising that one of the more popular women's magazines asked in December 1960, "Why Young Mothers Feel Trapped," when, as it correctly pointed out, "no women in the world's history ever had it so good."[49] As Betty Friedan called it, "the problem that has no name." The proliferation of tools that were supposed to make women's lives easier (such as fridges, dishwashers, vacuum cleaners, etc.) were not reducing the amount of time women were dedicating to house chores. Instead, they had intensified their desire for perfection. A Bryn Mawr College survey reported that women in 1960 were still spending 78 hours per week doing housework, not dissimilar to the early 1950s. However, the society placed an equally heavy pressure on man: "Those of us who came of age in the fifties had no choice. You had to be a husband, a provider, and a success,"[50] an obligation that caused anguish and what was described in those days as "maladjustment." Just as in the case of their wives, this led to increased drinking and excessive consumption of tranquilizers and antidepressants.[51] A failure to want to have babies or a family was generally regarded as a dangerous emotional disturbance to be treated through medical means, including electric shock therapies and even sterilization.[52]

While today's conservatives and neoliberals (especially in the US) harp back to what they perceive as the traditional family values of the 1950s, for its time, the family arrangement was actually unique and unprecedented, not only in the US but globally. The idea of teenagers or adolescents (i.e., a category between children and adults) had never existed in human history—you were always either an adult or a child. As Stephanie Coontz highlighted, the idea of a mother dedicating her time to home, children, and her husband was equally revolutionary and would not have been recognized by a majority of the population in either the 19th or the first half of the 20th centuries. At that time, the only value of a wife and a child was their usefulness as additional pairs of hands. Rather than being rooted in tradition, a strict segregation of duties between husband and wife was only applied to a small minority of truly well-off households. It was the above-described wave of prosperity that created the historically unprecedented division of family responsibilities of the 1950s–60s.

The drive toward societal consensus and conformity did not end with families. Any deviation from the perceived norms was punishable, sometimes severely.

The Truman administration required people to sign loyalty pledges, with anyone declining to do so treated as a suspect. In the late 1940s to early 1950s, more than 6.5 million people were checked for loyalty, with the accused benefiting from neither judge nor jury. Through the 1950s, schools and colleges fired more than 6,000 teachers and professors while television and radio producers discharged more than 1,500 employees for perceived crimes ranging from homosexuality to disloyalty. At that time, "speaking abusively of the US" was regarded as a criminal offense, punishable for life in states like Michigan and potentially even death in states like Tennessee. Any deviation from the "norm" in either political, moral, sexual, or behavioral aspects was punishable by sacking, fines, or, at the extreme, incarceration. Being a communist, for example, deprived one of unemployment benefits and driving and fishing licenses in New York, while in Texas, it could end in a 20-year jail sentence. The US State Department proudly proclaimed in 1950 that it was "firing one homosexual per day." Tom Clark, Truman's Attorney General, publicly stated, "Those who do not believe in the ideology of the United States… shall not be allowed to stay in the United States,"[53] and "Who could be more dangerous to the United States than a pervert."[54] Censorship was pervasive[55] and blacklists were the norm, not the exception.

At the same time, racial segregation and restrictions on black voting rights were supported by an absolute majority of white Americans. Various surveys through the 1950s revealed that 97 percent of southern and over 90 percent of northern whites opposed interracial dating while three-fourths of southern whites opposed having an African American as a neighbor, and even in the north, half of responders supported maintenance of segregation. It is not surprising, therefore, that Bill Levitt for two decades maintained his policy of not selling homes to black couples, not because he objected but because his clients did. In his own words: "The Negros in America are trying to do in four hundred years what the Jews in the world have not fully accomplished in six hundred years. As a Jew I have no room in my mind or heart for racial prejudice. But…I have come to know that if we sell one house to a Negro family, then 90 or 95 percent of our white customers will not buy into the community. That is their attitude not ours…as a company our position is simply this: We can solve a housing problem, or we can try to solve a racial problem, but we cannot combine the two."[56]

While too simplistic, there is an element of truth in Alan Ehrenhalt's portrayal of the 1950s and early 1960s America as an era of constrained affluence: "Your cereal was cornflakes; television was black-and-white; ballplayers generally stayed with one baseball team; life was structured."[57] One could add an unparallel barbarism of Deep South race relations as well as rabid homophobia to this laundry list.

Although Europe in the 1950s did settle into what can be best described as a controlled and ritualistic democracy, and until much later, it did not suffer from race-oriented violence, the societal norms were almost as strict as in the US.

Scandinavian countries, which are today regarded as beacons of freedom and democracy with the best scores globally on most human rights and democracy surveys, were practicing forced sterilization well into the 1970s. This practice of "racial hygiene" was embraced by parties on both the left and right, with over 100,000 people sterilized during this glorious era. Almost all countries exercised a considerable degree of control over the private affairs and opinions of the citizenry. Homosexuality was illegal everywhere and quite often punishable by prison terms. Similarly, abortion was illegal in most countries, and even contraceptives were technically against the law, especially in Catholic countries. Except for Scandinavia, almost all countries operated strict censorship of literature, news, theater, and cinema while the new television medium was almost everywhere (except for Britain) controlled by the government. In Italy and France, most of the fascist laws remained on the books well into the 1960s. In the case of Germany, the infamous Nazi article 175, which prohibited and punished homosexuality, was not reformed until 1969 and was not repealed until 1994. Britain was the first to embark on rapid liberalization, but once again, most of it had to wait until much later. In the 1950s, the British were not allowed to gamble or practice abortion, while getting a divorce was very hard, and censorship was harsh, with the infamous legal case of *Lady Chatterley's Lover* (a censored Penguin book) in October 1960 finally starting to crack the façade.

•　　•　　•

While Allen Ginsberg and Beatniks were the first to revolt against the stifling, restrictive, and discriminatory environment of the 1950s, the real breakthrough came on February 1, 1960, when four young black college students from the North Carolina A&T College sat down at the lunch counter of a whites-only venue in Greensboro, North Carolina, inaugurating more than a decade of turmoil that did not exhaust itself until a new societal consensus had formed in the late 1970s to early 1980s.[58] It was driven by the young generation later termed Baby Boomers, in reference to the postwar boom in marriages and births. These young people (born between 1946 and 1964) were not only the single largest cohort ever in either the US or European history, but also had very different views on almost every aspect of life—from bedrooms and private life to the role of the state and public sphere. As they matured, conflict with existing social, economic, and political structures was inevitable.

As color television sets gradually replaced black-and-white sets in the first half of the 1960s (and in the late 1960s in Europe), so did politics—with "black-and-white" stilted images of 1950s and early 1960s being replaced by the far more natural, colorful, alive, and violent world of the late 1960s and 1970s. This will be the topic for the next chapter.

Chapter 2
History Comes off Its Leash

*"I was using the symbol of a helter skelter...as a ride from the top to bottom—
the rise and fall of the Roman Empire...a demise."*
Paul McCartney on the origins of the song "Helter Skelter" (1968)

"Helter Skelter" was a lead song on one of the Beatles' last compilations, known as *The White Album*. The song referred to a fairground ride popular at the time in Britain in which people would climb a tower and then slide down a spiral ride on the outside of the tower. The song was meant to convey the impression that everything is liable to fall and disintegrate. However, after Charles Manson interpreted this song as a call for Armageddon, it acquired a far more sinister meaning. These words ("Helter Skelter") were painted in a victim's blood on the fridge of the murdered Leo and Rosemary La Bianca in Los Angeles (a day after Manson's gang had killed actress Sharon Tate, wife of director Roman Polanski) in August 1969. The song was an early precursor of the jarring and noisy metal bands of the 1970s.

What was going on, and why had the Beatles' love serenades of the early to mid-1960s morphed into "helter skelter," and more importantly, why was it interpreted by others as a call for Armageddon? It is not an easy question to answer, and there are hundreds of books and articles that explore it in far greater detail than I intend to. What made the second half of 1960s and the 1970s (frequently described as an extended "bad 1960s or 70s") so different from the preceding era?[1] As Jama Lazerow put it, the new age was the time when "everything was subject to question: political parties and private property, power and authority, sex roles and family arrangement, work and play, music, dress, language and thought."[2]

It is hard to find a more transformative time than the bad extended 1970s, which brought to the forefront an incredible number of forces that still shape our society today: freedom marches and the fight for civil rights in the US, anti-war and anti-imperialist movements across the world, the proliferation of hallucinatory drugs and "flower culture," student movements, the reappearance of neoliberal and conservative ideas, the beginning and then blossoming of women's, gay, lesbian, and Latino rights, as well as conservation and climate movements, and reemergence of terrorism. All of these had either started or were nurtured in this turbulent extended decade. It was a moment when, as one commentator argued, "history came off its leash."

•   •   •

What gravitational forces were responsible for such a dramatic shift from the tranquility of the 1950s and early to mid-1960s to the strife and disorientation of the late 1960s and especially the 1970s? It is for a good reason that what was described as the "glorious decades" turned into what was later termed a "kidney stone of a decade" or more colorfully and somewhat unfairly as a time of "bad hair, bad clothes, bad music, bad design, bad books, bad economics, bad carpeting, bad fabrics, and a lot of bad ideas."[3] In my view, there were several facilitators of this change.

First, neither the Beats movement of the 1950s nor the hippie counterculture of the 1960s would have been possible unless they were effectively underwritten by a strong postwar economy. Traditionally, convulsions are driven by a combination of despair and preexisting economic "fat" that fuels anger while allowing some members of society to drop out and ignore acceptable social norms without starving. Apart from more extreme expressions of dissatisfaction (such as the Red Brigades, the Black Panthers, and Weather Underground), disruptive movements of the era (whether social, economic, or cultural) were mostly led by young people coming from middle-class environments—the same middle class that was created by the two unprecedented decades of economic expansion. By 1968, the average American family income was $8,000, almost double what it was a decade prior, and triple compared to the late 1940s.[4] By the early 1960s, a teenager was judged to have the spending power of more than $10 per week,[5] with an increasing number able to satisfy their own spending preferences, whether in clothes, entertainment, or cars. More and more teenagers were driving to schools and colleges (as exemplified by Hollywood in *American Graffiti* and *Happy Days*). It is hardly surprising that one youth declared that "they were the luckiest teenagers in the history of the world."[6]

For the first time ever, a brand-new socioeconomic group had evolved: *adolescents*. They broke from the customs of their parents, developing their own language and norms, which were primarily influenced by their friends rather than their parents and teachers. James Coleman, an academic with Johns Hopkins University, was one of the first to identify this evolving trend. In his book (published in 1961 and based on surveys conducted in schools across northern Illinois), he argued that the sheer size of the Baby Boomer cohort, the massive expansion of educational opportunities unavailable to prior generations, and an unprecedented period of relative peace and prosperity created a new generation that was further apart from their parents than was normally the case. As a result, "levers by which children are motivated—approval or disapproval of parents and teachers—are less efficient."[7] The new generation perceived their circumstances to be so unique that it was their peers whose approval and admiration they were looking for, with parents and teachers taking a distant second place.

Corporations took notice of teenagers' purchasing power as well as their distinctly different views. This applied to both the US and Europe. In France, spending on magazine advertising aimed at adolescents rose by 400 percent between 1959 and 1962. Prior to World War II, teenagers who left school and started to work (usually at the age of fourteen) but lived at home were automatically expected to hand their earnings to the family. By the early 1960s, this practice had all but disappeared in the US, while in France and Germany, more than 60 percent of 16- to 24-year-olds who were still living with parents were retaining all their earnings and spending them as they wished.[8]

And spend they did, from miniskirts and long hair to new forms of entertainment, in the process, spawning rock and roll and pop music. Both style of dress and music were crucial as age-specific statements of independence, and quite often, as revolts against existing norms. The same was true of the desire to build a new world, giving rise to communal living (e.g., hippies) as well as a strong urge to redress deeply seated conformity, conservatism, and inequities of their era (e.g., student, civil rights, and anti-war movements). As Gitlin described: "In 1963, at twenty, I was elected president of Students for a Democratic Society, SDS, which numbered a grand total of six hundred paid members and harbored the modest ambition of shaking America to its roots."[9] However, all of this was only possible because in Europe and America, family budgets dispensed with teenagers' contribution.

Second, the younger generation did not share their parents' and grandparents' fear of the unknown. Growing up in the 1950s–60s, young Baby Boomers had not experienced anything as destructive as the Great Depression, pandemics, or World Wars. Instead, they witnessed growth, prosperity, and ample job and educational opportunities. The benefits were not equally shared, and the 1950s and early 1960s were still very much a WASP era in America, and in Europe past rigidities remained exceptionally powerful. However, almost everyone was better off than only a decade or two before. While more than 20 percent of Americans were classified as poor, even they were better off than those in most other countries or themselves in the past. In the hollows of Harlan County, Kentucky (one of the most impoverished areas in America), by the early 1960s, around 67 percent of households already had a television, and 59 percent owned a car.[10]

Baby Boomers were rejecting the stifling and conformist atmosphere of the 1950s, and the ever-present role of the "nanny state." Their ideas radically challenged what in the past had been commonplace: they insisted on freedom of movement between countries (which was tightly controlled in the 1950s–70s), freedom to marry or divorce anyone they like (again tightly controlled until well into the 1980s and sometimes even 1990s), the ability to change jobs (uncommon and not easy to do in the

1950s–70s), freedom to enjoy the outdoors (hence Boomers' support for environmental causes), and the elimination of discrimination (racial, ethnic, gender, or cultural). In other words, the new generation was insisting on equality and freedom of individual opportunities rather than guarantee of outcomes. It is not surprising, therefore, that, as we discuss later, quite a few disgruntled Baby Boomers had over time morphed into neoliberal or conservative leaders, with the linkage being a high value placed on individual rather than societal freedoms.

Whereas their parents and grandparents were willing to trade some of their rights to ensure that the worst possible outcomes did not occur and viewed the state as the guardrail against chaos that could at any time destroy their lives, Baby Boomers viewed the state and a broader society as an impediment to their freedom and a constraint that they were neither willing nor prepared to tolerate. In this context, it was not surprising that the Beatles' "Helter Skelter" coincided with the Woodstock music festival held in August 1969 in the Catskill Mountains, attracting more than 400,000 young people with a promise of music, LSD, and sex, or as it was described, "three days of peace and music." Similarly, 1968–70 was a period of violent student confrontations across the world, from US college campuses to the Latin quarter in Paris, from Brazil and Germany to Italy. While specific motivations and triggers were different, from calls for change in the educational curriculum to anti-war and racial policies, the underlying "heartbeat" was the same: "We, the younger generation, refuse to accept today's norms and demand a change."

Although each generation does rebel against their parents (it is just nature's way of asserting independence), radical shifts like those in the late 1960s and early 1970s are far less common and are driven by a deep cleavage in the prevailing economic, social, and political climate. While there were some differences between Baby Boomers and the following Generation X (born between 1964 and 1980), the gap was nowhere near as deep or disruptive, with the commonalities being far greater than the differences. However, the rift between Baby Boomers and their parents and grandparents was enormous. As this book will argue, a similarly deep ravine today separates the ageing Baby Boomers from the young Millennials and Generation Z (or those born after 1980).

Thus, the unique nature of the late 1960s and the early 1970s was due not only to the economic "fat" built up over preceding decades but also to the very different life experiences of Baby Boomers. It so happens that the 1950s–60s was generally not only a time of growing prosperity, but it was also a relatively peaceful time,[11] more so than in almost any other period in recent human history. As memories of the disasters of 1910s–40s gradually faded away, Baby Boomers no longer felt it necessary to sacrifice so much of their personal freedom for the protective but stifling state and societal constraints.

Third, one cannot overstate the importance of media, and especially the appearance of television and live broadcasting, in shaping and fueling these cultural and social changes. It was the live broadcasting of marches from places like Selma, Alabama, in 1965 that shamed the entire society, revealing the cruelty and bigotry of the Jim Crow Deep South. The same was true of 1960–63 broadcasts of sit-ins that spread in the wake of the Greensboro Four or the violent race riots of 1966–69. Between 1960 and 1965, at least 26 civil rights activists were murdered, but only one of the killers went to prison, with neither local nor state governments upholding the law.[12] Americans not only witnessed daily police brutality (accompanied by batons and vicious dogs) but also realized that in a black county like Selma, only two percent of blacks were allowed to register to vote.

And Selma was not unique. In a state like Alabama, with a large black population, only nine percent of blacks were registered to vote, and that figure was only four percent in Mississippi, with violent intimidation as well as various purported "literacy tests" ruling out the rest. Similarly, the Jim Crow laws of "separate but equal" led to a massive differentiation in educational opportunities. In Mississippi, the state was spending an average of $123 for each white student but only $33 for each black student, and the black graduation rates from high school were seldom more than two to three percent.[13]

Live broadcasting of the Vietnam War served a similar purpose, with an indelible image of a Buddhist monk sitting down at a busy intersection in Saigon and then pouring gasoline over his body and lighting the match in front of the world's cameras. The monk was protesting jailing of Buddhists by the Diem regime of South Vietnam. Similarly distressing were images of a burning nine-year-old Vietnamese girl running away from the US napalm attack on Viet Cong forces. The same was true of the live broadcasting of the Tet Offensive, the Battle of Khe Sanh, destruction of the ancient city of Hue, and the rescuing of South Vietnamese from the roof of the US Embassy in Saigon. Live broadcasting and instantaneous communication brought home the horror and hopelessness of the Vietnam War far more effectively than a more traditional print media could ever do, especially in times of stricter censorship.

A recent study by the Rand Corporation[14] shows that the evolution of media has always been a critical element that ultimately determined the intensity of disruption. Upheavals of the 1880s–90s were magnified by the appearance of the yellow press and the 1920s–30s upheavals were similarly magnified by radio. Television had even more profoundly driven the wedge in the 1960s–70s, and as I argued in my first book,[15] today's social media, is having an even greater impact. In the absence of a widespread TV audience and live broadcasting, it is doubtful that equivalent actions in the 1950s (like Rosa Parks or the Korean War) would have provoked a similarly deep societal impact.

Fourth, there is no doubt that the intensity of violence and disruption increased exponentially in the 1970s, with more extreme and disruptive confrontations becoming the norm. This was mostly due to a rapidly deteriorating economic environment as the glorious decades of strong growth, low inflation, and unemployment gave way to more than a decade of slow growth and high inflation (or what later became known as the longest period of stagflation in modern history). As always, it is changes in economic circumstances that amplified insecurities and determined the degree and depth of societal dislocation.

From the late 1960s, the global economy went into reverse. In the ultimate analysis, declining productivity and economic inefficiencies were pernicious side effects of heavy state involvement in managing economies through the 1950s–1970s as governments gradually took over more and more functions from the private sector. In Britain, the government nationalized National Gas in 1949, British Steel in 1967, the National Bus Company in 1969, Rolls Royce in 1971, and British Gas and British Petroleum in 1973–74. It then folded in the remaining car companies under British Leyland in 1976 and nationalized British Aerospace in 1977. In France, most banks, electricity and gas suppliers, and the Renault car company were nationalized in the late 1940s while further significant nationalizations occurred in the late 1970s and early 1980s. In Sweden, railways and some of the banks and mining companies were nationalized. In the US, this period marked the beginning of social investment under Lyndon B. Johnson's The Great Society programs in 1964–65, while the bulk of the railways were nationalized in the early 1970s. The list could easily go on; however, the key is that although the state involvement was absolutely crucial in rebuilding shattered economies, supporting inventiveness and innovation while also ensuring that human capital was raised to a much higher than hitherto level, governments in almost every corner of the world meaningfully overstepped the prudent pace of expansion and deeply intruded into many areas that should have remained part of the private sector.

Most countries were also pursuing lax monetary policies, effectively trading along the Phillips curve (named after the New Zealand economist who described the policy trade-off between employment and inflation). At that time, it was universally believed that one could tolerate some inflation in order to achieve and maintain full employment. A growing state industrial control was therefore compounded by rising social and government spending as well as the cost of the Vietnam War, mostly funded by lax monetary policies. In addition, unions had become much more dominant. In the US, trade unions covered 30 percent of the labor force in the 1960s compared to 10 percent today, while in countries like Australia and Britain it was closer to 45–50 percent compared to today's levels of around 15 percent. In OECD nations, the average trade union density was approximately 40 percent versus 16 percent now. Inflation-adjusted wage contracts started to widely proliferate. It is hardly surprising, therefore, that inflationary pressures picked up in the late 1960s. This was at least five years before the oil shock of 1973, which further exacerbated what were by then severe challenges facing most economies. As inflation went up, powerful forces entrenched and propagated it throughout economies—from trade unions to robust demographics, limited technological disruption (and hence, a strong corporate pricing power), and the government's reluctance to curb money supply.

In the US, the CPI jumped in 1968–70 from an annual pace of around 2 percent to 5–6 percent, reaching the heights of 10–12 percent in 1974–75 and staying mostly in the double-digits through the 1970s and early 1980s. The Phillips curve broke down, with inflation and unemployment rising at the same time. In that period, it was quite common to see both unemployment and inflation at percentages close to double digits. In the UK, inflation peaked at almost 25 percent in 1975 and remained close to or above 10 percent all the way through the mid-1980s while unemployment rose from 2–3 percent in the 1960s to the peak of almost 12 percent in the early 1980s. The inflation rate in France jumped to 14 percent in late 1974 and remained in the double-digits until the mid-1980s, while in Germany inflation picked up from less than 2 percent in 1967 to as high as 8 percent in 1974–75. In Italy unemployment peaked at 10 percent, while inflation throughout the period remained firmly in the double digits.

At the same time, GDP growth rates retreated around the world. In the US, after several decades of real growth rates averaging 3–4 percent per annum, the pace dropped to less than 2 percent through the 1970s and early 1980s, and the per capita growth rates declined to not much more than 1.5 percent. In countries like Italy deacceleration was even more disruptive with the per capita GDP growth rates dropping from 5.5 percent in the 1960s to only 2.5 percent in the 1970s, while in Japan the pace of increase in per capita income had fallen from over 9 percent to less than 3 percent. As with inflation and unemployment, the fall in growth was a truly global phenomenon, with growth retreating from around 5 percent in the 1960s to less than 3 percent, ushering in the stagflationary decade of the 1970s.

Figure 6. GDP per Capita Growth Rates (%), 1960–1969 vs. 1970–1983

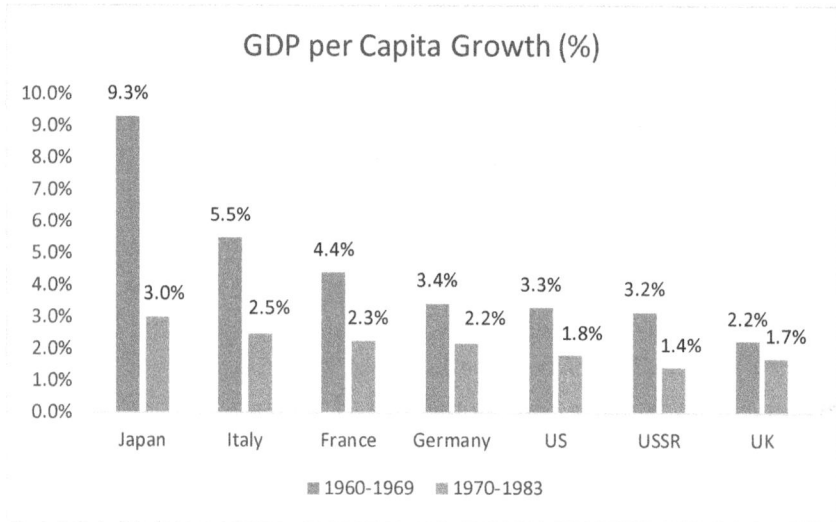

GDP per Capita Growth (%)

	1960-1969	1970-1983
Japan	9.3%	3.0%
Italy	5.5%	2.5%
France	4.4%	2.3%
Germany	3.4%	2.2%
US	3.3%	1.8%
USSR	3.2%	1.4%
UK	2.2%	1.7%

Source: Maddison Project Database, 2020

Figure 7. Average and Peak CPI (%), 1960–1969 vs. 1970–83

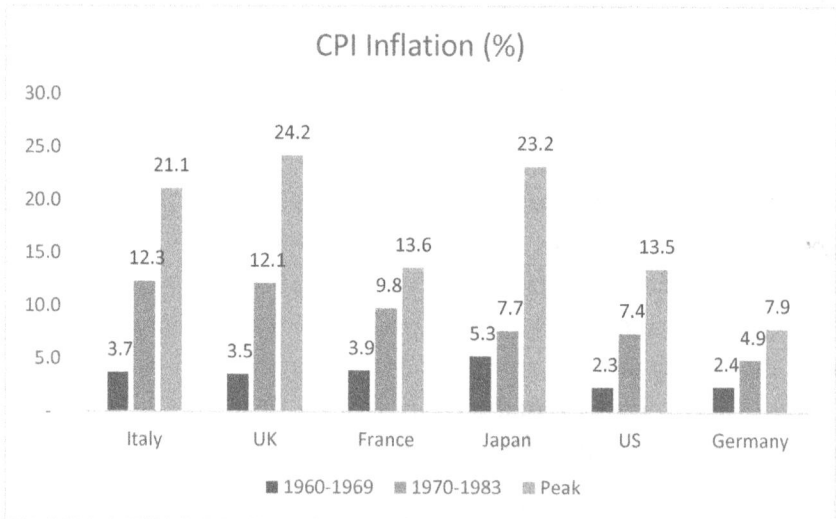

CPI Inflation (%)

	1960-1969	1970-1983	Peak
Italy	3.7	12.3	21.1
UK	3.5	12.1	24.2
France	3.9	9.8	13.6
Japan	5.3	7.7	23.2
US	2.3	7.4	13.5
Germany	2.4	4.9	7.9

Source: World Bank

Figure 8. *Average and Peak Unemployment, 1960–69 vs. 1970–83*

Unemployment Rate (%)

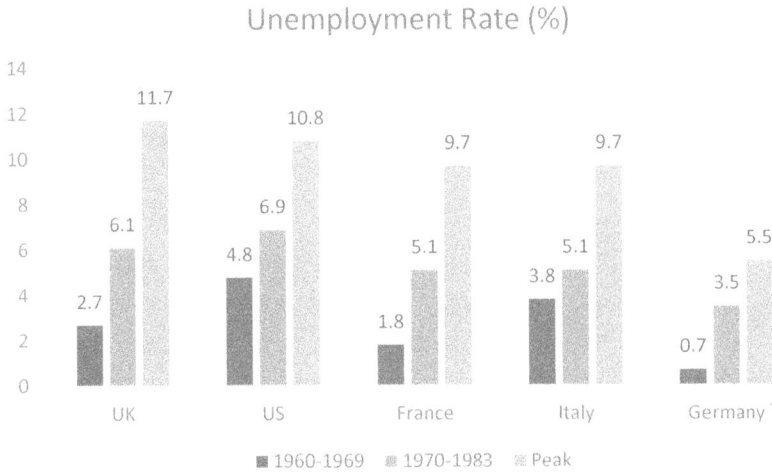

Source: FRED, World Bank

Ronald Reagan once said, "Inflation is as violent as a mugger, as frightening as an armed robber and as deadly as a hit man." It is, therefore, hardly surprising that the combination of rising inflation, high unemployment, and faltering growth "deflowered" the peaceful dreams and expectations of the 1960s, confronting young Baby Boomers with the unpalatable truth of scarcities and diminishing expectations. As the economic "fat" of the 1950s–60s burnt away, clashes became more violent and uncompromising.

In the US this was a time of Weather Underground movement (a far-left militant organization established in 1969–70, springing from Todd Gitlin's more moderate Students for Democratic Society, or SDS, of the early 1960s) that was responsible for multiple bombings (twenty-five in 1975 alone) across the US before it became defunct in 1977. It was also the time of the Black Panthers, which through the 1970s carried out dozens of bombings, assaults, and hijackings. The agenda for both was a violent struggle against what was perceived to be greedy capitalism and its lackeys (i.e., the state and the prevailing societal, racial, and cultural norms). In Germany, Baader-Meinhof (or the Red Army) was founded in 1970, and its activities (murder, kidnapping, and extortion) peaked in 1977–79 and included the murder of the head of Dresdner Bank and the kidnapping of the head of the German Employers' Association, while Alexander Haig, former NATO Supreme commander, barely escaped an assassination attempt. Italy, in the meantime, was savaged by the Italian Red Brigades, with the peak of violence also occurring in the late 1970s when hundreds of people were assassinated, kidnapped, or wounded in cities as diverse as Rome, Genoa, Monza, Bologna, Milan, and Turin, with the murder of Aldo Moro (former Italian prime minister) in 1978 being one of their more famous exploits. Neither organization became extinct until the late 1980s.

Not surprisingly, the Irish Republican Army (IRA) also got into business at about the same time (1969), and although the underlying cause was different from Red Brigades or terrorists in Italy or Germany, it was just as uncompromising and destructive until finally a political compromise was reached in the late 1990s. From 1973 onward, the battle moved from Northern Ireland to concerted IRA bombings in England. Other terrorist organizations (including PLO and its various offshoots) emerged in this turbulent decade. While there were many specific and idiosyncratic issues that offered fertile ground for the growth of these organizations, in most cases, the discontent was fueled by out-of-control inflation, declining standards of living, and rising unemployment. This is not to say that the Red Brigades, IRA, PLO, or Black Panthers did not have legitimate grievances, but to observe that the degree and the depth of their following would have been far less if not for the economic dislocations that was becoming manifest around the world from the late 1960s onward. None of these organizations, at least initially, had more than a few hundred dedicated "soldiers"; therefore they heavily relied on both the tacit and active support of thousands of civilians, with rising inflation and faltering growth fueling support for extremes.

The years of 1977 and 1979 saw the highest level of terrorist acts in mature economies on record with more than 1,000 each year. While not perfectly correlated, the intensity of terrorism activity does follow (with a lag) rising inflationary pressures and greater personal and financial insecurity. On the contrary, a period of higher security and lower inflation through the 1990s and the first decade of the 21st century witnessed a significant drop in terrorist acts with around 100 cases per year, with the exception of the collapse of the Eastern Block. However, the onset of the Global Financial crisis in 2008–10 saw once again an increase in terrorist acts (toward 300–500 cases per annum).

Figure 9. *Inflation vs. Terrorism Acts*

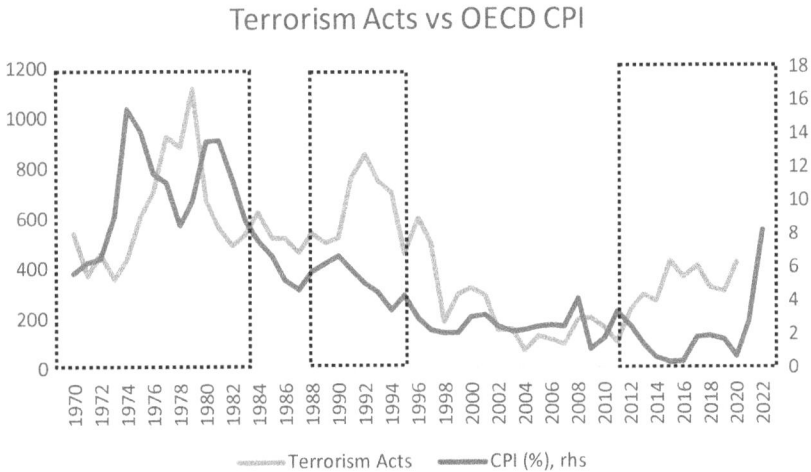

Terrorism Acts vs OECD CPI

Source: GTD. US, Canada, Western Europe, Australia, Turkey, and Japan

The late 1960s until early to mid-1980s was also a time of growing industrial militancy. In Italy, the hot summer of discontent in 1969 inaugurated an extended season of strikes, lockouts, factory occupations, and mass demonstrations throughout Northern Italy. The range of complaints was extensive, from pay to housing, transport, pensions, and even opposition to the Vietnam War. The intensity of strikes forced employers to grant large pay increases and allow for creation of workers' committees, with the government codifying these changes into law in 1970 (including inflation-adjusted wage contracts that further imbedded inflationary pressures). Striking activity in Britain through the 1970s was at a higher level than any time since the 1930s. In 1972 alone, almost 24 million working days[16] were lost (whereas in the 1960s, strikes usually resulted in less than 4 million working days lost per annum), mostly in nationwide coal miner strikes, with several other peaks occurring in the late 1970s and early 1980s. Beginning in May 1968, France was paralyzed for seven weeks by demonstrations, general strikes, and occupations of factories and universities, resulting in significant concessions and wage gains for workers and restructuring of educational institutions. Even in the US, strikes and work stoppages through the 1970s were at the highest level ever. In 1970 alone, there were more than 2.4 million workers engaged in large-scale work stoppages in addition to numerous wildcats, slowdowns, and aggressive and confrontationist negotiations.[17]

• • •

By the late 1970s and early 1980s, the backlash against the disruption, violence, disappointments, and vain hopes of the preceding decade was in full swing, bringing with it the next evolution of capitalism, or what Anatole Kaletsky described as Capitalism 3.0.[18] This new phase redefined our economies, politics, and societies and was the product of the maturing Baby Boomer generation redefining their needs and objectives. While most continued to want (and expect) greater individual freedom, there was less naivete and an even greater emphasis on free market solutions rather than government mandates.

In the words of George Packer, they made economies and societies that were "more entrepreneurial and less equal, more tolerant and less fair."[19] Although he was referring to the US, similar forces were at play in all other Western democracies. However, all of that was for the future. In the meantime, the world was being remade in the early 1980s, with the new societal consensus emerging which in turn would not be seriously challenged again until the Global Financial Crisis in 2008–10.

Chapter 3

THE AGE OF NARCISSISM

"In a nation that was proud of hard work, strong families, close-knit communities and our faith in God, too many of us tend to worship self-indulgence and consumption."

US President Jimmy Carter, July 15, 1979[1]

I n this insightful speech, given at the precipice of the new world, President Carter put his finger on the essence of the forthcoming age of the 1980s, the 1990s, and the first decade of the 2000s. The most accurate description of the new world was one of rampant *narcissism*. Christopher Lasch's book of the same name[2] perfectly captured the era's mood of despair and the emerging transformation in societal norms— from the common good and community service to individualism, self-improvement, and self-reflection.

By the late 1970s to early 1980s, the perception of economic, societal, and personal failures had become so extreme that the maturing Baby Boomers' cohort (which by that stage emerged as the dominant electoral group) had en masse made self-reliance, individual responsibility, freedom of choice without guaranteeing outcomes, self-worshipping, and the search for the meaning of life and individual happiness the cornerstone of the new societal and economic interactions. The trust in science, economics, and state institutions that was so strong in the 1950s and the first half of the 1960s was in the eyes of Baby Boomers betrayed by economists who misjudged the trade-off between inflation and unemployment, governments who dug economies ever deeper into a stagflationary hole, scientists who overpromised technically oriented solutions, and political parties that disagreed on most aspects of life (from wars and race to policing, law and order). Writing in real time, Lasch described the prevailing mood as follows: "Economic theory cannot explain the coexistence of unemployment and inflation; sociology retreats from the attempt to outline a general theory of modern society; academic psychology retreats from the challenge by Freud into measurement of trivia…natural sciences, having made exaggerated claims for themselves, now hasten to announce that science offers no miracle cures for social problems…historians admit to a sense of irrelevance of history."[3]

• • •

It was an era in which Western societies suffered from what can only be described as a nervous breakdown. As a sign of trouble, the consumption of antidepressants skyrocketed. The best-selling drug in the US through the 1970s was Valium, which peaked at an annual pace of 90 million bottles in 1978, the same year former First Lady Betty Ford admitted her own addiction. Marriage rates started their precipitous fall, divorce rates increased, and the baby boom of the 1950s–60s was well and truly in the rearview mirror as fertility rates dropped below replacement levels. Every year throughout the 1970s, one million Americans had themselves sterilized, and, as a result, throughout the decade around 10 million people had voluntarily decided not to have children.[4] People waited longer to get married (with an average marriage age for women increasing by more than two years) and were far more likely to divorce at least once in their life. In the 1960s, the US divorce rate was 9.3 per 1,000 married women, but by 1980 the rate had more than doubled to 22.6. Whereas in the 1950s and 1960s a typical American family consisted of a working father, a mostly-at-home mother, and several children, by the end of the 1970s this "typical" family constituted less than 15 percent of total households—ironically far less than single households, which increased from 10–11 percent of the total in the 1950s to 23 percent by the late 1970s.[5] Throughout the decade, an increasing number of surveys indicated that people were searching for self-fulfillment, with an overwhelming majority (over 70 percent)[6] spending a great deal of time thinking about themselves and their inner life.

Over time, however, as the electoral power of Baby Boomers rose, the political confusion evident in Jimmy Carter's quote and multiple surveys was slowly replaced by a new consensus. At the 1976 British Labor Party Conference at Blackpool, James Callaghan (the left-leaning British prime minister at the time), openly articulated how the state's spending and its excessive dominance over the economy and society had run its course and had become counterproductive. To quote, "We used to think that you could spend your way out of recession and increase employment…I tell you in all candor that that option no longer exists, and that in so far as it ever did exist, it only worked on each occasion since the war by injecting a bigger dose of inflation, followed by a higher level of unemployment as the next step."

This frank admission by a longtime supporter of the government's role was followed by iconoclasts such as Milton Friedman, Margaret Thatcher, and Ronald Reagan. The speeches by the new leaders were far more in tune with Baby Boomers' independent and individualistic streak, such as when Thatcher, as the leader of opposition, declared, "I place a profound—indeed a fervent faith—in the virtue of self-reliance and personal independence," and later in 1978 she argued that "once you give people the idea that all this can be done by the state, and that it is somehow second-best or even degrading to leave it to private people…then you will begin to deprive them of one of the essential elements of humanity—personal moral responsibility." Indeed, she went beyond that by suggesting that even the concept of a society as such does not exist and is nothing more than an artificial construct—there are individuals and families, but there is no society. It was then followed by Ronald Reagan (1981) with his famous quip that the "most terrifying words in the English language are: I am from the government, and I am here to help." Unlike their parents and grandparents, Baby Boomers never experienced an out-of-control private sector and the cruelty of free markets with their own multitude of externalities and negative feedback loops. Instead, they witnessed the inefficiency and stifling nature of an overbearing government and a society that attempted to control as many parts of the economy and private life as possible.

This transition inaugurated what Anatole Kaletsky described as the third stage of evolution of capitalism (or Capitalism 3.0).[7] As always, Hollywood and the entertainment industry were the first to pick up on the new trend, with the moody and discontented films of the 1950s–60s and the strife of the 1970s replaced by those glorifying greed and independence, with the free markets offering solutions for most economic or societal problems. In 1984, Madonna sang, "You know that we are living in a material world, and I am a material girl," and in 1987, Michael Douglas, who played an investment asset stripper named Gordon Gekko in the movie *Wall Street*, stated as a matter of fact, "The point is, ladies and gentlemen, that greed, for lack of a better word, is good. Greed is right, greed works, greed clarifies, cuts through, and captures evolutionary spirit." This moral debasement was perfectly in line with a laissez-faire approach to business and politics characteristic of Kaletsky's "Capitalism 3.0," where the public sector was invariably viewed as inefficient and wasteful, and free market mechanisms were deemed to provide the best resolution to any problem.

By the 1980s the Woodstock devotees of freedom, music, LSD, and sex morphed into tech titans, investment bankers, "Barbarians at the Gate" asset strippers, owners of overpriced organic food and well-being spas, yoga instructors, highly paid CEOs, grifters of various kinds, and real estate flippers. While some small hippy communities survived all the way into the early 1990s, they were the rare exception rather than the norm, with quite a few morphing into yuppies ("young urban professionals" who retained the hippies' preferences for healthy lifestyle and casual clothing but junked pretty much everything else that they stood for). What had started as a desire for personal liberty, self-expression, and decision-making independent of state and stifling community norms had morphed into a desire for financial independence and the unshakable belief in the ability of anyone to succeed if they tried hard enough, and if the state stopped interfering. In that world, there was no expectation of equality; indeed, striving toward it was now viewed as a path to a greater injustice. It then was just a small step from Woodstock in 1969 to financial market liberalization in the early 1980s and elimination of constraints of the Glass-Steagall Act in 1999. The essential idea was one of freedom and self-fulfillment, whether it was drinking, smoking, wearing long hair, traveling, trading stocks, or borrowing to satisfy one's desires.

Young people who in the 1960s and 1970s were manning barricades in Paris, staging attacks in the US, supporting the Red Brigades, or living in free spirit "decommodified" communities had become proponents of freedom from the state and societal shackles, and in the process, they forged a new consensus. Loretta Napoleoni is an example of this transition. Having in the 1970s failed admission to the Red Brigades' inner circle (in her own words, "I had failed the psychological profiling of a terrorist; the Central Committee of the Red Brigades had judged me too simple minded and too opinionated to become a good terrorist"), she graduated as a Fulbright Scholar from Johns Hopkins and as a Rotary Scholar from LSE and became an expert on security and terrorism, Another example is Daniel Marc Cohn-Bendit who was known as "Danny the Red." In the late 1960s, he was the key university organizer in Paris and was deported to his native Germany as a result. Subsequently, he rose to become the copresident of the European Free Alliance in the European Parliament and was awarded the EU European Initiative Prize for 2016. Bobby Rush, who established the Illinois branch of the Black Panthers in the 1960s, became congressman for Illinois's 1st district between 1993 and 2023, while Eldridge Cleaver—the Black Panthers' minister of information and inventor of slogans such as, "you are either part of the problem or part of the solution"—had by the late 1970s become a Republican and supported Ronald Reagan's election, even running (unsuccessfully) as a Republican for a Senate seat in California. Many of the leftist, communist, and/or Trotskyist sympathizers in New York and Boston in the 1960s became strong supporters of individual freedom and neoconservatism (including Norman Podhoretz and Irving Kristol). By the late 1970s and early 1980s, some of the older surviving Beatniks were advertising "Beatniks for Hire" to entertain and enliven Baby Boomers' parties.

It would be hard to find a better example of such transition than the life story of Jerry Rubin, one of the famous Chicago Seven, who was tried for conspiracy and incitement following violent protests and anti-war demonstrations that accompanied the 1968 Democratic National Convention in Chicago. He was also (together with Abbie Hoffman) one of the founders of "Youth International Party," known as "yippies," as well as an organizer of the Vietnam Day Committee which presaged later large-scale anti-war rallies. However, by the early 1980s, Rubin was better known as a yuppie capitalist. He even began a new career as a stockbroker and an early investor in various organic food and multilayered distribution businesses (employing Bobby Seale as one of his salesmen).[8] He remarked, "Money is power…I know that I can be more effective today wearing a suit and a tie and working on Wall Street than I can be dancing outside the walls of power."[9] In essence, a number of the 1960s radicals grew up and decided that implementing meaningful change required resources and compromises with the existing system. "Rubin and many other transformed Sixties radicals and hippies embraced the idea that socially conscious entrepreneurship was the best way to help people and the best alternative to the bureaucratic welfarism of the Great Society that Rubin and his compatriots had denounced most vociferously during the 1960s."[10] By that stage, many alternative and hippie communities became some of the first Silicon Valley investors, sponsoring companies like Apple, Amazon, and Google.

Another example is the now famous Burning Man Festival of crafts and music—an annual event held just prior to Labor Day in northern Nevada's Black Rock Desert that culminates in a pagan-like burning of a giant wooden man. Like the Hippie gatherings of the 1960s and 1970s, this festival had something for everyone—from music and crafts to dance parties, yoga, and spirituality classes. Although more of a 1980s and 1990s rather than 1970s phenomenon, it perfectly exemplified the persistency and the shifting priorities of Baby Boomers. For example, its code included "radical self-reliance, radical inclusiveness, and radical self-expression" but also "communal effort" and "decommodification" (initially everything at the festival was free). Over time, the festival attracted not just former hippies but also titans of technology and industry and many conservatives. One of the attendees was Grover Norquist, an admirer and propagator of the ideas of small government and low taxation. He clearly was attracted to the ideas of radical independence and self-reliance but not so much to everything being free. The festivals attracted luminaries like Larry Page,

Mark Zuckerberg, Sean Combs, Chris Rock, Ray Dalio, Eric Schmidt, and other tech, finance, and entertainment titans. It perfectly exemplified the Baby Boomers' conflicted transition. They still craved individualism, independence, self-expression, and community but also wanted self-gratification, and now that the Festival has grown to a size of up to 100,000 attendees, it is no longer free, with fees ranging up to $2,500 for tickets and several hundred dollars for car passes. Following the washout of the 2023 festival (as a result of a sudden torrential downpour), Arwa Mahdawi of *The Guardian* newspaper was correct to point out, "Once people such as Mark Zuckerberg and Elon Musk show up to your party, there is no longer anything countercultural about it. You are not rebelling against the man. You *are* the man."[11]

Steve Jobs, who just missed the 1960s revolution, had a great deal of admiration for this generation. The ideas of the 1960s and early 1970s shaped his business views. As he described it, Apple stood for "one person, one computer," compared to a titan like IBM, which stood for hierarchy and corporatization, or in his words, "remember in the Sixties, when people were raising their fists and saying, 'Power to the people?' Well, that is what I am doing with Apple. By building affordable personal computers and putting one on every desk, in every hand, I am giving people power."[12] Steve Jobs was a hippie in many other ways as well—such as his regular pilgrimages to India, diet restrictions, and love for 1960s music (especially Bob Dylan). However, as Jobs fully realized, there were also significant differences between him and the hippies. Essentially, he was playing a hippy rather than being one of them—they were aiming for destruction of the institutional order while he was building new, more profitable institutions.

Indeed, the same capitalism that the 1960s generation disparaged had proven to be sufficiently resilient to adjust to changing societal norms by effectively absorbing the Baby Boomers' culture of individual freedoms by defanging its extremes and mainstreaming the balance into the consumer culture. As Moretta described it, "Capitalist establishment succeeded in transforming non-conformity into profitable conformity, thus… turning hippies into parodies of themselves."[13] Corporations are nothing but creatures of society and therefore cannot exist and prosper outside of it. Whether it was patriotism and the reflection of general prosperity and an expectation of better things to come in the 1950s–60s, or the self-reliance, independence, self-indulgence, and narcissism of 1980s–2000s, capitalism had no choice but to adapt. As it adjusted, a wide range of new and wonderfully profitable opportunities appeared (e.g., looking good and casual, playing hippies without being one, organic food and worshipping at the temple of one's body).

• • •

There is a large body of literature that blames Baby Boomers for many of today's economic, political, and societal ills. In many aspects, it is true that, as Helen Andrews argued, Baby Boomers "had all the elements of greatness but whose effect on the world was tragically and often ironically contrary to their intentions. Their destructiveness came from their virtues as much as their vices."[14]

According to Tom Wolfe, by the mid- to late 1970s, many former hippies and yippies as well as other sixties' rebels and activists had morphed into what became known as a "Me Generation," with its emphasis on retrospection, self-realization, and self-expression. Various surveys highlighted that by 1979, 39 percent of Americans and around 60 percent of college-educated young Americans believed that "people should be free to look, dress, and live the way they want, whether others like it or not."[15] The previous era of civil and social responsibility and, most importantly, the requirement for conformity, had ended, and looking out for "number one" had emerged as the dominant ethos. As explained by Robert Ringer, "When you say, 'I should do this' or 'I should do that,' you are also in many cases allowing yourself to be trapped by the past, following rules set down by parents, teachers, and other mentors that may no longer have a real meaning for you in our current crisis culture."[16] This was hardly the final destination that sixties' rebels were expecting or planning for.

One of the best surveys tracking changing moral and ethical compass is an annual survey of the "American Freshmen," prepared by the staff of the Cooperative Institutional Research Program (CIRP) at the Higher Educational Research Institute of the University of California, Los Angeles. The key advantage of this survey is not only that it has been running continuously since 1965–66 but also that it asks broadly similar questions to each incoming college class, addressing exactly the same audience (age group of 18–20 years old, incoming freshmen). These surveys cover over 100,000 freshmen across 200 or so colleges and offer insights on a wide range of topics, from income and wealth to reasons for choosing a certain field of study, the influence of parents, friends, and media to religious beliefs.

Two questions are particularly revealing: 1. What is important to these young people when they embark on a lengthy and expensive educational journey; and 2. Why do they prefer to pursue certain majors or fields of study. In terms of reasons for attending college, surveys have been focused on several areas that go to heart of the question: whether community spirit and societal needs or individualism and money play the key role in a decision of young freshmen to attend colleges. The same is true regarding the choice of major areas of study.

There is no doubt that in the late 1960s, most freshmen were attending colleges in order to improve society, with the highest scores attributable to "help me develop a meaningful life philosophy" and "help others in need or difficulty." In the inaugural survey in 1965–66, approximately 83 percent of freshmen answered that the single most important factor for their decision to attend college was to "develop a meaningful philosophy of life," and the second highest (69 percent) was to "help others in need or difficulty." The same survey also indicated that 21 percent entered college to volunteer for the Peace Corps to help humanity. This was in line with the experience of JFK's administration several years earlier when the president's call to join the newly formed Peace Corps, designed to "help in the great task of bringing to man that decent way of life which is the foundation of freedom and a condition of peace," was met with an overwhelming response—more than 6,000 applications, with none mentioning salary.[17] On the other hand, the answer to a question whether or not they have decided to attend college primarily to be "very well off financially" attracted a relatively low score of 43 percent. Also, in line with a more communal and humanitarian spirit of the age as well as the legacy of exceptionally strong economy and labor markets of the 1960s, a significant proportion of responders (45 percent plus) expressed interest in pursuing majors in arts, humanities, education, and social sciences.

However, mirroring the above-described shift from hippies to yuppies or from Rubin the rebel to Rubin the capitalist, there was a clear shift in the mid- to late 1970s that meaningfully accelerated through the 1980s, with money and wealth becoming the primary reason for attending college, while community service, helping others, or developing a meaningful philosophy of life, fell backward in rankings. By 1987, the desire to be "very well off financially" had become the overwhelmingly dominant cause, rising from 43 percent in 1966 to 75 percent in 1987, while the perceived need to "develop a meaningful philosophy of life" slumped from 83 percent to less than 40 percent, and the "need to help others in difficulty" dropped from 69 percent to 58 percent. At the same time, in the last year when the survey asked the question whether your main reason for attending college was to volunteer for Peace Corp, the positive score collapsed to a mere 7 percent in 1988. Even the need to "clean up environment," which scored 42 percent in 1966, dropped to only 18 percent by 1987. The same started to occur with intended majors. An interest in humanities or education dropped precipitously while the desire to study business and finance started a steady climb. By 1987–88, around 27 percent of freshmen wanted to major in business management and finance, when compared to only 14 percent in the late 1960s, while arts, humanities, education, and social sciences halved to 20 percent, with arts and humanities alone dropping from 24 percent in 1966 to only 9 percent in 1987–88.

A similar study by Daniel Yankelovich, an American social scientist, was even more precise, highlighting the date of change as 1972–73. According to his analysis, "These few years of the decade of the 1970s point to vast changes in the complexion and outlook for an entire generation of young people. Indeed, so startling are the shifts in values and beliefs between the late 1960s, when our youth studies were first launched, and the present time that social historians of the future should have little difficulty in identifying the end of one era and the beginning of a new age."[18] Whereas in the late 1960s, US campuses were in rebellion, they had become relatively quiet by the early 1970s. He witnessed an almost total divorce between radical politics and new lifestyles, and the central theme was now finding self-fulfillment within a conventional career. Money and happiness, rather than societal improvements, was sought, while a new sexual morality was spreading both to mainstream college youth and to mainstream working youth. Yankelovich also noticed that the new Left was losing control, and there was no longer a clear-cut political center of gravity, with intensifying pressures in both directions—from the sunsetting new Left and from what later became known as a neoliberal Right.

As a Trilateral Report of 1975 (Crisis of Democracy) concluded, "In all Three Trilateral regions (i.e., US, Europe, and Japan), a shift in values is taking place away…from public-spirited values toward those which stress private satisfaction, leisure, and the need for intellectual and esthetic self-fulfillment. These values…are most notable in the younger generation. They often coexist with greater skepticism toward political leaders and institutions and with greater alienation from the political processes."[19]

•   •   •

Clearly, by the 1980s neither community support, helping others, nor the environment any longer played the key role. It was pretty much all about "looking after number one," with Gordon Gekko's "Greed is Good" mantra summing it up well, while the trust in institutions of state had collapsed. By the late 1970s and early 1980s, a new social consensus was being forged that prioritized individual self-expression, liberty, and freedom while downplaying the consequent side effects, such as inequalities or fairness.

These changes had profound economic and societal ripple effects. On the positive side, the new consensus has freed us from the conformity and shackles of a deeply unfair and hierarchical 1950s–60s culture. Baby Boomers ensured that the past traditional views on marriage, divorce, sex, race, and culture had become obsolete. Hippies and other sixties' rebels were the ones who spawned and promoted women's, gay, and lesbian rights and race-blind policies that became dominant through 1980s–2000s. Arguably, they broke more taboos than any other modern generation. Although somewhat excessively, they had also sponsored better organic food, exercise, and meditation that not only improved health but also offered attractive alternative lifestyle choices. By consciously rejecting their parents' faith in rationality, government, planning, and control, sixties' rebels created a more open and freewheeling way of life. Perhaps one of the greatest manifestations of the sixties' legacy can be found in contemporary music, especially modern rock and roll, black rap, and hip-hop.

However, freedom has its price. There is no doubt that the hippies' widespread experimentation with drugs opened a door for later use of much harder drugs and imbedded them into society's consciousness. Even more importantly, as George Packer suggested, Baby Boomers created a world that was more entrepreneurial but less equal, more tolerant but less fair, bequeathing to subsequent generations extreme economic, political, and social polarization with "institutions that had been the foundations of middle-class democracy, from public schools and secure jobs to flourishing newspapers and functioning legislatures...set on the course of a long decline."[20]

This will be the topic of the next three chapters: discussion of economic, social, and political consequences of the sixties' revolution and how it changed not only national balance sheets and wealth distribution but also political narrative, including the rise and eventual fall of neoliberalism.

Chapter 4
THE NEOLIBERAL REVOLUTION

*"The more dependent the position of the individuals or groups is seen to become
on the actions of government, the more they will insist that the governments aim
at some recognizable scheme of distributive justice; and the more governments
try to realize some preconceived pattern of desirable distribution, the more
they must subject the position of the different individuals...to their control.
So long as the belief in 'social justice' governs political action, this process must
progressively approach nearer to a totalitarian system."*

Friedrich von Hayek[1]

John Maynard Keynes once said, "Practical men, who believe themselves to be exempt from any intellectual influence, are usually slaves
of some defunct economist. Madmen in authority, who hear voices
in the air, are distilling their frenzy from some academic scribbler of a
few years back."[2] In the context of the intellectual revolution that Baby
Boomers brought to society, politics, and economics, it was the fusion
of Friedrich von Hayek and Milton Friedman, with a dose of Hannah
Arendt as well as Austrian and Geneva economic schools, that created a
powerful constellation of disparate and yet rather cohesive ideas on how
societies should be structured.[3] Over the years, these ideas have acquired
different labels—neoliberals, conservatives—and have a long intellectual
tradition dating back to the 17th and 18th centuries.

At the great risk of oversimplification, all of these threads point in
one direction: toward personal freedom, personal responsibility, and the
free market. Not surprisingly, many of these ideas found fertile ground
with Baby Boomers' longing for freedom and independence, colored
by their naivete regarding the ability of the free market to offer efficient
answers to almost any need—from the provision of medical services to
execution of justice, and from satisfying a multitude of competing, and

often contradictory, demands of independent consumers to social security and running research labs and fast trains. For many Baby Boomers, the government's provision of these services was judged to be suboptimum and inefficient while eroding their freedom of choice. As the above quote by von Hayek made clear, the more dependent people are on the actions of the government, the more they lose control—a process that leads to less freedom and ultimately a totalitarian system.

• • •

The question that neoliberals (if we settle on one standard label) struggle with: how do you protect freedom from encroachment by the state and messy democracy?

The answer according to neoliberals is that traditional morality and obedience to its naturally evolving laws (even if these might be viewed by most as unjust and cruel), when wedded to allocation of labor, goods, and services under the guidance of the "invisible hand" of the free market, maximizes freedom and reduces the tyranny. What is the role of the state? Highly constrained and subordinate. Apart from defense, law and order, ensuring freedom of navigation and safeguarding the integrity of money (explaining neoliberals' love for the gold standard), governments under this system are supposed to be restricted to enforcing the laws that society naturally developed, protecting the free market and safeguarding property rights from the excesses of democracy and the erratic politics that damage the edifice of freedom and efficiency. Most neoliberals agree with Thatcher and von Hayek that societies as such do not even exist. Instead, atomized individuals and families are real, but society as a concept is a dangerous and an artificial political construct which the state ought to fight against to safeguard the sanctity of the free market.

These ideas lead to a number of obvious policy prescriptions.

In this context, the fight for social justice (with "social justice warriors" becoming a pejorative term amongst most neoliberals) is viewed as a tool for tyranny because it limits choices and is contrary to the natural societal laws. In the same vein, social security nets are regarded as counterproductive, as they distort free market economic incentives, without, in the world of neoliberals, ultimately benefiting a person who draws on social security and, therefore, are intrinsically evil and should be constrained. To be sure, most neoliberals support state services for the elderly and those who are incapacitated to the point of not being able to participate in a free economy. However, even in these circumstances, the preference is to rely on charity and philanthropy of other members of society. "A thousand points of light" program, popularized by President George H.W. Bush, is an example of such ideas designed to promote private, nongovernmental solutions to social and poverty issues. In the same way, neoliberals believe that state provision of most services (such as healthcare, education, infrastructure, transportation, utilities, etc.) must be curtailed to the bare minimum with the responsibility delegated to an efficient private sector and, in many instances, relegated to individuals and families. Essentially, neoliberals hold that if individuals can be returned to the domain of families for financial support and other needs, they would voluntarily submit to the authority and the discipline of traditional morality rather than being confused by what they believe to be an artificially constructed morality of the state or that of broader society.

With this mindset, the state and democracy are frequently viewed as enemies of the "true freedom," explaining the neoliberals' desire to limit voting rights, gerrymander districts, create supra-national technocratic institutions to reduce the impact of politics on markets and to limit decision-making to the executive branch in order to lessen the influence of domestic politics. Some neoliberals even prefer the creation of a pure technocratic state protected from democracy under a totalitarian ruler. As Stephen Moore, a longtime fellow of the Heritage Foundation, once stated, "Capitalism is a lot more important than democracy. I am not even a big believer in democracy."[4] Similarly, Raymond Plant, a political philosopher, argues, "Democracy as it has grown up in Western societies may be inimical to the growth and maintenance of markets."[5] Steve Bannon, Donald Trump's advisor, has been advocating the "deconstruction of the state" and its conversion into a myriad of what can be best described as atomized private enterprises. Kevin Roberts, head of the Heritage Foundation, is calling for a destruction of the "administrative state" and its political influence by eliminating almost all constraints on the presidential authority.[6]

As quoted in Quinn Slobodian's extraordinary book *Crack-Up Capitalism*, the world that neoliberals envision is close to the one described in the *Red Pill* novel as a "system that would eventually find itself able to dispense with public politics altogether and put in its place the art of the deal: a black box, impossible to oversee, visible only to counterparties. There would be no checks and balances, no right of appeal against decisions of dealmakers, no 'rights' whatsoever, just the raw exercise of power."[7] It is hardly surprising that Jared Kushner, Trump's son-in-law, started the Office of American Innovation, designed as a "SWAT team aimed at fixing government with business ideas"[8] or effectively deconstructing the state into discrete units of production and consumption led by a benevolent autocratic force. Along the same line of thought, Marc Andreessen, Netscape cofounder, envisions a future where the technology-based elite will lead the world toward nirvana of ever-increasing scale and diminishing marginal costs, fighting along the way the perceived enemy of the state and its regulations—from social welfare and risk management to safety and environment.[9]

Ironically, for being such fervent believers of freedom, many of the neoliberals' ideas are not far-removed from communism or fascism, explaining a love affair that many seem to have with totalitarian and authoritarian states and their leaders across the world.

Although most Baby Boomers have remained consistently pro-choice, pro-sexual freedom, and pro-immigration, there is also a deep and a more conservative wing of the movement that highlights traditional family and religious values, creating a core of cultural attributes that are today publicly debated under the broad rubrics of "defending traditions" and "culture wars." These followers differ on a country-by-country basis but unlike educated and more progressive Baby Boomers, they tend to consist mostly of less educated and rural residents who feel that the Baby

Boomers' revolution has gone too far and is threatening their perceived identity and social status. They are in favor of strict segregation of the roles of husbands and wives and obedience of children to a point that they are almost regarded as the property of parents, including the right to dictate their education and even asking for state-sponsored permission to loosen work rules for the underaged. Their grievances focus on a diminishing status of this part of the population under the pressure of the deindustrialization, immigration, and globalization that Baby Boomers unleashed between the early 1980s and 2010s, and the perception that they no longer recognize their own country. As discussed above, the fact that moral and family values they aspire to were by themselves novel in the 1950s–60s, and do not reflect norms in the 19th or the first half of the 20th century, is irrelevant. To them, tradition means returning to the glory days of the 1950s when one salary could support a family, the wife's role was supportive of and subordinated to the husband, immigrants were kept in check, and the country lived under God.

These arguments also tend to link the love of the past with patriotism, and thus tarring objectors as intrinsically unpatriotic. Even in a more sophisticated dressing by academics like Patrick Deene and Yoram Hazony,[10] the essence of this conservative and nationalistic movement can be characterized as the unity of history, family, and religion within the confines of national borders. They strive to eliminate what they perceive to be a malign impact of globalism, cosmopolitanism, and "wokeism" (in its different interpretations). Although many of their criticisms of neoliberal order echo my discussion in these pages, their solution relies on strict adherence to what are perceived to be the right "truths." Democracy is an optional extra, preferably deconstructed, with strong echoes of the 1930s European fascist movements.

It is these divergent, often contradictory, and yet complementary strands that form the backbone of the support base for the likes of Viktor Orbán of Hungary, Georgia Meloni of Italy, Donald Trump and the broader GOP in the US, Recep Erdoğan in Turkey, the Law and Justice Party in Poland, and many others on the right side of politics who emerged as highly effective grievance merchants of "Us vs. Them," "Make America Great Again," "Hungary for Hungarians," "Pure Poland, White Poland," "Take Back Control," and other similarly divisive and highly exclusionary slogans.

These intellectual linkages also explain what unites individuals who profess freedom and yet are willing to risk women's lives to bar abortions. It explains how support for the life of an unborn child can be reconciled with a refusal to provide adequate prenatal and postnatal care. In the context of neoliberal views, life must be protected at all costs, but as soon as a baby is born, the direction reverts to a personal responsibility of the mother and the family, or at extreme, private philanthropy. Similarly, it explains why followers of these ideas are invariably against the expansion of social security and are constantly striving (mostly unsuccessfully) to "starve the beast" by reducing the nondefense portion of government spending. The waves of privatizations that swept the world in the 1980s–2000s (from utilities and water supply to trains, hospitals, and even prisons and mercenary armies) were equally in tune with this philosophy. It also explains a visceral dislike that most neoliberals have against policies aimed at alleviating climate change (such as electric vehicles, solar energy, etc.), as these involve considerable reliance on government financing and subsidies. Interestingly, they seem to have no problem expanding a far more polluting and hazardous nuclear energy, as it relies on private initiative with a more limited state involvement (even though most of the ingredients of nuclear technology were developed and financed by the public sector during 1940s).

The hobbling of state agencies, which have responsibility for antitrust and monopoly surveillance and enforcement, also makes sense. If one believes that the free market would invariably arrive at the best and most efficient outcome, then the state should exercise its power in a highly judicious and careful manner, and only when there is overwhelming evidence of considerable and pervasive market or consumer abuse. This interpretation of the state's role allowed for a significant concentration of corporate power across Western societies, especially in the US. As Maurice Stucke and Ariel Ezrachi argued in 2017, "The US has neither an antitrust movement nor much enforcement,"[11]—a radical departure from an era of much stricter enforcement in the 1950s–70s and even into the early 1980s. Whereas in the 1960s, around 25 percent of product value produced across the US belonged to oligopolies (i.e., dominated by four or less players), today, almost all industries have an oligopoly rating of 50 percent or above. An article in the *Economist* concluded that in the last two decades, around two-thirds of the 893 industries across the US have seen a significant increase in market concentration.[12] Up until the Biden administration, almost all acquisitions and mergers were essentially waved through under the rubric of "the private sector knows best." Although EU anti-monopoly agencies have always been more technocratic with a far lesser impact of the revolving door between the public and private sectors, even there, until more recently, there was a tendency to approve most mergers and acquisitions.

These deep cultural changes were inevitably reflected in how the private sector and corporations felt about their role in society and the economy and what interests they should be serving. Whereas in the 1950s–70s the US Business Roundtable (a key business lobby group) advocated a broad and inclusive view of corporate objectives that encompassed not only shareholders but also employees, creditors, quality of products, and national and societal well-being, by the 1990s, the objectives were massively narrowed to just one constituency: shareholders and profit maximization. Again, this was in line with Milton Friedman's view: "There is only one social responsibility of business—to use its resources and engage in activities designed to increase its profits." In other words, the free market would fix everything if only allowed to work without state interference. Hence, by the early 1990s, the Business Roundtable statement of corporate objectives was unapologetically neoliberal: "The principal objective of a business enterprise is to generate economic returns to its owners."

Paul Collier described how Bear Stearns investment bank displayed in the entrance lobby its core mission statement: "We make nothing but money."[13] In a different era, another simple mission statement belonged to what used to be the largest and the oldest British chemical company,

Imperial Chemical Industries or ICI, which in the 1950s and 1960s proudly proclaimed its mission: "We aim to be the finest chemical company in the world." Johnson & Johnson, in its first credo (or mission statement) dating back to 1940s–50s, simply stated that: "We believe that our first responsibility must be to the doctors, nurses and hospitals, mothers and all others who use our products." Both statements were easy to understand and in line with societal demands at that time that corporates' primary emphasis should be on products, customers, and society. However, by the 1990s, ICI's objectives narrowed to just the shareholder value, not dissimilar to a blunt statement from Bear Stearns.

Throughout the 1980s–2000s, the neoliberal mantra ruled, which implied that corporations increasingly were not paying attention to the damage their policies were inflicting on society, environment, and communities. Precious little attention was paid to widening inequalities, as CEO's compensation packages in the US rose to 300 times that of an average worker when compared to around 50 times in the 1960s, while explosion of share buybacks[14] distorted economic incentives for managements and corporates.

One of the most glaring recent examples of the neoliberal denigration of public services, when combined with the ideology that the private sector knows best, can be found in the problems experienced by Boeing over the last several years. Boeing, a storied US aircraft manufacturer that single-handedly invented mass tourism and connected the world with its pioneering 1960s–70s planes, has been suffering from increasingly severe quality and technology issues (e.g., forgetting to tighten bolts, leaving tools and debris inside aircrafts, software malfunctions that resulted in two of the greatest modern crashes—Boeing 737 Max). The underlying reasons for most of Boeing's problems can be directly traced to the short-term maximization of returns which emerged as the company's modus operandi. A company that in the 1960s–80s was renowned for its engineering skills and product quality has degenerated over the last two decades into one driven mostly by financial returns, share buybacks, and share price appreciation that in turn fueled executive compensation packages. Starving FAA (the Federal Aviation Authority) of funds by successive Republican and Democratic governments has also led to Boeing largely policing and certifying itself. Following its reverse merger with McDonnell Douglas, the culture change was complete: new sites were opened without union membership, assembly and production sites were offloaded to off-balance sheet and private equity vehicles—cost savings and efficiency became the overriding goal. Tellingly, in 2001, at the peak of the neoliberal wave, Boeing's headquarters were moved from its engineering heartland in Seattle (where it was based since 1916) to Chicago, one of America's largest financial hubs, and then to the political center of the US, the Washington, DC, area. While similar pressures were also evident at Airbus (Boeing's European competitor), the less intense penetration of neoliberal ideas led to longer-term product planning and less robust offshoring and consolidation of production sites. At the same time, European regulators never fully abrogated their supervisory function. It is hardly surprising that Airbus, a former underdog which in the 1980s needed to lease its aircraft for nothing to convince airlines to use them, has now emerged as the dominant global civilian aircraft manufacturer, while Boeing is facing a long road to rehabilitation.

Similarly, financial deregulation, which started in the early 1980s in the US and the UK but then massively expanded into the global arena by the late 1990s, made perfect sense within the world of neoliberal views of the role of the unfettered free market in delivery of the most efficient and optimum outcomes. As I described in my first book,[15] the last three decades were a period of the most intense financialization ever experienced by the human race, which anchored and predicated the entire economic system on the direction and volatility of asset prices and leverage. Although initially these changes did provide an extra boost to economic growth across the world, eventually the side effects became highly toxic, including extreme financial and economic fragility, a massive rise in income and wealth inequalities (as households closest to the fountain of debt and financial assets benefited disproportionately when compared to average households who relied mostly on salaries, wages, and household chattels), explosion of public sector deficits and debt, as well as an unprecedented separation of monetary and real economies.

What I describe as the "cloud of finance" has risen to as much as five to ten times the size of underlying economies when compared to their more equal positioning in the 1960s–70s. As I intend to discuss later in this book (Chapter Seven), this deep Financialization (and its globalization sidekick) is one of the twin pillars of what I call the Fujiwara effect[16] (or a merger and reinforcement of several powerful hurricanes), which has been reshaping our social, political, and economic interactions. The other pillar is the highly disruptive impact of the Information Age, which is redefining the role and functioning of both labor and capital. These two forces (i.e., Financialization and the Information Age) were unleashed by Baby Boomers, with Financialization massively turbocharging the pace and the depth of technological revolution, which in turn is powering an ever-deeper Financialization.

Finally, the same neoliberal strands drive an increasing judicial conservatism across the world, which is especially pronounced in the US. For neoliberals, the true nature of justice has nothing to do with what most people recognize as justice. Rather, as Wendy Brown, an American sociologist, describes it, according to neoliberals, "justice is only about correct principles, universally applied not conditions or states of affairs. Justice also has nothing to do with rewarding effort or the deserving."[17] Indeed, in that mindset, it would be an injustice to pursue what most people regard as justice, or as von Hayek highlighted: "It is probably true that men would be happier about their economic conditions if they felt that the relative positions of individuals were just. Yet the whole idea behind distributive justice—that each individual out to receive what he morally deserves—is meaningless...because the available product (its size and even its existence) depends on what is in one sense a morally indifferent way of allocating its parts."[18] In other words, according to von Hayek, wealth and position may or may not be the fruit of great labor and effort, and alternatively hard work may come to nothing. This might be disappointing, but it is not unjust, as the free market values each contribution (or lack thereof) differently, and getting the state involved in redistribution would be far worse, ultimately leading to an erosion of freedom. Hence, it is better to leave everything to the market and the prevailing morality. In the same vein, one could argue that strictly following rules and the exact letter of the law is preferable to interpretation, explaining how conservative judges tend to ignore appeals to humanity or fairness.

In summary, neoliberal theories envisage a cold and indifferent world ruled by evolved traditions under the guise of wise and all-knowing perfect markets, with democracy and volatile politics either completely eliminated, or at the very least, significantly constrained. Philipp Blom accurately described it as a religion rather than an objective science, and as any religion, "it has its own rituals, its own priests and prophets…we must bring them sacrifices, and like in ancient Greece, the priests keep the best pieces of sacrificial meat for themselves."[19] This is definitely not where hippies and yippies of the 1960s–70s or even yuppies of the 1970s–80s wanted or planned to end up. It is doubtful that they would have anticipated that their desire for freedom and self-expression would yield conservative justices, share buybacks and CEO compensation packages, environmental degradation, massive rise in income and wealth inequalities, empty factories and ghost towns, and a rising tendency to restrict the hard-won principles of civil, gender, and race equality. However, in the end, this was always bound to be the inevitable outcome of sidelining the state to the extent to which it had occurred in most Western societies over the last three to four decades.

• • •

The problem with the neoliberal agenda that has come to dominate many aspects of our lives is not that it is intellectually incoherent—in its own way, it is actually a rather coherent set of values—but that it does not work in the real world. Like most artificially constructed frameworks (such as communism or fascism), what looks good and coherent on paper fails in real life.[20] This is principally because neither of the core ingredients of traditional morality or free markets exist as immutable truths.

There are two case studies that neoliberals believe exemplify the benefit of adopting their principles, namely, Hong Kong and Singapore. It so happens that both are close to my heart, as I have spent almost two decades living in Hong Kong and frequently traveled to Singapore. I find the arguments that are put forward for the morality and free market principles as reasons for their success to be both misleading and incorrect.

Milton Friedman featured Hong Kong in his influential 1990 PBS series, *Free to Choose*, as an example of a neoliberal free enterprise environment, or in his own words: "If you want to see how the free market really works, Hong Kong is the place to go...the power of free market has enabled the industrious people of Hong Kong to transform what was once a barren rock into one of the most successful places." In fact, the best description of Hong Kong is not one of a free market but rather of an oligopolistic fusion between the consenting state and the powerful elite, represented mostly by select few merchant and real estate dynasties. For decades, Hong Kong's business model was premised on rising property values, as the government released land at a controlled pace and then sold it to oligopolistic developers, guaranteeing them high profits while financing state spending. Hong Kong never invested in new ventures, technology, or social programs, preferring to skim profits on transshipments to China and play a role as China's window for raising equity capital. Why bother doing anything else when monopolies, which gradually permeated all aspects of economic life—from pharmacies and supermarkets to highly restrictive professional guilds—are so much more profitable, with the government conceding to the private sector most of the initiative. After all, "the private sector knows best." As Donald Tsang (the second HK SAR CEO) stated, "Civil servants should not see their role merely as regulators but more as supporters and partners for business" while Carrie Lam (the fourth CEO) argued that the "private sector, through its enterprise and efficiency, can come up with more economic solutions to deliver a public service." It's doubtful that Milton Friedman could have put it better.

As a result of not having a coherent policy, Hong Kong failed to replace manufacturing jobs—in 1996, around 17 percent of the Hong

Kong labor force worked in manufacturing, which is now down to only 2 percent—with higher value-added and more satisfying occupations. At the same time, Hong Kong's early mover advantage of investing in China has largely evaporated as its businesses never progressed beyond real estate and low value-added and highly labor-intensive factories that are offering progressively less value to China. Apart from working for the government, transportation, restaurants, hospitality, hotels, or the real estate industry, Hong Kong offers few job opportunities. The city-state has never developed as an IT or technology hub, and neither has it established design studios, biotech, or information businesses, while its previously vibrant film and entertainment industries[21] are now pale shadows of their glorious past. The introduction of the national security law is now also leading to the exit of previously vigorous journalistic and news flow businesses, as well as Western executives and lawyers. It is not even clear whether or not in years to come information and social networks like Google or Facebook would be willing to run the risk of offering their products in Hong Kong, and the same might apply to the spread of AI and LLM services like ChatGPT.

The lack of social policies created even more glaring problems. One of the most catastrophic failures of Hong Kong administrators over the last two decades was their inability to provide sufficient housing for the population. The government consistently preferred private rather than public development. As a result, neither private sector developers[22] (who are primarily motivated to maintain high prices) nor the government could deliver a sufficient number of residential units to the marketplace. Despite the doubling of Hong Kong's population, the supply of flats dropped from 70,000–100,000 clip per annum under British rule (prior to 1997) to as little as 25,000–50,000. As a result, wait lists for public housing extend to six years or longer. Thus, whereas in the late 1990s and early 2000s, Hong Kong's housing crisis was almost solved, the situation has massively deteriorated over the last two decades under free market governments. Hong Kong as a city of slums in the 1950s–60s was transformed by the British active policies into a city of relative prosperity and comfort by the late 1990s. It is now again becoming a city of slums, with flat subdivisions (i.e., more than one family cohabitating in the same flat by dividing living quarters into separate units) becoming increasingly common. According to estimates by the Society of Community Organizations, more than 220,000 people or 3 percent of the population are residing in what are known "coffin homes" or "cages."[23] In addition, over 21,000 families live in temporary structures such as huts and rooftops while almost 6,000 families live in factory and commercial buildings. These add up to one of the highest levels of "invisible slums" among developed and relatively rich cities. An average Hong Kong family now lives in apartments that are only 172 square feet per person (and around 30 square feet for those residing in cages). This compares to 210 square feet in Tokyo, 260 square feet in Shanghai, 270 square feet in Singapore, 300 square feet in Shenzhen, and more than 400 square feet in New York.[24] Despite a recent drop in house prices, the median home price in Hong Kong is still nearly 19 times median household income, a far heavier burden than in Singapore, the UK, and US.[25]

Ironically, all of these wounds are mostly self-inflicted and not caused by a shortage of land (Hong Kong is almost double the size of Singapore), with woodlands, grasslands, and wetlands occupying around two-thirds of the territory, while housing takes up around 7 percent (compared to 15 percent in Singapore). It is lack of systematic policies and a laissez-faire approach to private developers that has condemned Hong Kong to slums and makes it next to impossible for the younger generation to get on the property ladder.

At the same time, low tax rates and the absence of inheritance tax stifles the government's social policies while ensuring that accumulated wealth becomes dynastic, further aggravating income and wealth inequalities while precluding the development of a broader social net. As a result, various studies have highlighted that the top ten richest families in Hong Kong control around one-third of the entire corporate sector while the top fifteen families may control as much as 80 percent of domestic assets.[26] Even subsequent dilution due to the influx of mainland companies still left Hong Kong as one of the most oligopolistic places on earth. At the same time, as studies by Piketty and Li Yang argued, Hong Kong has one of the world's highest levels of income inequality. They found a significant rise in wage inequalities following the handover of Hong Kong to China in 1997 when compared to the pre-handover period.[27] While deindustrialization played a significant role, lack of any consistent government policies to ameliorate the situation and stimulate alternative sectors played an even larger role. The study also found that not surprisingly, Hong Kong's top 0.001 percent of the population has the highest wealth share in the world (approximately 10 percent, on par with Russia but far higher than in the US, China, or even Brazil). Other studies found that the top ten billionaires in Hong Kong account for as much as 35 percent of wealth,[28] when compared to around 3-4 percent in the US. Pre-COVID-19, the income gap had also been widening for the top 1 percent versus the bottom 50 percent. In the decade leading up to 2020, the share of income commanded by the top 1 percent rose from 11 percent to more than 16 percent while the share commanded by the bottom 50 percent shrank from 19 percent to less than 12 percent.

I lived in Hong Kong in 2019 when up to two million people (or 28 percent of the population) were estimated to have marched against the proposed extradition treaty and to demand greater freedom and democracy. While every society has a sizable and determined part of the community who really does care for democracy, rule of law, and freedom, it is hard to believe that these issues alone would have animated such an outpouring. Instead, it is more likely that diminishing employment prospects (particularly for the younger generation), unaffordable housing prices, and extreme inequalities were the key factors that aggravated other political and social concerns. In a multitude of ways, one can trace most of this to the core perception that one must limit democratic and popular franchise while allowing the private sector to make decisions with limited interference from the state and bureaucracy. In 2014, Leung Cung-Ying, a Hong SAR CEO at the time and a former real estate developer, encapsulated von Hayek's and Friedman's ideologies. When asked about widening of the electoral franchise, he replied that it was all about the "numbers" game, and expanding franchise would increase the power of the poor and lead to politics in favor of social spending and a welfare state instead of business-friendly policies.[29] This is not a dissimilar argument to many of today's US conservatives advocating for a much narrower and more restricted voting franchise.

Not only is Hong Kong far removed from being a paragon of the free market (*Economist* magazine was right to rank it instead as one of the top "crony capitalism" places on earth), but it has delivered neither innovation, progress, growth, nor even a modest equality. Clearly, either Friedman chose the wrong place to profile his ideas, or, more likely, Hong Kong has proven that the core neoliberal principles do not work in practice and result in decidedly inferior outcomes.

Despite neoliberals' love affair with Singapore,[30] it is doubtful that Milton Friedman would have agreed. Indeed, in the 1970s he was concerned that the highly intrusive government would derail the growth and development of Singapore, and when he was proven wrong, he could only argue that perhaps it was a special case, or it might have developed even faster and better if not for state interference. In reality, Singapore is far closer to a controlled socialist society than to the principles of the free market. As Lee Kuan Yew (the founder of independent Singapore) once famously remarked, "If Singapore is a nanny state, then I am proud to have fostered one." Similarly, he argued: "At the end of the day, is Singapore society better or worse off? That's the test." Unlike von Hayek, he was a believer in molding society and was also completely ideologically agnostic. He would never have subscribed to the idea that the state should minimize interference in shaping both economy and society.

Lee's philosophy, if he ever had one, was that of a simple trial and error. As he openly stated, "We are not enamored with any ideology." One could laugh at the reach of some of his ideas (such as prohibition on chewing gum, or preoccupation with "breeding graduates" by sponsoring joint events open only to the top college graduates, or his firm belief in the benefits of Eastern Confucian culture), but the state also had many bright and constructive ideas such as how to transit from basic to more sophisticated industries (e.g., textiles to petrochemicals and onto biotech and labs) and from illiteracy to having some of the world's most sophisticated centers of learning. The state was also deeply involved in land planning, proactive building, and maintenance rules, and in facilitating the transit from simple shipping (and transshipments) to sophisticated value-added services of registration and insurance. The list could go on, but the bottom line is that Lee Kuan Yew would never have abrogated the state's responsibility for economic and social planning to the supposed "invisible hand" of the private sector, free markets, and evolved moral traditions. He would have never supported a moribund Soviet model, but neither would he ever have accepted the dogma that the private sector knows best, the way bureaucrats in Hong Kong seem to have done over the last twenty-five years.

While in the 1990s, one could have debated whether or not Hong Kong's laissez-faire and "state deconstruction" approach or Singapore's heavy-handed state model were better, by now, the verdict is in. Singapore has emerged as a reasonably coherent and prosperous society with a global outlook, while Hong Kong has not only regressed but remains a narrowly based merchant-run trading outpost, wrecked by social discontent that had to be repressed. It is not to say that Singapore is perfect; far from it. Singaporean citizens heavily rely on an army of foreign workers (around 30 percent of the labor force) who do not enjoy any of the benefits of Singaporean citizens or better-off expats. They reside in barracks and are transported to and from work by trucks to make them as invisible as possible, and whenever not needed, they are subject to deportation. Also, within Singapore, income and wealth inequalities have been meaningfully widening, fueled by the influx of better-off migrants, especially from China.

However, unlike Hong Kong, no one dwells in cages, with Singapore's government developing a far more flexible and coherent residential property market, primarily through a multidecade deliberate planning process of expanding and adding to the city's land bank through careful management of limited preexisting land resources and extensive land reclamation, which over the last three decades increased the overall size of the city by more than

20 percent. In addition, Singapore has consistently preferred to build and maintain a far greater proportion of public housing as compared to Hong Kong, where the government focused on private sector solutions. As a result, supply of new apartments was steadily rising, and today, about 75–80 percent of Singaporeans reside in publicly provided housing and have a much shorter wait time when compared to Hong Kong. The government also has deliberately avoided "ghettos" by insisting on different ethnic groups coexisting and mixing in all public housing developments. While it is almost as unequal (in terms of income and wealth) to Hong Kong,[31] the government's policies have been blunting the impact, as reflected in the housing market, real estate prices, and transfer benefits.

In terms of manufacturing, while Hong Kong was completely denuded with factories en masse moving across the border to China, Singapore has successfully avoided this hollowing out. In 1996, both Hong Kong and Singapore had around 500,000 employed in manufacturing. Today, it is down to less than 75,000 in Hong Kong, while in Singapore manufacturing employment still stands at 550,000 (or more than 10 percent of the workforce), delivering in excess of 20 percent of GDP; in Hong Kong, it is down to only 1–2 percent. While clearly not being a fully-fledged independent country and having a massive China on its doorsteps accelerated the hollowing out of Hong Kong, one should keep in mind that Singapore (like Hong Kong) does not have a viable domestic market, and it is sandwiched between Malaysia and Indonesia with a combined market of almost 300 million people. If left to the private sector, it is highly likely that Singapore would have lost a lot more of its manufacturing.

It was not a miracle but rather deliberate government policies that prevented this. The government proactively encouraged (through taxation, land grants, immigration, and direct investment) a shift from toys and textiles to petrochemicals and later electronics and biotech industries. Singapore launched its first national technology and innovation plan as far back as 1991, and over the following twenty-five years, there were five more national plans formulated, which cumulatively invested over S$40 billion (or US$30 billion). Singapore also has the National Research

Foundation and the Research and Innovation Council that coordinate and execute plans, including the establishment of Singapore as one of the key global biotechnology and biomedical centers. While Hong Kong is starting to accelerate its own investment plans, it is decades behind Singapore and has thus far failed to capture the entire value chain, from basic research to commercialization. Not surprisingly, whereas Singapore has been consistently investing in excess of 2 percent of its GDP into various forms of research and development, Hong Kong barely invests 1 percent, and this gap has been persistent over the last three decades. Similar trends are reflected in the number of full-time researchers.

It is Hong Kong's lack of technological sophistication that precluded it from achieving a much deeper and broader penetration of the mainland (China) markets. Although in the 1980s and for the most of 1990s, Hong Kong businesses were far ahead, both organizationally and technologically, of pretty much anything in China, by the early part of the 21st century, this was no longer the case. Hence, the earlier expectation of service and technology exports flowing into Hong Kong from China never crystalized. China now has better technologies and know-how than conventional real estate, toy, or plastic businesses that relocated from Hong Kong. Singapore, on the other hand, is gradually becoming one of the more important centers that exports royalty and license fees, based on indigenous R&D and acquired or transferred patents.

Neither state has a freely exchangeable currency (another blow against the logic of the free market), but unlike the Hong Kong peg or a hard fixed exchange rate, Singapore adopted a much more flexible approach to managing its currency, rates, and monetary policies, which offers it the ability to occasionally release liquidity pressures and manage policies from a holistically societal perspective. While neither are conventionally democratic, Hong Kong over the last five years has moved far closer to a closed system, while Singapore has been tentatively moving in the opposite direction.

The bottom line is that hyperactive public policies, some broadening of electoral franchise and, in many ways, the planned and guided economy and society of Singapore achieved far more than a laissez-faire economy of Hong Kong. While the two city-states had traditionally closely tracked each other, after 1997, a wide gap started to open, and today, Singapore boasts a higher income per capita, better managed inequalities, and higher productivity, while its private sectors (households and nonfinancial corporates) rely less on leverage than those of Hong Kong. Although neither place is what neoliberals might consider perfect examples of the free market and evolved morality, there is no doubt that Hong Kong is closer to those ideas than Singapore, and outcomes of the last two decades seem to defeat arguments that neoliberal policies lead to greater freedom and superior economic and social outcomes.

Figure 10. *Hong Kong vs. Singapore, GDP per Capita (US$)*

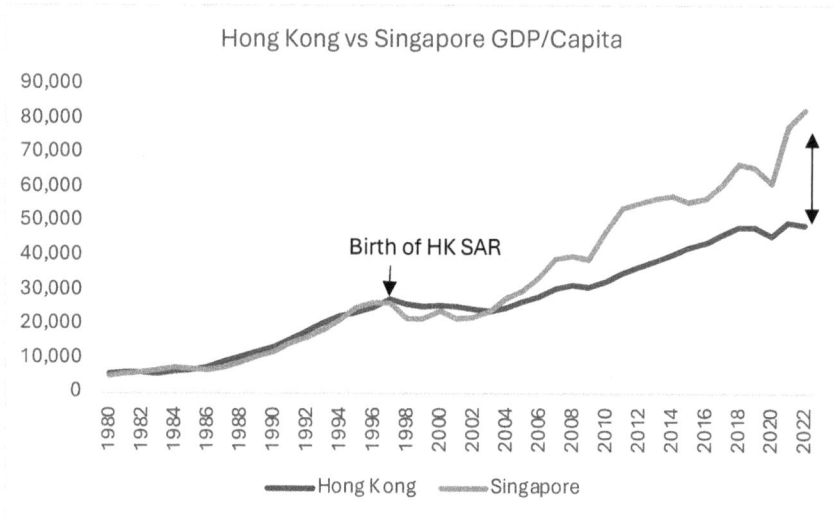

Source: World Bank

Other case studies that neoliberals highlight as examples of how their policies might be introduced are the Canary Wharf development in London and Dubai.

It is hard to find a place that elicits as many positive neoliberal reviews as Dubai. Theoretically, it satisfies most of the neoliberal agenda of tax-free capitalism without interference from a messy democracy, under the guidance of a benign king. Some describe it as "a society that has been designed by the Economics Department of the University of Chicago."[32] Instead of citizens, it has customers who seem to be happy with the terms of the contract between the ruler and the ruled.

However, even if it were desirable, replicating Dubai will be only possible in a place with few citizens (approximately 85 percent of Dubai's population is made up of expatriates, mostly laborers from India and Pakistan) and one that positions itself as an external beneficiary of global upheavals. Dubai mostly owes its success to the blockade of Iran and challenges that consistently flare up in Pakistan, Russia, Central Asia, and Afghanistan. Dubai has little to offer other than a highly successful financial and trade intermediation between various, sometimes hostile, places with efficient transshipment as well as a real estate and financial sanctuary. To be sure, Dubai has been willing to concede legal rights to a patchwork of English common-law and other jurisdictions, enabling it to offer a plug-and-play regulatory and operating environment to multinationals, which Baby Boomers' globalization allowed to widely propagate. However, even in this capitalism without democracy, overinvestment and the global financial crisis (2008–10) forced a bail-out from the oil-rich sister Emirate (Abu Dhabi), rather than confronting the more conventional free-market solutions of bankruptcies and liquidations. Finally, this model critically depends on the personality and the success of just one individual.[33] As history abundantly shows, such reliance usually leads to a far greater long-term volatility, as personalities, views, and/or global circumstances change. That's why some neoliberals are suggesting converting Dubai into a public company with external shareholders and a board of directors. However, as we have seen in corporate markets, this in turn creates its own pressures and contradictions—quarterly performance, share buybacks, and dividends—converting the key advantage of a king (ability to take a long-term view) into a disadvantage, which might not be much different from messy democracies so disliked by neoliberals.

In the case of Canary Wharf, there is no doubt that tax breaks, special zones, and less red tape can be of help. However, there is absolutely no evidence that Britain's propensity for such private sector solutions resulted in better outcomes. Do the British have a higher standard of living than key states of the EU (such as Germany, Benelux, Scandinavia, or France)? The answer is no. Do the British live longer? The answer, again, is negative. Is there more poverty and higher inequality in Britain? The answer is a resounding yes. It is not even clear whether the Canary Wharf development significantly enhanced the competitiveness of the British financial sector. It is more likely that British dominance in financial services owes far more to the English language, geographic position (in between North America, Africa, and Asia), common law, and the EU (pre-Brexit). Canary Wharf, as a project, could have been developed differently.

The history of the application of neoliberal policies in more conventional developed economies is not any better, especially in the countries that embraced it wholeheartedly, such as the US and Britain. Sufficient evidence has already accumulated over the last three to four decades to conclude that the idea of combining traditional morality with free market logic and sidelining the state does not lead to higher productivity. On the contrary, productivity in the US and UK stagnated throughout this period. Neither did it lead to improved income and wealth distribution. The opposite is true, as these policies resurrected something akin to the Gilded Age of the late 19th and early 20th centuries. Nor is there any evidence that it improves educational or human skilling outcomes, and unlike neoliberals' expectations that traditionally evolved morality would reduce social pressures and polarization, their policies massively aggravated both (Chapter Six).

While one could debate whether or not enough time has elapsed, and we could be open to the criticism of mixing long-term trends (such as the Information Revolution) with shorter-term outcomes (inequalities), and neoliberals might also argue that their ideas were not properly implemented, there appears little doubt that the actual outcomes thus far do not support most neoliberal ideas. Indeed, I concur with Joseph Stiglitz[34] that

96

if neoliberal ideas were properly implemented, outcomes might have been even worse. The neoliberal world is simply not a sustainable economic, social, and political system.

• • •

In 1979, the same year President Carter was despairing about the spirit of narcissism pervading US society, the neoliberal revolution began with the publication of Milton and Rose Friedman's manifesto, *Free to Choose: A Personal Statement*.[35] The book forcefully argued that it is not the private markets but the governments' interference with its workings that causes most of the distress and discontinuities. It is not that Milton Friedman ever advocated eliminating or completely sidelining governments; rather his argument was that as we have seen in the late 1960s–70s, governments tend to go too far, and that they cannot possibly possess enough information to second-guess market signals. While both claims are true, the opposite argument that free markets when left to their own devices would arrive at outcomes superior to governments' intervention—both in an absolute as well as distributive sense—is only true in a rarefied academic atmosphere of perfect information and competition, which unfortunately does not exist in real life. Similarly, his view that government interventions, especially in democratic settings, would be prone to be hijacked by powerful interest groups is equally true in an environment where the supposed free markets rule. Hence, his arguments for elimination of social safety nets, shrinkage of state functions, and curtailment of regulations (from monopolistic power to pollution), lead to opposite outcomes: greater pollution, higher industry concentration, rise in inequalities, and stagnating productivity.

Nevertheless, following the deeply traumatic stagflationary 1970s, societies were ready for something new, and Baby Boomers, who by that stage became the dominant electoral cohort, sponsored and supported politicians (from both left and right) who were either genuine believers (such as Ronald Reagan, Margaret Thatcher, and George Bush) or were willing to ride the wave (such as Tony Blair, Bill Clinton, or even Barack

Obama, and in many respects Deng Xiaoping). Although political realities are what they are, and no one could ever genuinely hope to cut the absolute size of government spending as a percentage of GDP, the backdrop had drastically changed, with the state significantly reducing its commitments to infrastructure, R&D, and education. For example, federal and state infrastructure investment in the US in the 1960s was approximately 7 percent of GDP, and by 2010s it was down to around 3 percent, while the proportion of basic R&D funded by the state dropped from over 70 percent in 1960s to less than 40 percent. As the environment changed, the same bureaucracy that would have carefully reviewed any major market transaction preferred to accept the societal consensus that the "private sector knows best" and avoid confrontation, with the break-up of AT&T and Microsoft lawsuits being the last major actions until Biden's administration in the 2020s. The same applied to the regulatory rulings by the Security and Exchange Commission (SEC) which carved out special protected niches that massively bolstered CEO compensation and share buybacks. Once again, it is only now (2023–24 as of this writing) that these regulations and rulings are being tentatively reviewed.

What went wrong with neoliberal ideas? This is a huge field that has been explored for years by economists, political scientists, historians, and curious amateurs and market participants. This is not the book to dwell excessively on and debate each issue; rather, I intend to provide a broad outline and leave it to readers to explore these topics in wonderful books and articles that specifically address this issue.

At the heart of the matter lies a deceptively simple question: Is capitalism—if left to its own devices and unchecked—a source of instability, chaos, and economic and social disorders? Or, if liberated from the clutches of well-meaning but inept governments, is capitalism a source of growth, innovation, justice, and freedom? While such stark questions contain numerous inconsistencies, every modern Western society tended toward either one extreme or the other. Following the Great War and the Great Depression, societies lost confidence in the ability of the private sector to guide them toward their desired outcomes—Lewis Mumford, at the height of the 1930s disruption, described the free market orthodoxy as a *theology* or *superstition* that delivered catastrophic results.[36] The prevailing mantra therefore shifted toward a greater role for the state or Kaletsky's Capitalism 2.0. People who witnessed the negative externalities and misallocation of resources as well as the cruelty that the private sector and markets are capable of inflicting, started to view governments as the guardrail against chaos and a much-needed curb on capitalism. This consensus lasted from the New Deal in the 1930s until sometime in the early 1970s. However, the stagflationary period of the 1970s as well as the assertiveness of the new freedom-loving generational cohort (i.e., Baby Boomers) changed the calculus, and by the early 1980s, a new consensus formed (solidifying globally by the 1990s) that prioritized private sector solutions while denigrating the state. This neoliberal consensus lasted for more than two decades until the Global Financial Crisis in 2008–10. Since then, the world has been in flux, transitioning toward yet another consensus.

So, what were the critical fault lines in the neoliberal view of the world? As both Keynes and Polanyi highlighted, limited government and the dominance of laissez-faire market systems will ultimately discredit liberal ideas in the eyes of the electorate. Polanyi[37] in particular was concerned that unfettered markets driven by monetary signals alone could easily undermine the social order, paving the way for dictatorship and far greater violence as people start to support more extreme ideas to ease their pain. This includes not only inequalities in assets and property rights but also a broader set of social rights, including the need to be heard and listened to. In a neoliberal view of the world, the market economy and the state must recognize the sanctity of property rights above all others, and ideally the state, while safeguarding these, should be separate from the markets. It then follows that markets would reward those who have more assets and wealth while the rest must hope that free market mechanisms would somehow miraculously take care of the rest. As von Hayek argued, hard work is not a guarantee of rewards, just as no work is not a guarantee of failure.

However, there are significant problems with this argument. In the absence of some countervailing force, businesses, power, and money tend to gravitate toward greater, not lower, concentration. As Thomas Piketty[38] argued in his groundbreaking study of economic trends over the last two centuries, the rate of return on capital is almost always higher than the rate of economic growth, implying that capital's share tends to rise, and it is only violent dislocations, such as revolutions or wars, that redress this anomaly by destroying capital. Indeed, the Great War and World War II were the key facilitators of such destruction, heralding the end of the Gilded Age of the earlier part of the 20th century, and the rise of relative fairness and equality in the 1950s–70s. This is not dissimilar to Marx's view that economic and political inequalities occur as a result of labor productivity consistently exceeding compensation. He also argued that markets in pursuit of profit maximization tend to hijack institutions of state, defanging government instrumentalities in the process, allowing for an ever-greater market concentration within and between industries, fueling the shift of national income from wages to capital.

Polanyi's answer was more subtle and, in my view, more realistic. In his book *The Great Transformation*—which interestingly came out the same year (1944) as van Hayek's revolutionary *Road to Serfdom*[39]—he argued that economists' core belief in an equilibrating system of integrated global markets does not reflect the reality of life (i.e., neoliberals believe that markets automatically adjust supply and demand through the medium of prices, and even if there are some market failures, they mostly view these as rare exceptions). Polanyi developed a concept of *embeddedness*, which is to say, unlike neoliberals who believed in separation of markets from societies (many of them did not even think that societies were real), he argued that economies and markets are embedded in societies and are subordinated to politics and social relations. To attempt to separate the two is, in his view, wishful and utopian thinking that could lead to catastrophic consequences. To put it bluntly, Polanyi did not believe that people would accept the degree of pain involved in free market adjustments (whether rising unemployment, bankruptcies, or the need to slash wages to maintain the gold standard), and will demand change, and if the change does not come, violence would invariably ensue. When established protagonists do not offer viable answers to people's concerns, space is created for extremists and populists. This, in his view, explained the rise of the Nazi Party in Germany or the Fascists in Italy, and the same goes for the Bolsheviks in Russia.

In other words, although a truly free market might redress issues of concentration of power (both economic and political), such conditions simply do not exist outside the narrow confines of academia. Instead, there is ample evidence of a strong tendency toward greater concentration of power and money. Apart from Piketty's destruction of capital in wars and revolutions, what other force is sufficiently strong to redress this concentration? The answer, to Polanyi as well as Sheldon Wolin,[40] is the government. Both argue that modern societies require that the state acts deliberately to reduce economic, social, and political inequalities. Indeed, the state is the only power with sufficient strength and legitimacy to be able to overcome market pressures and the power of oligopolistic elites.

While this might sound revolutionary and heretical in the domain of the neoliberals, it has been for centuries accepted as the most logical answer. As Athenians knew, democracy is not a natural human state, and to survive it must be nurtured. Alexis de Tocqueville and Jean-Jacques Rousseau discussed how democracies (or, for that matter, any stable society) can only exist if there is a degree of political equality which requires that inequalities (whether civic, education, or wealth) are minimized against the backdrop of a natural gravitation toward the opposite—greater concentration of power and wealth. Neither traditional morality nor the free market could ever dilute this. Only the state, through its legitimacy and monopoly power on violence and money creation, has sufficient strength. As I discuss later in the book, these periods of rupture are particularly pronounced during the cresting of technological revolutions. There is no doubt that if it were not for the state-led policies in education, welfare, and healthcare, the upheavals following the industrial revolutions through the 19th and 20th centuries would have been even greater. As outlined in my first book (*The Great Rupture*), the Information Age is unleashing changes of far greater strength than past industrial revolutions, requiring a complex balancing of freedom, fairness, and equality to minimize what is likely to be an extended period of disruption and disorientation that might last at least a decade or two through the 2020s and 2030s.

We shall return to these important themes later. However, in the meantime, the next chapter will examine the economic price of the Baby Boomers' neoliberalism.

Chapter 5

THE PAINFUL LEGACY

"They inherited prosperity, social cohesion, and functioning institutions. They passed on debt, inequality, moribund churches, and a broken democracy."

Helen Andrews's description of the legacy of Baby Boomers[1]

T he above quote from Helen Andrews neatly encapsulates key legacies that Baby Boomers with their neoliberal philosophy have passed on to next generations, including a widespread destruction of the middle class in more developed economies, addiction to assets and debt, pervasive inequalities (income and wealth), environmental degradation, and an uncontrolled and disorderly globalization.

• • •

Baby Boomers' desire to break down barriers to the free flow of information, ideas, lifestyles, finance, and trade led to the deepest ever globalization of trade, capital, and labor.

The level and sophistication of globalization that the world achieved in 1913, just prior to the Great War, was not again replicated until the early 1980s, with the intervening decades featuring tight controls on the flow of capital, goods, services, and people. However, starting in the late 1980s and until the Global Financial Crisis in 2008–10, external trade as a proportion of global GDP exploded, more than doubling from 25–30 percent to 65 percent at the peak of the wave. The neoliberal underpinnings of Kaletsky's Capitalism 3.0 (i.e., private sector always knows best, and there should be no restrictions or impediments to the flow of trade) was its primary driver, supported by a new societal consensus and actively facilitated by the new breed of politicians—from Margaret Thatcher to Ronald Reagan, Bill Clinton to Tony Blair, Bob Hawke and Paul Keating to Helmut Kohl and Gerhard Schroder.

As a result, tariff barriers came down to levels that the world had not seen since the British Navy forced them to zero in the mid-19th century. The drop was particularly pronounced in less developed economies. In 1989, the average tariff in Latin America was around 32 percent, and by 2008 it was down to only 4 percent, while in sub-Saharan Africa, tariffs collapsed from 25 percent to less than 7 percent. In more developed economies, including the US, average tariffs dropped to around 1–2 percent from levels closer to 5–10 percent two decades prior. It became much easier and cheaper for private sectors to build extensive global supply and value chains, which were no longer facing the same financial, bureaucratic, and cost constraints. This expansion was also facilitated by a technological revolution, including containerization[2] of trade, which drastically reduced the cost of shipping while increasing its flexibility.

The need to finance this burgeoning cross-border trade and the required investment had simultaneously resulted in a strong rise of cross-border capital flows, facilitated by deregulation of finance. Whereas in the 1980s–90s, the world's external assets and liabilities were generally below 100 percent of GDP, these more than doubled to over 200 percent by 2008 and are now closer to 250 percent, with FDI (foreign direct investment) liabilities rising from approximately 20 percent of GDP to around 70 percent today.[3] The nonresident credit outstanding (i.e., debt held in other nations' currencies) which was quite marginal in the 1970s, now stands at close to US$14 trillion. While these estimates imbed some double-counting, the late 2010s had marked the historical peak of the rapid rise in cross-border capital flows.

At the same time, labor markets became more flexible through lower union membership (down for OECD countries from almost 40 percent in 1960s to 16 percent in 2023) but even more importantly driven by an unprecedented wave of human migration. Baby Boomers' desire for unrestricted travel massively eased restrictions, with the number of people who today reside outside their country of birth approaching 300 million. If all these migrants constituted a country of their own, it would be the world's fourth-largest nation (after India, China, and the US).

Figure 11. *World Trade (exports and imports) (% GDP)*

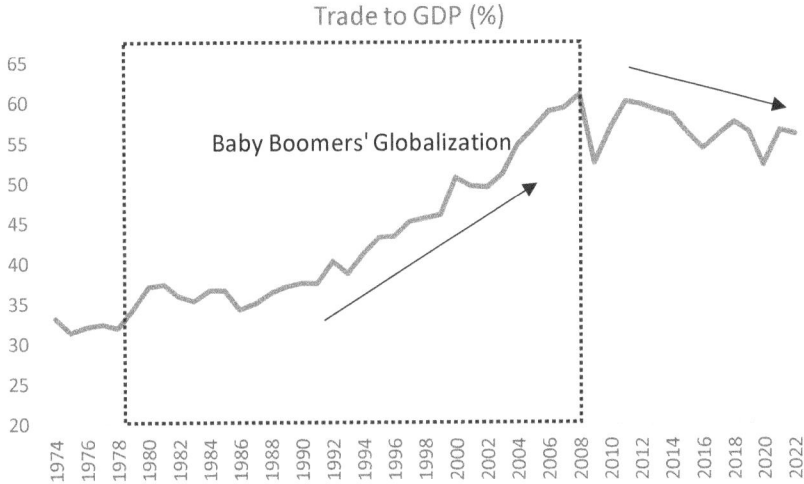

Trade to GDP (%)

Baby Boomers' Globalization

Source: World Bank, 2023

Relative to global population, it represents a rise from 2.6 percent in 1960 to around 4 percent by 2020,[4] with bulk of the flows occurring between the late 1980s and 2010s. My own family is an example of the Baby Boomers' thirst for freedom. While I was born in Ukraine, I lived most of my adult life between Australia, Hong Kong, Britain, and the US. My wife was born in Hong Kong but spent most of her adult life in Britain and the US, as have my two sons. The ability to move across borders and explore places and cultures while working in different jurisdictions, without excessively burdensome restrictions, was one of the greatest achievements of the Baby Boomers' revolution. My family and I were very lucky.

However, since the Global Financial Crisis, there has been an increase in tariffs (initiated by Donald Trump and continued under Biden) and a much more pronounced rise in nontariff protectionary measures (e.g., health certificates, intrusive inspections, bans),[5] accompanied by signs of a persistent erosion and stagnation of trade intensity. Essentially, in the last fifteen years, countries have started to deliberately place pebbles in the waters of globalization in an attempt to slow it down and reduce the damage inflicted on local communities. As with trade, a growing number of countries are now also doing their best to slow the pace of immigration through the usual means of visas, quotas, and deportations, sunsetting one of the freest periods in global migration since the mid-19th to early 20th centuries, when over 60 million Europeans migrated to the New World—mostly to the US, Canada, and Australia, but also to Argentina, Brazil, South Africa, and New Zealand.

These reversals are a clear vindication of Dani Rodrik's concept of the "Political Trilemma of the World Economy"[6] that he has been championing since the late 1990s. According to Rodrik, a professor at Harvard University, one can't have deep economic integration, nation-states, and local democracy. We can combine any two of the three but never all three simultaneously and not in full. The reason for this trilemma is that deep economic integration requires the elimination of transaction costs (such as reduction in tariffs and nontariff barriers, elimination of impediments to flow of capital and investment, increased flexibility of labor markets, and relatively free migration). However, this creates winners and losers, and even though the global economy as a whole wins, winners never compensate losers within an acceptable political timeframe, and, therefore, it is incompatible with the interests of a nation-state and its citizens. Also, winners and losers tend to be unevenly distributed, not only within borders but also between countries and among ethnic and racial groups. Rodrik argued that either one needs to abolish nation-states (unlikely), local politics have to perform global duties (difficult), or globalization has to go into reverse. Similarly, Peter Drucker, one of the founders of management science, argued in the early 1990s, that the growing internationalization and globalization also meaningfully heightens "tribal affiliations," as people feel that they need to belong to a community, and even though their employers might be based in the US, Japan, or Germany, they want to belong to a community (language, culture, religion) that they can comprehend. Hence, in his words, "The more transnational the world becomes, the more tribal it will also be."[7]

Globalization enabled businesses to take advantage of cost and efficiency arbitrage—cheaper labor and better supply and value chains. While lowering retail prices, improving global efficiency, and lifting millions of people in less developed countries out of poverty, globalization, at the same time, mercilessly destroyed factories, industries, and the middle class in more developed economies (witness reversal of fortunes of Michigan, Pennsylvania, Ohio, Glasgow, Birmingham, and many other places across the world through 1990s–2000s). Although over time everyone globally is better off, the domestic pressures for changing patterns of trade while supporting local employment and communities were always bound to rise, yielding the political stage to more extreme views, benefiting merchants of isolationism and populism who trade in these grievances. As the historian Stefan Linik argued, there is nothing natural or inevitable about globalization. Indeed, it is far from a "natural" state of affairs. The globalization causes mounting tensions between benefits of free trade on the one hand and equality, sovereignty, and popular politics on the other.[8] This has been one of the root causes for the rising tide of populism (in its various forms) and the extreme social polarization that engulfed most developed economies since the Global Financial Crisis.

Whereas in the 1950s–60s, Rodrik's trilemma was resolved by maintaining tight control over trade, labor, and capital flows (and as a result, enabling nation-states and local democracies to flourish), post-late 1970s, the world attempted to have all three and reconciled the trilemma by unleashing leverage and asset price inflation, which were supposed to compensate losers of global integration through better mobility, rising asset prices, and increasing wealth and by bringing future consumption to the present (i.e., borrowing) in order to take the sting out of rising inequalities. However, this temporary resolution of the trilemma has created its own set of challenges.

First and foremost, it unleashed a wave of debt and financialization on a scale that has never been seen before in human history. The rapid deregulation of finance, combined with policies that started to prioritize assets rather than income as the main, and indeed the only, way for most people to stay afloat and avoid sinking deeper into poverty, led to an explosion of debt and financial assets. This was completely unlike the 1950s–60s, when nominal and real wages were rising, and houses were for living, not speculation. Eventually, corporations and businesses had also accepted this debt and asset-driven logic, altering their operational and investment plans.

Whereas in the 1950s–70s, the global economy required not much more than US$1 or US$1.50 of debt for each incremental unit of GDP, by the 2020s, it needed at least US$3-4. In these decades, the world has accumulated a mountain of debt that has already surpassed US$300 trillion or almost 3.5 times GDP. Even as astronomic as these numbers look, the overall financialization is even higher. According to the Financial Stability Board estimates, as of 2022, the value of global financial assets surpassed US$460 trillion or close to 6 times GDP of correspondent countries (when compared to only US$120 trillion in 2002). And this is after valuing derivatives on a net rather than a gross basis and before accounting for unfunded liabilities carried by both the private and public sectors (such as pensions, social security, and medical costs), which in the US alone exceed US$50 trillion. Neither is this asset and debt dependency a strictly developed market phenomena, with an increasing of number of less developed economies (led by China) carrying a heavier than in the past burden, with debts rising from US$13 trillion in 2005 to more than US$100 trillion in 2023. In a relative sense, the leverage increased from almost equal to GDP in 1995 to more than 2.5 times today.

Figure 12. Global Debt Estimates (US$ trillion, % GDP)

	Households	Non-Financial Corporates	Financial Corporates	Government	Total
US$ trillion					
1990	10	10	7	10	37
2000	17	24	24	20	85
2007	35	43	54	35	168
2023	59	94	69	90	312
% of GDP					
1990	41%	41%	29%	41%	152%
2000	44%	72%	59%	55%	230%
2007	58%	76%	87%	58%	279%
2023	61%	96%	77%	97%	331%

Source: IIF, March 2024

Figure 13. Global Financial Assets (US$ trillion, % of GDP)

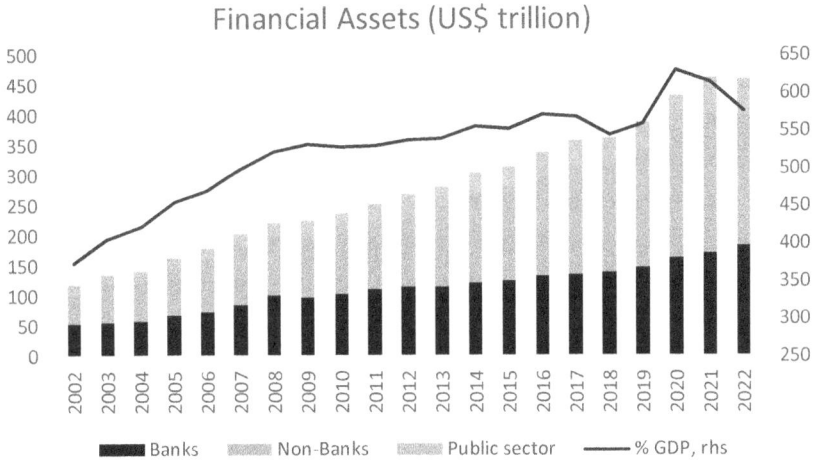

Financial Assets (US$ trillion)

Source: FSB, December 2023

While in the 1950s–70s, real and financial economies were broadly matched (or equal in size), today, depending on treatment of derivatives as well as off-balance sheet and unfunded commitments, financial economy is at least five times and possibly as much as ten times larger.

This, in turn, meaningfully destabilized the velocity of money and increased global economic and financial instability, pushing economies further into what Larry Summers, an academic and a former US treasury secretary, described as "secular stagnation" (or inability to grow).[9] As a result, ironically for freedom-loving Baby Boomers, this led to demands for persistent state-driven supports and stimuli through fiscal and monetary levers aimed at preventing neutral rates (i.e., rates at which economies neither contract nor expand) from falling at an even faster pace. This goes to the heart of Adair Turner's question as to why the global economy can no longer grow without generating a destabilizing level of debt. In his words, "We face a severe dilemma. We seem to need credit to grow faster than GDP to keep economies growing at a reasonable pace, but that inevitably leads to crisis, debt overhang, and post crisis recession. We seem to be condemned to instability in an economy incapable of balanced growth."[10]

A more intense dependence on leverage and asset prices has also gradually limited the government's ability to tolerate asset price volatilities, requiring a more robust management and compression of business and credit cycles that ultimately led to Greenspan's and Bernanke's infamous "put option" (i.e., intolerance to falling asset prices and markets). In other words, over the years global economies have been condemned to generating more liquidity and capital than real economies require in order to ensure not only that today's economic outcomes are in line with societal expectations, but that there is sufficient surplus liquidity (beyond current needs) to ensure that debt defaults and asset price volatilities are contained, and that over time, holistically defined assets continue to appreciate in value to lubricate the next cycle of economic growth. This converted free markets neoliberal ideas into a true state-dependent Frankenstein monster.

A rising tide of financialization of the global economy, while providing some short-term relief, also has a number of highly toxic side effects: it encourages financial speculation and rent-seeking behavior rather than productive investment, prevents clearance of excesses, encourages disintermediation of corporates and businesses from their products and brands as well as people from the fruits of their labor by massively accelerating the pace of the technological revolution, increases disinflation and lowers neutral rates, and most importantly, it aggravates income and wealth inequalities.

While popular literature is replete with examples of individual greed and failure (e.g., a "few rotten apples in the barrel;" misguided central banks; institutional and regulatory corruption and failures; crooks like the fictional "Gordon Gekko" and the real-life Bernie Madoff; or compliance and regulatory failures at Deutsche Bank, Wells Fargo, or Silicon Valley Bank), the underlying causes are far deeper. There are fundamental reasons why greed and misplaced incentives suddenly appear, why regulators look the other way, and why society as a whole rewards success irrespective of the means employed to achieve it.

110

As Charles Calomiris and Stephen Haber astutely observed, the conflict of interests between politics, taxpayers, citizens, and the finance industry makes "banking systems in most countries fragile by design."[11] People demand growth, wealth creation, and avoidance of pain, and politics delivers. In the last three to four decades, this was achieved through unprecedented financialization of the global economy. Although the banking system is *fragile by design* in any era, there are times when generational and societal expectations are particularly conducive to a more pronounced shift toward greed and exuberance. At the heart of the most recent wave was the Baby Boomers' insistence on endless growth, opportunities, and unrestricted freedom, irrespective of the ultimate consequences, either economic, societal, or environmental.

•   •   •

Intense financialization (and its equally important sidekicks, globalization and neoliberal tax cuts) were also significant drivers of rapidly rising income and wealth inequalities, mostly within states but increasingly between states as well. While the 1950s–70s was a period of middle-class creation and declining inequalities, the last three to four decades were the opposite: the weakening of middle class and rising inequalities. Whether one looks at the Gini coefficient (statistical measure of income inequality), share of income attributable to the top and/or the bottom of the pyramid, or gaps between the mean and median real household income, there is ample evidence of a rise in inequalities. For instance, according to Thomas Piketty, Emmanuel Saez, and Gabriel Zukman, the top 1 percent of US households today control around 15–20 percent of national income (and more importantly, 0.1 percent of households now control almost 10 percent), up from 8–9 percent five decades ago. Even more alarmingly, the bottom 50 percent of households which used to command around 21 percent of the national income in the late 1960s, are now down to only 13 percent.[12]

The concentration of wealth is even greater. Depending on the database, the top 10 percent of households own more than 70 percent, and the top 1 percent control an estimated 35–40 percent of the US national wealth when compared to around 25 percent in the 1970s. More importantly, no matter which database one uses, the bottom 50 percent own absolutely nothing, while the middle has been squeezed with the share of net wealth of those between the 50th and 90th percentile dropping from 34 percent of the national wealth in 1980 to around 25 percent in 2020.

While US outcomes have been historically more extreme (due in large part to a much more pervasive neoliberal influence and its corporate "star" culture), similar trends are evident in most other developed economies, even those with a history of more egalitarian income and wealth distribution, such as France, Germany, Japan, or Sweden. The share of European wealth commanded by the bottom 50 percent of households dropped from 9 percent in 1990 to around 6 percent by 2020, while that of the top 10 percent increased from 51 percent in 1990 to around 56 percent in 2020. In terms of income, the share of the bottom 50 percent declined from the high of 24 percent in 1980 to 21 percent today.

It is truly a global phenomenon. According to the Credit Suisse Global Wealth Report, as of 2020, 1 percent of the world's population had control over 50 percent of the global wealth, up from 42 percent in 2008 and 35 percent in 2000. On the other hand, the poorest 50 percent of the world only had around 2.7 percent of the global wealth. At the same time, forty-two billionaires owned as much wealth as around 4 billion people, while in 2009, one needed almost 400 billionaires to have the same relative weight. According to Forbes in 1998, there were 298 billionaires globally who owned 2 percent of global GDP, and by 2022, the number rose to 2,640, controlling 12 percent of GDP,[13] with a recent Oxfam report estimating that between 2020 and 2023, the wealth of billionaires increased by more than 34 percent.[14]

Figure 14. US Households' Share of National Wealth (%)

	1950	1971	1989	2007	2016
Bottom 50%	3.0%	3.0%	2.9%	2.5%	1.2%
-0%-25%	-0.1%	-0.2%	-0.1%	-0.1%	-0.4%
-25%-50%	3.1%	3.2%	3.0%	2.6%	1.6%
50%-90%	24.7%	26.3%	29.5%	26.0%	21.5%
-50%-75%	9.8%	10.5%	11.7%	10.2%	7.2%
-75%-90%	14.9%	15.8%	17.8%	15.8%	14.3%
Top 10%	72.3%	70.7%	67.6%	71.5%	77.3%
Middle Class (25%-75%)	12.9%	13.7%	14.7%	12.8%	8.8%
Top 1%	30.5%	26.4%	26.9%	34.1%	35.0%
Top 1%-10%	41.8%	44.3%	40.7%	37.4%	42.3%

Source: *Moritz Kuhn, Moritz Schurlarick, and Ulrike Steins, "Income and Wealth Inequality in America, 1949-2016," CEPR, June 2018; Saez Inequality Database, 2023*

Figure 15. Wealth Distribution, Europe and the US, 1900–2020

		Europe			US		
		Bottom 50%	50%-90%	Top 10%	Bottom 50%	50%-90%	Top 10%
The Gilded Age	1900	1.3%	10.2%	88.2%	2.5%	14.5%	83.0%
	1910	1.2%	9.2%	89.6%	2.2%	13.8%	84.0%
	1920	1.3%	12.8%	85.8%	1.9%	18.0%	80.1%
	1930	1.8%	11.2%	87.0%	1.3%	14.1%	84.6%
Pre Baby Boomers	1940	2.3%	16.2%	81.4%	2.0%	20.9%	77.1%
	1950	2.6%	23.2%	74.2%	2.7%	29.0%	68.3%
	1960	4.3%	27.7%	67.9%	2.6%	27.6%	69.9%
	1970	6.9%	31.2%	61.9%	2.1%	29.1%	68.7%
	1980	7.9%	37.9%	54.1%	2.2%	33.6%	64.2%
Baby Boomers' Era	1990	8.9%	39.6%	51.5%	2.7%	33.2%	64.2%
	2000	7.5%	39.2%	53.4%	1.8%	30.4%	67.9%
	2010	6.3%	38.9%	54.8%	0.9%	28.2%	70.9%
	2020	6.2%	38.1%	55.6%	1.6%	26.1%	72.3%

Source: *Thomas Piketty, Brief History of Equality (Cambridge: The Belknap Press of Harvard University, 2022). Europe is the average of Germany, France, Britain, and Sweden*

Figure 16. Income Distribution, Europe and the US, 1900–2020

		Europe				US		
		Bottom 50%	50%-90%	Top 10%		Bottom 50%	50%-90%	Top 10%
The Gilded Age	1900	13.5%	36.4%	50.1%		16.0%	41.0%	43.0%
	1910	13.1%	34.8%	52.1%		15.0%	41.0%	44.0%
	1920	15.7%	41.2%	43.1%		14.8%	41.0%	44.1%
	1930	16.4%	40.9%	42.7%		13.9%	39.8%	46.3%
Pre Baby Boomers	1940	17.4%	41.5%	41.1%		13.9%	37.2%	48.9%
	1950	20.7%	47.2%	32.1%		17.5%	43.4%	39.1%
	1960	20.0%	47.0%	33.0%		18.2%	46.3%	35.5%
	1970	21.1%	48.1%	30.8%		21.2%	45.5%	33.3%
	1980	24.2%	47.4%	28.4%		20.1%	46.2%	33.8%
Baby Boomers' Era	1990	21.8%	47.3%	30.9%		16.9%	44.7%	38.4%
	2000	21.0%	44.4%	34.6%		15.1%	42.3%	42.6%
	2010	21.4%	43.3%	35.3%		13.9%	42.5%	43.7%
	2020	21.3%	42.5%	36.2%		13.2%	40.9%	45.9%

Source: Thomas Piketty (2022)

As the Kuhn study of the US wealth inequalities amply illustrated, most of these differences were caused by an unprecedented growth of the "cloud of finance" relative to real economies. Households which were the closest to the fountain of debt and financial assets have significantly accelerated their wealth when compared to those which continued to rely mostly on wages and salaries, homes, and household chattels (such as cars, refrigerators, etc.). Whereas for the bottom 50 percent, housing accounts for more than 62 percent of their net worth, for the top 10 percent, that ratio is only 10 percent. On the other extreme, only 18 percent of the wealth of the bottom 50 percent of households are in financial assets (including 1 percent in equities), while for the top 10 percent of households have 49 percent of their assets in financial assets (including 20 percent in equities).

This is diametrically opposite of the 1950s, when most of the wealth was accumulated through wages. However, as money supply increased, and real wages and productivity stagnated through 1980s–2000s, the top 10 percent ploughed their resources into various forms of rentier activities (from financial speculation to real estate flipping) while the bottom 50 percent started to rely far more on debt to "keep up with Joneses" and maintain what they perceived to be the appropriate middle-class lifestyle. As a result, today the bottom 50 percent of US households have debt-to-assets ratio of 75 percent plus (compared to 38 percent in 1950), while the top 10 percent are virtually debt free.

•   •   •

As discussed in my first book, there are a number of structural reasons as to why the productivity miracle of the 1950s–70s reversed in subsequent decades, such as the onset of new technologies and migration to services. The above-described financialization of the global economy and perverse incentives imposed by the neoliberal free-market philosophy played a critical role by diverting energy and capital into either less productive or even destructive activities. As Joseph Stiglitz, an American economist, highlighted, the rapid growth of finance industry (and financialization) against real economy created strong incentives for rent-seeking and value-capturing activities while neoliberal sidelining of the government (and its competitive and enforcement functions) has also created a fertile ground for consolidation of industries and competitors, further amplifying inequalities and retarding productivity.[15]

In the US, output per hour grew through the 1950s, 1960s, and even into the early 1970s at around 2.5 percent per annum. However, since then US labor productivity dropped toward 1.3–1.5 percent. In other economies, the downshift was even more pronounced. In Japan, for instance, it declined from 7 percent to less than 1 percent and in Italy from close to 6 percent in the golden decades to almost zero. If we examine Total Factor Productivity, or TFP (i.e., after excluding contribution of labor and capital), since the mid-1970s, average economy-wide productivity in the US has fallen to not much more than 0.2–0.3 percent, when compared to 1.3 percent pre-mid-1970s. In France, Germany, Italy, and Japan, TFP pace has eroded from around 3 percent to either zero or negative. In other words, in many economies, the contribution of labor and capital now exceeds the growth in GDP per capita.

An eroding productivity (labor and economy wise) inevitably led to much weaker real wage outcomes. In the US, the average real (1982–84 US$) wages are currently less than 10 percent higher than they were in the late 1970s, and real wage trends are even weaker in Britain. In line with both Marx's and Piketty's arguments, US labor productivity since 1979 has grown eight times faster than sluggish wages, eroding the share of Gross National Income (GNI) attributable to wages while increasing the share of profits significantly above Warren Buffet's traditional "red line" (6 or 7 percent of GNI). Despite the COVID-19 pandemic and some recent shifts toward wages, profit share has been consistently at or above 10–12 percent. At the same time, the share of GNI that is allocated to wages and salaries is now closer to 52–53 percent when compared to the high of 59–60 percent in the early 1970s. And it is not only the US phenomena, with labor share of national income also declining in Australia, France, Italy, Spain, and even in some less developed economies, such as China, Mexico, and Thailand.[16] Although there is a great deal of debate whether or not COVID-19 has fundamentally altered these dynamics of division of income, I do not believe that this will prove to be the case until much later, when far more profound waves of disruption would alter the underlying nature and functioning of our societies and economies.

Figure 17. Global Labor Productivity (%), 1951–2023

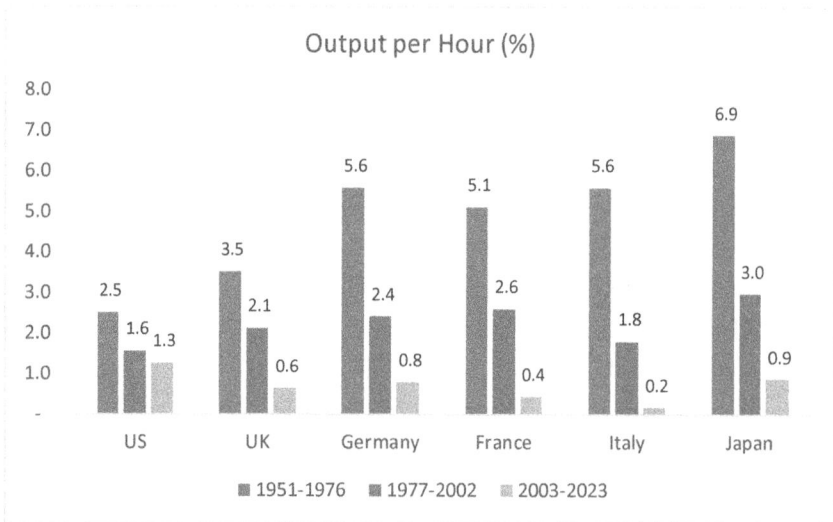

Source: TED, downloaded, December 2023

Figure 18. Global Total Factor Productivity (TFP) (%), 1951–2023

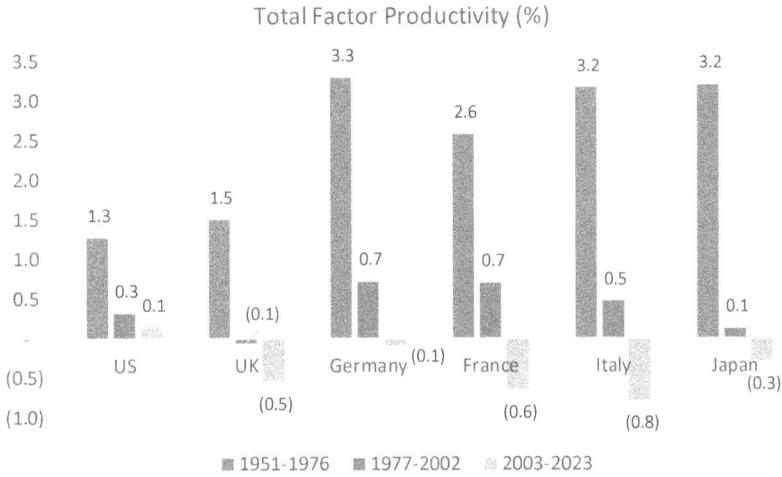

Total Factor Productivity (%)

1951-1976 1977-2002 2003-2023

Source: TED, downloaded, December 2023

Figure 19. US TFP (%), 1951–2023

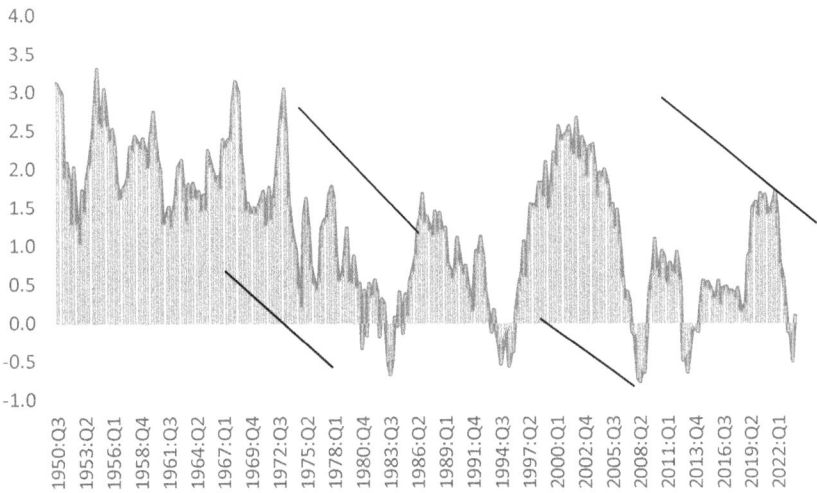

Source: San Francisco Federal Reserve, February 2024

117

Figure 20. US GNI, Wages vs. Profits (%), 1970-2023

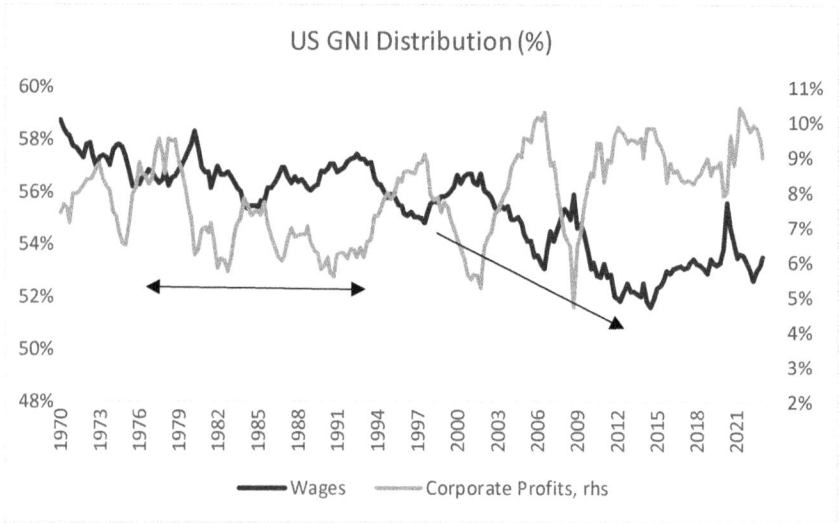

US GNI Distribution (%)

Wages ——— Corporate Profits, rhs

Source: Bureau of Economic Analysis, December 2023

•   •   •

An equally stunning reversal is evident when we examine changes in the approach to the role of the government and the private sector in the provision of healthcare. The American healthcare system is one place where the neoliberal ideas of the superiority of private sector solutions and the desire for a constrained ability of the state to curb private sector behavior are shown in their starkest relief. Over the last five decades, healthcare provision in the US has been effectively captured by various providers (from hospitals and pharmaceutical companies to private equity) with devastating results.

In the 1940s and 1950s, the US witnessed a dramatic fall in maternity and infant mortality, driven by better infrastructure, improvements in treatments, and various infant and maternity policies that were put in place by the government during these decades.[17] As a result, maternal deaths plummeted from 685 per 100,000 in 1930 to 37 in 1960, while infant mortality was down from 62 to 26 per 1,000. The fall was not just confined to white Americans, with non-white maternal deaths in that period also falling to below 100 and infant mortality to 40. In the 1960s and to some extent in the 1970s as well, the US was leading the world. However, subsequent decades were not kind to American infants or mothers.

Today, the US has one of the highest rates of infant and maternal deaths among developed nations. In 2020, maternal deaths in the US were above 20 per 100,000, representing no improvement when compared to the 1970s, while the average for key developed nations fell from 69 in 1960 to below 7, with a number of European countries at only 3–4. In other words, maternal death in the US is now perhaps 4–5 times higher than in many comparable nations. Even for non-Hispanic whites, maternal death is around 18–19. Although there is a debate regarding validity of cross-border comparisons and recent changes in the CDC's methodology, which could be inflating US death rates, even adjusting for these anomalies, the death rates in the US are still considerably higher than in most other mature economies, with an average closer to 10–15 per 100,000.[18] The same pattern of excess death applies to infants, with the US registering around 5–6 per 1,000 live births when compared to comparable nations which are closer to 3 per 1,000.

The deterioration of these health outcomes coincided with the neoliberal consensus from the early 1980s that public sector services are not just intrinsically inefficient but also constrain individual freedom of choice. This led to a considerable curtailment of the state's involvement and the political inability to agree on any meaningful healthcare policies, with freedom of choice becoming a political football in the tussle between "freedom and state dominance" against the backdrop of the institutional capture of the US healthcare sector. Three variables were largely responsible for higher maternity and infant death rates. First, there is a strong correlation of death rates with wealth and income inequalities, and as the US became significantly less equal, deaths followed. Second, the bulk of infant deaths occur sometime after birth, and the US is the only developed economy with neither compulsory nor free post-delivery care, nor does it have a guaranteed maternity or paternity leave. Third, the US now has one of the lowest densities of infant and maternity providers, at only 15 per 1,000 births, compared to 57 in Germany and 54 in Britain.

What are the economic consequences of allowing the private sector to capture this critical service, with limited state oversight? While it might sound harsh, the standard human life is actuarially worth around US$7 million. Thus, lowering infant mortality from 6 to 3 per 1,000, would be equivalent to an annual injection of approximately US$80 billion into the US economy, not to mention much better societal outcomes. While private initiative is crucial, only the state can provide requisite guardrails, especially in the critical areas like healthcare. Private sector cannot easily answer this question: What is the value of approximately 10,000 infants and several hundred women who perish in the US from excess death every year?

Figure 21. Global Maternal Death Rate (per 100,000 live births), 1930–2020

Maternal Death Rate	US	UK	Germany	France	Italy	Spain	Japan	Canada	Australia	Average
1930	695.0	472.4	N/A	N/A	N/A	N/A	260.0	N/A	529.6	489.3
1940	376.0	298.6	N/A	N/A	N/A	N/A	240.0	N/A	407.6	330.6
1950	83.0	91.4	183.7	N/A	N/A	N/A	176.0	N/A	109.1	128.6
1960	37.0	39.5	106.3	N/A	N/A	N/A	131.0	45.0	52.5	68.6
1970	21.5	18.0	51.8	28.2	54.5	33.1	52.0	20.0	25.6	33.9
1980	9.2	10.9	20.6	12.9	12.8	11.0	19.0	7.6	9.8	12.6
1990	8.2	7.6	9.1	10.4	8.6	5.5	7.0	2.5	6.1	7.2
2000	9.8	6.8	5.6	6.5	3.0	3.5	7.1	3.4	6.0	5.7
2010	15.0	5.0	5.2	10.2	2.9	4.1	4.6	6.4	4.3	6.4
2020	23.8	6.5	3.6	8.7	2.9	2.9	2.7	8.4	2.0	6.8

Source: World Bank, Our World in Data

Figure 22. Global Infant Death Rate (per 1,000 live births), 1930–2020

Infant Death Rate	US	UK	Germany	France	Italy	Spain	Japan	Canada	Australia	Average
1930	62.0	101.4	138.5	94.2	184.7	124.2	136.8	125.3	52.0	113.2
1940	47.0	75.8	89.3	74.2	149.3	120.6	107.0	86.1	39.0	87.6
1950	29.2	31.7	65.8	62.5	105.6	76.3	65.0	54.6	27.0	57.5
1960	26.0	22.9	23.4	23.6	44.1	51.0	30.4	27.8	20.3	29.9
1970	19.9	18.0	22.1	15.1	29.6	33.0	13.4	18.5	17.8	20.8
1980	12.6	12.1	12.6	10.1	14.2	12.4	7.4	9.7	10.8	11.3
1990	9.4	7.9	7.0	7.5	8.4	7.4	4.6	6.8	7.6	7.4
2000	7.1	5.6	4.4	4.1	4.7	4.4	3.3	5.3	5.1	4.9
2010	6.2	4.4	3.5	3.1	3.4	3.1	2.4	5.0	4.0	3.9
2020	5.4	3.6	3.1	3.4	2.5	2.7	1.8	4.4	3.1	3.3

Source: World Bank, Our World in Data

The same message comes across if we examine overall healthcare outcomes. Compared to other developed economies with strong public sector involvement across the spectrum of healthcare services, the US spends almost twice as much while yielding significantly inferior outcomes—life expectancy is shorter, prevalence of chronic disease higher, and even the average adult height is stunted.[19]

As can be seen below, over the last several decades, the American average lifespan has consistently lagged that of its peers. Today, an American lives roughly five years less than the average of the nine richest global economies and as many as seven years less than his or her Australian counterpart, despite the fact that the US spends almost 19 percent of GDP on healthcare compared to 9–10 percent in Australia and Italy, and 12 percent in France and Germany. The situation is even worse on the basis of "healthy life" (i.e., life span in a reasonable health), which is currently estimated in the US at 64–65 years, at least several years less than in most other jurisdictions. It is not surprising that healthcare has emerged as one of the largest and the most profitable industries in the US and one naturally with the strongest lobbying power in Congress, defending an unnecessarily complex but lucrative industry that delivers inferior societal outcomes.

Figure 23. Global Life Expectancy (years from birth), 1960–2021

	1960	1970	1980	1990	2000	2010	2021
Australia	70.8	71.0	74.3	77.0	79.2	81.7	83.3
Canada	71.1	72.7	75.1	77.4	79.2	81.3	82.6
Germany	69.1	70.4	72.8	75.1	77.9	80.0	80.9
Spain	69.1	72.0	75.3	76.8	79.0	81.6	83.2
France	69.9	71.7	74.1	76.6	79.1	81.7	82.3
UK	71.1	72.0	73.7	75.9	77.7	80.4	80.7
Italy	69.1	71.6	73.9	77.0	79.8	82.0	82.8
Japan	67.7	71.9	76.0	78.8	81.1	82.8	84.4
US	69.8	70.8	73.6	75.2	76.6	78.5	76.3

Source: World Bank

Figure 24. Global Life Expectancy vs. Health Care Spending, 2021

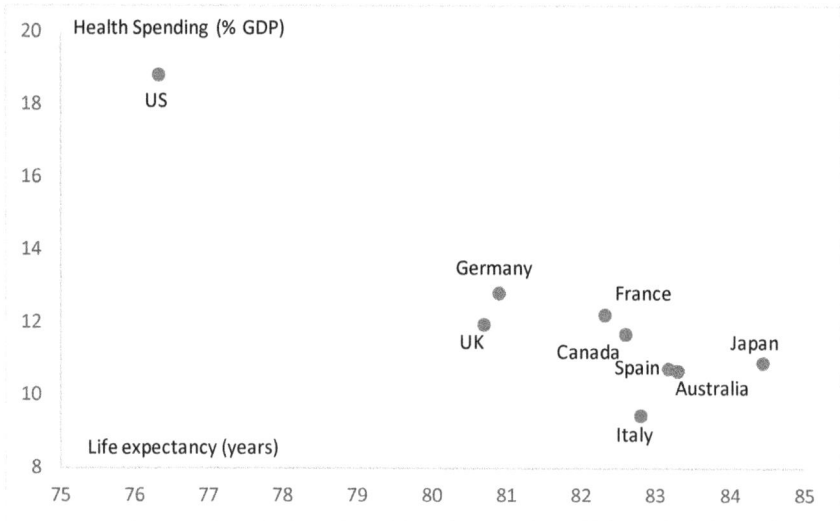

Source: World Bank

• • •

Finally, the neoliberal approach has significantly distorted public finances. There is an exceptionally vibrant field of research[20] that incessantly debates whether or not cutting taxes improves long-term growth rates, investment and innovation, and the extent to which subsequent inequalities and differences in compensation are addressed. However, from the early 1980s until the Global Financial Crisis, the idea of lower taxes had morphed into an exceptionally strong neoliberal political consensus, even though there was precious little proof of a relationship between lower taxes and growth, investment, and/or broadly defined prosperity.

As can be seen in figure 25, the degree of tax cuts implemented over these three decades has no precedent in modern history. In order to avoid the impact of World War II and subsequent reconstruction, the estimates below start in 1955 and end in 2020, with a dividing line between the two eras placed in 1985. While the first tax cuts were implemented in the early 1980s, most of the world joined in later that decade. In the case of the six key economies (US, UK, France, Italy, Sweden, and Japan), the average top income tax has dropped from around 75 percent between 1955 and 1985 to 48 percent for 1986–2020. At the same time, top estate tax rates were cut from around 60 percent (with some countries closer to 70–80 percent) to 37 percent. Also, corporate tax rates were cut from 45–50 percent in the 1980s toward an average that is closer to 25 percent, with effective tax rates even lower (e.g., US effective corporate tax rate is today below 15 percent when compared to the statutory rate of 21 percent).

This is the complete reversal of an earlier era that was characterized by high income, estate and corporate taxes that rose from almost nothing in the early 1900s to the highs in the 1950s–70s that were at almost extortionary levels (i.e., close to 100 percent). In the US throughout the 1950s and most of the 1960s, the top income tax bracket was above 90 percent, and the top estate tax bracket was 77 percent, while in the UK the top marginal tax rate through the 1950s–70s was above 90 percent (in some years as high as 98 percent), and the top estate tax rate was 80 percent through the 1950s-60s and into the early 1970s. It should be noted that the UK had no income tax until 1909 and the US until 1913, while estate taxes were minuscule in both countries. In France, the top income tax rate in the 1950s–70s averaged 60–65 percent, and it was closer to 75 percent in Japan.

Figure 25. Top Marginal Income and Estate Taxes (%)

	Top Marginal Income Tax Rate (%)			Top Marginal Estate Tax Rate (%)	
	Average (1950-1985)	Average (1986-2020)		Average (1950-1985)	Average (1986-2020)
US	76%	37%	US	74%	48%
UK	88%	43%	UK	78%	42%
France	63%	55%	France	21%	41%
Italy	76%	47%	Italy	41%	14%
Sweden	76%	58%	Sweden	63%	22%
Japan	71%	50%	Japan	73%	61%
Average	75%	48%	Average	58%	38%

Source: Piketty (2022)

The tax structure throughout the 1950s–70s was highly progressive, aimed at funding burgeoning state functions and expanding the role of the public sector while also deliberately aiming to reduce income and wealth inequalities. However, since 1980s taxation systems globally became far less progressive and sometimes regressive (especially after the proliferation of VAT taxes), and instead of funding the government, taxation systems have been increasingly designed to "starve the beast" in order to curtail government functions. Unfortunately for neoliberals, by the 1980s public functions had become so widespread and deeply imbedded into social and political fabric that even such firebrands as Ronald Reagan or Margaret Thatcher could do no more than slow down the pace of expansion while degrading public services, with any meaningful reversal no longer feasible. As a result, today, across most advanced economies (ruled by both right- and left-wing parties), government spending as a proportion of GDP is around 40–50 percent (with some closer to 60 percent). This compares to less than 10 percent prevailing prior to the Great War and no more than 15 percent in the lead-up to the Great Depression. Unlike the early 20th century when most state spending was on defense, law, and order, today the largest portion of the budget covers healthcare, education, pension, and social expenses. Again, it is worthwhile pausing for a moment to appreciate how neoliberal views on the undesirability of such spending have been consistently defeated at the ballot box. It is just another example of how unrealistic most neoliberal theories have proven to be in real life.

Although by the early 1970s state functions in most Western economies did expand beyond rational bounds, the subsequent curtailment of funding and a far more extreme hostility to the public sector against the backdrop of persistently high demand for public services led to a prolonged multi-decade period of fiscal deficits and, correspondingly, rapidly rising public debt. Outside of the wars (Napoleonic, the Great War, and World War II), today's public debt to GDP ratio is at the highest ever level, exceeding 100 percent for key nations, with some outliers like Japan at over 200 percent, compared to 50–60 percent in the late 1960s.

Figure 26. Government Spending (% GDP), 1880–2022

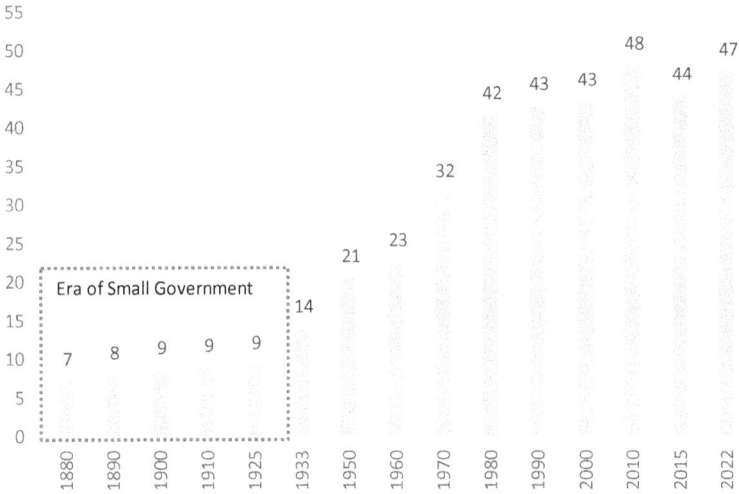

Source: Mauro et al (2013),[21] IMF, October 2023. Average of the US, UK, France, Germany, Italy, Japan, Canada, and Sweden

Figure 27. Composition of Government Spending (% GDP), 1880–2022

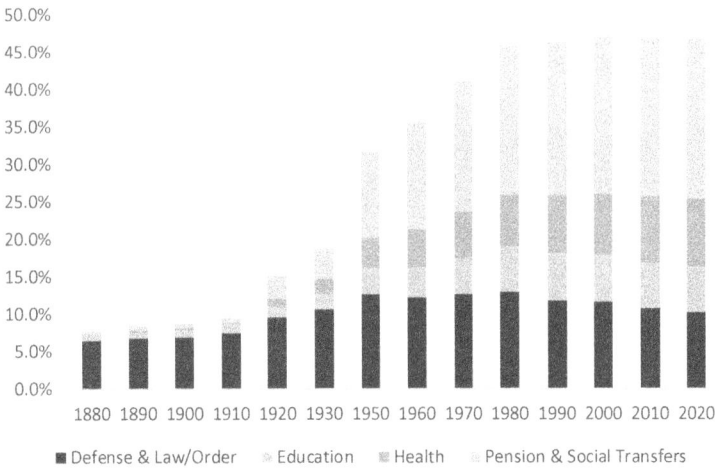

Source: Piketty (2022). Average of the UK, France, Sweden, and Germany

Figure 28. *Government Deficit (% GDP), 1960–2021*

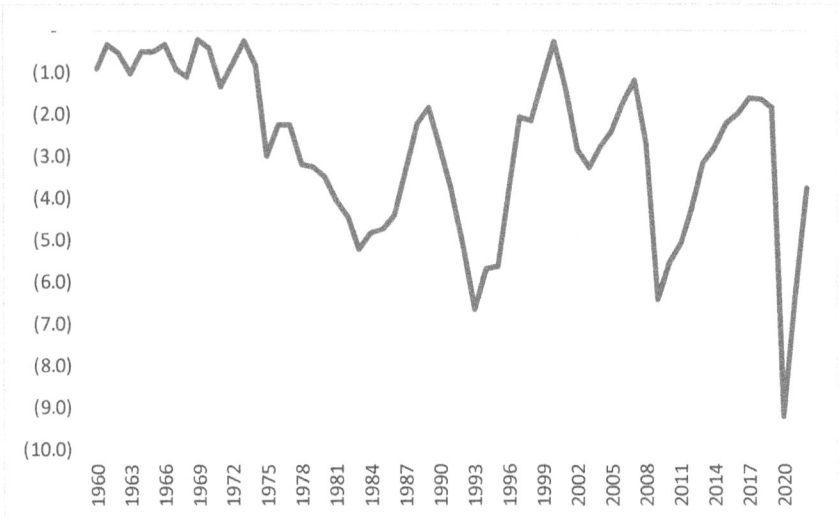

Source: Mauro (2013), IMF, October 2023. Average of the US, UK, France, Germany, Italy, Japan, Sweden, and Canada

Figure 29. *Government Debt (% GDP), 1870–2020*

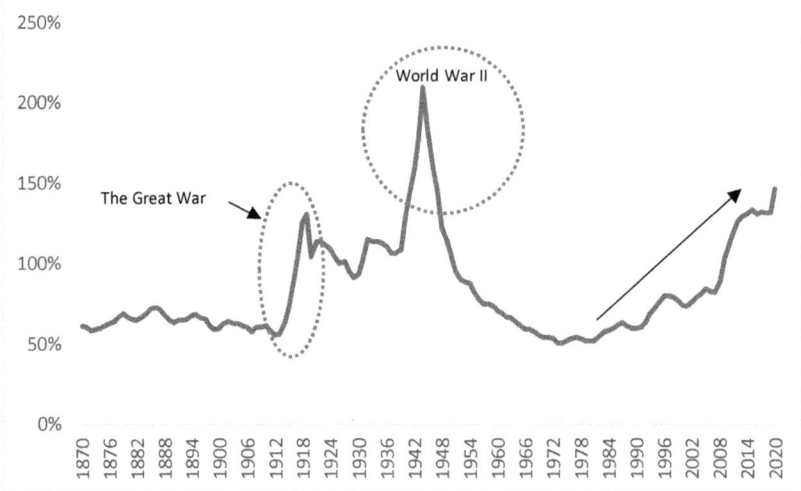

Source: Piketty (2022). Average of the US, UK, France, Germany, Italy, Japan, Sweden, and Canada

Whether or not cutting taxes actually leads to better outcomes remains the key ideological and policy battlefield. As highlighted above, there is a wealth of literature debating this issue. This is understandable, given that economies are highly complex, and taxation is only one piece of the puzzle, along with other factors like financialization, demographics, politics and technology playing a significant, if not larger, role. I have nothing to add to the intricacies of these arguments, other than to say that *prima facie*, it is hard to find much (if any) evidence that cutting taxes enhances either growth, productivity, or gross fixed capital formation, and it certainly amplifies inequalities. If one examines six key countries (figure 26: US, UK, France, Italy, Japan, and Sweden), GDP per capita growth rates of this cohort averaged around 3.5 percent per annum between 1955 and 1985 (when tax rates were high) and fell to below 1.5 percent between 1986 and 2022. While one could argue that the latter period included the Global Financial Crisis and COVID-19, the former encompassed more than a decade of stagflation through the 1970s. It seems like a fair match. A recent comprehensive study of tax cuts for those in the higher income brackets has similarly concluded that "tax cuts for the rich lead to higher income inequality in both the short and medium term. In contrast, such reforms do not have any significant effect on economic growth or unemployment."[22]

At the same time, as discussed above, there is no evidence that cutting taxes had improved productivity (on the contrary, it stagnated, at best). As far as gross fixed capital formation is concerned, the US private non-residential sector is today investing around 13–14 percent of GDP, the same as it did in the 1970s. A more recent indication of this lack of tax-driven investment stimuli can be found in the Trump administration's corporate tax cuts of 2018 that did not prompt any meaningful rise in investment, though they did boost dividends and share buybacks. Finally, there is no question that the era of the 1940s–70s was the single most productive period for inventiveness (funded and sponsored by governments), with most of today's products (i.e., innovation) derived from discoveries that were made in those golden decades. As I discussed in my first book, the global store of intellectual capital has been depleted over the last three decades, with applied research and innovation taking precedence over fundamental research and inventiveness, with the neoliberal philosophy leading to a considerable drop in state funding for research.[23]

• • •

The abandoning of the Bretton Woods system of fixed exchange rates that were tied to the USD and gold (1971–73), deregulation of the financial system through the 1980s and 1990s, a massive lowering of trade barriers, the withdrawal of state services and investment, tax cuts, and the liberalization of immigration flows have created a much freer and entrepreneurial, but far less fair and equal, world.[24] It led to unprecedented financialization and economic fragilities, destruction of communities, a significant rise in wealth and income inequalities, deterioration of public finances, and lower productivity. In some cases, it also resulted in decidedly inferior educational and healthcare outcomes.

In the midst of the Global Financial Crisis, Alan Greenspan, former Federal Reserve Chairman and arguably the highest profile neoliberal, confessed in his Congressional testimony, that the crisis exposed a mistake in the free-market ideology that guided his 18-year stewardship of US monetary policy. In his words: "I have found a flaw…I don't know how significant or permanent it is. But I have been very distressed by that fact…I made a mistake in presuming that the self-interests of organizations…were such that they were best capable of protecting their shareholders and their equity in the firms…I discovered a flaw in the model that I perceived is the critical functioning structure that defines how the world works." When asked by the committee chairman if he found that his ideology was not working, Greenspan answered, "That's precisely the reason I am shocked."[25]

As I will discuss in the next chapter, these negative economic outcomes also inevitably had a significant ripple effect through the society—further aggravating social fractures, with the deepest polarization since at least the late 1960s, and arguably, since the 1930s.

Chapter 6

Insecurity and Polarization

"Economic and physical insecurity are conducive to xenophobia, strong in-group solidarity, authoritarian politics and rigid adherence to their group's traditional cultural norms—and conversely secure conditions lead to greater tolerance of out-groups, openness to new ideas and more egalitarian social norms."
Ronald Inglehart[1]

Ronald Inglehart, late sociologist from the University of Michigan, made a number of contributions in the field of comparative politics. The best known are arguably his theories regarding how *generational replacement* causes intergenerational value changes. The quote above conceptualizes what he described as the *Evolutionary Modernization Theory*. Despite a complex title, it explains a simple concept: At times of crises and rising physical and economic uncertainty, humans fall back on millions of years of evolution and "circle the wagons," becoming less tolerant of strangers, more xenophobic, and intolerant of deviations from the strict interpretations of values of *their* group. As Kevin Drum, an American journalist, put it in one of his blogs: "Humans are just over-clocked primates. We have developed a thin layer of cognition that allows us to gossip more effectively and solve differential equations on request, but that thin layer lives on top of millions of years of primate evolution, and we are still bound by it. In particular, we are territorial, patriarchal, hierarchical, addicted to dominance displays and tribal."[2]

Correspondingly, times of greater *insecurity* tend to presage periods of more extreme partisanship, conflicts, restrictions on immigration, closures of borders, social violence, intolerance of unfamiliar ideas, and increased self-reliance. These periods also trigger what Inglehart described as the *authoritarian reflex*—people reaching out to demagogues and "strong leaders" in a desperate search for solutions to their mounting problems. Unfortunately, instead of building resilience and addressing root causes of discontent, most of these leaders end up creating more chaos and fragility. This is due in part to the psychological and emotional profile of many such "strong leaders." One of the more fascinating stories from Stalin's early years in power was when one of the world's most renown neurologists, Mikhail Bekhterev, was tasked with the responsibility of examining comrade Joseph Stalin. The year was 1927, when Stalin had not yet become *Vozhd* (Father of the Nation) and *Veliky Stalin* (Great Stalin), and hence, he agreed to the examination. Bekhterev's diagnosis was that Stalin suffered from extreme paranoia. The following day, the good doctor suddenly died and was immediately buried without autopsy, and his books were removed from Soviet libraries. In 1943, OSS (the predecessor of the CIA) commissioned a psychological profile of Adolf Hitler. The report diagnosed him as a paranoid neurotic narcissist and predicted that he would end his life in flames or suicide. Over subsequent decades the CIA created profiles of most authoritarian figures (from Mussolini and Mao to Saddam) that had a broadly similar narrative: a difficult and sometimes abusive childhood (for example, Stalin's father died in a bar brawl, and Saddam was an unwanted child), resulting in low self-esteem that later developed into narcissism (i.e., exaggerated sense of one's own importance and preoccupation with one's achievements, including a strong belief that they are the only ones who can fix things and save their country), paranoia, vindictiveness (i.e., lashing out at anyone who disagrees with them, and employing name calling), craving popular adulation, other psychological anomalies (e.g., "Stockholm syndrome"), and lack of empathy.[3] These individuals also tend to be micromanagers who do not easily delegate. They do not allow alternative power sources to flourish, and hence, they never have successors, and are surrounded mostly by yes-men and a small cohort of trusted advisors.

Many modern authoritarian leaders and budding dictators clearly exhibit the same qualities. While promising to strengthen nations, they, in the final analysis, weaken them. They also tend to inflame geopolitics while aggravating domestic social tensions. Although some of their economic policies are rational, ultimately, this is often offset by a greater volatility arising from their style of decision-making and lack of impartial expert advice. These leaders are also terribly preoccupied with their place in history, and, therefore, in order to leave a mark, they tend to accelerate and deepen conflicts and promote what ultimately prove to be highly undesirable and destructive structural changes.[4] Finally, given psychological profiles, their departures from power frequently signal an extended period of chaos until a new social and political consensus emerges.

The pace and the intensity of such disruptions and the emergence of authoritarian leaders tend to be especially extreme at times of major technological and financial upheavals (such as industrial and information revolutions, and financial and economic crises). Whether or not one agrees with Neil Howe's generational analysis and his specific subdivision of cycles into four distinct groupings (with the Fourth Turning Point representing upheaval and revolution),[5] there is sufficient evidence (Chapter Five) to support the idea that Baby Boomers' neoliberal legacy has been so deeply disruptive that it most likely qualifies as the entry point to a much more constrained, xenophobic, and violent period, calling for a greater demand for authoritarian leaders than in the recent past. I also agree with Howe, that we have passed this dividing line (US and globally) sometime in the aftermath of the Global Financial Crisis in 2008–10.

Conversely, of course, periods of rising economic and physical *security* tend to have the opposite effect of making societies more tolerant and open to new ideas and social and moral norms. These periods also tend to be times of proliferation of trade and freer circulation of capital and labor. Xenophobia and social conflicts become less pronounced, and democracies generally thrive while budding authoritarian leaders are far less popular. Generally, during such times there is a strong societal consensus as to what is important and how economies, politics, and societies should function.

• • •

In order to numerically support his theories, Inglehart launched the World Values Survey (WVS), which developed a consistent methodology for sampling views across a range of economies, both developed and emerging. Due to their complexity and scale, surveys are conducted in waves, with the latest covering a period between 2017 and 2022. While there are millions of data points spread throughout hundreds of questions, several are particularly poignant.

First, in line with other surveys (such as the Polity Project and the V-Dem Institute), WVS shows that over the last decade, democracies have been retreating everywhere.

According to the 2023 V-Dem report, the global democratic wave of the 1980s–90s has been completely reversed over the last decade, with the number of people living in autocracies (elected or closed) rising from 48 percent in 2009 to 72 percent in 2022. On the latest assessment, there are just barely more than thirty countries that still qualify as democracies, while the number of democratizing countries dropped to only fourteen when compared to seventy-two in 2011. Indeed, various forms of electoral autocracies emerged as the preferred governing system, with ruling elites gradually emptying institutions of state and removing as many checks and balances as possible (e.g., Turkey, Hungary, Poland, Mexico, India). Instead of seizing power by force, as happened in the 1950s–70s and which today would run the risk of considerable domestic and international opprobrium and potential sanctions, today's autocracies have come to recognize that a "salami tactic" of incrementally stripping institutions of their power while corrupting and manipulating them from the inside is a far better way of attaining and, more importantly, retaining power with minimum of negative repercussions.[6] At the current juncture, V-Dem identifies only a handful of advanced fully-fledged democracies, mostly in Scandinavia, Benelux, Australia, Canada, and New Zealand.

Figure 30. Democracies vs. Autocracies (% of global population)

	1972	2009	2012	2019	2022
Autocracies	64%	48%	46%	54%	72%
-Closed Autocracies	52%	22%	24%	25%	28%
-Electoral Autocracies	12%	26%	22%	29%	44%
Democracies	36%	52%	54%	46%	28%
-Electoral Democracies	19%	35%	38%	32%	15%
-Liberal Democracies	17%	17%	16%	14%	13%

Source: V-Dem, 2023

The latest WVS surveys paint a similar picture, with a rising number of responders agreeing with the statement that "democracy is a bad or fairly bad form of government." In the US, 15 percent agree, whereas two decades ago only 10 percent had this view. In Korea, approximately 30 percent of responders agree, double the level in the 1990s. Similarly, around a quarter of responders in countries like Colombia, Mexico, and the Philippines concur. At the same time, what is perceived as democracy is changing to be closer to what V-Dem describes as "electoral autocracies." The number of Americans who agree that it is a good idea to have a "strongman who ignores elections and parliaments" increased to almost 40 percent when compared to 25 percent in the late 1990s. In a country like Mexico, concurrence exceeds 70 percent (compared to 45 percent in the late 1990s), and in Turkey it is closer to 60 percent. Even in Germany, Britain, and France, around a quarter of responders agree. Another variation on the autocratic theme relates to the question of whether it is better to have governments run by experts rather than politicians. More than half of the US and French responders agree (versus around one-third in the 1990s) and almost two-thirds of those in Britain concur, and the affirmative answer exceeds 80 percent in Brazil. The atrophy of democracy has progressed so deeply that even an army-run government seems to be preferred by a large (and growing) section of the population. Over 20 percent of the US responders agree, and almost half in places like Malaysia, Mexico, and Brazil, and closer to two-thirds in Indonesia agree.

Surprisingly, this even applies to nations that have, in recent memory, suffered from brutal and destructive military dictatorships. There is even a tilt toward government structures that are guided by religious laws, with around 20 percent of Americans concurring.

Second, the above-outlined shifts in public views are underpinned by a loss of confidence in key pillars of functioning democratic societies.

Confidence in parliamentary institutions has eroded across most jurisdictions. In the US, a positive confidence score has dropped to only 15 percent, compared to 40 percent in the late 1990s, while in Spain it is down to around 33 percent, compared to over 50 percent in the late 1990s, and in Mexico, in the same time frame, it dropped to 15 percent from 43 percent. In Malaysia, the drop was truly unprecedented, declining from 70 percent to 43 percent in a space of just a single decade. In Colombia, confidence in parliament is down to only 5 percent, while in Britain and Australia it is languishing at 25–30 percent. This naturally translates into low confidence in political parties (down to 11–12 percent in the US from 25 percent in the 1990s, and only 15 percent in Britain), with an exceptionally high level of cynicism and skepticism across almost every country, even in Scandinavia.

Third, below the surface, there are even more worrying trends of either societies perceiving elections to be unfair or believing that their votes are somehow not counted or rigged. Only 39 percent of Americans currently believe that elections are fair and up to a quarter believe that votes are not counted fairly.

There is a similar decline in trust in everything from technology firms to judiciary. According to the WVS, around 40 percent of Americans do not trust the judiciary, with some of the more recent surveys indicating that in the wake of the Dobbs vs. Jackson abortion ruling and other recent conservative decisions, the level of distrust in the judiciary could be as high as 60–70 percent. In that survey, only 10 percent of democrats and, even more remarkably, only 53 percent of republicans approve of the highly conservative US Supreme Court.[7] According to a Gallup poll, in 2022 only 25 percent of Americans trusted the US Supreme Court, which is a far cry from levels that were closer to 50–60 percent in the 1980s–90s. In the same poll, democrats, republicans, and independents alike overwhelmingly agree that the US democracy is in crisis, and the US, as a country, is also in crisis.

Figure 31. US in Trouble: Country, Economy, and Democracy

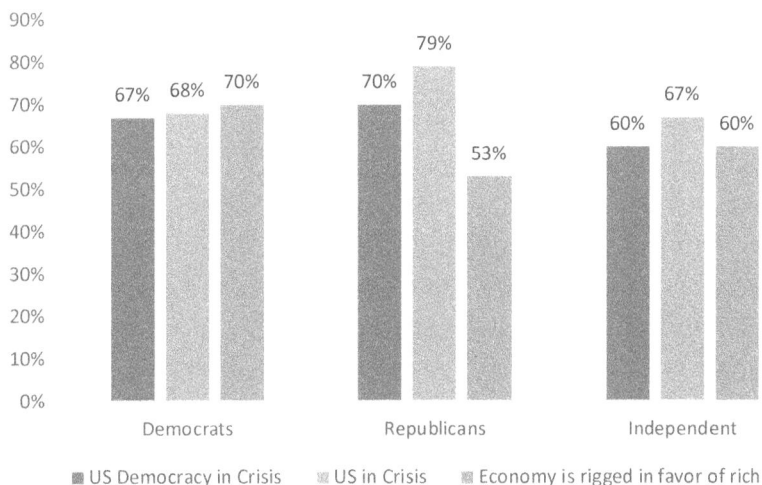

Source: Gallup, 2023

Fourth, over the last decade, there have been growing signs of conventional political partisanship degenerating into a highly toxic polarization. As described by Lilliana Mason, in the US context, "The competition is no longer between only democrats and republicans. A single vote can now indicate a person's partisan preference as well as his or her religion, ethnicity, neighborhood, and favorite grocery store. This is no longer a single social identity. Partisanship can now be thought of as a mega-identity, with all the psychological and behavioral magnifications that applies."[8] As defined by Jennifer McCoy and Murat Somer[9] in their groundbreaking study, the "pernicious polarization" is evidenced by the division of the electorate into two hostile groups where multiple cleavages collapse into one dominant boundary, and the political identity of the two camps becomes a social identity in which members feel that they belong to a "team" and show a strong loyalty to it. These identities are viewed as mutually exclusive, negating any possibility of discussion or debate, and as a result, the middle ground disappears.

It is hardly surprising that the topic of how healthy partisanship transforms into toxic polarization—presenting serious dangers to democracies, liberal order, and even national and state coherence—has become a hotly debated issue amongst political scientists.[10] Since the Global Financial Crisis, evidence has been accumulating that strong centrifugal gravitational forces are destroying the moderate political middle while strengthening the extremes. Whether one looks at Poland, Hungary, Turkey, Israel, Mexico, and Brazil or more advanced democracies, such as the US, France, the Netherlands, Italy, the UK, and Austria, the last fifteen years was a period in which populists demagogues, and "strong leaders" have become increasingly common, and, at the same time, a number of conventional middle-of-the-road political parties had to either adapt to the extremes and become virtually unrecognizable (such as AKP in Turkey, Fidesz in Hungary, PIS in Poland, BJP in India, and the Republican Party in the US) or run the risk of disappearing from the map.

While some polarization and partisanship are not inherently negative and often indicate a broadening of social and community debate, there are times when polarization becomes truly toxic and disruptive, creating virtually unmovable blocks that no longer have any meaningful incentive for discussion, exchange of views, or compromise. These blocks resemble fans of opposite football teams rather than political parties and are dominated by us versus them arguments, which eliminate any viable middle ground while massively narrowing room for a compromise. As Mason highlighted, it is not that countries or people do not have partisan identities (human societies always do that), but rather what we are witnessing is a creation of "mega-identities," which go way beyond political or policy disagreements and cover a huge array of traits, from race and religion to where one lives or shops and whether or not one is willing to have a member of an alternative party joining one's family or accepting them as friends.

Members of these tight groups do not necessarily want to make rational decisions but rather are driven by a desire to win against another group, even if both end up worse off. This explains why during times of stress, some poorer and more deprived sections of the population often vote for extreme right rather than left, even though financially and economically, the left-leaning parties usually have policies that are more aligned with their needs. This is because culturally and emotionally these individuals' identities (or what people perceive themselves to be) are more in tune with one block or another, irrespective of rational policy assessments, and the extreme right is frequently good at finding simple and easy-to-understand answers to people's problems (e.g., "blame the immigrants, foreigners, elites, godless governments," "we need a return to traditional values") when compared to the far more complex agenda of the left.

Indeed, some recent studies have illustrated that it is not ignorance that drives people to suboptimum outcomes. Even if explained what optimum outcomes are, the gravitational intragroup pull is so strong that any new evidence is used by the participants to buttress arguments as to why their team is better, is more honorable, and deserves to win, even if everyone loses and irrespective of the overwhelming evidence to the contrary. One recent experiment exposed republicans (who often get most of their news from Fox News or alt-right media outlets and social media feeds) to more mainstream news sources (such as CNN or BBC) to see whether polarization is caused by lack of correct information. No such luck. An exposure to more mainstream sources strengthened, not weakened, their conservatism and hostility to liberal ideas. The same happened to democrats and liberals who were for one month exposed to conservative media feeds—their liberal views and dislike of conservative ideas were further strengthened.[11]

This conclusion would not have surprised Henri Tejfel,[12] who in one of the early papers on group psychology described an experiment in which a group of school kids was divided into two competing teams, and even though they were close friends, this division created two opposite sides with members of each team willing to accept an obvious lie, as long as the rest of the team did the same. They were prepared to make everyone worse off as long as their team won. Since then, there have been dozens of similar experiments[13] conducted all around the world confirming that a group identity takes hold quickly and becomes the dominant trait.

However, this does not answer the following question: While some polarization and partisanship are healthy and inevitable, what are the conditions under which they turn highly toxic?

There is no shortage of culprits. Greedy elites, generational change, technological upheavals like the Industrial Revolution and the Information Age, out-of-control central banks and finance to environment. As discussed in Chapter Seven, the most obvious source for growing polarization is the interaction between technology and finance, a process magnified by other factors such as generational change and climate. What I describe as the Fujiwara effect (or the merger of the disruptive Information Age and deep Financialization hurricanes), fundamentally alters the functioning and relevance of both capital and labor, causing considerable disruption across all layers of society. As Inglehart highlighted, at times of stress people circle the wagons, becoming far less tolerant of strangers, more xenophobic, and intolerant to deviations from the strict interpretations of values of *their* group. This makes them susceptible to what sociologists describe as "polarization entrepreneurs" who in turn further amplify and fan these deeply held grievances, and benefit from them—financially and politically.

It is a self-reinforcing loop that is hard to break, with resets usually coming in the form of violence—riots, civil disobedience, revolutions, and wars (both external and civil). Indeed, dark clouds are gathering. As can be glimpsed from recent surveys, polarization is getting deeper and far more toxic. In the US, according to Pew in 2022, approximately 62 percent of republicans had a very unfavorable view of democrats. This is up from 43 percent in 2012 and 21 percent in 1994. In the opposite direction it is almost as bad with 54 percent of democrats having a very unfavorable view of republicans, up from 46 percent in 2012 and only 17 percent in

1994. The situation is even worse if we examine views of the independents who lean toward either democrats or republicans. In 2022, 47 percent of "republican leaners" had a highly unfavorable view of democrats when compared to only 10 percent in 1994, while 45 percent of "democratic leaners" intensely disliked republicans when compared to 11 percent in 1994. At the same time, according to a recent CNN poll (August 2023), up to 69 percent of republicans believe that Biden's administration is illegitimate, and that 2020 election was stolen, and up to 20 percent of Americans support the QAnon extreme conspiracy grouping.

Not only is there clearly strong dislike, but it has also increasingly gone beyond policy disagreements, and has become highly charged and very personal. In a recent survey 72 percent of republicans believe that democrats are both dishonest and immoral, up from 45–50 percent in 2016, with democrats reciprocating, 63–64 percent also viewing republicans as dishonest and immoral. In both cases, more than 50 percent of democrats and republicans regard each other as unintelligent, up from 30 percent as recently as 2016. Over 80 percent of democrats think that republicans are closed-minded and around 70 percent of republicans think the same about democrats while 62 percent of republicans think democrats are lazy. Similarly, in a recent Yahoo-YouGov survey (July 2023), both camps violently disagreed as to whether the problem of racism exists in the US and which group constitutes its primary victim. Almost 80 percent of democrats believe that Blacks are the main victims, and less than 20 percent believe that whites are victims of racism. For republicans, answers were almost diametrically opposite, with 71 percent believing that whites are discriminated against.

As with people under stress circling the wagons, both democrats and republicans are falling deeper in love with their own group. In recent surveys, around 52 percent of republicans said that other republicans are open-minded (up from 32 percent in 2016), while 74 percent of democrats think other democrats are open-minded. Similarly, 63 percent of republicans believe that other republicans are moral (up from 51% in 2016), while 51 percent of democrats think other democrats are moral (up from 38 percent in 2016). The number of republicans who think other republicans are honest is now 55 percent, compared to 39 percent in 2016, while for democrats the ingroup score is close to 50 percent.

Figure 32. US Parties, Highly Unfavorable View (%)

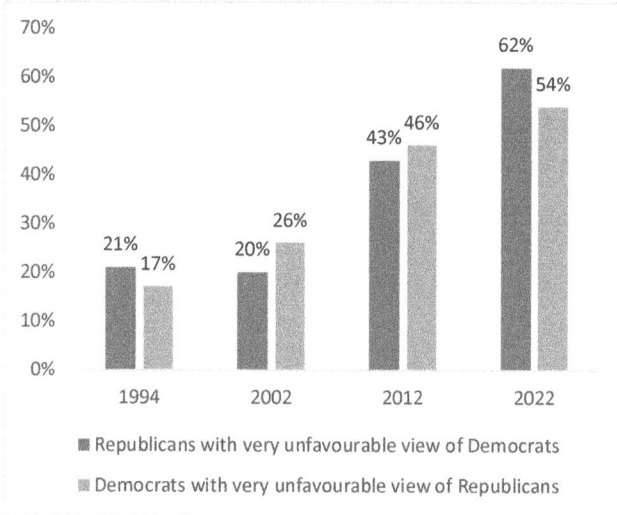

Source: Pew, 2022

Figure 33. US Parties, Personal Traits and Characteristics (%)

	2016	2022		2016	2022
Closed-Minded			Open-Minded		
-Democrats on Republicans	70%	83%	-Democrats on Democrats	67%	74%
-Republicans on Democrats	52%	69%	-Republicans on Republicans	32%	52%
Dishonest			Honest		
-Democrats on Republicans	42%	64%	-Democrats on Democrats	37%	49%
-Republicans on Democrats	45%	72%	-Republicans on Republicans	39%	55%
Immoral			Moral		
-Democrats on Republicans	35%	63%	-Democrats on Democrats	38%	51%
-Republicans on Democrats	47%	72%	-Republicans on Republicans	51%	63%
Unintelligent			Intelligent		
-Democrats on Republicans	33%	52%	-Democrats on Democrats	43%	47%
-Republicans on Democrats	32%	51%	-Republicans on Republicans	40%	49%
Lazy			Hardworking		
-Democrats on Republicans	18%	26%	-Democrats on Democrats	37%	34%
-Republicans on Democrats	46%	62%	-Republicans on Republicans	59%	67%

Source: Pew, 2022

Historically, this desire for in-group solidarity and corresponding hatred of outgroups is not unusual and spikes at regular intervals, and there has never been a shortage of people willing to fan and aggravate these divisions to solidify control over *their herd*. As far back as 1895, Gustave Le Bon argued that a gifted orator is able to create a powerful "crowd psychology," whereby individuals subsume themselves in something they consider bigger and more important than themselves, and thus they lose their ability for critical thought and engage in behavior that they otherwise would consider abhorrent. Populists exploit these rising insecurities and carnage by offering solutions wrapped in "abusive forms of violent affirmations, exaggerations, resorting to repetitions and never attempting to prove anything by reasoning."[14] In modern times, one of the first republicans to practice such art was Newt Gingrich who in the early 1990s counselled his colleagues to use such divisive practices. He recommended that when addressing opponents to use words like, "betray, bizarre, bosses, bureaucracy, cheats, pathetic, liberal lies, corrupt, sick, and welfare," and while when commenting on one's own side, he recommended using words like "common sense, courage, dream, duty, crusade, freedom, and liberty."[15] Facts were largely irrelevant, and these different monickers could be just as easily attached to one side as the other on exactly the same set of facts. There are times when people do not want facts but rather seek out an affirmation of their deeply held beliefs. The Boomers' globalization when combined with deep financialization and highly disruptive technological changes that have been progressing at a breakneck speed over the last several decades (refer to Chapter Seven), left many people unmoored from their traditional settings by shattering communities and questioning deeply held traditional values. Viktor Orbán of Hungary encapsulated well this feeling when he recently said that the liberal elites ignore the core values of "nationalism, tradition, and religion."

The polarization is now reaching a stage where two sides no longer even encounter each other as they used to, as neighbors, family, or friends.

According to recent surveys, republicans and those leaning toward them overwhelmingly (65 percent plus) prefer to live in large houses at some distance from each other and from shops and amenities, while most democrats prefer smaller homes within walking distance to schools, shops, restaurants, and other amenities. Similarly, there is nothing more personal that marrying into another family, and there is now ample evidence that whereas in the 1960s and 1970s, political affiliation played almost no part in the selection of marriage partners, today around 40 percent of democrats and republicans would be at least somewhat upset at the prospect of inter-party marriage. In 1960, only around 5 percent would have regarded such a marriage as either very or somewhat discomforting, and in 2008, that number stood at around 25 percent. The same message coincidentally comes from the UK surveys that show that at least 25–35 percent of Labor or Conservative Party supporters would unwelcome such marriages. Surveys also highlight that even having friends from the opposite party is becoming problematic. This separation is now personal, emotional, economic, and geographic.

Figure 34. US Parties, Neighbors and Marriage (%)

	Republican	Democrat
Larger houses, further apart, schools & stores miles away	65%	35%
Smaller houses, closer together, walkable to schools & stores	30%	61%
Upset or somewhat upset at the cross-party marriage, 1960	5%	4%
Upset or somewhat upset at the cross-party marriage, 2008	27%	20%
Upset or somewhat upset at the cross-party marriage, 2019	39%	38%
Friends from own Party		
-A Lot	57%	67%
-Some	21%	18%
Friends from other Party		
-A Lot	14%	9%
-Some	25%	22%

Source: Pew; Gallup

In 2022 for the first time ever, more than half of democrats self-identified themselves as liberals. This is a big deal for a country which continues to lean to the right, with conservatives outnumbering liberals by 10 percent. Whereas in 1994 around 24 percent of democrats were liberal, this rose to 54 percent in 2022. At the same time, the conservative wing collapsed from 25 percent to a mere 10 percent. By definition, a moderate middle was squeezed from a dominant 50 percent during Bill Clinton's presidency to 36 percent by 2022. The opposite occurred in the Republican Party, with the conservative wing strengthening from 58 percent in 1994 to 72 percent in 2022, while the liberal wing has all but disappeared (less than 5 percent), and the middle was squeezed, representing less than 25 percent of the party. This leaves almost no room for discussion or compromise, with the Republican Party in particular becoming an exceptionally "narrow church," demographically, economically, and ideologically.

This is reflected in the electoral and GDP map. In the 2020 presidential election, republicans captured 83 percent of electoral districts, but they were responsible for less than 29 percent of the US GDP and housed less than 40 percent of the US population. This is totally unlike Gore versus Bush in 2000, when republicans had just under 50 percent of the votes, but their winning districts accounted for 46 percent of GDP and 53 percent of the national population. Today, republicans are mostly confined to rural and poorer districts as well as noncollege educated white segments, while democrats dominate higher income and better educated coastal regions. Although inhuman and politically suicidal, Hillary Clinton's description of people from these republican-dominated areas as "deplorables" reflects this divide between the nostalgic past (that no longer exists and is unlikely to ever come back) and the future of the country.

Figure 35. US Self Identification, Liberal, Moderate, and Conservative

	Democrats		Republicans		Independents	
	1994	2022	1994	2022	1994	2022
Liberal	25%	54%	8%	5%	18%	21%
Moderate	50%	36%	34%	23%	51%	49%
Conservative	25%	10%	58%	72%	31%	30%

Source: Gallup, 2023

Figure 36. US, 2000–2020 Election Map

	Counties won	Population (m)	Votes (m)	% GDP
2000				
Gore	659	133	51.0	54
Bush	2,397	149	50.5	46
2016				
Clinton	472	177	65.9	64
Trump	2,584	146	62.9	36
2020				
Biden	520	198	81.3	71
Trump	2,546	130	74.2	29

Source: Brookings

Five, these fundamental differences translate into equally widespread cleavages in the assessment of appropriate economic and social policies. In a recent Pew survey (2022–23), there are wide differences in topics that animate each part of the electorate. For republicans, key preoccupations are crime, immigration, borders, religion, and traditions, while democrats are far more driven by issues like climate change, gender and race discrimination, economic fairness, cost of living, education, and healthcare.

Correspondingly, there are meaningful differences in how the two sides evaluate key institutional pillars. When asked whether they assess the role of colleges or public schools to be, on balance, positive, more than 72 percent of democrats agreed while republicans gave a positive rating of only around 35 percent. On the opposite side, when asked whether churches and religious organizations play a positive role, 68 percent of republicans agreed, while for democrats, the positive response was much lower at 41 percent. Not surprisingly, in response to a question about whether trade unions have a positive impact, almost 75 percent of democrats agree, but less than 40 percent of republicans concur. Democrats also are far more supportive of technology and technology companies, while republicans are more suspicious. The same applies to the perception of the role of the state, with democrats leaning more aggressively in the direction of a greater state involvement as the guardrail against perceived chaos and as the curb on capitalism, while the opposite is true of republicans.

However, there are also some commonalities. As democrats shifted to the left and republicans to the right, there are several overlapping areas where extremes converge, explaining why in the past, communists and fascists frequently found common ground. Both distrust and want to curb excessive corporate power. They are also suspicious of banks and financial institutions as well as large corporations. Both dislike billionaires and are in love with small businesses. There is also a strong support from democrats and republicans alike for the military as the only nationally unifying institution (positive score exceeds 80 percent).

Finally, it is important to highlight that differences between extremes might be less than they appear. The US remains a broadly conservative or a right-leaning nation. What many in the US decry as a radical left in most other developed economies would be classified as center or center-left, and what Americans regard as moderate would be closer to center-right or right, while conservatives would be more appropriately classified as extreme right. In other words, there is limited support in the US for truly left-wing policies. Ideas of freedom and self-reliance have such a strong societal resonance that they unrelentingly pull the US center of gravity toward conservative middle. Nevertheless, as surveys unequivocally show, the fusion of the Information Age and Financialization, fueled by neoliberal policies of the last three decades, has created the most extreme societal polarization since the late 1960s–early 1970s, and most likely since the 1930s.

• • •

While the underlying drivers are somewhat different, in Europe, the progression is not dissimilar to the radicalization of democrats and republicans. The highly heterogeneous set of right-wing parties in Western Europe initially held diverse positions on economic and social issues. However, over the last decade, similarly to republicans, most right-wing parties (such as PVV in the Netherlands, Brothers of Italy, National Rally in France, or AfD in Germany) became economic moderates (i.e., extreme economic policy prescriptions of heavy taxes on financial institutions or exit from Euro were jettisoned) and social conservatives (even converging with the neofascist extremes on immigration and racial purity issues).

A recent study[16] (utilizing Comparative Electorate Systems' database) attempted to estimate an average of in-party evaluation versus evaluation of people outside the party. As discussed above, in the US, there has been a growing gap between how democrats view other democrats versus republicans and how republicans reciprocate. This study showed a similar disparity in Europe. In ten countries of Northwestern Europe, the in-party rating (on a scale of one to ten) was as high as eight but evaluation outside of the party was less than four. The nine countries of Central and Eastern Europe exhibited an even greater polarization, with in-party evaluation of more than eight while out-of-party views were barely above three. Given significant post Global Financial Crisis disruption that occurred in Spain, Portugal and Greece, the polarization in Southern Europe is greater, with out-of-party scores down to only 2.7 when compared to 7.9 for in-party views. In many ways, European polarization might be more extreme when compared to the US, as there is a far greater proliferation of extreme parties, both left and right. In some European countries, polarization is clearly even deeper. Supporters of the two largest parties in Greece (left-leaning Syriza and right-wing ND) only assign a positive evaluation score to each other of 1.3 and 1.6, respectively. Not even extreme republican conservatives assign such a low score to the most liberal democrats. In Bulgaria, the situation is worse, with the dominant right-wing party (GERB) assigning values close to zero to the next two largest parties. Similarly low scores are evident in countries like Poland and Czechia.

Another study,[17] using a similar methodology, extended this analysis while expanding it over a larger number of countries and across time. They designed what is known as an *Affective Polarization Index,* a handy one-stop shop for observing the pace and the depth of polarization. In figure 38 below, Time One is an earlier survey (2005–2010) while Time Two represents follow-up observations (2015–2020).

Figure 37. European Political Polarization, 2010–2015

	In-Party Evaluation	Out-party Evaluation	Gap
North Western Europe	8.00	3.98	4.02
Central Eastern Europe	8.21	3.13	5.08
Southern Europe	7.89	2.74	5.15
US	7.72	3.33	4.39

Source: Andrea Reiljan (2020)

Figure 38. US and European Affective Polarization Index Over Time

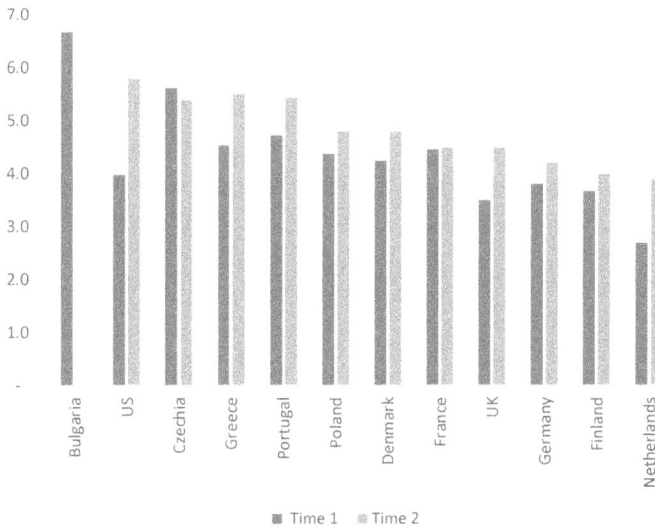

Source: da Silva et al (2022)

Finally, a recent OECD[18] study has confirmed that the degree of trust in governments across most European countries is now one of the lowest on record, with only around 34 percent in Poland, 35 percent in Italy, 39 percent in Britain, and barely 40 percent in France. While one can debate individual numbers and estimates, there appears no doubt that most European states are exhibiting a high, and generally rising, level of polarization and partisanship.

•   •   •

It would be hard, and maybe impossible, to come back from such deep divisions, distrust, and even hatred. However, there are some glimmers of hope. US independents have remained broadly moderate and there is evidence of less intense polarization amongst younger cohorts in both parties. The same message comes from other countries, with Millennials and Generation Z having radically different views when compared to the free-wheeling Boomers. As I discuss in Chapter Eleven, it is these differences that will determine the shape of a new societal consensus that is likely to emerge over the next decade or two.

The next section is dedicated to key underlying causes for such polarization or what I describe as the Fujiwara effect—the merger of two powerful hurricanes of deep Financialization and the Information Revolution, magnified by externalities, like demographics and climate—that is disrupting our economies, societies, and politics. I also intend to find historical parallels to our current predicament and project into the future. What will the future bring?

STARING INTO THE ABYSS

"When you stare into the abyss, the abyss stares back at you."

—Friedrich Nietzsche

Chapter 7

THE FUJIWARA EFFECT

"The Digital Revolution is going to be the biggest geopolitical revolution in human history…the industrial revolution changed the world, and all it did was to replace human muscle."

Kevin Drum[1]

While the Fujiwara effect is rare and usually requires two weather systems to be in relatively close proximity (less than 1,000 miles apart), it could spawn a much larger and more violent typhoon, or it might just feed on itself and divert the original path of either or both. Today's world is eerily reminiscent of the Fujiwara effect, with two to three large typhoons or hurricanes interacting and reinforcing each other, creating a potentially much more powerful force.

In my first book (*The Great Rupture*), which was published in 2020, I dedicated considerable space to discussing how the fusion of deep Financialization and the highly disruptive Information Age is reshaping our economies, societies, politics, and even interpersonal relations. In an economic jargon, there are considerable changes afoot in the role and functioning of both capital and labor while in political, social, and historical contexts, there are profound changes in every aspect of our societies—from the role of democratic politics to the relationship between the state and the individual, the structure of family units and what makes us happy, and even the essence of what it means to be human.

Apart from my book, there are many excellent academic and popular works that have over the years explored numerous aspects of these complex changes.[2] The question that readers of my book regularly ask is if there is such an abundance of material published on these subjects, why add to the pile? Or to put it another way, what did my book add to the debate? My consistent answer was that I could not find a single book that traverses the entire field. There are excellent works on futurology and technology (such as those by Martin Ford, Erik Brynjolfsson and Andrew McAfee, Mustafa Suleyman, Kai-Fu Lee, Ray Kurzweil, and many others). However, these books do not address, or at best do so only tangentially, the impact on societies, politics, or finance. Then there are many books that examine the impact on societies and politics (such as Yuval Harari's trilogy), but they do not discuss the role of financialization and debt. Books by Mervyn King and Adair Turner discuss debt and monetary economy, but they have little to say about the changing technological backdrop or the overall societal impact. Similarly, there is a range of excellent books that examine the historical evolution of technology and economies (such as those by Bradford DeLong and Joel Mokyr), but they do not link past to the future, and neither do they focus on either policy prescriptions or how to manage the "cloud of finance." There is a range of books that examine why certain countries, regions, or civilizations succeeded while others failed (such as those by Daron Acemoglu, David Landes, Jared Diamond, Douglass North, and others) but they do not discuss how the success formulae might change in the new digital age. There are also numerous books debating changes in the nature of capitalism and offering various policy prescriptions (such as those by Paul Mason and Mariana Mazzucato), but there is little discussion in these books of the role played by technology or how to manage "cloud of finance."

My book was a humble attempt to connect the past with the future, technology with finance, finance with markets, and then technology, finance, and markets with public policy prescriptions and to ask whether the recipe for absolute and/or relative success is changing under the pressure of the Fujiwara effect. Hence, the subtitle of the book "Do we need to free to be innovative, prosperous, or even happy?" Summarized below are the key takeaways of issues and topics, but for readers who wish to examine each argument in detail, I recommend referring to my first book.

• • •

We are currently at the precipice of the most profound disruption, or as I put it, "the world today is on the cusp of the fourth major turning point that in a matter of decades will reshape every human society as profoundly as anything that's happened since at least the fifteenth century."[3]

The last two decades witnessed an explosion of interest in the topic of what that future might look like and the implications for every facet of our existence: what we do and its value; how we are informed, entertained, and educated; and the nature of political and economic systems. Today's changes are not only faster, but they are also much deeper and broader. According to a study by McKinsey, the transformation driven by the Information Age is 300 times the scale and depth of industrial revolutions and is progressing 10 times faster, implying roughly 3,000 times the impact of the previous revolutions.[4]

Ray Omara, a late professor from Stanford University, once postulated that we tend to overstate the impact of new technology in the short run but understate its impact over the longer term. While the first decade or two after discoveries are usually full of unjustified fear, the third and the fourth decades are characterized by a relative complacency, followed by realization that the initial fears were justified after all. Whether we look at AI or robotics, there was a period of acute nervousness through the 1960s–80s (inevitably exemplified by Hollywood in numerous science-fiction movies). This was followed by decades of complacency or what were perceived to be "winters" of relatively slow progress. However, the pace of change started to meaningfully accelerate over the last decade or so, and the next decade or two is likely to be a period of rapid transition from complacency to extreme fear, with the 2020s–30s being the key time when the broadly defined AI, cloud computing, improving energy consumption, automation, 3D printing, and blockchain technologies revolutionize every aspect of our lives— social and political interactions, geopolitics, employment and economic policies, construction, logistics, manufacturing, property rights, the very nature of money itself. Nothing is safe from these radical changes.

• • •

Since the 1980s, scientists, historians, politicians, and even tech CEOs have been sounding the alarm that as societies we are nowhere near as prepared as we should be for what is coming down the pike. Even such positive and constructive technology advocates as Erik Brynolfsson and Andrew MacAfee are becoming increasingly concerned about the inevitable "timing gaps and dislocations"[5] while Joel Mokyr concedes that "the path of transition to this economy may be disruptively painful… we believe that there is a distinct possibility that wages…may need to be supplemented through some form of income redistribution…in addition, it may be necessary to expand the set of publicly provided goods."[6] At the same time, Laura Tyson and Michael Spence ask what will happen to a system based on the key premise that most people gain their income by selling their labor, when "labor of a large share of working-age population, regardless of their education, is rendered technologically redundant or no longer commands an income adequate to provide minimally decent or socially acceptable standard of living."[7] Arguably, the most frightening prediction came from Israeli historian Yuval Harari when, in his latest installment on the future of human race, he argued, "The merger of info-tech and biotech might soon push billions of humans out of the job market and undermine both liberty and equality. Big data algorithms might create digital dictatorships in which all power is concentrated in the hands of a tiny elite while most people suffer not from exploitation but from something far worse, irrelevance."[8] Following the launch of ChatGPT, Harari warned, "We have summoned alien intelligence. We don't know much about it, except it is extremely powerful and offers us bedazzling gifts but could also hack the foundations of our civilization. The first step is to buy time to upgrade our 19th century institutions for an AI world and to learn to master AI before it masters us."[9] Daron Acemoglu, an MIT economist, is warning, "If AI continue to be developed along its current trajectory and remains unregulated, it may produce various social, economic, and political harms."[10] In 2022, when 738 top academics and researchers were asked in a survey about the future risk of AI, almost half stated that there was at least a 10 percent chance of human extinction or a permanent and severe disempowerment from the future AI systems, and 69 percent of responders believe that societies should prioritize regulation and safety far more than it currently does.[11]

While most of these concerns and associated opportunities were known for a long time, the recent announcements of significant breakthroughs in language-based AI models (LLM) allowed these to burst from sci-fi and polemics into a much broader public universe. Following an avalanche of papers that prodded and tested the latest versions of ChatGPT on a diverse set of topics—from passing bar exams and completing tax returns to softer issues such as falling in love and marriage, from writing poetry to explaining complex mathematical models and assisting in computer coding—it has become clear that with each new iteration, outcomes are massively improved. The new models have also already progressed beyond words into images (e.g., OpenAI's other recent release of DALL-E 3) and sounds. The same is true of OpenAI rivals such as *Claude* from Anthropic and *Gemini* from Google, and new products from Baidu (*Ernie*) in China. One can confidently state that by the time this book is published, there will be many more products in the pipeline. There is a genuine arms race, with everyone from Meta and Google to Adobe and Microsoft, from Salesforce to BABA and Baidu experimenting with and developing AI tools and applications.

As these models are trained on ever more data, the number of parameters (or variables in the model that can be changed) is rising.[12] As OpenAI progressed from ChatGPT 1 to 4, the multiplier impact was at least 10x to 100x for each evolutionary stage. Although 1,000 billion or even 100,000 billion parameters are nowhere near the power of human brain (which has 100,000 parameters per neuron, and there are more than 100 billion neurons, implying 10 quadrillion plus parameters), the improvements could over the next five or six years get these models to be at least 200–300 times more complex than today's most powerful versions, further reducing the gap between human and nonhuman intelligence. Having said that, it will also require further breakthroughs, a significant reduction in energy consumption,[13] and more likely proliferation of quantum computing to get anywhere close to the flexibility and the power of the human brain. Ray Kurzweil is probably right in saying that it will take at least until 2029 to satisfy the Turing test and full integration with human brain is unlikely until sometime in the 2040s.

However, debates about the shortcomings of recent language-based AI models miss the point—the essence of AI is not to be better than human brain but rather to focus AI on a select number of tasks to perfect its performance in niches rather than across a wide terrain. There is already ample evidence that when the latest models were focused and intensively trained on more complex sciences (e.g., chemistry), they could easily beat the best students. As for much simpler tasks (such as accumulating and interpreting information, writing essays, assisting in construction of Excel spreadsheets and PowerPoint presentations, advising on transactions, etc.), current models are already nearly perfect, with gradually declining incidences of so-called hallucinations (i.e., when AI simply makes things up). One would imagine that as new variants are rolled out, imperfections would become even less pronounced, and reliability would improve.

This is the reason some have compared the burst of language-based AI models to the launch of Netscape in late 1994, which heralded the beginning of the Internet Age. While far from perfect, Netscape provided the first glimpse of the type of web browsing that new technology could deliver to one's fingertips. A decade of improvement followed, leading to the first primitive AI in the early 2000s which powers today's social media.[14] Recent language AI models represent the next step in that evolution, and even though it will take time, it is unlikely that techno skeptics will be proven right (e.g., In December 2000, *Daily Mail* in Britain famously ran the headline "Internet may be just a passing fad as millions give up on it"[15]). Not only are today's models offering an improved ability to accumulate data and information, but they are also acquiring the ability to act as de facto advisors, interpreting results and suggesting courses of action and outcomes. There are even glimpses of their latent ability to help advance science, inventiveness, and medicine.

One of the first business applications that has already come to the market is Microsoft's Copilot, which integrates ChatGPT into Outlook, Word, Excel, and PowerPoint. As it improves and others create similar business tools, it will largely dispense with many tasks performed today by more junior analysts and consultants (preparing presentations, summarizing talking points and calls, preparing descriptive notes, etc.). The next system updates will likely make it even less probable that investment banks or management consultants will be employing an equivalent number of graduates and/or junior professionals as before. Whereas in the past an investment bank might have recruited one hundred graduates to ultimately end up with twenty, it will now only need to recruit fifty to end up with ten, and later twenty to end up with just two. What about questioning and analyzing investment opportunities? One experienced banker or an analyst with the help of ChatGPT-like tools and Copilot could conduct interviews, assess data, and decide on the course of action. The same process of attrition of functionality has already been occurring in the legal profession, from paralegals and more junior associates to clerks,[16] while technological evolution has already been shrinking the pool of human financial traders. What about marketing consultants or product developers? As in the case of analysts, traders, or junior portfolio managers, one senior marketing executive or product development specialist with the support of AI (as his/her personal advisor) might be more than sufficient. What about scriptwriters? Well, there are already examples of AI-generated podcasts and some scripts. There is no doubt that more powerful AI will further accelerate these trends, and in as little as five or six years from now, white collar specializations and professions may undergo something similar to the deindustrialization that factory workers in Michigan, Ohio, Manchester, or Melbourne experienced in the 1980s–90s.

This, of course, is not the end of the story but just the beginning. The best way to look at AI is as a highly disruptive and invasive general-purpose technology (GPT) that impacts and shapes many other technologies (from robotics and automation to biotech), and as such, it is almost impossible to stop. Diffusion and sharp declines in marginal costs are bound to drive wider adoption. While not a straight-line process, history teaches us that once there is a breakthrough, there is virtually no way of stopping the wave, with many technology scholars describing the current environment as a "supercluster of innovation," with each new wave intersecting, buttressing, and boosting other innovations, not dissimilar to the impact of steam or electricity during industrial revolutions.[17]

The rapid progression of AI, combined with an equally robust development of sensors, cloud computing, and 3D printing is already starting to upend numerous industries, from manufacturing to logistics. This will, once more, refocus the spotlight on blue collar jobs, and while progression there will be slower than in the digital realm (more likely on a ten-to-fifteen year time scale), the pace is accelerating.

As described by Gill Platt from the Toyota Research Institute, we are now facing an environment comparable to the Cambrian explosion that occurred 500 million years ago and led to every single form of life on earth. In his words, "Today, technological developments on several fronts are fomenting a similar explosion in diversifications and applicability of robotics. Many of the base hardware technologies on which robots depend—particularly computing, data storage, and communications—have been improving at exponential rates."[18] The combination of cloud computing, deep machine learning, automation, and 3D printing are gradually redesigning how the world manufactures, trades, and distributes products as well as the role that robots play in both manufacturing and service sectors. As the consumer digital revolution over the last two decades altered music, entertainment, information gathering, and financial services, the next ten to fifteen years will witness a massive change in how we build houses (there are already technologies that can print houses at a fraction of the cost and in as little as 24 hours) as well as manufacture and distribute products as diverse as air conditioners with no moving parts to cars, turbo engines and furniture. As AI and robotics proliferate across agriculture, the nature and functionality of rural work and industries will also undergo a profound change, and as automation spreads through services, it will also determine who or what will greet us when we arrive at hotels or perform our open-heart surgery and look after us as we age.

According to the IFR (International Federation of Robotics), the number of industrial robots has already reached almost 4.5 million in 2023, up from barely 1 million in 2008, with annual additions now running at a clip of more than 500,000. It is expected that the stock of functioning industrial robots will exceed 6 million by 2026. In countries like Korea, industrial robot penetration exceeds 1,000 per 10,000 manufacturing jobs, with Japan and

Germany closing in on 400, and China passing 300, while the global average is reaching 150 when compared to less than 100 only five years ago.[19] And it is no longer just the automotive industry (an early adopter) that is driving this progression. The increasing dexterity and sophistication of sensors is allowing robots to penetrate a much wider range of industries, including electrical and electronics (26 percent share), metals and machinery (11 percent share), food industry and even such complex and human skill-driven industries as textiles and clothing. At the same time, more than 15 percent of robots are now coming from a far more sophisticated collaborative category (i.e., robots that work together and learn from each other). Invariably, deployment of robots results in lower marginal costs when compared to more labor-intensive factories. As always, the progression of new technologies accelerates at times of dislocation, and the COVID-19 pandemic in 2020–22 was not an exception. It further narrowed the cost and strategic advantages of employing human labor, driven by the declining cost and rising flexibility of automation relative to labor. Plus, of course, robots don't get sick, and they do not strike.

Figure 39. World's Industrial Robots ('000), 2011–2026

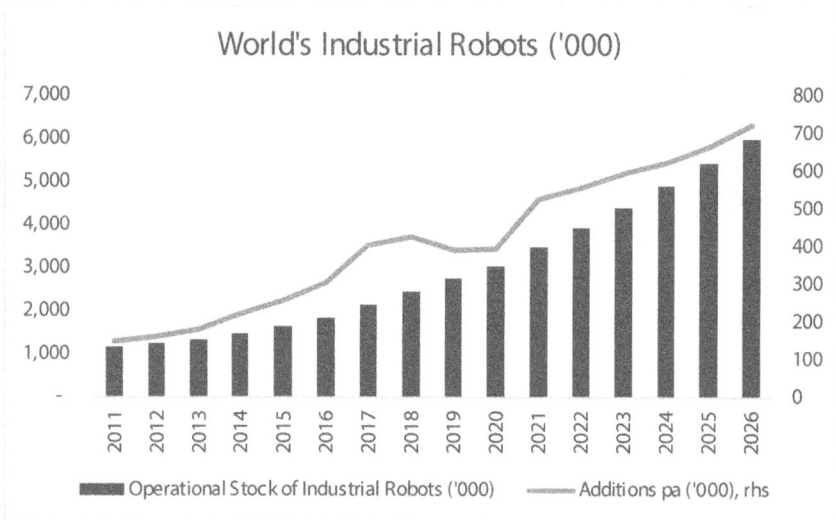

Source: IFR, 2023

The next area of robotics and automation coming into view is service (rather than industrial) robots. Between 2018 and 2022, the number of new service robot shipments averaged around 200,000 per annum, compared to almost none a decade ago. Most consultants expect growth rates to average at least 20 percent annually over the next decade. Service robotics covers a huge terrain, from logistics, agriculture, defense, medical, cleaning, public relations, and exoskeletons to construction. These are our future nurses, surgeons, cleaners, farmhands, logistics, and warriors.

We can already track this evolution through the proliferation of robots, the gradual elimination of moving parts in every product that we manufacture and distribute, and an increasing atrophy of intricate supply chains. Arguably, the scope of labor replacement and the significant decrease in marginal costs is even greater in manufacturing and logistics than in services. Tentative clues are evident when we examine the US manufacturing industry, which has been undergoing a significant renaissance. Over the last decade, the US share of the global manufacturing output stopped declining (stabilizing at around 15–16 percent or just over half of China's levels), with the pace of output growing by 3 percent per annum when compared to less than 1 percent in the previous two decades. Yet despite such vibrancy, manufacturing employment dropped from around 10 percent to just over 8 percent of the labor force. At the same time, although US nonfinancial corporations are investing the same 13.5 percent of GDP (as they did in the 1970s), the nature of investment is drastically different, with more than 50 percent directed to robotics, automation, IT, software, and intangibles, rather than traditional fixed assets (such as machinery, buildings, etc.). In other words, the US, having deindustrialized through the 1980s–90s, is now reindustrializing, but in a different fashion: almost no labor and less conventional fixed asset investment.

Over the next decade or two, the future will be one of "dark factories" (i.e., no need for light, as there will be few, if any, humans) and the elimination of bulky sites, replaced by much smaller and far more flexible automated producers with limited employment and fixed assets, located in close proximity to ultimate customers. This will essentially replace one global factory (like China) with a multitude of smaller sites at a much more flexible and lower cost structure. The future will feature products with almost no moving parts or break points, self-healing pipes, printed houses and cars, air-conditioning and refrigeration units without need for cooling or requirement for maintenance, autonomous driving cars, etc.[20] By the time robotics and automation replace blue collar as well as repairs, logistics, and transportation tasks, it is doubtful that there will be much else left for humans to do. This is completely unlike the Industrial revolutions when a peasant became a factory worker, or a buggy driver turned into a truck driver, and when machines needed humans to be their brains. By the end of the Information Age, there will not be many niches left unoccupied and available for human participation, including many higher value-added and cognitive tasks. The point is that robots do not need to be better than us—good enough will be sufficient, especially given robots' low operating costs and their exceptionally high flexibility and task leveraging.

This does not mean that new ways of spending time and getting rewards and social recognition would not emerge. Rather, these new sources of satisfaction might not be related to anything that we today recognize as jobs, professions, or career paths. As Andre Gorz highlighted in his 1999 classic, "We must dare to prepare ourselves for the Exodus from 'work-based society;' it no longer exists and will not return…work must lose its centrality in the minds, thoughts, and imaginations of every-one."[21] Or as one of the recent books on disruption put it, "Industrial revolutions pale in comparison to today's convulsions."[22] Andrew Keen argued, "Much of what we took for granted about industrial civilization— the nature of work, our individual rights, the legitimacy of our elites, even what it means to be human is being questioned."[23] Unlike previous waves that were supplementing human muscle power and eliminating the most routine of occupations, this revolution is aiming at replacing cognitive and higher value-added roles. Its objective is nothing less than turning humans into "freedom- and idleness-loving horses," just as automobiles and tractors eliminated working horses in the 1920s–30s.[24]

Whether one looks at an all-encompassing AI or a broader evolution of the Information Age, the key is whether or not technology will mostly replace or augment human labor?

I remain a firm believer that unlike the industrial revolutions, the Information Age is mostly focused on replacement not augmentation. It is about improving efficiency, reducing costs, and eliminating labor through various forms of automation rather than striving for complementarity. This outcome is especially likely if the evolution of technology continues along its current trajectory, dominated by large private sector groups, with limited, if any, oversight or regulatory constraints. This is what concerns Erik Brynjolfsson, who emphasized, "As machines become better substitutes for human labor, workers lose economic and political power and become increasingly dependent on those who control technology."[25] Similarly, Daron Acemoglu argues, "Even before AI there was too much investment in cutting labor costs and wages…AI, as a broad technological platform could have in principle rectified this, for example, by promoting the creation of new labor-intensive tasks or by providing tools for workers to have greater initiative. This does not seem to have taken place…many current uses of AI involve automation of work or the deployment of AI in order to improve monitoring and keep wages low."[26] In other words, as people lose a growing number of tasks to AI and automation, marginal utility (or the satisfaction that people feel) and marginal returns (or compensation) gradually decline. It is also possible that as the range of tasks shrinks, human ability to make decisions would also atrophy.

Instead of blindly believing that new jobs and occupations would somehow be miraculously created, societies need to proactively contemplate how these unstoppable, disruptive, and profound changes in the role of human capital can be mitigated to lower social and political pressures. There is a wider discussion of policy options later in this book.

How much of global employment and compensation will be impacted? While estimates vary, most assume a meaningful and, more importantly, a *growing* impact over time. A recent assessment of ChatGPT is that approximately 80 percent of the US workforce could have at least

10 percent of their work tasks affected, while close to 20 percent may see at least a 50 percent impact.[27] The UK Department for Education has similarly estimated that more than one-third of jobs might be impacted, with the highest degree of vulnerability in several higher value-added service-oriented sectors, such as management consultants, public relations specialists, credit controllers, university lecturers, accountants, psychologists, lawyers, and economists.[28] The International Monetary Fund (IMF) recently released its study of AI, which argued that in developed countries up to 60 percent of jobs are exposed, especially in the higher income brackets, with waves of AI-driven products further aggravating inequalities.[29] All of these assessments were made based on existing technologies, assuming no improvements, and were largely confined to services.

On a broader canvas, in 2017, the McKinsey Global Institute argued that "on a global basis...the adoption of currently demonstrated automation technologies could affect 50 percent of the world's 1.2 billion employees and US\$14.6 trillion in wages."[30] The study optimistically concluded that while few jobs are likely to disappear completely, at least 60 percent of global employees might have 30 percent or more of their functions automated. This was based on technology as it existed more than five years ago. A more recent McKinsey study increased their estimates of long-term economic benefit of AI (i.e., mid-to late 2040s) to as high as US\$11.0 to US\$17.7 trillion (up 15 percent on their estimates in 2017), but authors of the study were forced to admit that this would be only possible under *ideal conditions* of societies finding an equilibrium, or in their words, "Workers will need support in learning new skills and some will change occupations."[31] As Acemoglu and Restrepo illustrated, a job or a profession does not need to disappear completely to lower wages and erode marginal and average utility; a functional atrophy is sufficient.[32] An even earlier study by Carl Frey and Michael Osborne indicated that around 47 percent of US jobs are under threat of either extinction or a significant reduction in functionality, including 100 percent of telemarketers, 95 percent of accountants, 90 percent of technical writers, and almost half of economists and pilots, as well as a large swath of journalists, lawyers, consultants, and investment advisors.[33]

The disintegration of conventional labor markets is now proceeding at an accelerated pace, with an increasing number of people residing in what British economist Guy Standing described as a "precariat" state, stewing in a toxic mix of the four As: anxiety, anomie, alienation and anger.[34] On current estimates as much as one-third of the US labor force is already engaged (fully or partially) in various forms of alternative or "gig" employment (although "side hustles"—trying to earn or supplement income—would be a more appropriate description of these gig functions rather than a conventional classification as a profession or a formal employment).[35] In other developed economies, ratios vary from as little as 10–15 percent to as high as 30 percent. This "precariat" state is a perfect recipe for social polarization.

Erik Brynjolfsson recently argued that the next decade will witness, "Massive disruptions. Companies are going to be born and destroyed, as will occupations. Depending on how we use technology, we can use it in a way that is more likely to create shared prosperity, or more concentration of power."[36] When and how technological evolution will reconcile itself with existing political, social, and economic norms is open to debate, and that's why Brynjolfsson, a consistent cheerleader of technological evolution, suggested that the coming decade could be either the best or the worst in history. I am in the worst camp, as it is hard to see how we move from technology replacing labor to one that augments today's labor force. At the same time, arguing that we need to think hard how to structure regulatory and ownership structure of technology platforms will inevitably bump against today's oligarchic structures.

Having said that, over the much longer term (say 2040s), one can be more positive. It is likely that over time societies will adjust to the new technological backdrop, and although labor would not function the same way as it does today and the idea of a "work culture" will likely strike most people as something terrible that belonged to the world of their ancestors (equivalent to the way we think of slavery or feudalism), there will be new ways to utilize human talents, outside of the conventional work-based environment. A number of occupations will still prosper—mostly those emphasizing our humanity and high-touch services—entertainment of any kind, sports, coaching, the beginning of life (e.g., midwife), the end of life (e.g., priest), reassurance, support, and psychological advice (e.g., social workers, nuns, psychiatrists), making a case in front of a human jury, and executives who can motive and integrate people with technology.[37] It is also conceivable that Elon Musk's idea that ultimately the dilemma will be resolved by us ceasing to be human and becoming some form of sci-fi cyborgs might come to pass.[38] However, it is more likely that most people will embrace knowledge, leisure, friendships, religion, sports, or a multitude of other pursuits that under the new system will be separated from jobs and wealth. When we finally stop "hoarding labor" in what David Graeber, a late anthropologist from LSE, described as "bullshit jobs,"[39] productivity growth might mushroom to 5 percent or more, compared to today's levels which are closer to 1 percent, stabilizing societies and defanging the extremes.

Unfortunately, this does not describe the next decade. Between today's capitalism and work-oriented environment and the high-productivity future will be an awkward and hard to navigate twilight, torn by violence and heartaches, with raging debates on policy prescriptions for dealing with such fundamental changes. Instead of progression toward a utopia, it is more likely that the next decade will feature a further and deeper disintegration of conventional jobs and professions, and although not many jobs will disappear completely, the marginal utility and returns on labor will keep falling. Eventually, technology will progress to a point where most of the degraded labor can be replaced entirely. In the meantime, productivity will likely remain at the bottom of the U curve (i.e., stagnating), with technology not yet having progressed far enough to replace labor but far enough to reduce its usefulness and marginal returns.

There is also an important question of self-esteem and the psychological impact of these deep structural changes. As Eric Posner of the University of Chicago has recently asked, "How will people respond, psychologically and politically, to the realization that they can no longer contribute to society by engaging in paid work? People who derive self-esteem from their jobs do so in part because they believe that society values their work. Once it becomes clear that their work can be done better and more cheaply by a machine, they will no longer be able to maintain the illusion that their work matters."[40] As multiple studies have already found, life without work is a torture, as much psychological as it is financial.[41] These are radically different conclusions to conventional economics which views work as essentially a bad thing, with people needing to be induced to engage in work by offsetting cost of time and energy deployed against compensation (or wages). One way or another, it is clear that the diminishing utility of labor will likely lead to potentially devastating social and political consequences.

Many readers might stop here and argue that over the last three COVID-19 years, most economies have suffered from a shortage of labor, which seems incongruous with the above prediction of degrading labor inputs.[42] The key is to avoid confusing transitory changes with permanent ones. Technology is a permanent force that will strengthen overtime, while the COVID-19 pandemic has caused only a temporary dislocation of demand and supply curves for goods, services, and labor which, ironically, is likely to further turbocharge robotics and automation, fueling replacement not augmentation of humans.

•   •   •

The evolution of digital currencies, and especially the forthcoming introduction of Central Bank Digital Coins (CBDC), promises to also reshape banking and capital markets radically (Chapters Ten and Twelve). Unlike the conventional Industrial Age monetary system, where commercial banks were multiplying credit and transmitting the monetary impulse, the digital world will most likely dispense with commercial banks, as deposit-taking institutions, multipliers of credit, and assessors of risk. The same fate will most likely befall credit card companies. Central Banks, which are after all banks, would be able to issue digital currencies and directly stimulate or restrain credit demand while

doing a better job of controlling corruption and more rationally linking fiscal and monetary policies, especially following what I believe to
be the inevitable onset of the Universal Basic Income guarantee (UBI)
(Chapter Ten). What we perceive as money and credit might look very
different in as little as a decade from now.

The role and functioning of capital are also undergoing a significant
change.[43] New digital and intangible capital is becoming a more important driver than conventional fixed asset investment, and this new capital
has a number of unique properties.

First, intangible capital (such as robotics, automation, technology,
and software) offers a much stronger operational *scalability* (think of
the Coca Cola recipe when compared to constrained capacity of the
Coca Cola bottlers) and greater *synergies*, while delivering meaningful
spillover effects. In essence, digital capital is more flexible and scalable,
has a shorter duration, and can be simultaneously leveraged into multiple industries, thus blurring distinctions between various activities (e.g.,
Android software can be leveraged into advertising, travel, finance, and
distribution businesses while smart self-driving cars can have an impact
on real estate by lowering demand for parking spaces or on logistics by
replacing delivery vans). In the US, intangible assets already account for
as much as 60 percent of private sector GDP (as well as 55 percent of
incremental private non-residential fixed asset investment) when compared to around 40 percent in 1995 and less than 30 percent in the
1980s. In Japan and the EU intangibles account for as much as 35–40
percent of their respective private sector GDP or double the levels of
twenty-five years ago.[44]

Second, although there is a need for greater tangible investment
in digital infrastructure as well as climate and energy transition, it is
likely that the new age will be less, rather than more, capital intensive.
Depending on the timing of the energy transition (I am in a camp of a
multi-decade process, allowing both the private and public sectors time
to adjust), the overlay between tangible and intangible investment might
for a time raise overall capital intensity. However, this is likely to be a

temporary phenomenon, despite the dominant post COVID-19 narrative that we have over the last three decades overinvested in intangibles and underinvested in tangible assets. The shift toward higher energy efficiency and the technology-driven new methods of manufacturing and distribution are bound to keep reducing tangible capital requirements. We are essentially starting to reside in "capital lite" economies, or as Haskel and Westlake phrased it, our new world could be characterized as "capitalist economies without capital."[45]

Intangible capital behaves very differently, helping to create monopolies at a much faster than hitherto pace while also disrupting and demolishing these just as quickly, destroying existing jobs and business practices almost as quickly as new ones are created, and questioning both the importance and enforceability of property rights. The in-built properties of scalability, synergies, and spillover also generate strong disinflationary pressures, and as intangible assets become more important, marginal cost of almost everything falls toward zero. All one needs to prove the point is to look at charts of rapidly declining cost of new technologies that are progressing faster than Moore's Law. According to the NIH (US National Institutes of Health), the cost of genome sequencing has dropped over the last two decades from an astronomic US$95 million per genome to less than US$250 due to technological breakthroughs that moved sequencing from conventional to the next generation of technology. A similar trend has been evident in other areas, including transistor and semiconductor prices as well as solar panels, new age batteries, and other applications. Neither conventional businesses nor economies have an answer to zero, upending conventional capitalist business and economic models, based as they are on concepts of scarcity not abundance.

Third, unlike traditional capitalist economies, we are now residing in a world of excess rather than a shortage of capital. As I discussed in Chapter Five, one of the key legacies of the Baby Boomers' revolution was the unleashing of an unprecedented wave of financialization that has created a "cloud of finance" that is at least five and possibly as much as ten times greater than the underlying real economies.

Figure 40. Genome Sequencing, Cost per Genome

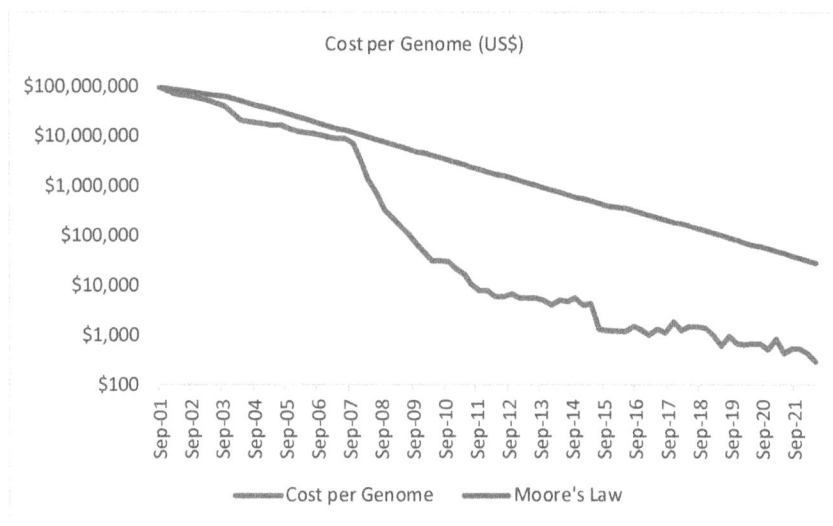

Cost per Genome (US$)

Source: NIH, 2023

While technological evolution is a natural human impulse, the pace at which it propagates depends on the availability and cost of capital, and one of the key side effects of the financialization revolution is the creation of excess capital and the compression of cost of capital. The deep financialization over the last three to four decades can be best thought of as pouring kerosene on the bonfire of the Information Age, with excess capital fueling technological innovation, which, in turn, creates even more surplus capital, reinforcing an ever-faster evolution of the Information Age. This mutual reinforcement is the beating heart of the Fujiwara effect. Although Carlota Perez[46] is correct in arguing that in the past, financial bubbles have always been an indispensable link in developing any super-cluster technology, the new world coming into view is one of abundance, not shortage or scarcity, of capital. This promises to radically alter (and to an extent even negate) established concepts of constrained capital and the need for a careful evaluation of projects through discounted cashflow frameworks to ensure optimum utilization of resources.

Finally, the above-described radical changes inevitably alter social and political climate. As Tyler Cowen keeps emphasizing, whenever dynamic technologies interact with static institutions, conflict is inevitable. It will clearly impact what he describes as "wordcel" class, by "displacing many jobs that deal with words and symbols, or make them less lucrative, or just make those who hold them less influential."[47]

It is worthwhile pausing for a moment to realize what profound change this will be. For centuries, Western civilizations (and the classical world before it) have traditionally awarded higher status to those whom Cowen describes as "ideas people," or those who can formulate, develop, and express ideas and trail the path toward transmitting those ideas into reality. Who will take their place in a social hierarchy? Similarly, the idea of "one man one vote" which became deeply imbedded in most societies throughout the 20th century, could be questioned, as contributions of people and cohorts will not only diverge but will become radically different. How would society decide who or what should lead them? There is an associated issue as to who ultimately owns robots and associated technologies. At the current juncture, most of the technological advances, although based on inventions that had largely occurred in the public sector (or were funded by the state), are owned by a select few private enterprises, creating an oligarchic elite that could feel empowered to control political and social life.[48] There are already disturbing signs that tech and finance elite (i.e., the beneficiaries of the Fujiwara effect) feel entitled to have an outsized influence on many social and political developments, especially in the US (e.g., Peter Thiel, Elon Musk, and Bill Ackman). As in the classical world, are we going to degenerate into narrowly based societies led by a few who disproportionately benefit from these technologies, or should we place limits on such power, including stricter supervision, regulation, and taxation? These will be difficult issues to navigate in the years ahead, and I shall address them in Chapter Ten.

Intangibles are also sharpening geopolitical tensions, explaining the emphasis that the likes of Vladimir Putin and Xi Jinping place on the evolution of AI and its incorporation into other technologies, including weaponry. What McAfee and Brynjolfsson called DANCE—data, algo-rithms, networks, cloud computing, and exponential improvement in digi-tal hardware[49]—has the ability to alter the relative power of competing geo-political blocks. For example, technology is already radically reshaping the battlefield, allowing far greater than hitherto asymmetric capabilities to be exercised by nearly stone age societies (e.g., Houthis of Yemen and Taliban of Afghanistan) against more advanced nations and armies.

•   •   •

In summary, the forthcoming digital age promises to be drastically differ-ent from the Industrial Age of the preceding two hundred years.

First and foremost, the new age will be the time of a rapidly rising capital-labor elasticity of substitution, when it becomes increasingly easy to substitute technology or capital for labor, aggravating societal polarization and unleashing significant waves of disappointment and frustration, espe-cially as rewards and pain are unlikely to be evenly shared. Second, technol-ogy will continue to significantly reduce the marginal, and eventually the average, costs of production and distribution until marginal and average costs converge at zero. Third, it will be a world where the role and function-ing of capital and money will undergo a profound change, and with it, the role of the state and what are regarded as its appropriate functions will also undergo considerable expansion. Fourth, the benefit of skilling and educa-tion will diminish. Unlike the Industrial Age when there was a need to move younger people to an ever-greater productivity and when college education was bestowing what seemed like a perpetually rising premium, the incre-mental benefits of education are likely to rapidly decline (Chapter Ten).

Fifth, the new world will question a number of key "givens"—such as the nature of political system, geopolitics, and the role of demographics and urbanization (i.e., having rapidly growing younger cohorts might not be the best outcome in a world of diminishing marginal utility of labor, turning the industrial age demographic dividends into feudal Malthusian curses). Sixth, the nature and functioning of corporations as the key orga-nizing structure is also likely to undergo significant changes, with decisions increasingly flowing from the bottom-up rather than being generated by more classical top-down industrial age structures. We are likely to witness a shortening of the lifespan of corporations to reflect declining marginal costs (production and transactions) and a greater importance of ideas and social rather than conventional tangible capital.

Summarized in figure 41 are some of the key differences between the industrial and information age. The new world might far more resemble the old feudal societies or an enlightened version of communism than a more familiar industrial capitalism, explaining the plethora of books exploring changes in the nature of capitalism and democracy. We shall return to this important topic later in the book.

Figure 41. Key Characteristics of Industrial vs. Information Age

Characteristic	Industrial Age	Information Age
Capital Requirements	High	Low
Capital Availability	Low	High
Operational Scale	Low	High
Spillover Effects	Low	High
Synergies	Low/Medium	High
Capital Labor Substitution	Below 1	Above 1
Labor Usage	High	Low
Skilling/Education Premium	Important	Declining
Middle Class Creation	Medium/High	Regression
Inequalities	Decline	Increase
Country & Regional Convergence	Low/Medium	Regression
Hierarchy	Important	Bottom-up

Source: Shvets (2020)

•　　•　　•

Is the future as uncertain, violent, and bleak as Yuval Harari, Laura Tyson, Andre Gorz, Daron Acemoglu, and many others fear, or could we argue that the human race has in the past successfully navigated many upheavals, and this time will not be any different?

The answer depends on whether one looks a century from now or perhaps only two decades out. Over the ages, the human race has consistently proven that ultimately, societies and economies adjust, and indeed become both more productive and prosperous. There is no need to believe that this time will be any different. However, we don't feel the pain of the generations that had the misfortune of personally experiencing such profound changes; we just remember the final glorious outcomes.[50] After all, the Luddites in the early 1800s were not wrong in their assessment regarding what looms would do to their jobs, livelihood, and self-respect. All three were destroyed as proud craftsmen were converted into factory slaves with appalling working and living conditions. Similarly, those fighting in the revolutionary barricades of 1848 or 1870 were not wrong assuming that changes sweeping the world were bound to increase both inequality and exploitation while today's discouraged and alienated former manufacturing and industrial workers are correct to assume that despite all the promises of high-quality jobs, none will ever come back.

Ultimately, though, capitalism did evolve; but it took more than a century of violent conflicts for a fairer world to finally emerge in the 1950s–70s. As the history of the first two industrial revolutions has amply illustrated, while technological revolutions ultimately significantly raise productivity, this only occurs over a very long timeframe (i.e., usually at least two generations).

For example, although the First Industrial Revolution had started sometime in the 1760s, neither productivity nor standard of living (as measured on biological outcomes, such as height, longevity, or luxury consumption) improved until sometime in the 1840s–50s. Technological revolutions start slowly and build momentum over decades until benefits spread throughout the economy, and then societies and economies adjust to the new environment. However, in between, turbulence reigns supreme. In the initial stages, productivity rises rapidly in niches of industries and occupations that directly benefit from these changes (e.g., cotton and steam in the First Industrial Revolution, automotive and chemical industries in the Second Industrial Revolution, or biotech and technology today) but tends to lag and/or erode in the rest of the economy as new business practices kill more conventional ones, one cut at a time.[51] It is only after societies and economies adjust to new technologies that the aggregate productivity responds.

It would be no surprise if the back end of the Information Revolution (most likely sometime in the late 2030s), were to see the pace of productivity rise to as high as 4–5 percent or more per annum—compared to around 1 percent following the First Industrial Revolution and 2 percent in the wake of the Second Industrial Revolution—as the role and functioning of both labor and capital changes beyond recognition. Unfortunately for us, in the meantime, the stagnating productivity that most developed economies have already experienced over the last two to three decades, as well as rising social and geopolitical polarizations, are likely to remain a persistent feature of the landscape until a new global consensus emerges. Through the 2020s and 2030s, and maybe even into 2040s, the fusion of a disruptive Information Age and deepening Financialization will likely continue to aggravate preexisting fractures while creating new ones at a speed that our societies might have difficulty adjusting to, summoning in the process dark forces of xenophobia, intolerance, and a desire to reduce pain by reaching out to a strongman, triggering an *authoritarian reflex*.

But this is not the first time the world has undergone such upheaval. What is the most comparable period in modern history, and what does it tell us about our likely future?

Chapter 8

BACK TO THE 1930S

"The era between the two world wars was defined by attempts to resolve
mounting tensions between globalization on the one hand and equality,
state sovereignty, and mass politics on the other."
Tara Zahra[1]

In 1941, Stefan Zweig, a Jewish Austrian writer, mourned the world of yesterday: "Before 1914 the earth had belonged to all. People went where they wished and stayed as long as they pleased. There were no permits, no visas, and it always gives me pleasure to astonish the young by telling them that before 1914 I traveled from Europe to India and to America without passport and without ever having seen one. One embarked and alighted without questioning or being questioned. The frontiers which, with their custom officers, police, and militia, have become wire barriers thanks to pathological suspicion of everyone against everybody else. Nationalism emerged to agitate the world only after the war, and the first visible phenomenon which this intellectual epidemic of our century brought about was xenophobia; morbid dislike of the foreigner, or at least fear of the foreigner."[2] Having lost his prized Austrian citizenship, and with it a large portion of his personal identity, and in despair for the future of Europe and its culture, Zweig had committed suicide in 1942 during his Brazilian exile.

Following the Great War, John Maynard Keynes also looked back to what he considered to be the glory days of the free movement of people, trade, and capital globalization. In his visionary book, *The Economic Consequences of Peace*, he remembered the pre-1914 times, when "The inhabitant of London could order by telephone sipping his morning tea in bed, the various products of the whole earth, in such quantity as he might see fit, and reasonably expect their early delivery upon his doorstep; he could at the same moment and by the same means adventure his wealth in the natural resources and new enterprises of any quarter of the world, and share, without exertion or even trouble, in their prospective fruits and advantages. He could secure forthwith, if he wished it, cheap and comfortable means of transit to any country without passport or other formality."[3]

The world, of course, had never belonged to everyone, and the experience of rich white males was radically different from that of the majority of the population. At the same time, xenophobic attitudes, and restrictions on movement of people bemoaned by Zweig and Keynes had already been growing for years prior to 1914 while trade barriers were steadily being erected around the world from the 1860s onward (with Britain and the Netherlands being notable exceptions). Nevertheless, it is true to say that two to three decades before the Great War witnessed the greatest ever flourishing of trade and capital flows while immigration was far easier than at almost any other time in history. There was also an expectation that the extreme inequalities that characterized the Gilded Age would gradually become less pronounced, and the benefits would be more equally shared. These expectations were not a fantasy but were rooted in the budding social and welfare systems that started to proliferate during that era, including decriminalization of poverty, improvements in healthcare, and income supports, as well as a meaningful easing of mobility barriers. As Keynes highlighted, while "the greater part of the population…worked hard and lived at a low standard of comfort… escape was possible, for any man of capacity and character at all exceeding the average, into the middle and upper classes."[4]

The world of 1920s–30s looked radically different from that of 1914 on a range of political and social indicators. Whereas prior to the Great War most democratic franchises were limited to males of a certain income and tax-paying power, after the war, the universal suffrage became the norm—first all-male and later females as well. This created a fertile ground for mass political parties (such as social democrats, communists, fascists), which in turn started to reflect the popular mood of xenophobia, antisemitism, racism, anti-globalism, class solidarity, and the desire for protection of local interests, even as some (e.g., communists) were propagating global ideas while still protecting locals. It was also the time when feminism got a meaningful boost while economic disruptions spawned culture clashes that far exceeded "bread and butter" issues, focusing on a range of family, race, and gender roles that were disrupted by an unconstrained flow of people, goods, and capital. In the aftermath of the Great War, governments prioritized local self-sufficiency over reliance on foreign supply and the protection of local communities while extreme organizations like the Ku Klux Klan (KKK) got a new lease of life as a "100 percent America" club (i.e., excluding anyone who was not of Christian, White, Northern European heritage).

From an economic perspective, military, political, and cultural disruption led to a collapse in trade and capital flows. The trade volumes of 1913 did not recover until 1924–25 but then dropped again during the 1930s and did not return to pre-Great War levels until the late 1970s to early 1980s.[5] The same happened to immigration. Apart from massive resettlements and ethnic cleansing at the end of World War II, the immigration levels of 1913 (when transatlantic traffic alone exceeded 2 million people) were not replicated until the 1990s. The period between 1930s and late 1970s or even 1980s can be best described as one of deliberately constrained flow of trade, capital, and people, reconciling Rodrik's political trilemma discussed above: ensuring the dominance of nation-states, local politics, and democracy at the expense of globalization.

•   •   •

One must always be careful when conducting a cross-time comparison. Having said that, as Mark Twain once quipped, "History does not repeat itself, but it often rhymes," and it is hard to escape the feeling that the 1930s, rather than the frequently cited 1970s, is probably the period most comparable to the one the world is likely to experience over the next decade or so. There are far too many persuasive parallels with the 1930s to be a coincidence.

First, both the 1930s and the last fifteen years have witnessed financial crises and recessions at a time when income and wealth inequalities were at historically high levels. Second, in both periods, investors and governments were haunted by the prospect of "secular stagnation" (or the inability to grow and recover). The term was popularized by American economist Alvin Hansen in 1939 and resurrected by Larry Summers, former US Treasury Secretary, in 2012. Even the reasons for such pessimism are similar. Hansen argued that the inability of the US to recover from the Great Depression was caused by a mix of technology, demographics, and finance (i.e., exhaustion of the ability to expand the western frontier, the disruptive impact of technology, and deteriorating demographics)—eerily similar to today's Fujiwara effect. While the idea of "secular stagnation" was forgotten for decades (as mere months after Hansen's speech, Germany invaded Poland, and the world changed forever), economists like Larry Summers and Paul Krugman resurrected the idea in the wake of Japan's lost decades of the 1990s and 2000s and the difficulties that the rest of the world encountered in recovering from the Global Financial Crisis of 2008–2010.

Third, the decade of the 1930s witnessed significant societal polarization. It was the time when Hitler, Franco, Mussolini, and Stalin had either come to power or strengthened their rule, while Mao and the CCP were embarking on their Long (and bloody) March, and in the US, Huey Long, a socialist populist, threatened to unseat FDR. It was a time when people were willing to experiment with extreme economic and political models and were susceptible to the siren calls of authoritarianism. The last fifteen years have similarly witnessed a rollback of the democratic revolution of the 1990s, with proliferation of "anocracies" (i.e., states with a democratic façade, cleansed of most of its substance, with only around 30 countries still qualifying as liberal democracies and over 70 percent of today's population living in autocracies, when compared to less than half in 2010). Whether Donald Trump, Giuseppe Conte, Jair Bolsonaro, Viktor Orbán, Boris Johnson, Recep Erdoğan, Geert Wilders and many other recent populists, it is unlikely that any of them would have ever been allowed to grab control unless people were angry, dissatisfied, and disoriented. The same is true for the political landscape. Over the last decade, parties were forced to migrate to extremes or face extinction. Most the conventional parties that ruled countries like Italy, France, or the Netherlands since the World War II have already disintegrated while parties that managed to stay relevant have changed beyond recognition (such as the Republican Party in the US, Fidesz in Hungary, or the Law and Justice Party in Poland).

Fourth, culture and race wars were raging throughout the 1930s, and calls for a return to what was advocated as "traditional values" were the go-to theme for successful politicians and other merchants of grievances. As discussed in this book, it is eerily similar to today; even the slogans are almost identical. One of the more popular of Goebbels's 1920s propaganda posters featured Hitler with a taped mouth, and the declaration that everyone but Hitler was allowed to speak. Freedom of speech and whether it should be universal or constrained, a topic hotly debated today, had its echo in the decaying 1920s Weimer Republic.

Fifth, throughout the 1930s, the world was divided into camps (i.e., democracies versus fascists and communists). This is not much different than the growing division between what I describe as "Illiberal Eurasia" or "Sinosphere" on the one hand (China and its dependencies like North Korea; Russia and its diminishing empire; Central Asia; Iran, Pakistan; Afghanistan; etc.) and the "Anglosphere" (i.e., US, UK, Australia, Canada, New Zealand, Japan, and to a lesser extent South Korea) as well as a broader West (the Anglosphere plus the EU). Other fractures are also becoming deeper, including the role and responsibilities of the broadly defined south or less developed economies. For the first time since the 1930s and 1940s, there are radically different alternative political, economic, and social models that are being promoted to replace democratic orders.

Sixth, the breakdown of relationships between key players and the refusal of the US to join the League of Nations fatally undermined the legitimacy of that institution, formed in the wake of the Great War. After its inability to act against Japan's invasion of Manchuria, Italy's attack on Abyssinia and following withdrawal by Nazi Germany, and the Soviet invasion of Finland, the League of Nations, designed to prevent conflicts, ceased to exist. Today, trust in the UN is at a historical low, at only around 50 percent in the US and France, 48 percent in Italy, and below 40 percent in Japan.[6] UN's inability to act on Russia's invasion of Ukraine as well as its impotence to address other burning issues like climate change, the Israeli-Palestinian conflict, and China's unilateral militarization of the South China Sea is emasculating this latest variation of the global will to avoid wars and peacefully negotiate conflicts.

Seventh, the 1930s marked the beginning of a major phase of heavy government interventions and the sunsetting of the first iteration of liberalism, with a government-led world lasting until the end of the stagflationary period of the 1970s. Similarly, the last fifteen years has witnessed a slow death of neoliberalism (which was dominant over the preceding three decades), and its replacement by a much more activist role allocated to the state and public sectors. The government "umbrella" has been getting wider and broader, encompassing not only fiscal but also monetary and industrial spheres. Whether it be central bank activism and the reemergence of industrial agendas (in neoliberal times, the consensus held that the public sector was inherently inefficient, and therefore, should avoid picking winners) or more proactive social policies, as with the 1930s New Deal, today's public, having lost trust in private sector solutions, seems to be demanding far more from the state.

Summarized in figure 42 are key differences between the most cited comparable periods (i.e., 1930s and 1970s). As can be seen below, our times are indeed likely to be far closer to the 1930s than 1970s.

Figure 42. Key Characteristics of 1930s vs. 1970s and 2020s

	1930s	1970s	2020s
Institutional Trust	Low	Medium	Low
Social Tension	High	High	High
Geopolitical Tensions	High	Medium	High
Competition between alternative systems	Yes	No	Yes
Government reach	Rising	Falling	Rising
Pandemics, Climate & Health Disruption	Yes	No	Yes
Demographics	Inflationary	Inflationary	Disinflationary
Wealth Inequality	High	Low	High
Disruptive Technology	Yes	No	Yes
Unionization	Low	High	Low
Inflation Adjusted Wage Contracts	No	Yes	No
Financialization	Low	Low	High
Loose Monetary Policy	Inconsistent	Yes	Yes
Stimulatory Fiscal policy	Yes	Yes	Yes
Energy Intensity	High	High	Medium

• • •

Although one could argue that we are more globalized than in 1913 or the 1930s, and the intricate chains linking the world today are far more complex, it is doubtful that rationality and economic arguments would be the dominant zeitgeist of the new age. Instead, as Zweig and Keynes highlighted, the world is more likely to be ruled by anger, distrust, disappointment, and disillusionment, the flames of which "merchants of grievances" would be more than happy to fan (and benefit from), creating an environment that pays a premium on destruction rather than construction and on ideological purity rather than governance and compromises. As in the 1920s and 1930s, burning down the house (or "deconstruction of the state" in the words of Steve Bannon, Donald Trump's advisor) is likely to be the fervent wish of a significant minority, and in some countries, even a majority.

In his book, *Decline of the West*, published in 1918, Oswald Spengler argued that the West was facing severe challenges, and that a long period of "Caesarism" (or rule by dictators) would be ushered in, eventually leading to the disintegration of Western societies. His views were influential (from comparative sociology of civilizations to Arnold Toynbee and Samuel Huntington) and were highly popular in the 1920s–30s, as they seemed to rationalize the collapse of the Weimer Republic and the destruction of liberal orders in a number of Western nations, even though Spengler (who died in 1936) was never a Nazi supporter and presciently predicted that the Thousand Year Reich would be unlikely to survive longer than ten years. He was right—the Third Reich collapsed in 1945. Modern versions of the inevitability or even benefit of such Caesarism is found in the writings of extreme right-wing and conservative groups in the US, including Michael Anton and the Claremont Institute who believe that the US is facing an existential threat that can be only redressed by the replacement of democracy with some form of authoritarian rule.[7]

Although Spengler is not as well known today and has been broadly criticized, with many of his views roundly discredited, it remains valid to argue that civilizations do collapse and there are times when democracies and liberal orders are replaced by Caesars. While one can debate the extent to which cultural and historical factors matter and whether collapse of civilizations is predestined (as Spengler argued), or whether economic, technological, and demographic factors are the key and these are within human power to change, Inglehart's concept of "insecurity" described above seems the most logical answer: at times of severe stress, a thin veneer of civilization tends to fall off, and more primitive and raw emotions take over.

In the early 1900s, Italy was a vibrant but a relatively new democracy. In 1913, the Liberal Union (mainstream centrist party) gained 48 percent of the vote and other center-left-right parties took the rest. None were extreme, and Benito Mussolini was still a young firebrand and a journalist not convinced as to whether he wanted to be a nationalist, socialist, or communist. However, Italy's entry into the Great War, resulting in high level of casualties, economic disruption, and rural and industrial upheavals, followed by lack of any meaningful gains from the war, and finally the arrival of a pandemic, radicalized the Socialist Party, shifting it from the social democratic end of the spectrum to one with the Russian Bolsheviks as its model. By 1919, it became the largest party, gaining 32 percent of the vote. A recent academic study by Daron Acemoglu, De Feo, and De Luca[8] tied the rise of extreme right fascists between 1919 and 1922 to districts where new socialists and communists were making the strongest gains, with urban middle class, *petite bourgeoise*, conservative rural dwellers, and peasants switching allegiance, due not only to economic, but also cultural and traditional values. Fascist Parties rose as a direct response to a significant left-wing shift in the country, which in turn, was a by-product of geopolitical, economic, and pandemic-related upheavals and the fervent desire for some stability. By 1921, fascists of various colors captured approximately 20 percent of the vote while Socialists and Communists claimed another 30 percent. In other words, the nation had become polarized with no space for any meaningful compromise or debate, with more than half of the electorate voting for some form of destruction or "burning down" the house. A period of left-right violence ensued, and in the elections of 1924 (no longer fully free), the Fascist Party claimed 65 percent of the vote, and Italy's move away from liberal democracy was set in stone until the destruction of the state in the wake of the World War II.

In the 1920s, the Weimer Republic was also a vibrant democracy with its capital (Berlin) on the cutting edge of modern art and architecture as well as sexual and political freedoms. There were more venues for the LGBTQ community in Berlin than conventional cabaret while German women secured full civil rights in 1919, compared to French women who did not achieve that until 1944–45. In the elections throughout the 1920s, the conventional center-left parties dominated, and as Germany's economy recovered from the war, the share of the Reichstag vote commanded by extremes (Communists and Nazis) was down to only around 12–13 percent. However, the Great Depression that hit Germany from late 1929 through 1932 (ultimately causing unemployment to rise to more than one-third of the labor force), as well as the neglect of Germany's extensive and unproductive rural estates had changed the dynamics. Unemployed men mostly gravitated toward the Communists while artisans, small businessmen, lawyers, housewives, and peasants abandoned mainstream parties for the Nazis.[9] In the elections of 1931–33, the extremes had consistently commanded in excess of 50 percent of the vote. As in Italy in 1921–24, support for the Nazi Party was a direct response to the perceived dangers of Communist dominance and the fear of an assault on property rights, higher taxes, and changes in moral and family behavior. Clearly, the middle ground had by that stage collapsed irretrievably, and it was just a question as to whether the extreme left, or extreme right would have success in uniting the nation. Given the simplicity and the emotional appeal of extreme right (anti-immigration, family values, national pride, etc.) when compared to the much more nuanced and complex agenda of economic, taxation, and social issues that tends to dominate left-wing politics, it is usually (but not always) the right wing that succeeds.

Figure 43. Italy, National Elections (% of vote), 1913–1924

	1913	1919	1921	1924
Democratic/Liberal				
Italian People's Party	-	20.5	20.4	9.0
Liberal Union	47.6	8.6	-	-
Italian Socialist Party	17.6	-	-	-
Italian radical Party	10.4	-	-	-
Italian Republican Party	2.0	0.9	1.9	1.9
Other	22.4	33.6	27.6	9.5
Extreme Right				
Combatants' party	-	4.1	1.7	-
National Blocks	-	-	19.1	-
National list	-	-	-	64.9
Extreme Left				
Communist Party	-	-	4.6	3.7
Italian Socialist Party	-	32.3	24.7	5.0
Unitary Socialist Party	-	-	-	5.9
Democratic/Liberal	100.0	63.6	49.9	20.4
Extremes	-	36.4	50.1	79.5

Source: Italy Ministry of National Economy

Figure 44. Weimer Germany, Reichstag Elections (% of vote), 1924–1933

	May'24	Dec'24	May'28	Sep'30	Jul'32	Nov'32	Mar'33
Democratic/Liberal							
Social Democratic	20.5	26.0	29.8	24.5	21.6	20.4	18.3
Center Party	13.4	13.6	12.1	11.8	12.5	11.9	11.7
Nationalist	19.5	20.5	14.2	7.0	5.9	8.8	8.0
Bavarian People's	3.2	3.7	3.0	3.0	3.2	3.1	2.7
Other	24.3	24.2	27.7	22.3	4.8	5.8	3.1
	80.9	88.0	86.8	68.6	48.0	50.0	43.8
Extremes - Left & Right							
NSDAP (Nazi)	6.5	3.0	2.6	18.3	37.4	33.1	43.9
Communist	12.6	9.0	10.6	13.1	14.6	16.9	12.3
	19.1	12.0	13.2	31.4	52.0	50.0	56.2

Source: Gonschior.de

While Russia's semi-democratic life between 1905 and 1917 (described in my first book) was far more turbulent and parties were less established, in 1906, the Constitutional Democratic Party (Kadets) which was a liberal mainstream party, captured around 38 percent of the vote with the moderate Labor Party (Trudoviks) claiming a further 25 percent while the extreme Social Revolutionaries and Social Democrats secured only around 5 percent. However, the Tsar's persistent attempts to negate 1906 constitution and to disenfranchise the parliament (Duma) fueled polarization, which following Russia's entry into the Great War became truly extreme. By the time the last elections were held in 1917, Lenin's Bolsheviks secured 23 percent of the vote, the Mensheviks took another 3 percent, and Social Revolutionaries got over 50 percent of the vote, while the Kadets attracted less than 5 percent. By 1917, the die was cast; it was just a question of what type of revolutionary change Russia was bound to face.

It is debatable whether various Weimer leaders, such as Konrad Adenauer, a former mayor of Cologne, the president of Prussian State Council, and eventually the first post-war chancellor of West Germany, could have put differences aside and derailed the rise of Hitler. The same applies to the people surrounding the aging and increasingly senile President Hindenburg (especially Kurt von Schleicher). Similarly, could Russia's interim leader, Alexander Kerensky, and the leaders of a more moderate Menshevik wing, have stopped Lenin and the Bolsheviks? What would have happened to Mussolini, if King Victor Emmanuel agreed to Prime Minister Luigi Facta's request to declare martial law? These are some of the history's "what-ifs." But one thing is clear, that beyond a certain point of no return, whether it was Russia in 1917, Italy in 1922–24, Germany in 1933, or Spain in 1936, societies had already become so polarized that neither compromise nor meaningful discussion was any longer possible. In each case, extremes were consistently polling close to or above 50 percent of the electorate, and the other side was treated as an immoral and treasonous enemy to be destroyed and swept away, not to be negotiated with.

Whenever commentators argue that the US is different, they tend to forget that in the 1930s, Huey Long, one of America's wildest populists, had almost defeated FDR, and he could have changed history if he had not been assassinated in 1935. He had the perfect psychological makeup of a populist dictator. Long ruled the state of Louisiana with an iron fist, brooding no dissent, blackmailing, and smashing anyone who stood in his way. As described by one of his contemporaries, he was "blatant, profane, witty, unscrupulous, violent, possessed of the demagogue's habit of promising the impossible."[10] His "Share Our Wealth" program envisaged, among other things, effective basic income guarantees for everyone, paid for by wealth taxes on the richest sections of the population. Prior to his assassination, polls were giving him at least three to four million votes in the forthcoming presidential elections. Father Charles Coughlin was another extreme firebrand. A Catholic parish priest from Michigan, he had a weekly radio sermon with an unimaginable following (in those days) of more than 30 million listeners. He mercilessly attacked speculators and Jewish bankers while arguing for wholesale expropriation of wealth and nationalization of industries and banks, with his popularity peaking at the height of the Depression and the Dust Bowl. Even the Communists, never very popular in the US, were attracting a growing following. On the other end of the spectrum, the KKK, which in the 1920s–30s became so powerful that it was frequently described as the "invisible government of the US," fought hard to restrict immigration and to deport anyone it considered to be unfit, with the number of deportations rising six-fold in the 1930s when compared to the 1920s.[11] The early 1930s was also the time of the only documented attempt to overthrow the US government by creating a fascist army of 500,000 veterans, as described by the McCormack-Dickstein Committee.

It is true that the US Constitution has so many checks and balances that governing is frequently impossible; however, the same blockages make it harder (but not impossible) to elect individuals who are able to undermine the core pillars of democratic and liberal order. As the near win by William Jennings Bryan in 1896 and the election of Donald Trump in 2016 illustrated, the US is not immune to similarly divisive, populist, and polarizing waves. Steven Levitsky and Daniel Ziblatt highlight[12] that modern revolutions are seldom conducted through coups, but rather the state itself steadily erodes conventional norms and then legalizes these through legislature, and in the US through judiciary. In most cases, it is justified under the pretext of fighting extremists and is promoted as "strengthening democracy"—improving efficiency and supposed legitimacy of the electoral process while fighting some mysterious "deep state." These changes are also usually defended on the narrower ground of "reflecting the will people," particularly of those perceived to be the "right type of people"—excluding foreigners and the supposedly corrupt cosmopolitan elite. The playbook is as old as history itself, but it always works, reflecting Kevin Drum's cynical view of humanity as being little more than "overclocked primates."

•   •   •

It is hardly surprising that such extreme polarization of the 1920s–30s ultimately led to the "world on fire" of the 1940s. At the time (as in 1913–1914), war was perceived to be the only way to resolve disputes and "clear the air." Although there was nowhere near the same enthusiasm as in the lead-up to the Great War, the consensus throughout the 1930s accepted that some form of confrontation was inevitable, and hence, most discussions focused on merely trying to minimize, not prevent, conflagration through appeasement and abortive attempts to utilize the good offices of the League of Nations. History is not deterministic, and clearly the ultimate conflict did not have to be as savage and inhuman as it turned out to be, but some form of conflict was inevitable.

The same is true today, with strategic policy statements emanating from Washington, Brussels, London, Berlin, Tokyo, Moscow, and Beijing highlighting an increasingly hostile geopolitical climate and a desire to weaken the opposite side to lay ground for the confrontation. It is clear that over the last decade, elements of either cold or hot war have been falling into place—restrictions on technology transfers as well as education and skilling of the opposite camp; removal and localization of critical supply chains; constraints on acquisition of assets and land in the opposite block, while making it more difficult for countries like Russia or China to access Western capital markets. As Jake Sullivan, US National Security Adviser, has said recently, "Ignoring economic dependencies that had built up over the decades of liberalization had become really perilous—from energy uncertainty in Europe to supply-chain vulnerabilities in medical equipment, semiconductors, and critical materials…these were the kinds of dependencies that could be exploited for economic or geopolitical leverage."[13] The world is fracturing into several antagonistic and competing blocks, in a way that Zbigniew Brzezinski was presciently warning as far back as 1997, when he argued that the most likely and the most dangerous geopolitical outcome would be a "grand coalition of China, Russia, and perhaps Iran, an 'antihegemonic' coalition united not by ideology but by complementary grievances."[14] This was a remarkably accurate prediction, considering that this was the age when China's global integration project was in full swing and the reformist Zhu Rongji was the premier with an aggressive agenda of remaking China, while Putin was still a complete unknown (outside of a narrow circle of KGB officers and St. Petersburg municipal council). Alas, no one listened, and his suggestions of how one could construct a system of "carrots and sticks" to minimize the impact of such a coalition fell on deaf ears.

Although Beijing blames the US for this escalation, in reality, if not for the US, it is highly unlikely that China would have entered the World Trade Organization WTO in 2001, and it was the US that did more than any country to create today's China through a consistent bipartisan engagement policy across six administrations (from George H. W. Bush to Obama). It was a meaningful shift in China's policies, after the Global Financial Crisis in 2008–2010, that changed the US view of China, its direction, and its role in the post-World War global system. It seems indisputable that the Global Financial Crisis was such a shock to China's leadership that it no longer believed in the Western global order and the superiority of liberal policies. As discussed above, not a dissimilar process of distrust has also been playing out in the West, but in China, it is overlayed by its complex history, deep memory of the "century of shame," absolute dominance by the Communist Party (CCP), and the two-thousand-year history of a highly centralized state with limited civil rights. In the wake of the Global Financial Crisis, Wang Qishan, China's Vice Premier at the time, told Hank Paulson, the US Treasury Secretary: "You were my teacher. But now I am in my teacher's domain, and look at your system, Hank. We aren't sure we should be learning from you anymore."[15]

At least four years before the elevation of Xi Jinping, China had already ended the erosion of state control over net national wealth (which was down from over 70 percent in 1978 to around 32 percent in 2008[16]) and redefined the role of state-owned enterprises from efficiency and toward much broader goals (including numerous social and political objectives). Since the Global Financial Crisis, the state's share started to climb again. China also ended grassroots local democratic initiatives while tightening control over information and clamping down on internal debate. Over the subsequent decade, Xi took this reversionary trend to a brand-new level, including elimination of most of the free space between private and public sectors, and state and non-state actors, while at the same time massively increasing the extent of state and party control over most key decisions, including the allocation of capital. Under Xi Jinping's leadership, the idea of separating the party from the state and bureaucracy (which was championed by Deng Xiaoping in the 1980s and by all subsequent leaders) was scrapped, with policymaking functions progressively moving from the bureaucracy to the party organs and its various commissions, most directly controlled by Xi. Within the party, the decision-making power has also been channeled into an ever-smaller group of leaders. Unlike the collective leadership era (i.e., the early 1980s to 2010–2012), the new China has emerged as less programmatic, and far more paranoid and ideologically dogmatic.

Since 2010, China has proceeded to actively reshape global governance and the preexisting five-decades' old system by trying to redraw rules across most key areas—from trade to the role of the state and community relative to individual rights, Internet and information flows to the resurrection of the18th century concept of an absolute national sovereignty (i.e., a country is free to do almost anything it wishes within its borders), while championing ideas of spheres of influence and a much more constrained sovereignty allotted to smaller countries on the periphery of the big powers. Essentially, over the last decade China faced a choice: change its own domestic system to accommodate the prevailing global order or try to change the global order to accommodate China's political, social, and economic system. While previous generations of leaders were mostly aiming to integrate and change China, ever since the Global Financial Crisis, China has decided to change the world to make it a more hospitable place for its own system.[17]

As Yang Jiechi, China's former Foreign Minister once said at the Association of Southeast Asian nations (ASEAN) forum (2010), "China is a big country, and you are smaller countries, and that is the fact." The same coercive and "wolf diplomacy" policies were on full display during the China-Australia stand-off that included bans on Australian soybeans and coal, tariffs on wine as well as warnings for Chinese students to avoid Australian educational institutions; its aggressive moves against Lithuania, Norway, and the Czech Republic; the government-fanned boycotts against Korea and Japan as well as unilateral militarization of the disputed South China Sea islands and introduction of the national security legislation in Hong Kong.

For over a century, the world worked hard to enmesh big countries in a variety of international commitments and rules (from the EU to the WTO and the UN) to prevent them from dominating smaller nations while creating a more holistic and universal concept of human rights within an acceptable rules-based order. China has been trying to redefine these, with its policies mostly designed to strengthen control over its periphery, weaken Western policies, and safeguard the CCP's domestic dominance. It is not that China is intrinsically evil, but as its standing improved and economy developed, it has simply followed the ancient Athenian dictum: "The strong do what they think they can and the weak suffer what they must." And China increasingly does what it wants rather than what it must, as the world from Beijing's vantage point looks very different than from the Western perspective.[18] China today is not satisfied with its position in the global system, disagrees with most of its value and policy preferences, and aims for redistribution of power to give it greater freedom of action and insists on changes in existing mechanisms of how the global community makes decisions and solves disputes. This is the beating heart and the driving force behind China's recent "Belt and Road," "Global Development," and "Global Civilization" initiatives.

Most Chinese officials had interpreted the Global Financial Crisis not just as the "calamity made in the United States but also as a symbol of the transition of the world economy from American to Chinese leadership,"[19]expecting that China's inexorable rise has become the defining trend in international relations, with the West (especially the US) unreasonably resisting what China believes to be its proper place in the world. This is eerily (almost word-for-word) similar to complaints that officials of the Imperial Germany directed against what they perceived to be "unfair British practices" in containing the historically preordained rise of Germany. Today, Beijing levels similar accusation of "unfairness," with China's Ministry of Foreign Affairs White Paper (June 2022) stating, "What the United States has constantly vowed to preserve is a so-called international order designed to serve United States' own interests and perpetuate its hegemony... The United States itself is the largest source of disruption to the actual world order."[20]

During the latest (20th) Congress of the Communist Party, Xi Jinping stressed the need to prepare for conflicts, hardship and self-sufficiency: "We must strengthen our sense of hardship...be prepared for danger in times of peace, prepare for rainy day, and be ready to withstand major tests of high winds and high waves."[21] In line with this philosophy, Xi has introduced a comprehensive national security agenda to cover almost everything from economics, politics, and corruption to defense, culture, and ecology to cyberspace, deep sea, data and artificial intelligence, with every aspect designed to reinforce self-sufficiency and protect party control in preparation for what China regards as "stormy seas and trials ahead."

It was inevitable that these ideas and policies would ultimately clash with Western- and US-led order, turning China from a global "integration and stake holder" project of 1980s–2000s, into its own force —occasionally hostile, sometimes cooperative, and consistently prickly, aiming for a comprehensive redesign of global norms, not dissimilar to what Germany or Japan tried to do in the late 19th and early 20th centuries. A complicated history, economic development, and wounded pride have always been a toxic mix, especially when concerning larger powers, and expectations through 1990s and 2000s that economic links, flow of trade and capital, and a rising standard of living will overcome these challenges were naïve. These did not lead to better understanding and integration but to even more bitter grievances. As I will discuss in Chapter Nine, this will not be easy or trouble free, especially as the economic and societal trends and fortunes of both China and the broader West are in a state of extreme flux.

The change in the attitude of the US toward China became visible toward the end of President Obama's second term (2015–16), but the reformulation has massively escalated during the Trump and Biden administrations. By now, China has morphed into one of the few bipartisan issues in what is an incredibly fractured political landscape. Whether democrats, republicans, or independents, there is now a solid majority that views China as a long-term adversary. A similar message comes from most other Western nations—from Japan and Korea to the EU and Australia.

A recent Pew survey (2022–23) shows that 83 percent of Americans have a negative view of China, when compared to 73 percent in 2020 and 33 percent in 2002, while positive views plunged from 41 percent in 2002 to only 14 percent with the net view collapsing over two decades from a positive 8 percent to a negative 69 percent. Although EU has been attempting to find a middle ground, China's "wolf warrior diplomacy" as well as the Russia-Ukraine war meaningfully shifted its view of China. A survey by the ECFR shows that only 3 percent of Europeans believe that China shares their values while 38 percent now view China as either an adversary or rival. In the top ten Western nations, the average unfavorable view of China has increased to 74 percent in 2022 from 47 percent in 2002, with the steepest rises in nations that are closest geographically to China, such as Australia, Korea, and Japan. The average net Western view deteriorated from a positive 14 percent in 2002 to a negative 53 percent in 2022.

Numerous recent surveys have also highlighted a significant widening of areas where people across the West feel there are irreconcilable differences with China: human rights, military power, competition and trade, and China's interference in domestic affairs. Finally, there is a strong public unanimity in the West that China cannot be trusted to do the right thing in global affairs.

Figure 45. Net Public View of China, 2002–2022

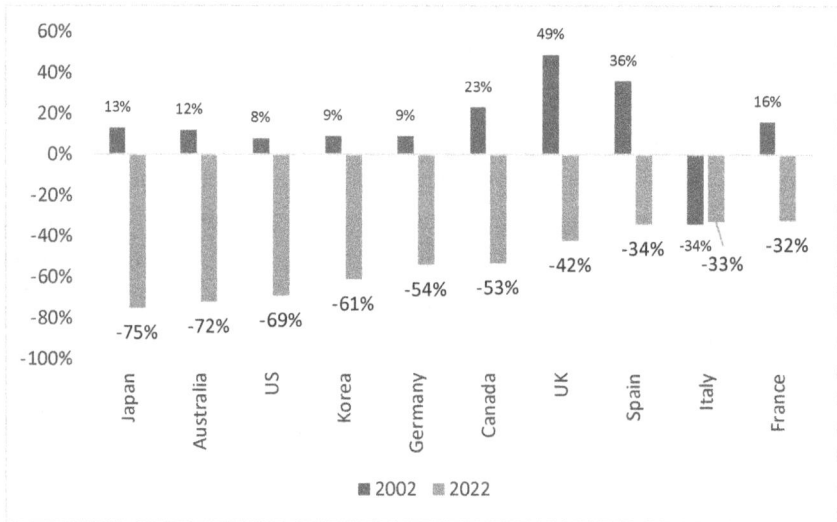

Source: Pew, 2022–23

Figure 46. Confidence in China Doing the Right Thing in Global Affairs – Negative Score

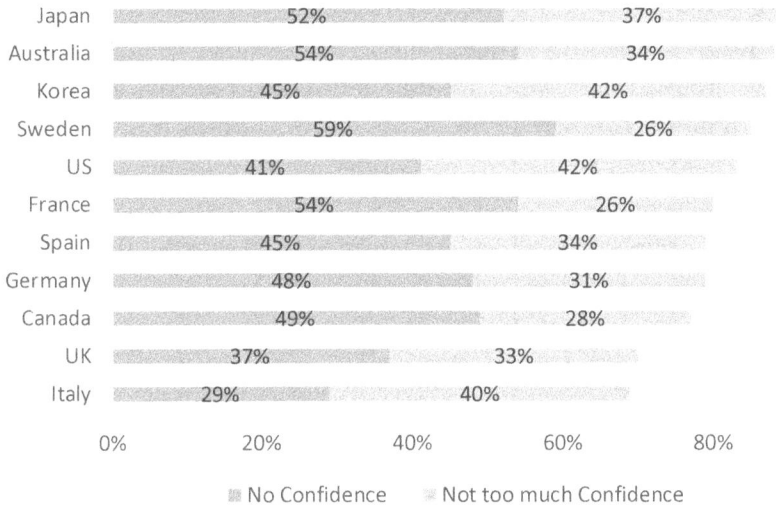

Country	No Confidence	Not too much Confidence
Japan	52%	37%
Australia	54%	34%
Korea	45%	42%
Sweden	59%	26%
US	41%	42%
France	54%	26%
Spain	45%	34%
Germany	48%	31%
Canada	49%	28%
UK	37%	33%
Italy	29%	40%

Source: Pew, 2022–23

Although there are not many reliable and/or independent surveys in China (under pressure from national security laws, most reputable agencies have gradually exited China, including Gallup which announced the shuttering of their China operation in November 2023), a recent CEIAS survey highlighted that 59 percent of China's responders reported that their view of the US worsened between 2019 and 2022, while only 24 percent indicated an improvement. In totality, the negative view of the US was in excess of 60 percent while the negative view of Japan stood at around 55 percent, and over 60 percent preferred a tougher China policy toward both the US and Japan. On the other hand, the responders' view of Russia has significantly improved, with 79 percent reporting a better view in 2022 when compared to 2019, and only 16 percent reported a worsening.

While Russia is not in the same league as China and remains essentially a kleptocratic nuclear petrostate, it has numerous unresolved issues arising from the collapse of the Soviet Union. As Zbigniew Brzezinski (former national security adviser to President Carter, and in his time, one of the best-known experts on Eastern Europe), once said, "Without Ukraine, Russia ceases to be an empire, but with Ukraine suborned and then subordinated, Russia automatically becomes an empire." He also argued, "Russia can be either an empire or democracy, but it cannot be both." While in the early 1990s, it was not clear which road post-Soviet Russia would take, by the early part of the current century and following social and economic chaos of the 1990s, Russia turned away from the liberal and democratic path and had reverted to an empire. Although this was never the preferred course for the elite in Moscow and St. Petersburg, the rest of the country (which is what matters) wanted to get back to a more conventional stability. As discussed in my first book, the violent and chaotic history of Russia created a highly centralized environment with limited history of civil and human rights. Stability, rather than progress, has always been the primary objective.

Prior to the Ukraine war, most of Vladimir Putin's policies (since he came to power in 2000) were in line with both people's perception of economic imperatives and the historical and emotional views of most Russians. He restarted the moribund Soviet industry and got the country to a point where trains ran mostly on time; hospitals were open, over three hundred single-factory towns continued to work, and pensions were paid. Were his answers economically efficient? Of course not. Have they positioned Russia to prosper over the longer-term? Definitely not. But these questions miss the point. Unlike Westerners who emphasize marginal returns and impact ("Am I falling behind and am I doing better today than yesterday?"), most Russians are *average* rather than *marginal* actors, and averages change slowly, but marginal impacts do so rapidly. For Russians, the salient comparison is not whether one is better off today than yesterday, rather whether on average one is better off than in the past, including one's parents and grandparents. Most people understand that their country is deeply inefficient and corrupt, and they can do better elsewhere, but the environment remains stable and far from catastrophic. In my view, it is this inertia and average, rather than marginal, mentality that explains why it took two lost wars (i.e., the Russo-Japanese War and the Great War) as well as a pandemic to finally get rid of the Romanoff dynasty and the slavery-based and productivity-sapping system that it ran for three centuries. Despite various attempts at reforms throughout the 18th and 19th centuries (from Catherine the Great, Speransky to Witte), most were still born with the country taking at least one step, and sometimes two, backward for every reform package.

Unlike Germany or Japan, which were defeated outright, Russia and the Soviet Union did not suffer outright defeats either in the Russo-Japanese War, the Great War, World War II, or the Cold War. As a result, it never confronted an equivalent process to that of de-nazification that Germany went through, and hence, the culture had not undergone any meaningful change, with no comprehensive repudiation of Tsars, Stalin, or Gulags. To this day, it continues to be dominated by the legacy of the country's thousand-year history, including a disproportionate value placed on its heroic past and its desire to be perceived as a great power.

Neither the state nor its people have ever reconciled themselves to losing more than 20 percent of the Soviet territory, returning Russia to broadly the same borders it occupied during the reign of Peter the Great in the early18th century. Most Russians do not care about large areas of Central Asia (which were only incorporated relatively recently), while the Baltic regions had always been a useful but awkward part of the empire. However, most people feel strongly about "brother nations" of Ukraine, Belarus, and Kazakhstan (especially the northern portion of the state that used to belong to Russia). Even Aleksandr Solzhenitsyn (Soviet dissident and the author of *Gulag*) advocated in the 1990s for the establishment of what he called "historic Rus" or a union of Russians, Belarus, and Ukrainians, as well as northern Kazakhstan. In his pamphlet "Rebuilding Russia" published in 1991[22] he argued: "We all together emerged from the treasured Kiev (Russian spelling of Kyiv), from which the Russian land began, according to the chronicle of Nestor…in Lithuania and Poland, White Russian (Belarussians) and Little Russians (Ukrainians) acknowledged that they were Russians and fought against Polonization and

Catholicism." Vladimir Putin, in his wide-ranging and pseudo-historical 5,000-word essay published in 2021, argued, "I am confident that true sovereignty of Ukraine is possible only in partnership with Russia. Our spiritual, human, and civilization ties formed over centuries and have their origins in the same sources, they have been hardened by common trials, achievements, and victories. Our kinship has been transmitted from generation to generation...Together we have always been and will be many times stronger and more successful. For we are one people."[23] Margaret MacMillan, professor of international history at Oxford, recently highlighted that from Putin's perspective, "malign outside forces—Austria-Hungary before World War I and the European Union today—had tried to divide Russia from its right patrimony."[24]

As in most long-cherished ideas, there is a grain of truth in what Solzhenitsyn and Putin described—Russia had indeed arisen out of Kyivan Rus of the 10th to 12th centuries, which in turn was an amalgam of Viking warriors and various Slavic and Finno-Ugrian tribes that populated regions between the Baltic and the Black Seas. In the 11th and 12th centuries, when Kyiv, Novgorod, Chernihiv, Starai Ladoga, and others were major merchant cities, and Kyiv itself was the religious and administrative capital, Moscow was just a small fishing village, founded by the prince of Kyiv (Yuri Dolgoruky) as Kyivan Russia expanded northward. The peak of Kyivan Russia was in the 12th century. However, subsequent division of power between branches of royal linage and, most importantly, the Mongols' assault in 1237–1241 had destroyed any degree of unity. The areas that we today regard as Russia (apart from Novgorod) came under the direct control of the Golden Horde, while the areas that we identify as Ukraine and Belarus had come to be dominated by Poland and Lithuania. In the early decades after the Mongol invasion, it was not even clear whether it would be Poland, Novgorod, Vladimir, Tver, or Moscow that would ultimately unify Russian lands and shake off the Mongol yoke.

As discussed extensively in my first book,[25] ultimately it was Moscow that between 1380 and 1477 succeeded and, as a result, emerged as Russia's political, administrative, and religious center. However, it took another several centuries before areas of today's Ukraine and Belarus started to be gradually integrated into the fledgling Russian state, facilitated by the collapse of the Polish Commonwealth and partitions of Poland throughout the 18th and early 19th centuries. Still, some areas of western Ukraine were not integrated into the Soviet Union until the Nazi-Soviet pact of 1939, and others had to wait until 1945. In other words, Ukrainian and Belarus branches were developing separately from the Russian branch for at least three hundred years, and in some cases for up to eight centuries.

This explains significant cultural, linguistic, and political differences between the three branches. To argue that they are one would be equivalent to believing that the Germanic Franks, who defeated the Gauls in the late Roman period, make France a Germanic nation; or that there are no differences between people of Denmark, Norway, and Sweden; or that Austrians are German; or that Canada and Australia are British. Indeed, as Serhii Plokhy, one of the best-known experts on Eastern Europe and Russia-Ukraine in particular, highlighted, "It was the Kyivan myth of origins that became the cornerstone of Muscovy's ideology as the polity evolved from a Mongol dependency to a sovereign state and the empire." And this had serious implications, as ruling dynasties and people at large could no longer divorce themselves from that founding myth, and as a result, "Russia today has an enormous difficulty in reconciling the mental maps of Russian ethnicity, culture, and identity with the political map of the Russian Federation."[26]

This is not an unusual post-imperial syndrome that countries like Britain or France had to go through (and indeed still do, with the Brexit being one such manifestation), except it seems far more poisonous and too deeply ingrained in the popular psyche. If one were to ask ordinary Russians whether Ukrainians or Belarus were their friends, relatives, cousins, and uncles, the answer would be in the affirmative. If one were then to follow up and ask whether Ukraine or Belarus should be allowed to become enemies or drift too far away from Russia, the answer would likely be strongly in the negative. Though it is doubtful that ordinary Russians ever truly supported the war (despite official and semi-official surveys claiming otherwise; people are conditioned to answer questions the way they are "expected to"), it was always going to be hard to reconcile their views of close kinship with the desire of most Ukrainians and the Belarus people to be treated as independent nations and their will (in large part due to their differentiated history) to be closer to the West.

While the US public is almost as anti-Russia (despite recent Republican resistance to renew US military support for Ukraine) as it is anti-China, the shift in the European views over the last several years (and especially in the wake of the war) has been nothing short of profound. Most nations seem to be determined to disconnect from Russia (with few notable exceptions, like Austria, Hungary, or Bulgaria), including permanently eliminating the region's dependence on Russia's energy supply. It is interesting that in the recent ECFR survey (2022), around 18–20 percent of surveyed people were prepared to cut all ties with Russia, even if the Ukraine war ended tomorrow, with some countries (e.g., Poland, Sweden, and Denmark) being even more robustly anti-Russian. At the same time, in Germany, which traditionally had the deepest historical ties with Russia, it appears that only around 25 percent of responders would favor a full restoration of the relationship.

Figure 47. Europe-Russia Relationship After the War

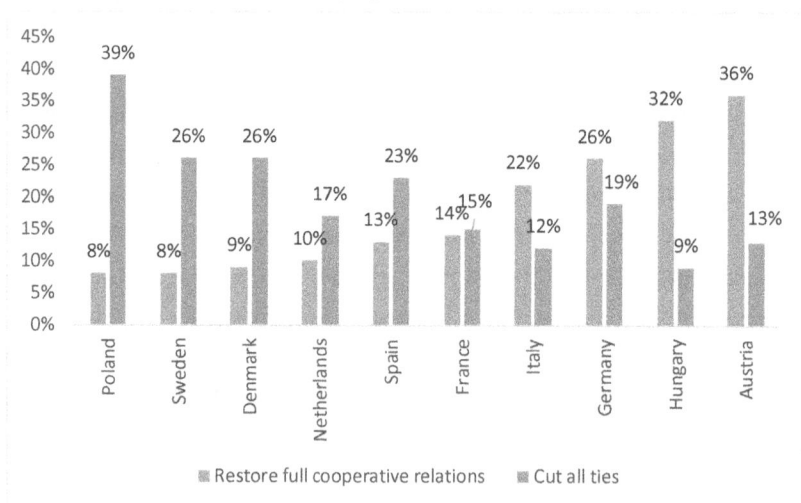

Source: ECFR

There are no obvious solutions: what Russia wants, Ukraine cannot willingly accept, and what Ukraine wants, Russia can never willingly concede to. The same linkage is clearly obvious in the way China treats Taiwan. Just like most Russians do not fully recognize the independence of Ukraine or Belarus, so China cannot accept even a partial independence of Taiwan under a similar rubric: "We are the same people." There are no obvious or easy answers, especially as Xi Jinping has consistently highlighted that the resolution of the "Taiwan problem" cannot be delayed to the next generation. The conflict is of course much wider than just Ukraine and Taiwan, and embraces the entire gambit of political, economic, and geopolitical issues, or as Vladimir Putin put it, "The historical period of the West's undivided dominance over world affairs is coming to an end…we are standing at a historical frontier: ahead is probably the most dangerous, unpredictable, and at the same time, important decade since the World War II."[27] The entire thrust of China's and Russia's economic, political, and social policies cannot be fully, or even partially, reconciled with the existing global order and Western societal norms.

While there are significant differences between China and Russia, and their interests are not identical (offering a narrow window for diplomacy), there is far more that unites China and Russia than what divides them. Both believe in the leading role of the state and the subordination of individuals and the private sector to the directive of the state, in service of what it judges to be the best interests of society as a whole. Both subscribe to the concept of absolute national sovereignty and a constrained sovereignty for their smaller neighbors, and both aim to resurrect spheres of influence and insist on these being recognized and respected by the global community. Both want to redefine human rights while subjecting information flows (such as news and Internet) to strict state control. Neither have independent and impersonal judiciary or institutions of state. I view both countries, as well as large portions of Central and South Asia and the Middle East (such as Iran, Afghanistan, Turkmenistan, Myanmar, and to some extent even Pakistan and parts of Africa) as belonging to the same "church," singing from the same "hymn book" and sharing the same "grievances." Hence, it is likely that most of these nations will continue to have each other's backs and cooperate across a range of spheres that overlap to a far greater extent than with the broadly defined West.

Similarly, while there are differences between what I regard as the twin pillars of the Western order (i.e., the Anglosphere and the EU), both are ultimately permeated by Western culture and societal values, including human rights, the role of the state versus non-state actors, the importance attributable to impersonal judiciary, as well as independent institutions of state, free press, democratic election processes, and rules-based order. Although no nation is perfect, and as described above, the last decade has witnessed considerable backsliding across most Western nations, there is a strong core that still unites nations as diverse as the US, Britain, Germany, Japan, France, Italy, the Netherlands, Spain, Australia, and Canada.

· · ·

Today, as in the 1930s, there are numerous hot spots with a potential for conflict, fueled by similar preconditions: secular economic stagnation, disruptive technological changes, demographics, financial instability, extreme inequalities (within and between states), rise of new powers, and, most importantly, lack of consensus as to acceptable social, political, and economic models subscribed to by most of the world. The Fujiwara effect ensures that for years (possibly decades) to come, people within countries will be moving in different directions and at different speeds; the same will be true for countries and blocks, ensuring a festering pain of domestic polarization as well as geopolitical conflicts.

Hence, the question that the next chapter attempts to address is not whether conflicts can be avoided (by now, proliferating conflicts should be taken for granted), rather where they are likely to occur, the severity of outbreaks, and the likely impact: political, societal, and economic.

Chapter 9

FACING COLD, HOT, OR HUNGRY WAR?

*"It follows that it was not very remarkable action or contrary to common practice
of mankind, if we did accept an empire that was offered to us and refused to give
it up under pressure of three strongest motives: fear, honor, and interest."*
Thucydides on reasons for the Athenian-Sparta rivalry

As discussed previously, the global neoliberal consensus of the 1980s–2000s broke down following the Global Financial Crisis, but the new consensus has not yet emerged and might not solidify for at least another decade and possibly later. In the meantime, chaos and confrontations are likely to remain the norm rather than exception. The question is whether the nature and destructive power of these conflicts will be akin to hot wars (such as the Napoleonic War, the Great War, or World War II) or something resembling a Cold War à la 1950s–70s. As in the 1930s, one can even identify regions where conflicts are likely to break out. A *ring of fire* runs through the bloodlands of Ukraine and Belarus, then winds down toward the Balkans (especially Serbia), snaking across the broadly defined Middle East and Central Asia, rising toward the Himalayas, then dropping to the South China Sea and Taiwan, and finally traveling north toward the Korean peninsula. There is no doubt that there will also be conflicts in other parts of the world (such as Africa or Latin America), however, it is unlikely that any of them will be globally systemic.

Political science has a concept of "enduring rivals" or nations that identify themselves as near equals, viewing each other as long-term rivals. In different eras, Romans were confronting the Carthaginians and Persians, Ottomans were fighting the Habsburgs, British were confronting the French, Germans were competing against the French and British, while the Soviets battled Americans. Decades ago, China identified the US as its primary rival, and the US more recently reciprocated. According to political scientists, even though such durable rivals represent a small fraction of states, in the past, up to 80 percent of all wars were between such pairs, and at least 90 percent of major rivalries ended with a shock to the global system (e.g., the rise of Islam and the collapse of Communism).[1] This of course, became known as the Thucydides Trap, named after one of the fathers of history who believed that "Fear, Honor, and Interest" have always been the key drivers of geopolitical competition. In other words, when one nation's search for honor tramples on another nation's interest, conflicts are inevitable; it becomes only a matter of time and a question of what form these will take.

However, history teaches us that while conflicts are frequently unavoidable, they can take different forms and yield radically different outcomes, and while all are suboptimum, some are better than others. Rivalry can lead to utter destruction (e.g., Carthage, Germany, Japan); it can result in an economic collapse but fall short of destruction (e.g., the Soviet Union); or it can morph into a Cold War with persistent confrontation mostly fought by proxies, as in the 1950s–70s. At another extreme, rivalries might lead to a rise of another power or some form of global calamity that threatens to overwhelm them both, encouraging rivals to cooperate (e.g. US-China rapprochement in the 1970s–80s and British-French accords). Final outcomes are never predetermined, but as conflicts become inevitable, nations feel the need to prepare for the worst, and hence, Xi's frequent calls for self-sufficiency and the US State Department's emphasis on isolating and relocating sensitive supply chains and materials.

Today, political scientists and policymakers are struggling to clarify the emerging relationship between the China-led Illiberal Eurasia and the West, with ill-defined statements of "de-coupling" and "de-risking" proliferating with irreconcilable differences between these filling pages in the financial press. The bottom line is that no one can realistically decouple from China. It remains the world's second largest economy, the world's largest trader, and an integral part of almost every supply chain. However, inability to decouple does not imply the lack of ability to gradually and carefully "grind" China out of the Western economic, financial, and trading systems. It will take time (a decade or longer) but ultimately, the flow of goods, services, people, ideas, information, and capital between blocks is likely to diminish while strengthening and broadening within blocks. Although China insists that it is against de-coupling, many of its own recent policies (such as national security legislations, militarization, insistence on the localization of key technologies and supply chains) encourage and facilitate such decoupling and self-sufficiency. In my view, it is an unstoppable process, until the mindset and policies of either China or the West change.

Therefore, most of the required ingredients for something resembling a cold war (or walking a tightrope of constraining and degrading one's opponent without causing a hot war) are already in place. As George Kennan argued in his famous 1946 Long (X) Telegram from the US Embassy in Moscow, "Gauged against the Western World as a whole, Soviets are still by far the weaker force. Thus, their success will really depend on the degree of cohesion, firmness, and vigor which the Western World can master. And this is a factor within our power to influence…much depends on health and vigor of our own society…we must formulate and put forward for other nations a much more positive and constructive picture of the world we would like to see…we should be better able than Russians to give them this. And unless we do, Russians certainly will."[2] Despite Kennan's mercurial nature and frequently contradictory views, this has become the essence of the containment policy that the US and the broader West maintained against the Soviets.

As in Kennan's time, today, the broadly defined West maintains a significant and, in many ways, overwhelming superiority in most key economic, technological, and military spheres. In figure 48, I have summarized some key statistics. Although the West only houses 13 percent of the world's population, it is responsible for 56 percent of global GDP (at market prices). The West also controls almost 70 percent of global R&D and as much as 85 percent of basic or fundamental research, while its military spending (driven mostly by the US) captures over 60 percent of the total. The West also has more than a 52 percent share of global trade (exports plus imports). In terms of triadic patent families, the West houses over 80 percent of all global patents and completely dominates newer areas of biotechnology, life sciences, new materials, advanced computer, and chip technologies.

Despite persistent headlines about the sunsetting of the USD as the global currency and the medium of exchange and value, nothing could be further from the truth. Although over the last decade the USD share has declined somewhat, it still accounts for around 60 percent of global foreign exchange reserves (with the Euro, Yen, and Pound adding a further 30 percent). According to the Bank of International Settlement (BIS), USD's share of global foreign exchange turnover is 88 percent (or in other words, it is on one side of almost all transactions), and the USD, Euro, Pound, and Yen account for almost three-quarters of SWIFT transactions. At the same time, Western settlement system (CHIPS) is around 30 times larger than China's version (CIPS). The West remains dominant across the entire range of capital market instruments.

Depending on how one defines the Sinosphere and/or Illiberal Eurasia, its share of global GDP is closer to 20–25 percent (or less than half of the West), and it is responsible for not much more than 25 percent of global R&D and, at best, only 10 percent of fundamental research. Although China is now the world's second largest R&D spender, and it has created highly innovative products, the nation has thus far contributed very little to the global pool of knowledge, as reflected in its much lower share of fundamental R&D as well as an almost complete absence of China in Nobel Prize categories across all sciences. This explains the ease with which both the Trump and Biden administrations have managed to undercut China's technology giants and chips progress. While China's military budgets are a national secret, and, therefore, one needs to rely on estimates provided by international consultants, it is unlikely that the Sinosphere captures more than 20–25 percent of global military spending.

In terms of capital markets, the internationalization of China's currency (Rmb) is progressing at a slow pace, hampered by lack of convertibility, limited liquidity, and the fact that China benefits from trade surpluses. China, therefore, has a constrained capacity to place sufficient amounts of its own currency into foreign hands. China's currency only captures around 4-5 percent of SWIFT transactions and has less than 5 percent of global foreign exchange reserves, while its share of foreign exchange transactions is below 10 percent. As far as other Illiberal Eurasian currencies are concerned, most are either non-convertible, sanctioned, or, for all practical purposes, invisible. No matter how one cuts the numbers, the weight of a broadly defined Sinosphere or Illiberal Eurasia is less than half of an equally broadly defined West.

Figure 48. West vs. the Rest (US$ billion), 2021–2022

	GDP (US$ bn)	Population (m)	R&D Spending (US$ bn)	Military Spending (US$ bn)
US	25,463	333	721	877
EU	16,641	448	453	258
Japan	4,231	125	174	46
UK	3,071	67	56	69
Canada	2,140	39	30	27
Australia	1,675	26	22	33
Korea	1,665	52	113	46
NZ	247	5	3	3
Other (Swiss, Norway, Israel)	1,909	24	57	42
Broadly Defined West	**57,043**	**1,119**	**1,629**	**1,401**
China	17,963	1,412	583	300
Russia	2,240	144	45	91
Iran	389	89	3	7
Pakistan	377	236	1	10
Central Asia	316	78	1	4
Afghanistan	145	47	N/A	N/A
Belarus	73	9	0	1
Myanmar	59	54	0	2
North Korea	50	26	N/A	N/A
Sinosphere & Illiberal Eurasia	**21,612**	**2,094**	**633**	**415**
India	3,385	1,417	35	82
Brazil	1,920	215	19	20
Indonesia	1,319	276	4	9
Saudi Arabia	1,108	36	5	75
Turkey	906	85	24	11
South Africa	406	60	3	3
Other	12,863	2,649	1	191
Other	**21,907**	**4,738**	**91**	**391**
World	**100,562**	**7,951**	**2,352**	**2,207**

Source: World Bank, OECD

Figure 49. West vs. the Rest, Currency and Financial Markets (%), Q2 2023

	FX Reserves	FX Turnover (%)*	SWIFT Share (%)
US	60%	88%	47%
Other	35%	90%	38%
West	95%	178%	85%
Sinosphere	4%	10%	9%
Other	1%	12%	6%
* Adds up to 200%			

Source: Swift, BIS

Figure 50. Basic or Fundamental Research (% Global Share), 2019

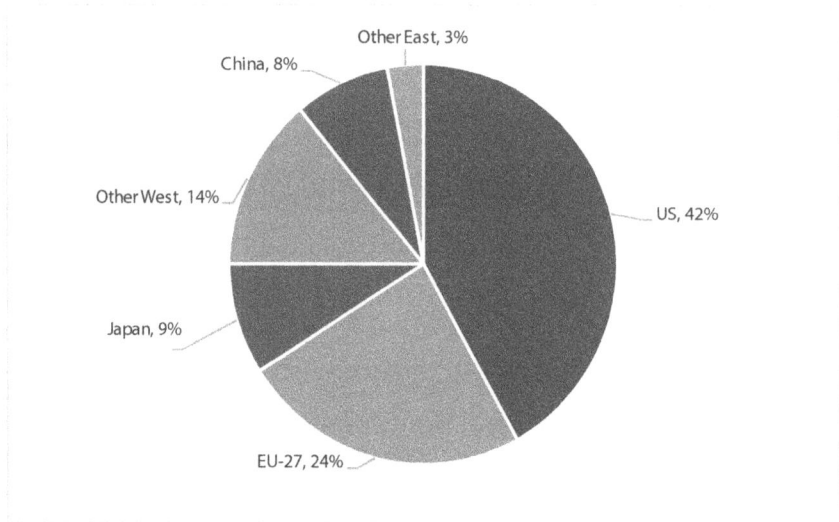

Source: OECD

More recently, however, there has been a growing debate as to whether China and Russia might in fact lead a much wider non-Western world, including nations across Africa, Latin America, and Asia, collectively known as the Global South. These views were considerably boosted in August 2023 when BRICS—a loose grouping that includes Brazil, Russia, India,

China, and South Africa—was expanded by adding Iran, Argentina, Egypt, Ethiopia, Saudi Arabia, and the UAE.[3] There are a number of other less developed countries also interested in joining. Will this expansion make a difference? The answer is probably no. The original BRICS has never been a coherent grouping, and now the expanded BRICS is becoming an even more heterogeneous and unwieldy club, with members having almost nothing in common. It includes some of the world's largest (though imperfect) democracies (such as India and Brazil), authoritarian regimes (China, Egypt, and Russia), a theocratic state (Iran), and outright monarchies (Saudi Arabia and the UAE). Economically, they range from nuclear petrostates (Russia and Iran) and some of the most successful global exporters (China) to sanctioned economies (Iran) and recidivist debt defaulters (Argentina). None have fully developed transparent regulatory and judicial systems or impartial institutions of state. Militarily, some are totally dependent on Western (mostly US) support, while others are in a near hermit state. It is hard to see how this grouping could agree on anything useful other than relatively empty slogans arising out of their genuine fear and distrust of the West.

What motivates this coalescing of interest? As the father of history knew more than 2,500 years ago: "Fear, Honor, and Interest." Similar to the Soviet Union, which in the 1950s–70s sponsored and supported Non-Alignment Movement, the logic behind these strategies is that any nation (however small) that moves from one side of the ledger to another weakens the principal rival and provides an extra backing in building a global order more in tune with the Soviet's and, today, China's policies. Eventually, the Soviet plan failed, and the Kremlin leadership was forced to recognize that the entire exercise was a monumental waste of time and resources, yielding little in return. Still, proxy fights and attempts to redraw global rules remained for decades the essence of Soviet diplomacy. It is likely that China is destined to learn as the Soviets did that such broadening seldom yields the desired outcomes.

Perhaps even more importantly, the most viable (economically and militarily) parts of the broader Global South (such as India, Brazil, Turkey,

Indonesia, or South Africa) have very little in common with either China or Russia, and neither their interests nor their views of the world coincide with those of China or Russia. Essentially, these larger nations are what can be best described as "too small to be big, and too big to be small." Therefore, they do not fit neatly into any grouping, but neither do they have sufficient strength to take an independent stance. Instead, they are trying their best to "play" both sides of the fence, with each camp courting them and offering greater latitude and strategic space than otherwise would have been possible. These nations also have their own trade protection and industrial policies which are in conflict with China's need to export its domestic excess capacity. At a time when there is no globally accepted consensus of the appropriate global rules and standards, China and Russia are trying to offer an alternative. However, outside extremes and near-hermit states (such as North Korea, Iran, or Afghanistan), it is unlikely that they will find a meaningful number of genuine converts.

But the fact that there is such a considerable gap in economic, technological, military and "soft power" capabilities between the West and Illiberal Eurasia does not preclude a cold war morphing into a much more disruptive hot war. After all, the Axis Powers in World War II were on paper much weaker than the opposite side. As Kennan highlighted, the answer critically depends on the degree of cohesion and determination that either block is capable of mastering. What is the difference between hot and cold wars, and when will we know that one might be morphing into another?

• • •

Hot wars are by their nature highly destructive and deadly, massively disrupting global demand and supply curves while causing unprecedented shifts in state policies and fiscal spending.

The experience of the First and Second World Wars indicate that the death rate in intense hot conflicts—ones which spread globally and directly involve key protagonists—could be as high as 200 per 100,000 people. However, cold wars (mostly fought via proxies and not globalized) tend to have death rates of closer to 5 to 7 per 100,000. At the other extreme, during the extended period of peace dividend (following the collapse of the Soviet Union until the Global Financial crisis, between 1990 and 2010), death rates dropped to as little as 1 per 100,000.[4] Over the last several years (due mostly to the Ukraine-Russia and Israel-Hamas Wars as well as conflicts in Syria and Yemen),[5] the ratio has already picked up toward 3 per 100,000. Similarly, if one examines military spending, the last decade witnessed a steady rise to more than 2 percent of global GDP (or US$2.3 trillion), and in the case of the US, defense spending rose toward 3.5 percent. This compares to Cold War spending in the 1950s–80s that was closer to 5–6 percent. However, during the Great War, US military spending rose from less than 1 percent to 15 percent of GDP, and during World War II, it peaked at almost 40 percent. For a number of direct combatants (such as Britain, Germany, and Japan), military spending rose to as high as 80 percent of GDP.

It is, therefore, critical to determine what type of conflicts nations and economies are likely to face. At this juncture it seems more likely that current conflicts will persist for years (possibly decades) but closer resemble the Cold War of 1950s–70s rather than a series of hot global conflicts. Although the distinction is highly fluid, outcomes will be driven by the cohesion of opposing camps and the degree to which one protagonist weakens and thus decides to either preempt stronger rivals or relieve domestic pressures by embarking on wars of honor. In 1910–14, the prevailing feeling among German military strategists was that in years to come, the opposite camp would grow much stronger. This accelerated preparations for the war, turning what at the time were numerous smaller conflicts in the Balkans and the Middle East into a much wider than anticipated war. Similarly, an injury to the honor and pride of the nation inflicted on Germany following the Treaty of Versailles (including a partial loss of sovereignty and crushing reparations) made the Second World War a highly probable event.

Three key developments need to be monitored to determine whether an extended cold war of the 2020s–30s could morph into a much more direct confrontation: (a) the relative economic and military position of the US versus China (with both excessive strength and weakness signaling danger), (b) the future of the remnants of the Russian colonial empire, and (c) the degree of cohesion that the United States will be able to master. In addition, immigration and demographic upheavals have the potential to significantly alter the equilibrium.

• • •

Not long ago, economists, commentators, and investment banks were competing on who would be the most accurate in predicting how quickly China overtakes the US and becomes the world's largest economy. However, by the end of 2022, the ground started to shift with recognition not only that China might never overtake the US (at least not on market prices), but also that it is starting to lose ground against other nations, such as India. While the immediate reason for this change of views was the inability of China to fully recover from the extreme COVID-19 restrictions imposed by the government over the previous three years, there is also a growing realization that China's political and policy frameworks have undergone such a major shift that they could retard long-term growth while considerably raising risk premia.

As discussed above, these changes predate the Xi administration by at least several years and can be traced to the shock of the Global Financial Crisis. However, over the last decade, the pace of change has meaningfully accelerated with the elimination of Deng's principles of the separation of the party (CCP) from the state and bureaucracy and the full subordination of the private sector to the state-led social and political agenda being the main differences compared with a prior epoch. While many of the societal challenges that China is trying to address (such as the role of digital media, pollution, unaffordable housing, education, medical care, and extreme wealth inequalities) are not dissimilar to what the US and other Western nations are grappling with, the difference is the high degree of concentration of economic and political power in China. Unlike the US or the EU, China does not have an independent and impartial judicial system, neither does it have any meaningful freedom of press or speech. Also, unlike the US, where power is widely dispersed between the federal, state, and local governments as well as between the executive, legislative, and judicial branches, China exercises a unitary top-down form of governance with no meaningful checks on the raw exercise of power. Although during the extended period of "collective leadership" (between the early 1980s and 2012), there was a window of opportunity to openly discuss and debate policies and their impact, under the current Xi administration, that window has been firmly shut.

These shifts are not unusual for communist-led countries that function under what is known as the principle of "democratic centralism," an oxymoron invented in the early 1900s by Vladimir Lenin[6] who tried to work out how the Russian political system (i.e., dictatorship of the proletariat under the guidance of its vanguard, the Communist Party) would function without degenerating into a stagnating dictatorship. Like most made-up ideas that proliferated under both communist and fascist regimes, it ultimately broke down under the weight of its own contradictions. But throughout the 20th century, it had become the core constitutional principle for most communist-led nations, including China. What is "democratic centralism"? The idea is to permit freedom of discussion and debate within the party without any fear of penalties, retribution, or repercussions. This represents the democratic element. However, as soon as the leadership settled on the course of action, there is supposed to be no room for any further disagreement, and everyone is expected to pull together or face potentially highly unpleasant consequences. It is not dissimilar to the way most private corporations actually function, except that the Communist Party has no oversight (market, judicial, or popular), and its decisions are utterly unappealable.

Whether in the Soviet Union, China, Vietnam, or former communist states in eastern Europe, the strength and durability of two parts of the oxymoron varied across time. For example, while Vladimir Lenin was still alive, he fostered the democratic principle. However, when Joesph Stalin came to power, and especially after he strengthened his grip in the

1930s, an extreme form of centralism became the norm. Toward the end of Stalin's life, even the politburo seldom met, and all key decisions were made by Stalin and a small cohort of functionaries around him. Following the death of Stalin and a subsequent period of confusion, under Nikita Khruschev, the democratic principle was encouraged and tolerated, until Leonid Brezhnev reversed the course. Another reversion toward a more democratic and collective style came back under the last Soviet leader (Mikhail Gorbachev). The same has been true of CCP. An initial burst of ideas was extinguished by Mao's authoritarian and dictatorial leadership which after his death led to an extended period of "collective leadership" that over the last decade was once again replaced by an autocratic and centralized Xi administration.

Such highly centralized stages are characterized by the elimination of discussion and debates and an almost complete eradication of alternative views. As a result, nations tend to become less flexible and far less pragmatic with a longer and more unpredictable reaction time to events, whether political or economic. In extreme cases (like Stalin's and Mao's times), the decision-making process becomes akin to the ancients consulting the Oracle, with bureaucracy no longer willing to take an independent stance or initiate any major new policies, unless the Oracle explicitly supports these. In such a system, consequences and penalties for taking initiative could be deadly, not only for the bureaucrat but his entire family.[7] Nothing illustrates these risks better than the description of Moscow's opulent House of Government (where in Stalin's days more than 2,000 senior Party and government officials and their families lived) as a "mortuary." In the 1930s–50s, entire families would frequently and suddenly "disappear" (mostly at night, after a not so gentle knock on the door by the KGB), with children taught never to ask, "What happened to little Ivan, and why I can't play with him anymore?"[8] In my own family, as a little child, I once came across someone who suffered such a terrible fate. In the 1960s, we lived in a small communal flat (i.e., several families sharing facilities like a kitchen and bathroom) with a very pleasant old lady who mostly kept to herself. Later I learned that during Stalin's purges of the army in 1937–38, she was sentenced to ten years in the gulags. After serving time, her sentence was arbitrarily extended, and she was not freed until Khrushchev came to power in the mid-1950s. Her crime: When asked about a certain Soviet general, her answer was that he was a nice man. This was sufficient proof of treachery or at the very least lack of proletarian vigilance against the "enemies of the people" who were supposedly lurking everywhere. As Nikita Khrushchev wrote in his memoirs, "Stalin instilled in us the suspicion that we are all surrounded by enemies." Many of Mao's victims had comparable stories to tell.

Although these authoritarian phases are frequently viewed as times of strength and structural reforms, the reverse is unfortunately true. Instead of strength and endurance they frequently lead to chaos and fragility. While the above discussion focused on communist states and the idea of "democratic centralism," the same process also works in most right-wing dictatorships. The origins of such centralized control-and-command systems can be traced to a familiar concept of "economic and physical insecurity," which in turn triggers what Ronald Inglehart described as an *authoritarian reflex* or reaching out to supposed strong leaders to address people's mounting problems (Chapter Six). Unfortunately, these leaders, instead of solving problems, frequently make them worse and instead of increasing resilience make these nations more fragile.

This is the challenge facing China, potentially threatening to reverse decades of exceptional progress. Over the preceding thirty years, its economy grew rapidly under the influence of four interdependent factors. First, the unleashing of the popular entrepreneurial spirit after centuries of constrained existence. As I discussed in my first book,[9] it is debatable (and unprovable) whether the significant structural changes (political, social, and economic) that were bubbling to the surface in the early part of the 20th century would have ultimately developed into a fully-fledged liberal economy. However, Japan's invasion of Manchuria as well as KMT's kleptocratic policies had made such a transition impossible. Indeed, depending on indicators, China has been in decline from the time of the Zheng He voyages in the early part of the 15th century, with every glimmer of hope quickly extinguished by China's sclerotic social and political environment. This makes three decades from the early 1980s truly unique in China's history—uninterrupted progress fueled by the entrepreneurial energy of the Chinese people. Second, while domestic policies (starting with the agricultural revolution and then progressing to special economic zones) were the critical backbone, China's evolution was boosted by the Baby Boomers' world of globalization and the opening up of trade routes as well as capital flows, which China assiduously courted. And with trade and capital came greater freedoms, expertise, and technology. The key date in this transition was China's ascent to the World Trade Organization (WTO) in 2001. Third, until a decade ago, China consistently pursued the policy of separation of the party from bureaucracy and state, making rules more transparent while redefining and eroding the power of state-owned enterprises (SOEs) and fostering a free space for the private sector. The state also experimented with tentative forms of local democracy while strengthening judiciary, at least in simpler commercial cases that did not directly involve the government or the party. In that period, the CCP's cells at an enterprise level atrophied into nothing more than comfortable retirement jobs and social clubs. Fourth, while China had never abandoned the desire to fully retake Taiwan or Hong Kong, it left both untouched, with Deng's view that solutions can wait until the next generation, or even later, remaining dominant. This offered China an opportunity to raise capital in Hong Kong and acquire technology via its relationship with Taiwan.

While not everything was perfect, and China's rapid development also featured a rise in extreme wealth inequalities and pervasive corruption, per capita income increased from less than US$200 in 1980 to around US$10,000 by 2013, moving the country from poverty to middle-income status while capturing as much as 15 percent plus of global GDP and trade. In other words, China progressed from being nothing more than a rounding error to the world's second largest economy and the world's greatest trader. Over three decades, China tapped into what, at the time, was perceived to be an almost unlimited pool of cheap labor which when combined with an accelerating capital intensity, urbanization, and higher productivity, created what has become known as China's miracle. While the country continued to grow through the early 2020s, the pace markedly slowed, and, more importantly, risk premia that investors and corporations started to demand from China significantly increased.

Although this is not the book to explore in-depth economic challenges facing China, it is important to highlight how these might have an impact on the topic at hand—geopolitical tensions and the potential for transition from cold to hot conflicts. In a nutshell, after decades of powering global growth, China is unlikely to ever play such a dominant role again. Instead, it is more likely that China is entering an extended period broadly comparable to a 1990s Japan-style stagnation, with much shallower than in the past nominal and real growth rates. When in late 2023, IMF reduced China's long-term (beyond 2027) growth trajectory from 5 percent to 3.5 percent, it was viewed by many as too negative. The opposite might be true, as China's position is far more complex when compared to Japan's decades of malaise, potentially leading to an even sharper and longer contraction.

First, as with Japan of 1990s–2000s, the main source of China's problems lies in its gigantic misallocation of capital. In the case of Japan, through 1970s–80s, the high national saving rates and the Plaza Accord drove exceptionally high investment rates that were over time misallocated from productive to unproductive uses (mostly real estate and financial speculation). The single most important issue facing China is also its persistently high national saving rates (45 percent of GDP). As an accounting identity, there are only two ways of handling it: either China needs to raise consumption, and therefore lower saving rates, or it must invest and export. However, there are strong cultural, historic, and economic reasons why China is encountering difficulties in lowering saving rates. These include lack of viable, equitable and comprehensive social and healthcare services (despite recent improvements), extreme reliance on real estate to support household balance sheets, limited alternative investable opportunities, and, perhaps most importantly, a growing and stifling state dominance in setting growth targets while steering corporate investments into sectors that the government prioritizes.

As a result, China has been consistently investing well over 40 percent of GDP, which currently amounts to as much as US$9–10 trillion per annum (more than 30 percent of the world's total) or double Japan's entire GDP. Such a rapid pace of investment compressed into a short timeframe has inevitably led to misallocation of resources (especially in real estate and infrastructure). In order to appreciate the pace and depth of the investment spree, one can look at the IMF estimates of total capital stock. In 2004, China's was woefully short of capital, with total stock of around US$4 trillion or only $3,000 per capita, compared to the capital stock of the US at the time of US$26 trillion or US$93,000 per capita. However, by 2019 China had already bypassed the US with capital stock of US$53 trillion versus US$47 trillion for the US, and on the current path, by 2028, China will likely have capital stock of more than US$105 trillion when compared to around US$75 trillion in the US. Although on a per capita basis, this will still be less than the US, China is a much poorer nation, and capital stock would at that point represent around 4 times China's GDP, when compared to closer to 2 times GDP for the US.

Are there signs of capital misallocation? Definitely. Apart from empty towers, more than 2 billion square meters of empty residential flats, and fast trains to nowhere, the last decade witnessed a steep rise in incremental capital output ratios (i.e., how much investment is needed to generate an incremental unit of GDP) as well as steep declines in returns on equity across China's corporate sector (down from the highs of around 20 percent to 9 percent). The declining efficiency capital can be also observed in rapidly rising debt levels (i.e., inefficient capital never generates returns to repay debt), with China earning the distinction of the world's fastest ever accumulator of debt (up from US$3 trillion in 2005 to US$65 trillion in 2023, or from 1.5 to almost 4 times GDP). Similar symptoms were abundantly evident in Japan through the 1980s to early 2000s. For example, Japan's debt burden rose from around 1.5 times GDP in the 1970s to over 4 times in early 1990s (and it is closer to 6 times now), while corporate return on equity slumped from 12–13 percent in the early 1980s to almost zero in the early 2000s. One can also see it in many other indicators (e.g., China, between 2011 and 2013, consumed more steel and cement than the US had in the entire twentieth century).[10]

While China's policymakers understand that overcapacities are getting worse and misallocation of capital is growing (e.g., it is constantly urging provincial governments to constrain excessive investments, especially in narrower and newer industries like EVs, batteries, or solar), there is no way out from the constraints of an accounting identity—excess savings must be invested, further aggravating misallocation of resources and increasing overcapacities, causing and perpetuating strong disinflationary pressures.[11]

Figure 51. China vs. the World, National Saving Rates (% GDP)

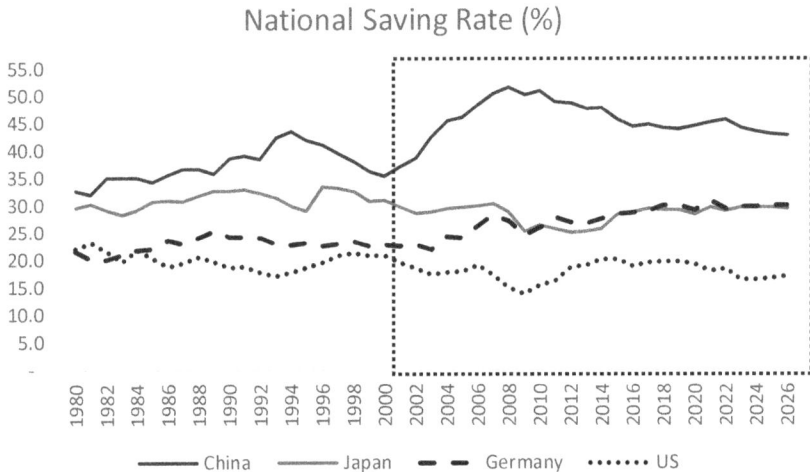

National Saving Rate (%)

Source: IMF, 2023

Figure 52. China vs. the World Investment (% GDP)

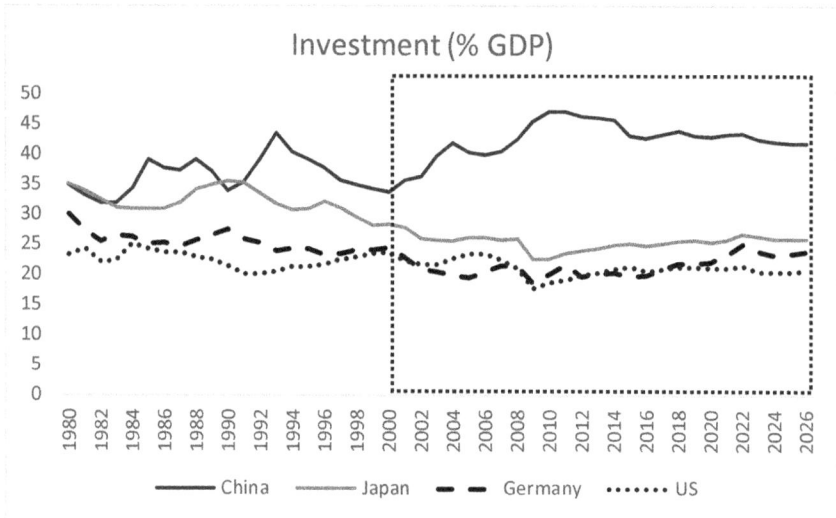

Source: IMF, 2023

Figure 53. China vs. the World, Stock of Capital (US$ trillion)

	2004	2010	2019	2028E
China	4	14	53	107
US	26	36	49	74
Japan	19	23	18	20
India	1	3	6	15
Germany	8	9	10	14
France	6	8	8	10
Korea	2	3	5	8
UK	5	6	6	8
Italy	5	6	6	6
Indonesia	1	2	3	6

Source: IMF, 2023

The second challenge facing China is that its misguided policy of population control between 1979 and 2015 (i.e., the one-child policy) is now resulting in an accelerated population ageing, with the labor force starting to contract (not dissimilar to what Japan has been facing since the late 1990s). The demographic dividend that China enjoyed for three decades is now rapidly reversing. Even if one adjusts for the quality of human capital, there is unlikely to be any meaningful labor contribution in the years (or even decades) ahead. Although, as discussed above, technology makes demographics a less relevant factor, it is still a headwind.

The third challenge is that not only is efficiency of capital utilization dropping and China is unable to add labor, the economy has also been delivering low and erratic multi-factor, or Total Factor, productivity. In an absolute sense, China's labor productivity is only around 25 percent of the US's, one-third of Germany's, and less than half of Japan's, while multi-factor productivity (after contribution of labor and capital) has been stagnating despite China's recent push into various technology niches, from solar panels and EVs to batteries and robotics. As can be seen below, almost all of China's GDP growth rates were due to capital deployment, which is now becoming a negative factor.

Thus, it appears that unless China embarks on a significant policy paradigm shift, growth rates might continue to erode, potentially below IMF's recently lowered long-term 3.5 percent target. As with Japan of the 1990s–2000s, overcapacities (in some instances as much as three-to-five times global demand) will likely generate strong disinflationary pressures, even further lowering nominal GDP growth rates. The only rational answer includes delegating more decisions to individuals and businesses and actively encouraging consumption by writing checks to households, strengthening social nets, creating a "no limits" resolution trust for its troubled real estate sector (around 25 percent of GDP) and moderately widening free private sector space. At this stage, there is limited evidence that China is willing to entertain such choices, primarily because these would lead to a reduction in state and party control over the economy and society, and because of the focus of Marxist economics on *productive forces* and *productive capital* that places an overly strong emphasis on supply rather than consumption and finance. Indeed, more in line with classical economists (such as Francois Quesnay, Adam Smith, David Ricardo), China and Marxists pay far too much attention to what are perceived to be value generating sectors while harshly penalizing those they regard as either rearranging or capturing other people's value, with finance and capital markets in particular treated as mostly "value capturing" activities. Although, as described throughout this book, excessive financialization of the last four decades had many toxic consequences, and the obsessive preoccupation with market prices by neoliberals led to devastating outcomes in the West (Chapter Four), the opposite tilt of assuming that finance and capital are intrinsically evil while understating importance of consumption, results in equally bad outcomes.

This leaves China with only one other option—export surpluses and excess capacities at discounted prices to other countries (mostly the US, the UK, Japan, and the EU). Unfortunately, China's concurrent attempts to remake global rules to be more in line with its own system creates impediments to such a flow of trade. Over the last twelve months, there were already numerous examples of both the EU and the US either putting up barriers or threatening to contain China's ability to export its rapidly growing excess capacity. As Jay Shambaugh, the US Under Secretary of International Affairs, recently stated, "We are worried that Chinese industrial support policies that are more focused on supply rather than... demand...[we] are careening toward a situation where overcapacity in China...is going to wind up hitting world markets."[12] Similarly, Janet Yellen, US Secretary of the Treasury, has been recently warning China to avoid dumping state-sponsored and subsidized products. This is in addition to the EU anti-dumping probe into China's electric car industry which was launched in September 2023 and debates regarding a possibility of similar actions against China's solar energy industry. In the past (under the Bill Clinton or George W. Bush administrations in the US or under Angela Merkel in Germany), the priority was to integrate China into the global order, and hence, issues like China's aggressive state industrial policies or forced technology transfers, were deliberately underplayed. Today, the attitude is radically different.

It feels like a "Catch 22," with no easy answers. Indeed, China's position might be more problematic than that of Japan's lost decades. First, when Japan was hit by the collapse of the asset bubble in 1990, it was already a wealthy and highly homogeneous society with egalitarian wealth distribution (comparable to Denmark). On the other hand, China's slowdown is occurring when it is only a middle-income economy with a highly heterogeneous society and wealth distribution comparable to Brazil. Second, Japan in 1990 was looking forward to two decades of rapid global growth, underwritten by financialization of the US and reemergence of China itself. Hence, it could settle for a strategy of stability and maintenance of the relative standard of living by riding global growth waves. Unfortunately for China, I believe that the next decade or two would feature much more constrained global growth rates, and, quite possibly, a prolonged secular stagnation. Third, although the government agencies in Japan had always exercised a considerable degree of sway over the private sector, it never had anything like the intensity of China, where there is no independent central bank, commercial banks are not commercial, and the private sector is not truly or conventionally private. Finally, Japan was a fully paid-up member of the Western-led global order, while China is trying to remake the world. Hence, through capital, trade, skilling, and technology restrictions, China is likely to face a higher investment risk premia as well as a tougher road to the exporting of its products.[13]

George Magnus, a research associate of Oxford University's China Center, summarized well the challenges facing China, "The country is suffering from slowing economic growth, stagnating productivity, a malfunctioning property sector, the misallocation and inefficient use of capital, debt-capacity constraints, and weak household income and demand."[14] There are solutions but all are highly complex, and will take time, and will be difficult to implement without considerable economic, political, and institutional changes.

Figure 54. China, Economic Growth Drivers, 1990–2023 (%)

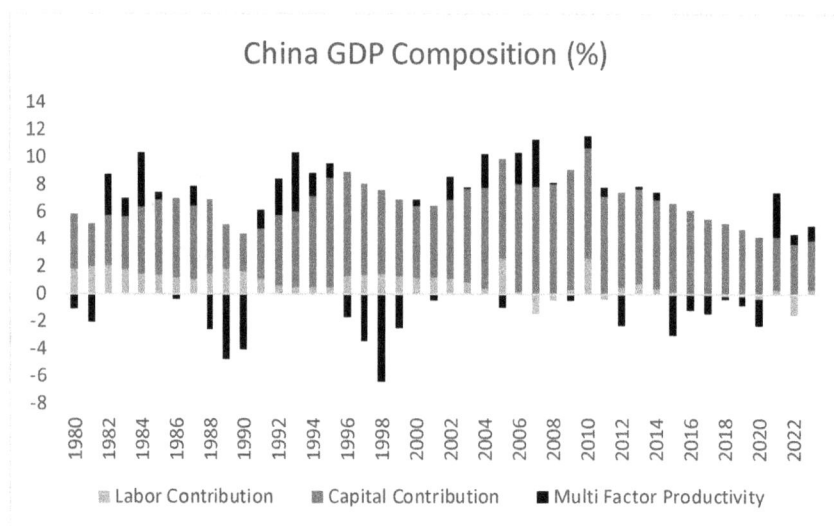

China GDP Composition (%)

Source: Total Economic Database, December 2023

However, unlike Japan, which in 1990 operated an open capital account and had a fully convertible currency, China today operates a "walled garden" (i.e., closed capital account and non-convertible currency) and, therefore, is unlikely to suffer from an instantaneous collapse. Rather, it is likely to face growing headwinds. It is therefore conceivable that as global tensions grow, economy slows, and domestic social tensions rise, China might need to contemplate a significant policy pivot, similar to what occurred in November 2022 when China suddenly and chaotically abandoned harsh COVID-19 restrictions. How China pivots would determine its long-term growth trajectory, risk premia, as well as the country's role in the global cold or hot conflicts. The greater the disparity (strength or weakness) between China and the West, the more likely the conflict would progress toward the hotter end of the spectrum.

• • •

What about Russia? Arguably, the best and the most prescient description of Russia was provided by the *Economist* magazine during the Crimean War in 1854 when editors argued that Russia's vast empire is in a "great measure composed of spoils which she has torn from surrounding nations…her frontier provinces are filled with injured, disoriented hostile populations…many of whom wait, with patience and desire, the blessed day of emancipation and revenge." Despite Putin's frequent references to Western colonialism, Russia remains the world's largest surviving colonial empire. Although it lost around 20 percent of the territory in the 1990s, the rump still includes over two hundred nations and one hundred distinct linguistic groups that have little or nothing in common with either East Slavic languages or the Orthodox religion. The best way to look at Russia is as a mini-Soviet Union-type empire that could be as prone to nationalism and the desire for de-colonization as any other part of the world. National minorities occupy around 40 percent of Russian territory, where most of the country's natural resources are located and constitute over 20 percent of the country's population. Especially troublesome for Russia are autonomous regions around the Volga River and the Caucasus. When the Soviet Union broke up, two of the largest autonomous republics in these areas (Tatarstan and Chechnya) refused to sign the Federation treaty, which led to a protracted Chechnya War. While Chechens are today loyal to Moscow, this could change quickly, as families of current leaders fought Russians as recently as the late 1990s. The same is largely true of many other minorities, from Dagestan to Bashkir, Chuvash to Saha, and Ossetia to Ingushetia.

The country is also beset by deep geographic fault lines. Tellingly, during the Wagner mutiny in June 2023, some of the tanks were splashed with the word "Siberia."[15] This is the largest part of Russia, occupying around 75 percent of the territory, but it is a home to only 32 million people (or 22 per cent of the population of Russia), consisting of ethnic Russians and more than a hundred different tribes—the legacy of the dissolution of the Mongol Golden Horde and Sibir Khanate in the 15th century as well as unequal treaties imposed on Imperial China in the 18th and 19th centuries. Even though ethnic Russians are in the majority, these are fiercely independent people, and Siberia and the Far East were the last regions to finally be brought under Bolshevik control in the early 1920s. Wagner's tank commander was likely fighting not just for Russia but for a greater freedom of Siberia. Though it contains the bulk of Russia's treasure trove of commodities, Siberia has been neglected for centuries. A brief Yeltsin's independence spring of the early 1990s was quickly replaced by the traditional robber baron-style approach to the periphery, with money and resources sucked out to Moscow and St. Petersburg, with very little, if anything, left for the locals.

Given its deeply corrupt and rentier-type economy, it is highly unlikely that Russia would ever reclaim its past strength and economic vitality. Hence, it has to rely mostly on political suppression and an extensive security apparatus to keep the country intact. It is not that ethnic minorities or Siberian Russians necessarily want independence. Rather, the problem is the inability of the highly centralized state that Russia has built and nurtured over the last eight centuries to adapt. The country remains largely a kleptocratic petronuclear state with limited ability to either raise productivity or add incremental labor or capital. Over the last decade, its GDP growth rates averaged less than 1 percent per annum, and it has neither savings nor investment pools to propel growth rates onto a higher plateau. Even adjusting for the purchasing power parity, which significantly flatters Russia's real position, its relative GDP per capita standards continue to stagnate at not much more than 30 percent of the US levels, while at current market prices, GDP per capita is far less at only 15 to 20 percent. Although Russia remains an important supplier of various commodities (from oil and gas to agriculture, copper, and nickel), its share of the global economy has shrunk to not much more than 2 percent, a rounding error when compared to 8–9 percent that Russia commanded during the last years of the Romanoff dynasty (1913).

Despite considerable immigration (mostly from Central Asia and the Caucuses), Russia's working-age population has shrunk from 101 million in the early 2000s to less than 95 million today, and the number of child-bearing women (15 to 45 years old) is down to only 29 million, with birth rates barely above 1.4 live births per woman, significantly below what is needed to just maintain Russia's population. The combination of economic, military, and physical insecurity is perpetuating low birth and high death rates as well as rising emigration (and brain drain), further shrinking Russia's population while limiting its creative potential. UN estimates that by 2050, the country's population might drop to around 130 million people when compared to more than 145 million in 2020. It is worthwhile to recall that at its peak in the 1980s, the Soviet Union had a population of 280 million people. In its most strategically exposed region (Far Eastern Federal District, bordering on China, Japan, and the US), population has already shrunk to less than 8 million people, occupying almost 40 percent of Russia's territory.

Figure 55. Russia, Economic Growth Drivers, 1990–2023 (%)

Source: Total Economic Database, December 2023

Figure 56. Russia and China vs. US (=100%), GDP/Capita (at market prices)

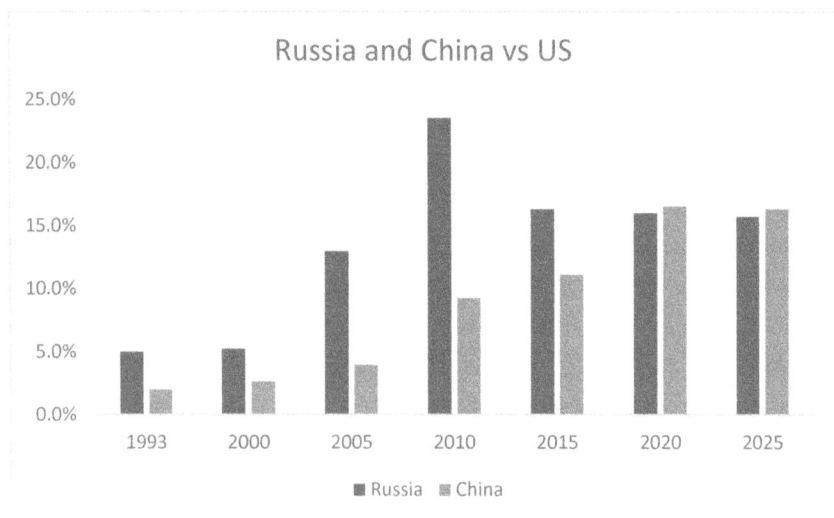

Source: *World Bank, IMF, December 2023*

As described in my first book (written before the war in Ukraine), Russia is likely to remain a "danger to its neighbors as an unsatisfied and sullen but ultimately unsuccessful and deformed giant, eventually morphing into a modern-day equivalent of Mongol warriors in the service of Chinese emperors."[16] Dependence on China is likely to increase as Western sanctions and Russia's inability to clarify its objectives and/or clearly delineate where the East ends and the West begins, draw Russia and its periphery (Belarus and Central Asia) deeper into China's orbit. While this will create frictions and would be highly unwelcome in the Kremlin, there are no other options available to Russia unless the country changes direction as a result of either domestic and/or international disorders.

The greatest fear is that some combination of hot and cold wars, as well as a stagnant economy dominated by military needs, might lead to uncontrollable domestic upheaval and a fracturing of the Russian Federation itself or what Stephen Kotkin described as the disastrous "Russia in chaos" outcome.[17] This would be the nightmare scenario for the world at large, which has thus far been avoided by the deliberate policy of the US (and the broader west) to provide sufficient help to avoid an outright Ukrainian defeat but not enough to truly cripple Russia. US has thus far spent less than 1 percent of its GDP on supporting Ukraine, and this was sufficient to inflict a massive damage on Russia; what would have happened if the spending rose to 2 percent? However, this balancing act, ultimately remains nothing more than a fine judgement call.

•　　•　　•

A hot war is not predestined, but the more China's economy underperforms and the stronger domestic pressures in both China and Russia become, the greater the chance that today's 1930s-style environment could evolve into a far more violent and destructive 1940s rather than a more contained world of the 1950s–70s.

These fractures might get even deeper and broader if, in fact, the other main protagonist (i.e., the US) were to undergo highly disruptive social dislocations. As discussed in Chapter Six, the US today is far more polarized than it was in the late 1960s–70s, and arguably at any time since the 1930s, the 1880s–90s, or the Civil War. Disagreements have now progressed far beyond differences regarding specific policies and prescriptions, and encompass a never-ending array of cultural, racial, and historical disputes. The protagonists no longer socialize with or even marry each other, and neither do they shop in the same shops or listen to the same music or news. Their educational, work, and cultural attributes are diametrically opposite, aggravated by the Baby Boomers' globalization, deindustrialization, and uncontrolled flow of people, goods, products, and money over the previous three decades. As it has always happened in the past, "pain," "grievance," and "ethnic" entrepreneurs are proliferating at a rapid clip, fanning hatred, and insisting on uncompromising answers, blocking the ability of the political system to find common ground to resolve disputes. Republicans increasingly view democrats as immoral, dishonest, lazy, and closed-minded, with democrats largely reciprocating. The two sides resemble members of opposite football teams, where the aim is to hurt the other side, even if everyone is ultimately worse off. One can also compare the current situation to the attributes one finds in religious cults or extremes of communism and fascism, where people believe so strongly in the righteousness of their own views that the opposite side must be morally bankrupt and/or unpatriotic if they don't see the right path. Hence, opponents must be either destroyed or reeducated. This is the primary reason communist states (like the Soviet Union or China) have been operating "re-education" centers while also relying on psychiatry to lock up their opponents (after all, in that world, by definition, anyone who does not see the light must need psychiatric treatment).

As discussed by Barbara Walter,[18] professor at the University of California at San Diego and one of the foremost experts on civil wars, the US is exhibiting a number of disturbing elements that might result in a civil war, as evidenced by recent calls for a "national divorce" as well as academic and popular arguments that the US is in so much trouble, that it requires either a messiah (with many believing that Donald Trump is anointed by God) or some form of dictatorship to right the ship. As Walter highlights, the most dangerous stage is when democracies start to degenerate into various forms of *anocracies* (i.e., democracies in style but not substance) or when tyrannies start transiting toward a democratic rule. In both cases, instabilities become more pronounced, as one section of the population loses power and control while another has not yet decided how to deploy their newly found power. As the Republican Party migrates to the extreme populist end of the spectrum while the Democratic Party proves unable to sell their policies of minority protection, economic supports and welfare state, the middle ground will likely continue to shrink, and each election could become a knife-edge exercise of extreme swings, from left to right and back. While the same uncertainties are visible across most other nations (e.g., recent right-left pendulum swings in Poland, the Netherlands, and Italy), the US is so critical to global equilibrium that a similar volatility would pose a far greater danger to the world.

While the environment is clearly grave, it is comforting to remember that over the last seven decades, there has been no precedence of a country as sophisticated, modern, rich, and democratic as the US having descended into a civil war. It is true that if not for FDR's policies and a great deal of luck, US democracy might not have survived the 1930s. However, while today's societies are polarized, and inequalities are disturbingly high, the level of pain that the US and the world endured in the 1930s was significantly more intense. It should be also kept in mind that power in the US is far more dispersed than in most other parliamentary democracies, split as it is between federal, state, and local governments as well as between legislative, executive, and judicial branches, making it much harder to accumulate dictatorial power. The country still maintains robust and impartial institutions of state while its armed forces are professional and largely apolitical, and bureaucracy is capable of "dragging the chain" (as Donald Trump recognized during his presidency) to avoid implementing destructive decisions.

Thus, it seems somewhat premature to argue that the US could become so paralyzed that it would disintegrate into competing domestic camps, degenerate into a tyranny or even a highly illiberal democracy. Uncertainties are clearly high, but at the current juncture, it seems more likely that China and Russia will go through a great deal more volatility and dislocation while the US, with a bit of luck, just might maintain its coherence (at least relatively), remaining the bulwark against the illiberal tide.

•   •   •

The reason the title of this Chapter included "hungry wars" is because I believe that there is another element that although outside conventional rivalry, could have a significant bearing on the final outcome: the pressures of demographics and immigration from the least and less developed nations.[19]

My first book went to great length to discuss prerequisites for successful states and preconditions for failure; hence, I do not wish to repeat the exercise except to highlight that most of today's least or less developed states (failed ones like Somalia, Niger, Yemen; semi-failed, like the Democratic Republic of the Congo, Nigeria, Lebanon, and Venezuela; or states where either there are no functional institutions or such institutions have been comprehensively hijacked, such as Egypt, Bolivia, Pakistan,

Iraq, Algeria, and Ethiopia)[20] are places that will see the greatest increase in population over the next two to three decades.

The population of sub-Saharan Africa, the least developed region in the world, is projected to have 2.1 billion people by 2050, compared to less than 1.1 billion estimated in 2022. This will include 1.3 billion people of working age (15–64 years old), up from 0.6 billion in 2022. To put it in perspective, this region's share of the global population will increase from less than 14 percent to over 20 percent, while the proportion of the working age cohort will skyrocket from 10 percent of the world's total in 2022 to 19 percent by 2050. The population of Northern Africa and the Middle East will also increase greatly from around 0.5 billion to 0.8 billion people, implying that Africa and the Middle East might within two decades house almost 3 billion people (or the equivalent of the population of the entire world in 1960). This is in addition to a continuing strong growth in Central and South Asia, where the population is expected to grow from 2.1 billion in 2022 to almost 2.6 billion in 2050, with the working age cohort expanding from 1.4 to 1.8 billion people.

Figure 57. Population of Africa, the Middle East, and Central Asia (million)

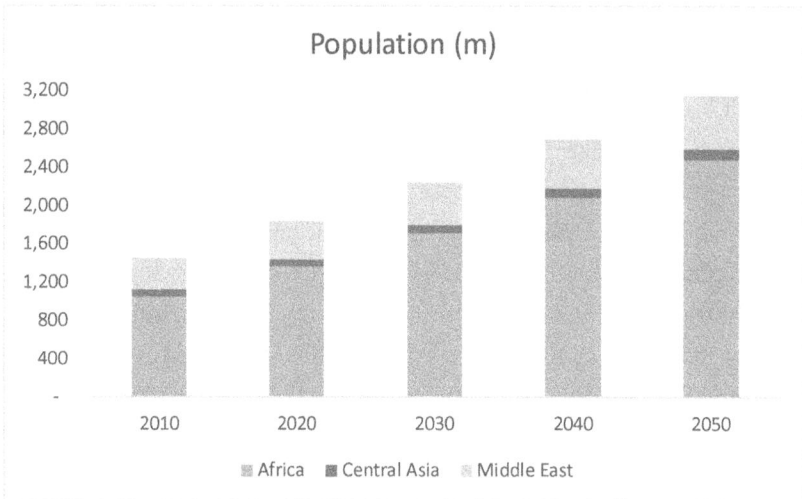

Source: United Nations, December 2023

Unfortunately, these geographical areas are stuck in low productivity, corruption, nepotism, and pre-modern societal relations while also facing a truly unprecedented demographic bulge caused by a collapse in infant mortality (due to the effectiveness and availability of modern medicines) against the backdrop of still high female fertility (as societal norms of how many children a woman is expected to bear change at a far slower pace).[21] The bulge is especially severe in Africa, parts of the Middle East, and South and Central Asia, and according to the UN estimates, the mismatch will not crest until sometime in 2040s. Over the next two decades, less developed economies (excluding China) will likely add up to 1.5 billion people of working age (out of the current global pool of less than 5.5 billion), with no obvious utilization for this surplus labor. As I discussed in my first book, "While in the past, these younger people would have been allowed to 'vegetate' in subsistence agriculture, hunting, and gathering, today, this is no longer a viable option. Even in Africa, illiteracy is rapidly disappearing. Also, modern means of communication inform them of alternative and far more desirable lifestyles elsewhere."[22]

Figure 58. *Change in Working-Age Cohorts (million)*

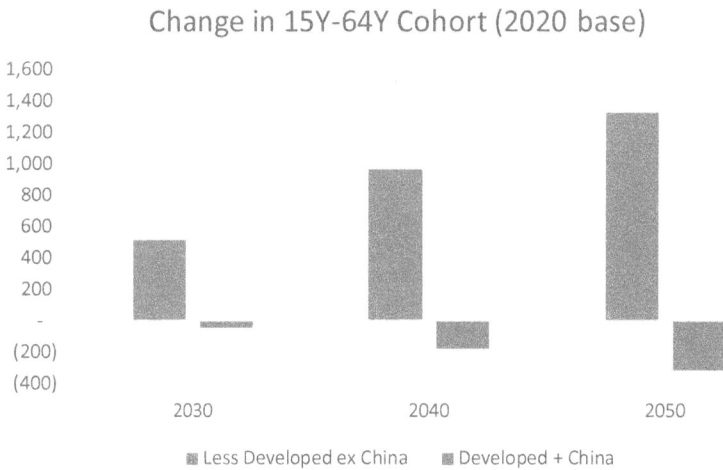

Change in 15Y-64Y Cohort (2020 base)

Source: United Nations, December 2023

The mismatch is also occurring at a time when opportunities for employment in manufacturing and global supply chains are likely to dwindle as the need for cheaper labor diminishes. Even in such labor-intensive industries as textiles, clothing, and footwear, the share of costs allocated to labor has more than halved over the last two decades, while in newer industries, labor is quite often no more than 10 percent of costs, with intangible assets, technology, branding, and new materials dominating. It is likely that over the next decade, the global economy will simply not need these people, even at $1 per hour wages (Chapter Seven). As Dani Rodrik in his article on "Premature Deindustrialization" highlighted, the less developed economies are already deindustrializing at income levels that are 25–50 percent lower than those of more developed economies going through the same process during the Industrial Age.[23]

Why is this important? Because over the last two-to-three centuries, manufacturing and global trade were the King's Road to development and progress. Whether one looks at Germany, the US, or Japan in the late 19th and early 20th centuries, or China, Korea, and Taiwan in the late 20th and early 21st centuries, it was the ability to participate in global flows of manufacturing, trade, and capital that propelled these nations forward, and the inability to do so that hobbled others such as Brazil, Mexico, India, the Ottomans, or Imperial China. At the same time, Daron Acemoglu and James Robinson[24] have persuasively argued that it is traditionally the case that manufacturing and trade play a fundamental role in creating democratic politics. Hence, our Fujiwara effect is not only steadily closing the most viable and proven ways for the least and less developed economies to progress, but it is also making it harder to foster civil societies and institutions of state.

The challenge facing more developed nations is that if only 10 or 20 percent of the younger cohorts decide to leave their place of birth, immigration systems will be overwhelmed, and the refugee population will explode. According to the latest statistics on refugees and displaced persons, as of May 2023, more than 110 million people have been displaced globally, including almost 40 million refugees.[25] Immigration and border control, which is already a highly sensitive touchstone issue in the US, Europe, Australia, and Canada, will become far more extreme, raw, and violent. And there are no obvious ways of containing this. After all, Roman galleys patrolling the Danube and Rhine could not stop waves of people, whom Romans called "barbarians" (from Franks to Visigoths, Vandals to Lombards, and Goths to Burgundians), driven toward the Roman Empire by extreme climatic and economic necessities. Similar economic and environmental imperatives drove Mongols, and later Turks, across Eurasia in the 13th to15th centuries, and neither Russians, Persians, nor Greeks could stop them. Disparities in relative income and well-being ultimately equalize, either by raising productivity and offering opportunities at home or by invasions and destruction of lives and capital through desperate immigration-driven conflicts. Building and strengthening borders and walls never helps.

So, what is the answer? A wide-ranging and highly intrusive Marshall Plan for the least and less developed regions of the world seems to be the only rational response. However, these proposals always bump against five hard-to-navigate political hurdles. First, why should we spend resources on faraway places when we still have poverty at home? Second, why should we subsidize others (e.g., if the US for instance offers more help than, say, Europe)? Third, how do we know that money will be appropriately invested when levels of corruption and theft in these countries are so high? Fourth, we are ready to spend it on countries on the same ideological platform as us, but we will try to undermine others (e.g., a typical Cold War "domino" theory). Five, how do these countries pay us back?

Answers and solutions seem to be obvious, but historically, these were seldom implemented until it was too late. Even for the Romans, who were far more flexible than anyone else at the time, it took a while to figure out what to do with the barbarians. The key question is whether the US or Europe would prefer a radical change in the racial, ethnic, and religious composition of their societies by opening borders, or whether they would rather try to develop economies and institutional systems in the less developed nations to meaningfully reduce immigration flows. Given that ultimately money will need to be spent anyway and/or blood also might need to be shed, is it not better to try to get ahead of the storm?

Although all developed nations will be ultimately impacted, at least initially, it will be largely a Eurasian problem (places like the US, Australia, and Canada are separated by oceans). My first book wistfully suggested that Europe and China cooperate and contribute as much as 10–20 percent of their GDP (or upwards of US$3–4 trillion), similar to what the US had done in spurts between 1946 and 1956 to rebuild Europe and Japan. I also suggested that in order to avoid excessive wastage from local corruption, both design projects be directly controlled by Europe and China, not dissimilar to China's "One Belt One Road or Belt Road Initiative," except structuring these not on commercial terms but rather as supervised enlightened donations. I suggested coupling these projects with meaningful state and institutional construction and the realistic threat of withdrawal of support.

Unfortunately, over the last four years since my book was written, it has become abundantly clear that China is continuing to pursue projects as largely commercial transactions (and as a result saddling the least developed nations with an unsupportable level of debt, usually at a premium to risk-free rates). At the same time, geopolitical and political considerations have remained the dominant driver, and China continues to bypass Western-dominated, but experienced and well-developed, IMF systems for surveillance and debt restructuring. And today's cold war-style separation into competing blocks is clearly making cooperation that much harder. In a similar vein, outside of Mexico and a few other countries, the US has no meaningful programs to lead in building political and economic systems across large areas of Latin America, Africa, the Middle East, or Central Asia.

My first book also anticipated that climate and the rising specter of pandemics could be another reason for substantive policy changes. The drying up of the Sahel, the increasing unpredictability of monsoons, and other climate-driven changes could easily escalate distress and force even stronger migratory moves. When I was writing my first book (finished just prior to the COVID-19 pandemic), it was already clear that if there were to be any major pandemics that would threaten the survival of humanity, they would be likely to originate and propagate from the least or less developed nations. Therefore, instead of being concerned about how funds will be repaid, it might be more rational to consider that returns might take the form of healthcare and survival rather than DCF-inspired financial returns.

This is a hard and contentious subject, full of social, political, economic, cultural, and religious landmines, not to mention a poisonous colonial legacy. The least and less developed regions include some coherent nations that are already in the process of creating viable state institutions, but the grouping also includes many others who have not yet even solidified the idea of a single unified nationhood. Not that long ago, some of these nations had their borders carelessly and casually drawn by their former colonial masters without any regard for ethnic, religious, or linguistic differences (especially across Africa and the Middle East). Many have neither coherence nor shared historical, cultural, or linguistic bonds and are still largely a collection of warring clans and tribes. In the case of other less developed states that have been around longer, there are numerous instances of failures in the construction of state institutions and judiciary, with most levers of power hijacked by vested interests. There are no easy answers.

Depending on economic, climate, and geopolitical considerations, one could envisage that the intensity of migratory waves (especially into Europe), could shift the center of gravity either toward hot wars or, maybe, and perhaps more hopefully, toward a greater global coordination between main protagonists fighting a common "enemy."

·　　·　　·

It is never easy to judge such fine distinctions as cold versus hot wars and even harder to delineate the hungry wars,[26] as societal, political, and economic interactions are so complex that even small variations could lead to a "butterfly effect" of radically different outcomes. However, I am hopeful that a sequence of cold wars might ultimately lead to greater cooperation in dealing with common global challenges (such as climate and immigration). In part, my optimism rests on the impact that younger generational cohorts will have in shaping and sponsoring policies that stabilize societies and develop common solutions, thus guiding us closer to the 1950s–60s rather than the "world on fire" of the 1940s.

This is the topic of the next section which examines what policies we might wish to deploy over the next decade or two in an attempt to diffuse domestic polarization and blunt extremes of geopolitical tensions.

BUILDING A BRIDGE FROM TODAY TO TOMORROW

"Things fall apart; the center cannot hold."

—William Butler Yates

Chapter 10
STATE AS A GUARDRAIL

"We are already moving rapidly away from industrial capitalism as we understood it in the twentieth century, and there is little chance that we will move back in that direction."
Peter Frase[1]

I f one were to ask people in the early 1930s whether their system was in severe trouble and no longer working for the majority of the population, the answer would have been a resounding yes. Did anyone know how it would end? The answer would have been no. There was no single widely accepted political, economic, or social model. In such a world of no consensus, people were prepared to experiment with a diverse set of rules—from fascism and communism to democracies.

In the wake of the Great War, with depressions, hyperinflations, deflations, and unimaginable levels of unemployment, not many would have given democracy a high, or even a moderate, chance of survival. Hence, the prevalence of travel and political books throughout the 1930s praising the ability of the Soviet Union, Nazi Germany, or Fascist Italy to get things done while ignoring or downplaying Stalin's purges, depravations of the Holodomor, or Hitler's concentration camps,[2] with journalists, academics, and occasional businessmen invariably declaring both communism and fascism as the future when compared to the past of the crisis-prone West. One of the bestsellers of the era was a book[3] by Anne Morrow Lindbergh (wife of the aviation pioneer Charles Lindbergh) in which she argued that despite the extremes of the Fascist and Soviet regimes, totalitarianism was the future and a "new, and perhaps even ultimately good, conception of humanity trying to come to birth…the wave of the future is coming and there is no fighting it." While clearly not fully comparable, these reactions were not dissimilar to the 1950s and 1960s,

238

when the generations who survived the abyss were willing to sacrifice a great deal of independence and freedom to stabilize their world and to lower risks. People wanted peace, jobs, family, moderate prosperity, and lack of volatility. In return they accepted a stifling political and economic environment dominated by the state and a very narrow societal consensus as to what was perceived to be right and wrong, whether in personal, political, or economic matters.

As discussed in Chapter One, for two decades after World War II, improvements were indeed beyond anyone's wildest dreams, and, in turn, these deeply scarred generations had a difficult time explaining to their children how grateful they should feel for living in the miraculous world of the 1950s–60s. For the young Baby Boomers, however, who were not exposed to the horrors of the 1930s–40s, the world was one of plenty, whether educational and entertainment opportunities or jobs. Having by the late 1970s attained the demographic and electoral majority, they commenced an unrelenting multi-decade process of dismantling societal constraints—from the ability to marry or divorce whomever one wishes with minimum fuss and the elimination of many of the past racial, gender, or age discrimination practices to insistence on discussion and debate of almost any topic. The constraints of work practices and labor markets were equally swept aside as union membership plummeted, and the cultural backdrop no longer penalized those who were willing to frequently change jobs or professions. This ushered in a world far more closely aligned with the neoliberal philosophy of personal freedom, personal responsibility, and the free market. But freedom has its price and the cost and externalities of these policies (the collapse of state functions, a massive rise in inequalities, uncontrolled globalization, environmental degradation, etc.) finally arrived in the wake of the Global Financial Crisis (2010) (Chapter Five). Now a new world beckons, but its outlines remain vague, and uncertainties are as high as they were in the 1930s.

•   •   •

In 1941, in one of the most prescient papers on the compromises and challenges that democracies regularly face, an American historian, Carl L. Becker, asked during the greatest test of democratic values, "Can the flagrant inequality of possessions and of opportunity existing in democratic societies be corrected by democratic method? If it cannot...the resulting discontent and confusion will be certain, sooner or later, to issue in some form of...dictatorship. This then is the dilemma which confronts democratic societies: to solve their economic problems by the democratic method or cease to be democratic societies."[4] This was later amplified by Ronald Inglehart in his "Evolutionary Modernization Theory" which argues that at times of rising physical and economic insecurity, a thin veneer of civilization falls off and people circle the wagons, and are willing to accept extreme answers to their problems, triggering an "authoritarian reflex" or desire to reach out to strong leaders whom they believe would ease their pain and discomfort. As the ancient Greeks were acutely aware, democracy is not a natural human condition and to survive, it must be carefully nurtured with the degree of inequality (civic, educational or wealth) minimized against a natural tendency toward the opposite.

In the wake of FDR's New Deal, Carl Becker argued that while there were significant differences between communism, fascism, and democracy, underneath, all three systems were trying to address similar economic and distributional challenges by adopting a common strategy: "They are all carrying us, so to speak, toward an extension of governmental regulation of social enterprise."[5] In other words, all three responses to the crises of the 1930s involved a significant expansion of the government into political, regulatory, and economic spheres. Communism went the furthest in completely eliminating private property rights and freedom of discussion and debate. Fascism was in some ways a milder version, allowing a degree of freedom in the private sphere, but it had completely subordinated the private sector to the diktat of the government and also eliminated dissent. FDR's New Deal attempted to find the middle ground by expanding the government's tentacles while trying to preserve as much private freedom and initiative as possible. Becker asked, "The question that chiefly concerns us is whether the necessary social regulation of economic enterprise can be affected by the democratic method—that is to say, without a corresponding social regimentation of opinion and political freedom. Can the *possessors be sufficiently dispossessed and the dispossessed be sufficiently reinstated without resort to violence, revolution, and the temporary or permanent dictatorship?*"[6] (Italics are mine.) As Becker highlighted, communists would have clearly said no, arguing that revolutions are inevitable, while fascists would have suggested that a totalitarian state is the most optimum way of running both economy and society. Indeed, a number of today's neoliberals and conservatives concur with this sentiment, and there were similar voices in the 1920s–30s (for example, Carl Schmitt[7]) who focused on frailties and fault lines of democratic orders. Alas, with the benefit of hindsight, their solutions turned out to be far worse than the disease itself.

Again, it is best left to Becker to sum up the predicament: "Common men, when sufficiently distressed, instinctively turn to 'inspired' leaders; and dictatorship in our times, as in past times, is the normal price exacted for the failure of democracy to bind common men by their hopes and their fears."[8] As discussed in Chapter Six, people occasionally reach a stage of such extreme polarization (e.g., 1930s and the last decade) that they are no longer susceptible to rational arguments and instead of being responsible citizens resemble fans of competing football teams,[9] with the objective of destroying the opposite side, even if everyone is ultimately worse off. In these circumstances, conspiracy theories flourish and can never be debunked, no matter how much evidence is presented, and those of the opposition are no longer viewed as fellow humans but rather as immoral and debased heretics who are not only wrong but also unpatriotic and profoundly against what is perceived to be the natural order. It is difficult to get back from this, and the deadlock is therefore frequently broken in revolutions and wars.

However, it does not have to be so. Although those in power do not surrender their advantages easily or freely, there is plenty of evidence that a more peaceful resolution is possible, with societies occasionally transformed from within. In the 18th and 19th centuries, English landed aristocracy was not happy surrendering its privileges, but through the evolution of the common law system and property rights protections, they gradually and step-by-step surrendered them. The same applied to the proliferation of social security, unemployment support, and health care insurance from the 1870s to the 1900s, which meaningfully redefined the relationship between labor and capital. In ancient times, Roman patrician classes had also surrendered their absolute power gradually through the 3rd and 1st centuries BCE. There are no infallible answers, and there are no perfect political and societal orders, and anyone who ever claimed otherwise (such as the communists and fascists) was consistently proven to be offering solutions that were far worse than the alternatives.

It is therefore a question of experimentation and attempting to redress the underlying causes leading to extreme polarization while trying to keep as many freedoms (personal, political, and economic) as possible. What policies might lower the temperature and reduce polarization and tensions? As in the 1930s, the government is the only actor with sufficient strength and legitimacy to get the job done. No one else would be able to offer any meaningful answers.

$$\bullet \quad \bullet \quad \bullet$$

One of the most important policies to be considered is the introduction of some form of basic or universal income guarantee (UBI). Although decried by neoliberals as encouraging laziness and discouraging initiative, UBI is likely the only way in Becker's words of "dispossessing possessors while reinstating dispossessed" without outright expropriations, revolutions, dictatorships, or wars. This was the insight of the FDR's administration in the early 1930s, despite frequent complaints that the US was creating a state-controlled Bolshevik economy. On the contrary, what FDR had achieved was a realistic compromise between freedom, democracy, and the economic challenges of that age. The alternative would have been turning the US toward either fascism or communism.

I outlined in my first book that "as the free space for human endeavors becomes more and more constrained, societies must consider alternative ways to liberate humanity from the hell of declining usefulness and destruction of self-respect that goes with it."[10] To put it another way, as Yuval Harari phrased it, "Most people are likely to suffer not from exploitation but from something far worse—irrelevance."[11] In economic jargon it basically means that as a result of profound changes in the functioning of both capital and labor (due to the Fujiwara effect), marginal utility of labor is eroding, and, as discussed in Chapter Seven, it is unlikely that this process of diminishing utility (and consequently growing popular unhappiness and dissatisfaction) can reverse by itself.

UBI's underlying concept is that every citizen is entitled to a certain amount (above the poverty line), irrespective of whether they are rich or poor and whether they work or not. Over the last six decades, this has already been tried in various places, from Kenya and Uganda in Africa to the US, Canada, Japan, the UK, Netherlands, and Finland.[12] It is an appealing concept as it allows nations to dismantle the current complex bureaucracy that was built up to administer and police a web of welfare benefits while also blunting corruption (especially in less developed economies), intractable identity-based politics, and favoritism. UBI also promises to provide support for consumption and aggregate demand while our economies transit toward a new world of post-conventional capitalism as technologies change and redefine the nature and functioning of labor and capital. I believe that within a decade or two, labor markets will undergo further deep dislocations, eliminating a significant portion of tasks performed by humans (without any obvious replacement beyond non-work satisfaction).

In the words of Esping-Andersen, UBI "decommodifies labor"[13] and by doing so undermines one of the key pillars of a traditional capitalist society. However, the reality is that our societies and the essence of work as well as relations between employers and employees are already changing, and this process is unstoppable. The question, therefore, is not how to return to some idealized neoliberal classical capitalism, but what type of policies would make this inevitable transition easier, smoother, and less violent while protecting as many of our freedoms as possible.

Another major objection frequently expressed by detractors of UBI is that offering unrestricted basic income will be prohibitively expensive (although today's benefits already exceed US$4 trillion in the US alone) and could undermine support for the neediest sections of the population.[14] No question, it would be expensive, and for most countries, UBI would likely require a higher and more progressive tax structure. However, there are increasingly various ways to pay for it, including utilization of exceptionally long-dated government paper, using central bank liquidity (refer to the discussion below), or altering tax brackets on the few individuals and firms that prosper in such an environment (including the frequently discussed tax on robots, minimum global taxes, and wealth tax on billionaires[15]). Most commentaries also ignore the simplicity of UBI (sending checks and direct payments), which will result in a significant reduction in administrative costs and wastage while meaningfully improving human flexibility (residence, work, or study), compared with the current complex quilt of constrained and overlapping programs. Most importantly, it is likely to restore human dignity and enable people in a post-work era to experiment with various ways of contributing to societies and staying happy. Abraham Maslow said, "A musician must make music, an artist must paint, a poet must write, if he is to be ultimately at peace with himself." While undoubtedly true, it does not describe the real-life experiences of the bulk of humanity today. Most people work because they must, rather than for any sense of fulfillment. In a world of diminishing returns on humans, UBI will liberate people to discover themselves and their IQ and EQ without the pressures of student loans, SAT tests, GPAs, or the nonsensical idea that education is a human capital and that a recipient of that capital must pay for it.

Finally, there are objections that UBI could undermine "work ethics" and incentives for improvement and innovation. Again, as with most other objections, there is a plethora of controlled experiments that have shown that the need for social hierarchy and interactions is so deeply ingrained in the human psyche that dropout rates are low (around 1–3 percent, at most). Similarly, as discussed above (Chapter Five), there has never been a strong link between levels of taxation, on the one hand, and innovation and prosperity, on the other, offering another proof that the rational economic creature assumptions of neoliberal economics do not have much (if any) relationship with how human societies work.

This is not the book to debate the intricacies of various UBI proposals (e.g., Should it be directed and more constrained? Should it be combined with work incentives?). However, despite vociferous opposition,[16] it is clear to me that UBI in its various forms is the future, even though it will take time for societies to coalesce. There is mounting evidence that the resurrection of this rather old idea (e.g., Richard Nixon and LBJ considered it in the late 1960s and early 1970s, with the seeds planted well over a century ago) is no longer regarded as a "fringe" mumbling by people who do not understand economics. UBI has already gone mainstream, not only in academia but increasingly in technology, business, and political circles (e.g., support for UBI from Andrew Young, an unsuccessful Democratic challenger in the 2020 elections, but also support from the likes of Bill Gates, Sergei Brin, and Elon Musk). This is encouraging, particularly considering that American culture considers failures as a personal, not systemic, shortcoming. In more culturally attuned Europe, Canada, Australia, and Japan, there is an even greater acceptance of UBI's logic and benefits.

$$\bullet \qquad \bullet \qquad \bullet$$

Another key policy plank rapidly coming into view is the nature and functioning of public finances. Having recognized that fiscal spending is not just irreversible but also the key to avoiding an even deeper and faster fall in neutral rates (i.e., inability to grow), most commentators have now turned their attention to the best way to fund the public sector.

Though this still excludes many governmental bodies (such as the IMF and World Bank) and editorials of financial press—which are persistently sounding the alarm regarding what is perceived as out-of-control spending and the dangers of excessive public sector debt—there is a growing recognition that ideas not long ago described as fringe (such as the Modern Monetary Theory or MMT) might hold the key for handling this burgeoning debt and placing public financing on more stable footing.[17]

A classic example of a conventional push back is the recent *New York Times* editorial, "America Is Living on Borrowed Money," which while not degenerating into fear mongering, offered a somber assessment of dangers facing the US.[18] The editorial ominously stated that on the current path, US federal debt will within a decade reach as high as 120 percent of GDP (actually, overall public debt is already higher than that), as if there were something magic about that number. Experience over the last several decades has consistently proven that while rising debt coincides with slower growth and lower money velocity, there is only weak evidence of causation, while there is plenty of evidence that there is nothing special about any specific threshold (despite the often quoted "red line" of 90 percent, contained in a highly influential book by Reinhart and Rogoff).[19] Most advanced economies already have public sector leverage that is either close to, or significantly above, these levels.

In addition, what these commentaries tend to ignore is that what matters is the overall financialization of economies rather than just its public sector. As discussed in Chapter Five, finance has over the last three decades permeated all parts of our economies and has become the single most important variable driving outcomes. While one can debate reasons why in the 1980s we embarked on such intense financialization (my answer is Baby Boomers' desire for growth and wealth creation irrespective of consequences, compounded by slowing productivity), by now, there is no longer any off-ramp. The financialization train, so to speak, left the station several decades ago, and at anywhere from five to ten times global GDP, the "cloud of finance" is now the "dog," and the real economy is just the "tail." The task at hand, therefore, is not to deleverage but rather manage this "cloud of finance" to ensure that "the dog does not sit on the tail." Indeed, management of risks and liquidity (mostly through communication policies and emergency support lines) has already become the cornerstone of central bank policies globally. It is the height of naivety to assume that some form of "sound money" can actually return in any meaningful way.

Today, central bank balance sheets have already expanded to almost US$40 trillion, representing approximately 50 percent of GDP of the correspondent nations surveyed by the Financial Stability Board (FSB), compared to levels closer to 10 percent in the 1980s–90s. This rise was particularly pronounced in the wake of the Global Financial Crisis in 2008–10 and throughout the COVID-19 pandemic (2020–22). At the same time, central banks have fully embraced the need to control volatilities and minimize bad debts through a myriad of highly intrusive and proactive policies. These range from emergency repo lines that make sure that monetary plumbing works (e.g., Federal Reserve introduced this in 2019 following a repo crisis), policies addressing specific vulnerabilities (e.g., "The Bank Term Funding Program" that converted treasuries into cash, created by the Federal Reserve in 2023 to stem the regional banks crisis in the wake of collapse of Silicon Valley Bank) and ensuring a smooth functioning of government securities (e.g., European Central Bank's "Monetary Policy Transmission Facility" that enables the ECB to step in to correct what it perceives to be a mispricing of spreads). This is in addition what in the last two decades has come to be regarded as conventional policies of "Quantitative Easing and Tightening," whereby central banks directly buy or sell government and sometimes corporate securities, in order to relieve pressure, lower the cost of debt, and help with setting policy rates.

Over the last several decades, central banks and policy makers have been de facto nationalizing capital markets, not because there is some hidden conspiratorial agenda, but rather due to unprecedented economic risks that highly leveraged and financialized economies pose. This is in addition to increasingly proactive fiscal policies (especially in the wake of COVID-19) and what effectively amounts to direct funding of the state through central banks, even though it is still conducted through market mechanisms. Bank of Japan, which has been conducting these operations the longest, currently owns around 50 percent of Japanese government securities. In the case of most other central banks, ratios vary between 10 and 30 percent. Relative to GDP, Bank of Japan assets are covering 120 percent of Japan's GDP, Swiss National Bank assets are close to 100 percent of GDP, European Central Bank covers almost 50 percent of the eurozone's economy while the Federal Reserve is above 25 percent of the US GDP.

Figure 59. Central Bank Assets (US$ trillion, % GDP)

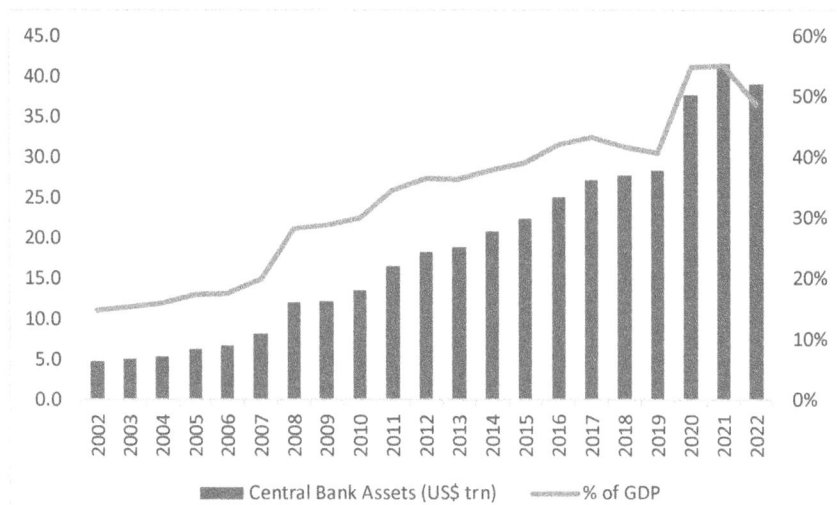

Source: FSB, December 2023

Finally, most of the commentary seems to treat national accounts as if these were similar to a family budget. Nothing could be further from the truth. Unlike households, nations effectively "consume themselves," whereas households trade with other households and corporations. If a nation enjoys a high degree of monetary sovereignty (i.e., predominantly issues, uses, and borrows in one's own currency—this applies to the US, Japan, the UK, and most other developed economies but not to the bulk of emerging economies), then the treasury departments, central banks, and people are all one and the same. We borrow from each other, and so repayment does not increase national wealth. Monetarily sovereign nations do not need to look for money, rather they create money. Unless they lose their sovereignty or face binding demand-supply constraints (and hence, a possibility of uncontrolled inflation), popular headlines of choices between paying interest or spending on social security, guns, or butter are fairly meaningless.

While I do not intend to debate various aspects of the Modern Monetary Theory (MMT), the experience over the last three to four decades has conclusively proven that running large public sector deficits does not necessarily cause inflationary pressures and/or currency debasements. All one needs to do is to look at Japan which has been running high deficits for more than three decades without any inflationary pressures or debasements. Similarly witness a meaningful rise in deficits in the wake of the Global Financial Crisis without inflation. On the other hand, there were various episodes (such as during Bill Clinton's presidency) when budget surpluses coincided with rising inflation. Although opponents might argue that the strong inflationary spike that inflicted global economies in 2021–23 is proof that high fiscal spending can cause a significant run-up in inflationary pressures, it is hard to make that judgement, as at least 50 percent (some would argue well over 70 percent) of the inflationary overflow was not caused by excessive demand but rather supply issues, as COVID-19 and the Russia-Ukraine war meaningfully dislocated demand and supply curves for goods, services, and labor. As long as these dislocations normalize, inflation should have retreated. Indeed, this is exactly what has occurred thus far, with G5 inflation (US, UK, Eurozone, Japan, and China) coming down from the high of 7–8 percent in late 2022 to around 2.3 percent by April 2024 without causing global or even localized recessions or leading to any meaningful rise in unemployment rates.

At the same time, I do not find credible arguments that state spending is inherently inefficient and causes a fall in productivity. As discussed in Chapter Four, this is the backbone of the neoliberal views that dominated the policy landscape for almost three decades, but which ultimately led to weaker, not stronger, productivity, greater inequalities, and rapidly rising financialization. It does not mean that everything done by the governments is efficient; rather I do not subscribe to the view that whatever the private sector does is always necessarily and automatically more efficient. Finally, there are various moral hazard arguments imbedded in the discussion of state spending, especially when it is directly or indirectly funded by central banks. This is a serious objection that has a great deal of validity. The only countervailing argument is that most developed economies have reasonably robust and independent institutions of state, and, therefore, the chances of descending into the hell of hyperinflation (à la Zimbabwe, Venezuela, Argentina, or the Weimer Republic) are quite low. However, even if there is concern about these outcomes, there is no evidence that issuing government paper through bond markets precludes these episodes (after all, these defaulting nations were all issuing bonds).

Thus, I maintain the view expressed in my first book that it is highly likely that over the next decade, state spending and the range of policies over which the state would exercise a considerable degree of control will continue expanding. Although it is not yet clear how many MMT concepts will be absorbed, there is a reasonable chance that the ongoing state expansion will be increasingly funded directly by central banks. With the inception of Central Bank Digital Coins (CBDC), the role and functioning of commercial banks as multipliers of credit would undergo a massive change, with central banks not only indirectly steering markets and rates but directly managing demand, including various forms of UBI. What would happen to the underwriters of state debt? They would most likely no longer be needed, as indeed, even today policy makers already have such a high degree of control over yields, spreads, and rates that most of the underwriting is becoming far less relevant when compared to more traditional capitalist economies.

The de facto nationalization of capital markets is progressing primarily because they are perceived to be far too important and dangerous to be left to the private sector. This also explains why over the last decade, most economists and investors were surprised by low market volatilities. Why should volatilities rise, when they are no longer determined by the free market but instead are corralled and constrained by central banks and policy makers? In 2008–09, it took the Federal Reserve more than nine months to become comfortable with quantitative easing (even though Japan pursued it for years), and in 2019 it took more than a month for the Federal Reserve to roll out an unlimited emergency repo facility, but in 2023 only 72 hours were needed to develop a program to convert treasuries into cash. In time, and if needed, we are likely to see policies specifically tailored to other "land mines" (e.g., commercial real estate, private equity and debt, parity trades) rolled out in seconds. The migration of decision-making away from the private sector and investors and toward policymakers has been ongoing for more than two decades, but the pace has accelerated in the wake of the Global Financial Crisis and COVID-19, and this process cannot not be reversed without suffering severe economic and social upheavals.

This is another remarkable contradiction—the freedom-loving Boomers have now become totally dependent on the state to protect their assets. However, from a policymaker's point of view, the Boomers' thirst for growth and wealth led to a "cloud of finance" that is at least five (and possibly ten) times larger than the underlying economies. Do policymakers, therefore, have any realistic choice but to constrain volatilities? The question yet to be answered, however, is whether these state intrusions and proactive policies further aggravate global "secular stagnation" (or inability to grow without fiscal and monetary supports) that gripped the world economy over the last several decades, or whether they in fact constitute the necessary and indispensable bridge between the capitalism of the past and the future.

• • •

Although this subsection might strike some readers as too technical and not as relevant, I believe it is important to clarify why state policies were becoming so proactive over the last three decades and why I do not believe this will radically change, at least not in the next decade.

Jerome Powell, the current chair of the Federal Reserve, has frequently referred to monetary policies as navigating by the stars. What he meant was that neutral rates or r^* (i.e., real rates that maximize employment and growth with stable inflation) are at the heart of policymakers' mandates. But, in the same speeches, he also discussed difficulties in using r^*, u^* (i.e., natural rate of unemployment) and π^* (i.e., inflation) as policy tools. Not only neutral rates are not observable and necessarily deduced from how the economy behaves, but over the last several decades they have become much more volatile, or in Powell's words, "Our assessments of the location of the stars have been changing significantly." In more nautical terms, Powell has been describing the Fed as navigating under "cloudy skies," meaning that policymakers have at best only a vague idea as to the location of the "stars" and their direction (rising or falling).[20] This creates major problems for central banks, corporations, households, and investors.

While hard to compute and far from perfect, r* is the single most important policy tool. The idea of neutral rates dates back more than a century to Knut Wicksell and basically argues that inflation and growth (and the balance between the two) depend not on rates per se, but rather on where rates are relative to what he described as "natural rates." Although forgotten for a while, the idea was revived over the last three to four decades as policymakers searched for the right benchmark to manage the rapidly growing "cloud of finance." In theory, if central banks set policy rates higher than "neutral" or "natural" rates, this would slow economies and defang inflation, and vice versa.

However, the battle has always been on how to define r* and what forces shape it. Almost everyone agrees that neutral rates are driven by long-term structural forces, such as technological evolution and demographics. But there are plenty of disagreements as to other variables. One of the key issues is the interaction of demographics with other factors such as increasing longevity and extreme wealth inequalities. Normally, the ageing of societies would imply lower savings (as retirees consume their previously accumulated savings pool), implying rising neutral rates. However, a significant increase in longevity requires longer saving periods, while inequalities lead to fewer cohorts accumulating savings at a pace that they cannot possibly consume and far in excess of their retirement needs, implying falling neutral rates. As I have illustrated in Chapter Five, in most economies today the top 10 percent of households own as much as 70 percent of national wealth, a far greater share than several decades ago. Similarly, there are disagreements about the role and importance of asset bubbles. As Paul Krugman,[21] Adair Turner, and Larry Summers have highlighted, the last four decades featured an inordinate number of asset bubbles, raising the question as to whether the highly financialized and leveraged economies need bubbles in order to grow and avoid more extreme outcomes. Do bubbles cause a decline in neutral rates, or do they help policy makers to soften the rate of erosion? There are also debates on how public sectors impact location and direction of neutral rates, harping back to the neoliberal efficiency views as well as arguments of overactive policies precluding or at least delaying normal market clearances.

One could easily go on about the role of tangible versus intangible and intellectual assets, the importance of capital flows, and reconciliation between short-term policies and the long-term structural nature of r* drivers. However, for most economists there is no doubt that for a range of reasons, real neutral rates across developed economies have been consistently and systematically falling for a long time, going back as far as the early 1980s. The Laubach-Williams and Holston-Laubach-Williams models (HLW), currently published under the New York Federal Reserve umbrella, are some of the most consistent and frequently used guideposts. What HLW shows is that US real neutral rates fell from around 4 percent in the 1980s to as low 0.5–0.7 percent prior to COVID in 2019, and even today (late-2023). In the case of the eurozone, the model indicates an erosion from around 3 percent to a negative 0.5 percent. Consensus Economics, another provider, suggests that eurozone real neutral rates might be below negative 1 percent. Forecasts for Japan indicate an even steeper fall from as high as 8 or 9 percent in the 1980s to a negative 0.5 percent today. In Canada, estimates suggest a decline from around 5 percent in the 1980s to somewhere closer to 1 percent. While there are not many reliable estimates for less developed economies, there is no doubt that over the last three to four years, China's real neutral rates have undergone a significant derating, potentially reaching levels not dissimilar to those of Japan.

Figure 60. US and Eurozone Real Neutral Rates (%)

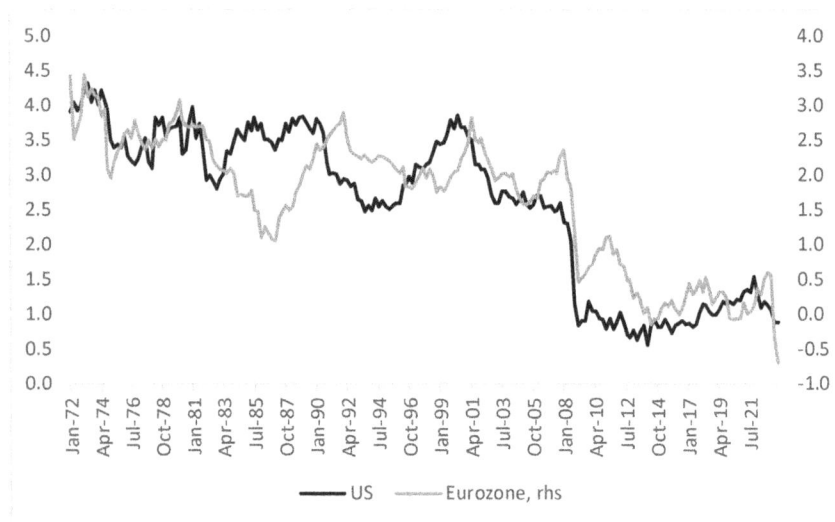

Source: HLW, December 2023

This precipitous fall, accentuated after the Global Financial Crisis, perfectly correlates with the onset of the intense financialization of the global economy, which by now completely depends on leverage and asset prices (i.e., bubbles). From the days of Paul Volcker in the early 1980s to Greenspan's put option in the late 1980s, our economies have been consistently using leverage and asset prices to offset declining productivity and take the sting out of rising inequalities. Alas, it had led to the opposite: further erosion of productivity and even steeper inequalities (especially wealth). The declining r* also perfectly coincided with the growing impact of the Information Age revolution with its powerful disintermediation of both capital and labor and strong downward pressure on marginal pricing. Finally, the long process of r* erosion aligns with aggressive monetary policies over the last three decades. This is what I describe as a Fujiwara effect, or several hurricanes merging into a much more powerful upheaval.

It was this reality of a low (and declining) r* and a correspondingly low inflation that trapped central banks over the last several decades, forcing them to adopt an ever more complex set of tools (such as quantitative easing, emergency support lines, etc.), requiring policy makers to place policy rates below declining neutral rates in order to support growth and prevent an uncontrolled rise in the bad debts that a highly leveraged and financialized economy would inevitably generate. As discussed in Chapters Seven to Nine, it is likely that over the next decade or two, the world will be convulsed by proliferating, and by their nature unique, "black swan" events (from domestic polarization to geopolitics, and from migrations, pandemics to climate). Will there be more volatility than in the past? The answer is a resounding yes. Despite this, I think the structural forces that have relentlessly driven neutral rates down for over three decades are so powerful that they will most likely offset these volatilities, keeping neutral rates under pressure. The Fujiwara effect will keep retarding productivity, constraining spending, and lowering inflationary pressures, forcing central banks and policymakers to constantly reach out for controls, or at least exercise a stronger influence, over ever-wider segments of the economy and capital markets.

These pressures will only relent when economies and societies have fully adjusted to the new environment (including the likely disappearance of the conventional work paradigm) with the functioning and role of capital and money having already undergone an equally radical transformation. A decade or two from now, the world will look very different in almost every respect: economically, politically, and socially, with UBI as well as profound changes in the role of the state (and how it is funded) being the most critical bricks in the bridge from today to tomorrow. However, there are several other policies that promise to be almost equally as important.

•   •   •

There is an urgent need for a new Marshall Plan for the least and some less developed economies (essentially almost everyone outside of the US, Canada, Europe, Japan, Australia, and New Zealand, as well as a select few other nations, like China, Korea, Chile, Singapore, etc.). As discussed in

Chapter Nine, the least and less developed economies, especially in Africa, Middle East, and Central Asia (and to a lesser extent, South Asia) are facing an unprecedented demographic bulge, at a time when the demand for and the utility of labor is likely to keep declining and while climate change will continue to amplify monsoon and rainfall variations, especially in the Sahel and South Asia. Unlike previous migratory waves, today we are far more connected and better informed, and hence, the pressures are likely to be more severe and compressed into shorter time frames. As discussed above, over the next twenty-five years, less developed economies (excluding China) are likely to add as many as 1.5 billion young people of a working age while the population of Africa, the Middle East, and Central Asia will double from around 1.5 billion in 2022 to more than 3 billion by 2050 (including over 2 billion of working age cohort), and this demographic wave will not crest until sometime in the 2040s. Even if as little as 10–20 percent of this younger cohort decide to leave home in search of a better life, the current number of displaced persons and refugees (around 110 million) could easily double or even triple, with hundreds of millions of people on the move.

This more than amply explains how the internal dislocations that are already becoming acute in more developed economies are being seriously magnified by concerns and fears of uncontrolled immigration. Unfortunately, as the Romans discovered in the 3rd to 5th centuries and the Greeks and Russians in the 13th to 15th centuries, these migratory waves can never be stopped, as they are driven by extremes of inequalities and environmental and climate change. This will likely continue to shift the political map in both Europe and the US (as well as other developed economies like Canada and Australia) to an even greater hostility toward migrants, despite the obvious impotence of this achieving any meaningful results.

These developed nations face three equally unpalatable choices. First, a de facto recolonization through military means to ensure that people stay in their home country. Second, acceptance of the need to spend considerable resources (potentially up to 10–20 percent of GDP) on developing economies and institutional structures in less developed regions. Third, opening the borders (as Romans ultimately conceded to settling barbarians on their frontier) but as a result, meaningfully altering their ethnic, racial, cultural, and religious composition. Insistent cries for border security and walls, though understandable, are unlikely to be a fruitful response (just ask Emperor Hadrian or the Byzantines). It seems inevitable that nations will try to explore all three options, even though the second choice should be the best answer—balancing humanity with the need to protect local communities while avoiding the extremes of wars, forced recolonization, drowning of migrant ships, and loss of qualities that make us human.

The good news is that these less developed regions are not beyond help. Unlike more mature economies, there are ample opportunities to raise productivity (from exceptionally low levels) while utilizing some of the best stores of natural resources (energy, industrial, and digital age) and expanding currently constrained land resources for food and agriculture. For example, Africa today has some 60 percent of the world's arable land, but the agricultural yields are so low that the continent remains a major food importer (US$43 billion in 2019).[22] This is mostly due to the region's political instability, poor infrastructure, highly inefficient utilization and ownership of land, as well as an extremely low use of fertilizers.[23] As a result, Africa's yields from cereals are only half of those in India and less than a fifth of the US. In addition, there are other significant benefits from developing more efficient agriculture and land usage, such as protecting the earth's biosphere (Africa has the richest and the world's most diverse biosphere) and preventing, or at least mitigating proliferation of life-threatening pandemics.

While initially this is likely to be largely a Eurasian problem, with Europe at the sharp end of these migratory waves, it will ultimately be everyone's problem. Preparing for it and formulating plans for supporting these economies while also minimizing wastage and corruption and strengthening (often rebuilding) institutions of state, should be occupying minds at both the national and global level. Alas, today's preoccupation is mostly with the shorter-term priorities of strengthening borders, deporting refugees (only to see them come back again), redirecting refugees to other countries (e.g., the infamous Rwanda plan by the British government or de facto bribes paid by the EU to Tunisia, Turkey, and Libya), and/or the scoring of cheap political points (witness border debates at the US Congress).

The next decade is likely to be the key period in this transition from unrealistic to more realistic answers. The unresolved question is what volatility, disruption, and violence would need to be endured between points A and B and what the impact these will have on other polarization and geopolitical tensions such as cold versus hot war between the Sinosphere or Illiberal Eurasia and the West.

•   •   •

We are already witnessing the beginning of a new age of industrial policies. Not long ago, I presented at a conference where one of the speakers discussed pitfalls of governments picking winners. I suggested that the paper might soon belong to a museum, as most future papers will be debating how industrial policies can be best optimized for the new age (while trying to avoid the glaring excesses of the late 1960s to mid-1970s), rather than ominously warning about the pitfalls of state involvement. It is likely that for environmental, social, and geopolitical reasons, nations will increasingly try to tilt the balance toward sectors and areas where the private sector, if left to its own devices, would either not proceed or would do so inefficiently and with considerable time lags. Whether it is chips, quantum computing, new energy and transportation platforms, security and surveillance, new agricultural techniques, or new materials, industrial policies and much deeper state intrusion seems inevitable.

A recent example of such an industrial policy paper was the White House review published in June 2021.[24] In many ways, it could be regarded as the new age Sputnik moment, with US policymakers clearly and concisely outlining competitive challenges facing the US, focusing not on the conventional industrial age but on new leading-edge technologies such as (a) semiconductor and advanced packaging, (b) large-capacity batteries and new energy, (c) critical materials and minerals, and

(d) biotechnology. This paper was followed by a number of other studies conducted by research bodies with close links to the US establishment, such as the Kennedy School at Harvard and Georgetown's Center for Security and Emerging Technology. These papers emphasized the need for the rapid progression of new technologies as well as the dangers of close integration of China's military and commercial spheres and its "all-in state and integrated national approach."[25] As a foretaste of the future, there is also an increasing flow of academic papers[26] that highlight how the state is likely to return to its prior functions of the 1950s–70s in having active industrial and developmental policies.

On a step-by-step basis this is already being translated into real life projects from the Inflation Reduction Act (IRA) and the US$280 billion CHIPS Act by the Biden administration to a greater attention paid to basic research and NASA as well as evolution of industry-specific plans in countries as diverse as Japan (New Direction of Economy and Industrial Policy), the EU (e.g., setting aside €160 billion of its COVID recovery funds toward chips, batteries, and climate transition as well as the Green Deal Industrial Plan), Korea (the K-Chips Plan) and Australia (US$10 billion fund aimed at revitalizing manufacturing).[27] Clearly China, with its ambitious "Made in China 2025" and other highly interventionist industrial policies, is no longer unique. The IMF estimates that in 2023 alone there were 2,500 industrial policy interventions across the world, with more than half originating in China, the European Union, and the US.[28] Although at this stage, most of these Western projects have a narrowly defined geopolitical agenda (such as securing vulnerable supply chains as well as chips and technology), the range of issues and topics is getting much broader than would have been conceivable even a decade ago. While everyone accepts that there is a need to balance competing interests and objectives (such as fiscal and financial stability, promotion of growth, and the desire to support national champions), bureaucrats and policymakers are increasingly embracing these challenges.[29]

Although it is true that conventional economics still remains solidly in line with the neoliberal view that state-sponsored or supported industries reduce efficiency and create externalities (e.g., lower productivity, higher subsidies, and greater fiscal instability), there is a growing flow of studies that take a closer look at the upstream and downstream benefits of state-supported industrial policies and their flow-on impact on exports, rather than focusing exclusively on domestic protectionism, even from bastions of traditional thinking such as the IMF.[30] Most of these studies conclude that if crafted appropriately, the net benefits are considerable. Classic examples of positive feedback loops are Airbus in Europe, South Korea's Heavy-Chemical Industry Drive (an industrial policy pursued in the 1970s), and Taiwan's semiconductor policies throughout the 1980s–2000s. Given that academic studies tend to follow the prevailing mood, the mere appearance of industrial policy research illustrates how far the consensus has already moved (in the 1990s, anyone wanting to embark on a PhD project suggesting that industrial policies are beneficial might not have found a supervisor, especially in top US colleges).

The debate is no longer about ideological objections to state involvement but rather about more optimum ways of encouraging, persuading, and incentivizing private sector participation (via regulatory mandates, tax incentives, subsidies, and guaranteed returns) while ensuring upstream and downstream benefits. History teaches us that the state ultimately overextends (e.g., the late 1960s to mid-1970s). But in the context of the disruption facing the world over the next decade or two, this is hardly the most important issue; rather, the main objective must be to moderate social and polarization risks.

• • •

State spending on basic or fundamental research is also rising. In my first book, I illustrated differences between inventiveness and innovation. The former includes major breakthroughs that the latter (sometimes many years down the track) utilizes for innovation purposes, ultimately leading to actual products and services. As Vannevar Bush, former head of the US Office of Scientific Research and Development, remarked in his report to President Truman, "Basic research leads to new knowledge; it provides scientific capital…it creates the fund from which the practical applications of knowledge must be drawn…new products and new processes do not appear fully grown…they are founded on new principles which in turn are painstakingly developed by research in the purest realms of science."[31] At the time, he was justifiably concerned that with the end of the war, the US government would pull back from its extensive funding of basic research. However, given that society at the time continued to trust state institutions to do the right thing, he did not need to worry; the federal government continued to fund (directly and indirectly) over 70 percent of all of the nation's fundamental research throughout the 1950s–60s and into the 1970s, from which sprung later products (or innovation) from chips and MRI scanners to microwave ovens, Internet, wireless telephony, and GPS.

However, since the 1980s there has been a considerable contraction of state funding for basic research (another example of Baby Boomers' preoccupation with short-term returns and their desire to limit government reach). Whereas in the mid-1960s, federal government spending on fundamental research was around 2 percent of GDP, this dropped to 0.7 percent by 2019 with the private sector not picking up the slack. Non-defense fundamental research in the US is now less than US$100 billion per annum out of the total R&D budget of more than US$700 billion. Google X-labs openly admits that the private sector does not do "undirectional research" (i.e., research initiated by curiosity and the desire to explore, not monetary rewards). As Mariana Mazzucato illustrated in her study of the role played by public sector funded fundamental research, almost everything inside Apple's iPhone was either invented or funded by the federal government.[32] Returns from undirectional research are simply too volatile and uncertain for the private sector to pursue. There are also meaningful conflicts of interest: Would a private pharmaceutical company pursue a line of research that would significantly strengthen its direct competitor, even though it might be advantageous for humanity at large? Also, fundamental research (long term with highly uncertain outcomes) does not work well with short-term quarterly financial reporting requirements and today's executive compensation packages. This does not mean that the government will directly conduct research; rather as in the 1960s, it would offer larger and less restricted budgets to enable independent agencies, universities, and private sectors to pursue it (from NASA to Bell Labs and Berkeley).

Enhancing emphasis on fundamental research will also play an increasingly important role in geopolitical conflicts. Today, almost all of the inventiveness (or science) still resides in the West (mostly the US and, to a lesser extent, the EU and Japan), with China and the Sinosphere having contributed little, explaining the emphasis in most of Xi's recent speeches on boosting science. However, as the *Economist* magazine presciently stated, "The idea that you can get either truly reliable science or truly great science in a political system that depends on a culture of unappealable authority is, as yet, unproven. Perhaps you can. Perhaps you cannot."[33] As effectiveness of Trump's and Biden's restrictions on chip technology transfers to China amply illustrated,[34] the West continues to have an absolute stranglehold on fundamental research. Although China remains an exceptionally innovative nation (i.e., improving on what has been proven to be true in science and delivering final products), its entire tech industry is built on the foundations of Western science. I expect that the West will be gradually grinding China out of its system, with China reciprocating. This will be putting an increasing emphasis on the ability of China to invent, which as the *Economist* article suggested, might not be easy in a climate of unappealable authority. Whether Putin or Xi, both are counting on AI and quantum computing replacing human ingenuity, and hence, the subtitle of my first book: "Do we need to be free to be innovative, prosperous, or even happy?" The lesson of the last five centuries was an unequivocal yes—only freedom could drive inventiveness, growth, and prosperity—but in a digital age, it might no longer be true.

•   •   •

Another key policy that I highlighted in my first book is the need to rethink education and skilling systems and institutions. As discussed above, in most developed economies, various types of gig and unconventional methods of generating income already cover as much 25 percent of the labor force while "formal" hours of work have been on a declining curve almost everywhere. Although the recent pandemic disruption (2020–22) was characterized by a persistent shortage of labor, it is likely to have been just a temporary aberration rather than a new trend. The same is true of the premium that college education has traditionally bestowed on graduates—it has already been falling for at least a decade with returns diverging and overall net benefit eroding.

As conventional industrial-age capitalism sunsets, the requirement of a highly specialized expertise will diminish, and instead the future will be about bringing up a person with a broad mind and many interests, rather than narrowly specialized human capital. In a world of the diminishing marginal utility of humans and an increasing replacement of tasks currently performed by people through the application of AI, robotics, automation, and other technologies (Chapter Seven), the "humanity of humans" and associated interpersonal skills are likely to be the last line of defense. As I described in my first book, "In a world of irrelevance, what is the value of human capital, other than humanity itself."[35] Unfortunately, as a number of studies[36] have conclusively illustrated that our innate ability to think creatively and outside of the box as well as our capacity for finding unexpected and unpredictable connections is neither enhanced nor encouraged by today's schools and colleges. Current preoccupations by colleges on buildings, endowments, donations, stadiums, acceptance yields, and narrow vocational training are becoming a historical anachronism, harking back to the Industrial Age when people needed to be skilled to a progressively higher level to take full advantage of new machinery that demanded an ever narrower field of specialization. Alas, I am not a believer in the Information Age augmenting labor. Instead, it is far more likely that the range of tasks that humans can perform as efficiently and cheaply as technology will continue to narrow, leaving us to fill a multitude of social, caring, interpersonal, and entertainment roles ("humanity of humanity") rather than rewarding narrow experts.

One of the claims in my first book was that in as little as two decades from now, the campus of Harvard University might be abandoned for lack of demand and probably reclaimed by nature or, perhaps, function as a museum of past educational systems. Today's bachelor's degrees and GPAs will disappear apart from the few individuals who want to commit themselves to an academic path, and these would be replaced by rapidly alternating certificates and educational and enrichment classes, from sculpture and art history to cooking, and from yoga and meditation to psychology and gaming. Most of these would be taught online, with the best teachers leveraging a global audience rather than a few students who somehow made it to Harvard. As Julio Frenk, president of the University of Miami, recently remarked, we need to abandon the idea that "education is something that happens to people during a specific time in their lives, a time when they go into a tunnel and come out with a diploma."[37]

• • •

Governments around the world will also need to grapple with challenges that technology platforms in their various guises pose to economic equality, wealth distribution, monopolistic power, and competitiveness as well as social intercourse.

Most of today's anti-monopoly and anti-trust regulations are predominantly based on the 19th- and 20th-centuries' concept of price gauging and consumer loss. However, the challenges today are not about brutal monopoly power in the style of Standard Oil, AT&T, or Microsoft but rather the growing impact of technology platforms that accumulate an almost unparalleled power. As discussed by Foyer and Keen,[38] the core of new age regulatory issues is not so much pollution, dominance within narrowly defined industrial niches, unsafe products (à la rotten meat that was sold across the US prior to Roosevelt's legislation in 1906 and dangerous cars prior to the Road and Car Safety Acts of the late 1960s) or rising consumer prices but a far more subtle abuse of power. It is the power to leverage dominance in one area (Android software, for example) to benefit a company in other areas (say, Google maps, or the selection of shopping or product venues) that is starting to emerge as the essence of modern regulations by reflecting the ability of technology platforms to leverage their strength across a wide terrain, with significant and almost overwhelming network impacts. Unlike the industrial era, the key is not consumer pricing loss (indeed, the opposite is true, as network impacts reduce marginal costs and prices), nor is it deterioration in the quality of products (again, the opposite is true) but rather control over monetization of people themselves and the extent to which it occurs due to loss of privacy and/or choice. At the same time, as new technologies arise there is a need to foster competition and help these to find their niches rather than being smothered by giant platforms with near zero marginal costs. Over the last three years, this was the essence of campaigns by Lina Khan (Biden's chair of the Federal Trade Commission) and the EU against Amazon, Google, Apple, and other platforms. The lack of meaningful breakthrough successes so far illustrates the degree to which regulations and legal practices need to adjust.

There is an equally important question as to how far technologies can be allowed to shape societies as well as social and political interactions, and how these should be regulated (e.g., bots imitating people's browsing habits or the creation and dissemination of fake news to influence mood and voting patterns). This is such a large and complex field that it will take years (if not decades) for policymakers to come to terms with it. In the meantime, whether it is creating demand for products that either do not exist or do not have the extent of following that systems attribute to it; prepackaging knowledge that short-circuits and, in many ways, negates structured education; gaming and other addictions that are inflicted on younger people; or constant concerns regarding electoral interferences and fanning of polarization, it is hard to see how governments will be able to stop this flood and channel it into more constructive venues. However, without it, societal tensions are likely to get worse. The latest Edelman Trust report showed that most societies are broadly dissatisfied with the way governments are regulating and managing innovation, with 56 percent of responders in the US believing that the government is not managing innovation well and only 14 percent thinking that innovation is well regulated and managed. In Germany and the UK, the negative score is 49 percent (when compared to positive scores of around 15–16 percent) and negative views stand at 48 percent in France.[39]

Finally, there is the question of distribution. As Richard Freeman[40] correctly highlighted, those who will own these robots and platforms will own the world, aggravating inequalities, starving the state of revenue, and potentially creating a feudal-type structure with indentured labor rotating between various short-term assignments without any meaningful progression path and with almost no rights. Who should own these technology platforms (especially if a significant portion of their technologies have been either sponsored or funded by the state), and how should they be regulated to prevent abuse while also reducing their monopolistic power in order to encourage further innovation? These are hard questions to answer and would undoubtedly face fierce opposition as well as political and lobbying resistance.

•　　•　　•

While there are many other policies currently being discussed in academia and popular press, I feel that a number of the suggestions are neither practical nor realistic (such as converting corporate ownership into community trusts, replacing market prices with broader values, or implementing UBI's "cousin"—guaranteed jobs).[41] Although admirable, many such proposals fail to fully consider technological evolution and its highly disruptive impact while downplaying imperfect human nature.

Having said that, changes are afoot and chances are that Ronald Reagan's infamous line from his 1981 inaugural address, "the government is not the solution to our problem, government is the problem," is bound to be decisively rejected in the coming years and decades, with the government reemerging as the key guardrail and an indispensable element in the transition from Kaletsky's "Capitalism 3.0" (neoliberal world spawned by Baby Boomers) toward another, yet to be defined, social and economic system. As in the past, it will be facilitated and driven by the new generation (i.e., Millennials and Gen Z), who will determine the extent of freedoms that societies will be prepared to accept and how much our social, economic, and political relations will change. This will be the topic of the next chapter.

Similar to the New Deal, the best compromise might be a return to a world broadly in line with the 1950s–60s: heavy state involvement in most aspects of the economy and our lives with somewhat constrained freedoms.

Chapter 11
MILLENNIALS AND THE ABYSS

"Amongst democratic nations, each generation is a new people."
Alexis de Tocqueville[1]

A s Alexis de Tocqueville, a perceptive and influential observer of the early American republic, once observed, each generation is a new people. What he meant is that in a relatively free society—and, by the way, it does not need to be an open democracy in a modern sense, as indeed the US in the 1820s could hardly be described as a democracy—each generation brings new experiences and views, and ultimately stamps history with its own distinct footprint. There are many sociologists and historians who have developed their entire perspective of history around concepts of generational changes, with Neil Howe being arguably the most well-known and consistent advocate of the importance of generational change in driving history, but similar ideas were also percolating in the writings of Ronald Inglehart, Daniel Elazar, Samuel Huntington, Arthur Schlesinger, and many others.

I have already discussed in Chapters One to Four, how the experiences of the two world wars, depressions, deflations and hyperinflations, the Dust Bowl, pandemics, and other disasters inflicted on humanity between the 1910s and 1940s had so deeply scarred what later became known as the GI and Silent generations that it had a profound impact on almost all social, cultural, political, and economic choices that these cohorts made through the 1950s and 1960s. The emphasis was very much on avoiding risk and safeguarding stability above everything else. Similarly, I have discussed how the unprecedented bulge of the Baby Boomer generation moved the center of gravity away from stability and reliance on the government as the guardrail and toward much greater freedom—personal, economic, social, and political. The following Generation X had maintained the Boomers' razor focus on freedom, and as a result, in George Packer's words, these two cohorts between the late 1970s/early 1980s and 2010 created societies that were far more tolerant and liberal but less fair, more entrepreneurial but significantly less equal. They also set most Western societies on a long-term decline in the efficacy and stability of institutions of state and democracy by embracing key tenets of the neoliberal philosophy, with its emphasis on free market solutions and denigration of state functions. The consensus placed an inordinate emphasis on freedom of choice without due regard for the consequences of such freedom on the environment, inequalities, etc.

Although dividing lines between generations are by necessity hazy and exceptionally hard to delineate (for example, did the Baby Boomer generation end in 1960 or at the more accepted date of 1964?), there is no question that generational analysis is a powerful phenomenon. What drives these generational changes are people's individual experiences as well as some sense of common beliefs and a collective identity. As multiple surveys highlight, when asked which variable had the greatest bearing on defining "who one is and how one sees the world," the most common answer was, "my generation."[2] There are times when differences between generations are relatively minor (e.g., between Boomers and Gen X). But equally, there are also times when such differences are unbridgeable ravines, as was the case between Boomers and their parents and grandparents. Similarly, today, the differences between ageing Boomers (like me) and young Millennial and Gen Z, or those born after the early 1980s, promise to be as wide, deep, and dislocating as in the 1970s, when history came off its leash.

What determines whether one generation slips relatively smoothly into another or if they clash are individual experiences. At times of relative stability (technological, financial, and economic), two generations see the world in a broadly similar light, and while there are some differences, and emphasis might shift somewhat, on the whole, the two cohorts see eye to eye. However, at the peak of technological disruption when societies encounter meaningful dislocations compared to the previously accepted *modus operandi*, and when concurrently one witnesses a growing societal polarization and the inevitable financial and geopolitical shocks, a new paradigm is called for. Although older generations try to minimize the impact and resist change, it is of no use, as ultimately, the new generation becomes the dominant demographic and electoral voice. Eventually, a new consensus is forged in the cauldron of fire, and societies coalesce. However, as we saw through the 1920s–30s as well as the late 1960s to early 1980s, it could take a decade or two, and sometimes longer, for a new consensus to emerge. As I highlighted in the earlier chapters, the Global Financial Crisis was the watershed moment (2010) that commenced the dismantling of the Baby Boomers' consensus which had dominated our world for the prior two to three decades. A new consensus has not yet emerged, but ultimately, it will; it is just a question of time and how much disruption and violence the world would need to endure as we search for that new consensus.

How different are Millennial and Generation Z from the preceding Baby Boomers and X cohorts? The answer is a lot. As in the past, it is the fusion of technology (Information Age) and finance as well as demographic shifts that create much deeper than normal ruptures that challenge almost every aspect of our lives, from the functioning of labor and capital to societal interactions and the importance of such key elements as the nature of work and how we are informed or entertained, and even what is meant to be human. Today, the younger generations are not only witnessing the disintegration of conventional labor markets, professions, and jobs, but they are also confronting extreme inequalities, severe domestic political and social polarization, as well as the end of the peace dividend era and a return to more brutal norms in international relations and geopolitics, from the never-ending war on terror to China and Russia. Baby Boomers have also left younger generations an "unpaid check" of the environmental and financial degradation arising from their obsession with never-ending growth and wealth creation, irrespective of consequences.

How are Millennials and Gen Z reacting to such complex challenges? In many respects not dissimilar to the way their great grandparents did in the 1950s–60s.

•　　•　　•

The last two decades have witnessed a proliferation of surveys attempting to assess how these younger cohorts view the world and the extent to which their priorities differ from the previous consensus. Just like the GI and Silent generations, Millennials and Gen Z distrust private sector solutions and want to curb perceived excesses of capitalism (from profit maximization to disregard for externalities like the climate). They are looking to the government and the community for support rather than emphasizing self-reliance while wanting to return corporations to the type of objectives that management teams embraced five to six decades ago (e.g., quality products, looking after employees and society). However, unlike the generation that dominated the 1950s–60s, today's younger cohorts prefer to keep some of Baby Boomers' freedoms, especially hard-won victories in the areas of race, sex, marriage, and alternative lifestyles, even though surveys also show that they are willing to trade in some of their rights for stability.

According to the US Congressional Institute Survey,[3] 71 percent of Millennials believe that the key role of the state and governments is to promote support and community spirit rather than independence. This is distinctly different from Baby Boomers who tend to prefer independence. In the case of democratic-leaning Millennials, the ratio is closer to 83 percent, and even more interestingly, around 62 percent of republican-leaning Millennials also support the community role of the government when compared to only 30 percent of Baby Boomers. Broadly similar answers come back when these questions are asked: "Should the government help the younger generation plan for their future?" And: "Should the government do more to resolve economic and social problems?" In that survey, 73 percent of Millennials believe that the state should be more actively involved in preparing people to plan for their future, compared to 56 percent for Baby Boomers, and 68 percent of

Millennials believe that the government should do more to resolve problems facing societies and economies versus 51 percent of Baby Boomers. At the same time, a far lower number of Millennials (42 percent) agree with the statement that "when something is run by the government, it is usually wasteful and inefficient." By comparison, the republican-leaning Baby Boomers peg that answer at almost 75 percent. It is also interesting to note that the gap in views on the government's role between democratic- and republican-leaning Millennials is not as pronounced when compared to democratic- and republican-leaning Boomers. A more recent survey by Pew[4] asked not only Millennials but also some older Z cohorts whether the government should be doing more to solve problems. An overwhelming majority of 70 percent of Generation Z and only a slightly smaller share of Millennials (64 percent) concurred when compared to 49 percent of Baby Boomers.

Figure 61. The Role of the Government in Solving Problems (%)

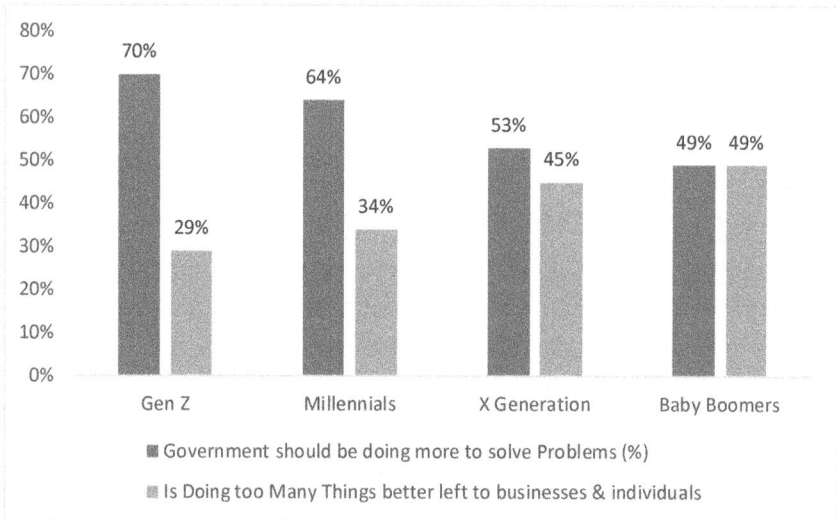

Source: Pew, May 2020

As multiple surveys highlight, the same desire for the community and support is also translating into a much higher acceptance of a positive role played by trade unions. A recent Gallup poll indicated that 67 percent of US responders approved of the role the trade unions play, up from 48 percent in 2009, and on par with the support that unions enjoyed in the 1950s–60s, and 43 percent argued that unions should have more influence, the highest since 1999. The support from Generation Z is even greater, exceeding 70 percent, and the gap between democratic- and republican-leaning Gen Z cohorts is nowhere near as large as it is for Baby Boomers, Gen X, or even Millennials, with as many as 57 percent of republican Gen Z expressing support for trade unions. This chimes with a recent Pew survey indicating that a majority of Americans (54 percent) now believe that a decline in the share of union labor over the preceding four decades was bad for the US, with even 40 percent of republicans concurring. At the same time, 59 percent of Americans agree that this was also bad for workers.[5]

This is not only a US phenomenon. Similar findings are evident in surveys of EU Millennials,[6] which show that 52 percent of Millennials believe that tackling poverty and reducing social and economic inequality should be the most important EU priority. In addition, an overwhelming 83 percent of EU Millennials believe that the government should ensure a minimum livable wage for all workers, with strong support for trade unions. It is worthwhile to pause for a second and realize how diametrically opposite this is to Baby Boomers' desire to have unlimited opportunities without guarantee of outcomes. An even broader survey by Deloitte,[7] covering forty-four countries, found that Millennials and Gen Z place improvement in social mobility primarily on the governments' shoulders (rather than individual effort). This survey also highlighted their insistence that the private corporate sector should focus on quality of products and services as well as looking after employees and the environment rather than on profit maximization. As I intend to discuss in the next chapter, corporations are already responding to these societal changes, with a meaningful shift underway in how they set their core objectives.

At the same time, Millennials and Gen Z are more open to alternative employment and work arrangements. This shows a growing understanding that the job markets of their parents and grandparents no longer exist, and so they adjust. In the Deloitte survey, over 80 percent would consider gig engagements, and around 60 percent think that the gig economy helps innovation. In other words, these unconventional ways of generating income are losing their stigma with younger cohorts, even though surveys clearly show that they realize that these would lower their future income. Interestingly, in line with the GI and Silent generations, these younger cohorts seem to have a much stronger moral fiber, when compared to the more transactional nature of Boomers. For example, in a 2018 McKinsey survey, 75–80 percent of Millennials and Z cohorts would stop buying brands and would strongly advocate for other people to boycott brands implicated in macho, racist, and homophobic behavior. Similarly, they are more tolerant of issues like sex and interracial and same sex-marriage and are far more climate-change attuned. Only 14-15 percent of Millennials and Gen Z believe that climate change is due to natural processes rather than human activity, while for Baby Boomers and X cohorts that ratio is closer to 25 percent.[8] At the same time, almost 50 percent of younger cohorts think that same-sex marriages are good for societies whereas for Baby Boomers, these views are below 30 percent.[9]

Another survey that we have been extensively relying on in Chapter Three is "American Freshman—National Norms," prepared by the staff of Cooperative Institutional Research Program (CIRP) at the Higher Educational Research Institute of the University of California, Los Angeles. As discussed, key advantages of these surveys are that they have been continuously running since 1965–66 and ask consistent questions to the same audience (18- to 20-year-old freshmen), covering up to 100,000 freshmen at more than two hundred colleges across the US.

These surveys show that sometime in the mid- to late 1970s there was a significant break with previous generations away from community service and helping others in need and toward self-fulfillment, earning money, and success. This was reflected not only in responses to questions as to why one was entering college but also what majors one would like to pursue. Between mid-1970s and the early 2000s, the primary reason became "the desire to be well-off financially" which rose from 43 percent in the 1960s to 75 percent in the late 1980s, while the need to "develop a meaningful philosophy of life" slumped from 80 percent in the 1960s to less than 40 percent by the late 1980s and early 1990s, and "the need to help others in difficulty" dropped from 69 percent to 58 percent. At the same time, during the last year when a survey asked whether the main reason for attending college was to volunteer for the Peace Corps, the score dropped from over 20 percent in the 1960s to a mere 7 percent in 1988. Even the need to clean up the environment, which ranked at 42 percent in 1966, dropped to only 18 percent in 1987.

By the late 1980s, neither community support, helping others nor the environment played a key role. It was all pretty much about satisfying Baby Boomers' desire for freedom and self-fulfillment. The same process worked in the selection of major fields of study. Whereas in the 1960s and early 1970s over 45 percent expressed interest in studying arts, humanities, education, and social sciences, by the late 1980s the largest cohort (27 percent) intended to study business and finance while arts, humanities, education, and social services halved to 20 percent, with arts and humanities down to only 9 percent.

However, as Millennial and Gen Z started to have an impact from the late 1990s and especially from the early part of the 21st century, there is evidence that younger cohorts have different priorities, with most much more closely aligned with the 1960s than the 1980s or 1990s. In other words, today's students are more like their grandparents and great-grandparents. For example, enrolling in order to "develop a meaningful philosophy of life" increased from 40 percent in the late 1980s to 50 percent, while college attendance due to a "desire to help others in difficulty" skyrocketed from 58 percent in the late 1980s to 80 percent in 2019. Environmental protection has also emerged as one of the key reasons for enrollments, with this being the primary motivation rising from less than 20 percent in 1987 to 45 percent in 2019. At the same time, attending college in order to prepare oneself for "community action" rose from 19 percent in 1987 to 43 percent in 2019. Similarly, enrollment in business and finance more than halved when compared to the peak in the late 1980s and early 1990s, replaced by biology, health, and life sciences, which by 2019 rose to 27 percent when compared to 14 percent in 1987–88, while hard sciences (i.e., mathematics, physics, chemistry, computer science, and engineering) rose to around one-third of the incoming class versus 17 percent in the late 1980s. Even the arts and humanities are making steady upward progress.

Clearly, younger generations are attracted to the opportunities offered by the Information Age (hence, choices of biology, computer sciences, etc.). Although they value money far more than the 1960s generation of freshmen did (i.e., they no longer have any illusions that money does not matter), they prefer to deploy their success not just for making themselves well-off but to help the environment, others in the need of assistance, or community efforts.

On the darker side, Millennial and Gen Z are more likely to support extreme political views when compared to democracy-loving Baby Boomers. As their great-grandparents, the younger cohorts have witnessed the inability of democratic systems to cope with extreme polarization. It is increasingly triggering Inglehart's "authoritarian reflex" or search for a strongman who can get to the heart of the matter and address their mounting problems. The World Value Surveys that we relied on in Chapter Six indicate that the generation under the age of 30 tends to have the lowest respect for democracy and its institutions. In the US, less than 30 percent of younger cohorts think that it is "absolutely important to live in democracies" when compared to 57 percent of those who are fifty years or older. In Australia, young cohorts' support for democracy is higher, but it is still below 42 percent when compared to 72 percent of those who are fifty years or above, and the younger cohorts' support for democracy is only 20 percent in Japan. Similarly, around 47 percent of the US younger generation thinks that it would be good to "have a strong leader who does not bother with elections and laws," when compared to only 28 percent for older cohorts.[10] It is not surprising, therefore, that support for younger firebrands and populists on the extreme left or right tends to be the highest amongst those younger cohorts.

The youngest generations (Gen Z, between the ages of 18 and 26) also appear to have virtually no trust in key institutions of state and democracy. According to a recent Gallup survey,[11] trust in the US Congress stands at only 10 percent while trust in the Supreme Court is below 20 percent or roughly half the national average, and trust in traditional media outlets is below 15 percent, and it is not that much better for Internet and social news. Although for the country as a whole, trust in the military is very high (around 80 percent for democrats and republicans), it is only 30 percent for adult Gen Z, and even for republicans of this generation it is around 60 percent. It is ironic that the same generation that seems to asks so much more of the government has no trust in key institutional pillars of democracy or state, reinforcing evidence that these cohorts are willing to entertain more extreme answers to their predicament, including various forms of totalitarianism.

Figure 62. Generation Z Trust in US Institutions of Democracy and State

	Democrats	Republicans	Independent	Overall
Science	92%	50%	73%	75%
The Presidency	25%	5%	7%	13%
News	22%	8%	10%	14%
Medical System	43%	38%	34%	38%
Information on Internet	24%	21%	15%	20%
Large Tech companies	9%	12%	10%	12%
Congress	11%	14%	6%	10%
Supreme Court	11%	33%	16%	17%
The Criminal Justice System	11%	41%	12%	18%
The Military	14%	62%	26%	30%
Police	12%	71%	23%	28%

Source: Gallup, September 2023

Also, similar to the GI and Silent generations (but very different from Baby Boomers), an increasing number of younger cohorts seem willing to tolerate a degree of speech suppression that they find either uncomfortable or contrary to their core moral values, with surveys suggesting that as many as one-third of college students would be prepared to suppress news coverage of demonstrations and canceling speeches as well as invitations to presenters who are not in line with their views. The Cambridge University Centre for the Future of Democracy has predictably concluded, "We find that across the globe, younger generations have become steadily more dissatisfied with democracy—not only in absolute terms, but also relative to older cohorts at comparable stages in life."[12]

Thus, on balance, it seems Millennial and Gen Z are more socially conscious, less independent, and more demanding of state services and protection. They seem to value the feeling of community and are prepared to sacrifice some of their democratic and other freedoms to achieve these goals. At extremes, democracy becomes largely optional. Just like Silent and GI generations, they are searching for stability and are more risk averse than either Baby Boomers or Gen X. These cohorts are also far more sharing and having been sheltered and protected all their lives by their Baby Boomer parents, they tend to look for support, not judgement, and experience difficulty accepting criticism. The independent Boomers were trying to create "winners" out of their children by providing the most nurturing environment. Instead, they have created a greater dependency rather than the hoped-for independence. Helicopter parenting, Megan Law, childproof homes, SAT tutors, and "prizes for losers" have all become the hallmarks of the new age for most younger Western generations, especially in the US. At the same time, having grown up in the environment of pervasive and all-encompassing social media, the younger cohorts (especially Gen Z) have become accustomed to penalties that societies and employers inflict on imprudent or even free-thinking expressions of personal feelings, making them more cautious than Baby Boomers would ever have found acceptable. Similar to the Silent generation who in the 1950s and 1960s were carrying the scars of McCarthyism and penalties that the House Committee on Un-American Activities could exercise without any appeal or due process, Millennials and Gen Z are acutely aware of the pitfalls of openly expressing their views.

As can be seen from the following summary, younger cohorts resemble older GI and Silent generations far more than they do their parents (i.e., Boomers and Gen X), even though there are some differences. For example, Millennials and Gen Z have more liberal social values,[13] are less willing to take trenchant criticism and have a greater appreciation of money. In figure 63, I have ended Gen Z in 2015, even though there is a debate as to whether the dividing line should be as early as 2010. Similarly, I have ignored the early years of the GI generation, as these were far too close to the preceding "Lost Generation," and instead I started the clock in 1910 rather than a more accepted timeline of 1901.

Figure 63. Summary of Generational Differences

	"Late GI + Silent" (1910-1945)	"Boomers + X" (1946-1980)	"Millennial+Z" (1981-2015)
Importance of Stability	High	Low	High
Risk Aversion	High	Low	High
Planning for the Future	High	Moderate	High
Teamwork	High	Low	High
State as a guardrail against chaos	High	Low	High
Value of Community support	High	Low	High
Importance of Self Fullfillment	Low	High	Moderate
Importance of Money	Moderate	High	High
Importance of Service	High	Low	Moderate
Focus on Environment	Moderate	Low	High
Freedom of choice not guarantee of outcomes	Low	High	Low
Ability to take crtisism	High	High	Low
Focus on Liberal Social values	Low	High	High
Willigness to sacrifice rights	High	Low	High

• • •

When will these younger cohorts start having a decisive influence on societies and politics? As we saw in prior chapters, Baby Boomers were already exercising a considerable pull from the late 1960s onward. But in most countries their impact was not decisive until the late 1970s and early 1980s when Boomers and Gen X cohorts had become a majority of the adult population (above the age of 18). Boomers and Generation X crossed 50 percent of the US overall population in the early 1970s, but they did not overtake the GI and Silent generation adults until the early to mid-1980s. In my view, this explains the rising intensity of neoliberal policies which moved from being of marginal importance in the 1970s to being the dominant ideological and policy strand from the early 1980s until 2010, with politicians like Ronald Reagan, Margaret Thatcher, Bill Clinton, and Tony Blair, economists like Milton Friedman, and management consultants like Ronald Coase rising to prominence on Baby Boomers' shoulders.

In 2015, US Millennial and Gen Z cohorts had already edged out Baby Boomers and Generation X in population terms; however, they still had a considerably lower proportion of adults (i.e., around 31 percent when compared to 57 percent for Boomers and Gen X). By 2020, Millennials' and Gen Z's share of adults increased to almost 39 percent, and these younger cohorts should be in a majority (i.e., over 50 percent) by 2028–29. According to UN estimates, their share is likely to peak at 56–57 percent of US adults sometime between 2035 and 2040. At the same time, Boomers' and Gen X's share should be down toward one-third of adults. At that point, the battle between generations will be over.

Figure 64. US Generational Cohorts (% of Population)

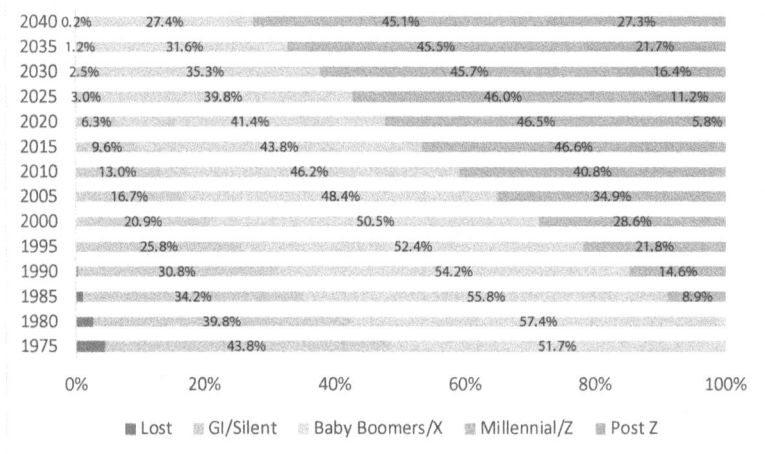

Source: United Nations, December 2023

Figure 65. US Generational Cohorts (% of Adults)

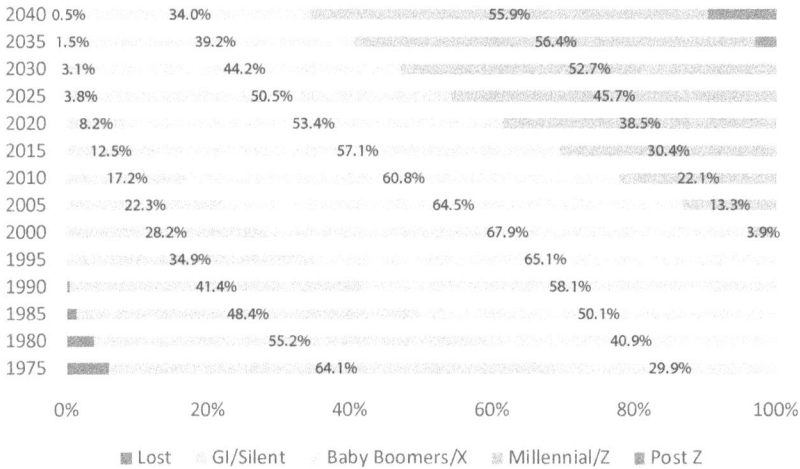

Year	Lost	GI/Silent	Baby Boomers/X	Millennial/Z	Post Z
2040	0.5%	34.0%	55.9%		
2035	1.5%	39.2%	56.4%		
2030	3.1%	44.2%	52.7%		
2025	3.8%	50.5%	45.7%		
2020	8.2%	53.4%	38.5%		
2015	12.5%	57.1%	30.4%		
2010	17.2%	60.8%	22.1%		
2005	22.3%	64.5%	13.3%		
2000	28.2%	67.9%	3.9%		
1995	34.9%	65.1%			
1990	41.4%	58.1%			
1985	48.4%	50.1%			
1980	55.2%	40.9%			
1975	64.1%	29.9%			

Source: United Nations, December 2023

While timetables vary on a country-by-country basis, and experiences as well as views of younger cohorts in less developed economies are clearly meaningfully different, in most Western nations, Millennial and Gen Z will reach adult and electoral majorities sometime over the next decade, and certainly, by the early 2030s. In the top eight western nations (i.e., the US, the UK, Germany, France, Italy, Japan, Australia, and Canada), the unweighted average share of these cohorts is likely to rise from around 41 percent in 2025 to 48.5 percent in 2030 and peak at around 52–53 percent in 2035, persisting at that level into the early 2040s. The post-Gen Z cohort (those born after 2015, and who are referred to as a Generation Alpha) should start having an impact toward late 2040s, although at this stage, this cohort is far too young to be meaningfully assessed, and it is unlikely that their full transformative impact will be felt until sometime in the 2050s.

Figure 66. Millennial and Z Generations (% of Adult Population)

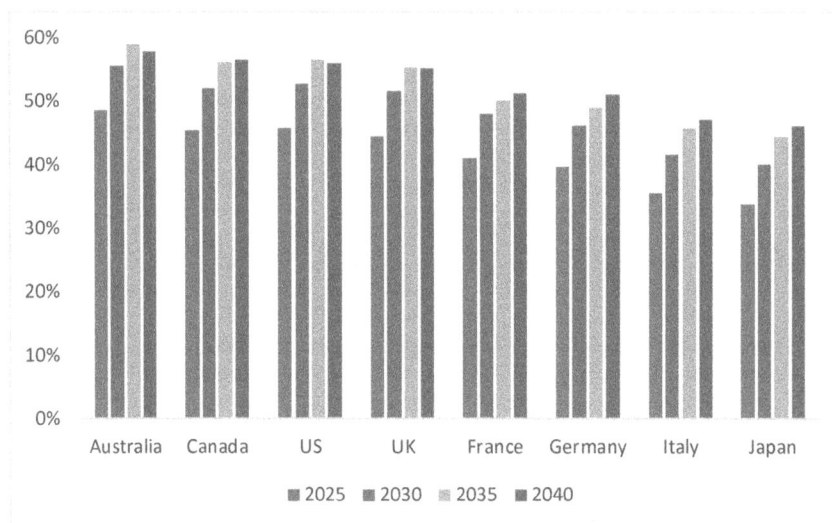

Source: United Nations, December 2023

• • •

Arguably the best description of broadly defined Millennials was provided by the renowned expert in this area, Neil Howe, when he wrote, "Millennials seek no risk, but security. Not spontaneity, but planning. Not a free-for-all marketplace, but a rule-bound community of equals."[14] This is far closer to the philosophy of the GI and Silent Generations rather than Baby Boomers or Generation X, and therefore, the world they create will also be closer to the 1950s and early 1960s than 1980s–2000s.

It is inevitable that as Millennials and Gen Z become the main demographic and electoral force, their values and views will come to dominate societies and, by implication, the political and economic landscape. Just as the GI and Silent cohorts had rebuilt the world destroyed by the Second World War, it will be the responsibility of these younger generations to glue the world back together and do their best to overcome the tremendous challenges unleashed by the Fujiwara effect.

Chapter 12

Dawn of a New Day

"The darkest hour is just before the day dawns."
Thomas Fuller

In 1993, Peter Drucker, one of the fathers of management science, ominously warned that governments were increasingly trying to control not just the "climate" (i.e., extreme severity of outcomes) but also the "weather" (i.e., making sure that the temperature remains at a comfortable 70–80 degrees Fahrenheit, and that there are no major thunderstorms, and definitely no floods). In his words, "The Great Depression gave rise to the belief that the national government is—and should be—in control of the economic weather."[1]

Three decades have passed since his pioneering study of what post-capitalism world might look like and more than ninety years since the Great Depression, and despite neoliberal hostility, the state has remained on a persistently expansionary path throughout, under both left- and right-wing governments. As economies and societies struggle with disruptions caused by deep Financialization and the Information Age, it is likely that state tentacles will spread even further, and the free space will continue to shrink. John Gray, a professor from Harvard University, compared it to a migration of Hobbes's Leviathans from "being an institution that claimed to extend freedom" to "one that protects human beings from danger. Instead of a safeguard against tyranny, it offers *shelter from chaos*."[2]

We are standing at the dawn of a new day, and the question is not whether our economies, politics, and societies will change but rather what lies on the other side of the "black hole" and the role that the Leviathan will play.

•　　•　　•

Nothing illustrates better the scope and the breadth of today's state control than the metamorphosis of capital markets and the government's growing sway over economic cycles. Central banks and policymakers have already been for decades expanding their reach in incremental steps, prompted at every turn by exogenous shocks such as Black Monday in 1987, the collapse of Long-Term Capital Management in 1998, dot-com in 2000–01, the Global Financial Crisis in 2008–10, and the COVID-19 pandemic in 2020–22.

As economies financialized and leverage increased, so has the potential for shocks. The Financialization-driven global excess capital (i.e., five to ten times GDP), when combined with trading and market digitization as well as instantaneous repricing, has the ability to change financial conditions rapidly and excessively, while also offering numerous opportunities for policymakers to continue tightening their control over capital markets. As discussed earlier in this book, there is no off-ramp for the Financialization train; it is no longer about recreating "sound money" or deleveraging but rather managing an increasingly risky and a potentially highly volatile "cloud of finance." At this point, conventional de-leveraging (through inflation or otherwise) is one of the most dangerous strategies that central banks could possibly pursue. This also explains the growing focus on what central banks describe as macro and micro prudential controls, which range from broad regulatory rules to a proliferation of dedicated policies designed to address specific issues. A few examples of the latter include regulations of what policy makers regard as an "inappropriate" widening of spreads, curbing volatility in interbank plumbing and repo markets, and addressing various risks such as real estate (residential or commercial) or specific alternative financial niches (from private debt and equity to parity and basis trades).

Given the depth and breadth of financialization, returning to policies designed, in Drucker's words, to control "climate" rather than "weather" is neither feasible nor desirable, as the flow-on impact on real economies would be devastating. Anyone wishing to limit the degree of state interference should be careful what they wish for. Given that across most countries, money supply over more than three decades grew at least two to three times faster than nominal GDP (unlike the 1950s to early 1980s when money supply was growing more or less in line with underlying economies), there is no feasible way of converging these two variables. Any attempt to do so is bound to result in an uncontrollable repricing of assets, with people quickly realizing that their pensions might no longer exist or that their homes might be worth a fraction of what they paid for them. If we wished to debate virtues or vices of financialization, we should have done so when Paul Volcker (former Fed Chairman who is better remembered for squashing inflation in the early 1980s but whose far more pertinent legacy was to unleash an uncontrollable wave of debt and financialization) launched our modern world.[3] Or perhaps in 1987 when Alan Greenspan (Volcker's successor) brought his policy to its logical conclusion by launching what became known as "Greenspan's put" (or inability to tolerate volatility of asset prices), reinforced by his successors (Ben Bernanke and Janet Yellen).

Thus, the idea of market participants determining the most efficient allocation of capital and pricing of risk through free market signals, with limited prudential oversight by policymakers and regulators, survives only in economics and finance textbooks with limited (if any) relevance to today's capital markets. Going forward, the complexity of global capital markets and their increasing interconnectedness (no one knows the second, third, or fourth derivative of any event) implies that major bankruptcies (à la Lehman Brothers in 2008) or market clearances are completely unacceptable. Instead, careful management of volatilities is required, as the "cloud of finance" gets ever larger.

Policy tools have already been proliferating at a breakneck speed, and we should soon arrive at a point where one could seriously question whether there is any room for markets. If central banks determine both prices and spreads, why does one need bond markets? Few investors any longer pay much attention to spreads between the German *Bunds* and Italian government paper, as the European Central Bank's "monetary policy transmission" facility can be engaged at any time to narrow such spreads if policymakers disagree with market pricing. Similarly, it is unlikely that the Federal Reserve would ever again lose control over the front end of the curve (as it did in September 2019), due to the presence of its unlimited emergency repo facility, while Silicon Valley Bank's solution of converting treasury balances of different duration into cash (2023), could be replicated in similar incidences at a moment's notice. Since 2008, the relationships between central banks were buttressed by extensive swap lines that can be activated at any sign of stress in FX markets. Over the last decade, investors also witnessed central banks involved in direct lending to the main street (during the Global Financial Crisis and COVID-19 pandemic) as well as the lending and buying not only of government securities but also loan books and corporate bonds and, for the Bank of Japan, even equities. There is also a great deal of pretending that government spending is not financed by central banks, when in fact it frequently is, with governments selling bonds into private markets only to see them bought by central banks. Why not eliminate intermediaries altogether, especially if the state has already determined volumes, rates, and spreads?

Over the next decade or two, the degree of control is likely to be meaningfully increased not only as a response to growing risks but also due to the progress of technology, including proliferation of Central Bank Digital Coins (CBDC). Although central banks must be careful how and when they disintermediate commercial banks, and what role such banks will have in this new world, it seems inevitable that many functions today performed by commercial banks (like Citibank, Barclays, or JP Morgan) will shift to central banks.[4] This particularly applies to the propagation of monetary policies through maturity transformation of commercial lending and deposit taking (or the fractional deposit system that has been in existence for more than two centuries). The same is true of credit card companies like Visa or Mastercard or payment systems, with central banks able to offer such products at almost zero incremental cost. The key question that policymakers are currently trying to address is: *What is the role of commercial banks, in a world where transaction costs collapse, ability to access deposits and assess risk gets easier, and central banks are not just purveyors of trust but also direct market participants?* It seems increasingly likely that within a decade or so, CBDC and stablecoins (but not Bitcoin and its imitators, which are only useful as a hedge against an uncontrolled melt-down of the global monetary system) will dominate the landscape, displacing conventional currencies. Despite many concerns, these will likely be the only instruments with the requisite degree of trust and scalability to become the "new" money.

Thus, today's capital markets no longer reflect conventional think-ing and theories regarding rates, spreads, liquidity, and most other factors that were at the heart of the traditional capitalist economy. Under the pressure of intense financialization and rapid technological evolution, key ingredients of economic and capital cycles are degrading. The fragility of both real economies and finance and their destabilizing interactions imply that central banks and policymakers can no longer tolerate volatilities of economic and capital market cycles. This is not because of conspiracies, "dark forces," or "deep state," but rather the fear of highly unpredictable and destructive outcomes for real economies.

Hence, in Peter Drucker's words, we have been for decades manag-ing "weather" and not "climate," preventing clearances of both real and financial economies. This is worlds away from Robert Lucas's and Thomas Sargent's (two of the most influential Nobel Prize winners from the 1970s–90s) economic orthodoxy of rational expectations and self-equil-ibrating systems. The previous decades were characterized by Boomers' persistent attempts to emasculate the state, but their thirst for freedom was only made possible by an increasingly robust state interference in the operation of what were reputedly free markets. This is probably the greatest irony of the most ardent proponents of neoliberal ideas—that their theories (though wonderfully modeled) failed to reflect how human societies work. If there were no meaningful government interference, and people were prepared to accept consequences of equilibrating markets, and markets were efficient with perfect information, then the neoliberal world might have worked. Alas, as Karl Polanyi explained, economies are not separate from societies but rather are imbedded in and derivative from them (Chapter Four), with liberalism, and its most recent "neo" iteration, making demands on people (bankruptcies, wage adjustments, lack of state support, etc.) that are simply not sustainable and will never be accepted for any length of time. People would simply refuse to tolerate periodic dramatic fluctuations in their daily life and would mobilize to protect themselves from such shocks.

FDR's New Deal represented one such compromise that avoided extremes by responding to these pressures through expansion of the government, aimed at reducing inequities, inequalities, and suffering.[5] The principal reason why today's social dislocations are not as extreme as they were in the first or second iteration of liberalism (i.e., in the 19th and the first half of the 20th centuries) is precisely because societies have been pushing back. Boomers' expectations of forever growth and wealth led to an ironic side effect of aggressive compression of business and capital market cycles (neoliberal theory be damned), in the process, morphing Boomers' ideas of personal freedom and responsibility into an ever-heavier dependence on the state to manage increasingly fragile economies and markets.

When was the last time that the US experienced a deep recession and meaningful clearance of excesses? Ignoring a short-lived but sharp contraction during the COVID pandemic (2020), one needs to go back to the 1860s–1930s to see what recessions and adjustments looked like in the true neoliberal world. From the end of the Civil War until 1950, there were 22 recessions with an average output contracting each time by more than 20 percent. However, since 1950, there have only been 11 recessions, with an average (peak to trough) output contraction of a mere 3 percent and with many closer to 2 percent. In prior eras, these would not have even qualified as recessions. Also, the average time elapsing between recessions has significantly expanded to more than six years when compared to less than two years in the preceding eight decades. Thus, we have been experiencing less intense and far less frequent recessions, certainly nothing of the scope and devastation of the Long Depression of the 1870s–80s or the Great Depression of the 1930s.

Figure 67. *US Recessions, 1918–2023*

US Recessions - 1918-2023

Source: BEA

However, there are no free lunches, and the side effect of a multi-decade lack of clearances is that over time recoveries have become much more muted. *Risks do not just evaporate—instead they migrate to other areas (e.g., social, political, geopolitical, climate)*, something that has been especially evident after the Global Financial Crisis. While economic cycles have not entirely disappeared, they have been compressed to a point where it is getting difficult to identify where one cycle ends and another begins. The Fujiwara effect has been accelerating the replacement of products, brands, operational and marketing systems while central banks and policymakers have been simultaneously trying to take as much risk and volatility out of the financial system as possible.

The net outcome is that neither economic nor capital market cycles look or behave the way theory argues they should. How does one assess where neutral rates are and, therefore, what central bank policy rates should be? Are neutral rates going up or coming down? How does one assess risk premia if it is no longer driven by conventional economic and capital market cycles? Should it be 1 percent or 5 percent? Both might be the right answers, explaining why central banks have recently become so data dependent— another way of saying that policymakers have only limited confidence in their knowledge as to where stars are. This has significant implications for private sectors, investors, and policymakers (Chapter Ten). The greater the uncertainty and more volatile neutral rates become, the more complicated is the environment facing private sectors in gauging future demand. It also simultaneously undermines the usefulness of discounted cash flow analysis and estimates of the weighted average cost of capital. Should one expand capacity or build a new factory, or should one close the factories? Without reasonable confidence in the final demand and a degree of certainty as to what the weighted average cost of capital is likely to be, it is becoming far more difficult for most corporations to answer this basic question.

Over the last three to four decades, Boomers have reluctantly permitted the state to engage in robust economic and cycle management and capital market policies. The younger cohorts (i.e., Millennials and Gen Z) are likely to truly embrace the state as the natural answer and the most obvious guardrail against evolving chaos, covering an ever-wider terrain— from proactive income, industrial and redistribution policies, to a de facto nationalization of capital markets.

Most commentators and economists might be aghast by such dramatic shifts and especially the extent of reach and control that governments and public sectors will exercise. The next decade could be, therefore, characterized by vociferous disagreements on what it all means and its implications on topics as wide ranging as economic efficiency, growth, productivity, and personal freedoms. These concerns are legitimate and must be debated. However, the world is already profoundly changing, and the pace is likely to keep accelerating, touching on every aspect of our lives—from social interactions and politics to the role of the free market and the nature of capitalism. There is no conceivable way of returning to any point that is even remotely close to conventional industrial capitalism, just like in the 19th century, there was no way of returning to the early stages of mercantilist capitalism.

• • •

The profound changes are also becoming far more pronounced in the social sphere. Boomers' freedom to discuss and debate pretty much any issue is already being curtailed by societies beset by insecurities and fueled by the willingness of younger cohorts to sacrifice some of their freedoms. It is even possible to see a return to the 1950s' style of McCarthyism. One could recently witness this on full display when Republican Senator John Kennedy of Louisiana was persistently asking Melissa Dubose, Biden's nominee for the US District Court of Rhode Island, whether she was a communist, and despite answers that she has never been a communist or a Marxist, Kennedy persisted on the same line of questioning. After it was pointed out that Kennedy himself was for decades a democrat before becoming a republican, Senator Lindsey Graham of South Carolina had to laugh, saying, "Let's agree on the following…a Louisiana democrat is probably not a Marxist."[6] However, this is far from a laughing matter, as the same line of argument was already used against a nominee for Comptroller of the Currency in late 2021. This is uncomfortably close to the questioning by the Committee for Un-American Activities, described in Chapter One, with the infamous starting question, "Are you now or have you ever been a communist?" followed by unbearable pressure applied by the committee to name names and threats of "black books" which condemned thousands of people, without benefit of either judge or jury. At the peak of his influence, McCarthy boasted a 50 percent approval rating, and over one-third of the electorate supported the work of the committee. When in June 1950 Republican Senator Margaret Chase Smith accused McCarthy of promoting "fear, ignorance, bigotry and smear,"[7] only six other republicans joined her. It was not until later that both parties recognized the danger McCarthy posed, and this was only after public opinion turned and became less fearful of the Soviet threat. Many of today's republicans believe that merits of McCarthy's 1950s crusade outweigh the negatives of his character and style, and hence, the myth of his victimization by the elite endures to this day.

The same intolerance is becoming evident in the penalties that societies are starting to exact from anyone who raises sensitive issues—from the Palestinian-Israeli conflict to various topics associated with diversity and inclusion or types of books and material that should be available at schools and colleges, with the inevitable proliferation of "wokeism entrepreneurs" (from Ron DeSantis in the US to Nigel Farage in Britain) who fan polarization pressures. The path of free communication and debate is getting ever narrower, with protagonists using social media, monetary donations (witness the recent billionaire donor's strike in the case of the elite US colleges), and the judicial system to label certain types of behavior inadmissible and deserving of severe punishments, while favoring their own versions of "truth" as the only right and patriotic path. As in the 1950s, what is meant by academic freedom is extensively questioned, with most US conservatives and some neoliberals genuinely believing that educational and cultural institutions had been captured by "extreme left Marxists" with progressives pushing back against perceived conservative overreach. While Western countries do not yet have the 1950s' official censorship, many of today's nationalist-conservatives are advocating for exactly such constraints, with extreme progressives responding in kind. Surveys also highlight that a sizable portion of younger cohorts seem to accept the benefit of more constrained debate and limited free space for discussion. In more authoritarian countries, like Russia or China, the space for debates and exchange of views has by now been completely extinguished.

All over the developed world borders are tightening, slowly reverting to the frontiers of the 1950s–60s, which were hard to cross, requiring extensive documentation, and where mass deportations of migrants were a common occurrence. For example, in 1954 the Eisenhower administration embarked on what was described as Operation Wetback, which voluntarily and compulsorily deported up to 1.1 million Mexicans. Both the Trump and Biden administration have already stepped up deportations, with anti-immigration emerging as one of the few bipartisan issues and with Trump indicating that if he is elected in November 2024, he plans to deploy the entire might of US law and order and military resources to expel those whom he describes as "alien invaders." The UK has been also persisting with its Rwanda plan of deporting illegal migrants to the African country, and the EU is now customarily bribing countries like Tunisia, Libya, Lebanon, and Turkey to contain migrant flows while de facto allowing thousands to die in the Mediterranean. Although in the long term, it won't make much difference (as borders can never contain human flows and, indeed, Eisenhower expulsions ultimately were not successful), it is illustrative of an increasingly angry and scared populace, demanding border closures and separation from other nations.

In the US, a greater conservatism is even spreading toward numerous topics of private morality, something that Baby Boomers struggled to overcome in the 1960s–70s, from sex before marriage to the ease of divorce and from reproductive rights to questions of sexual orientation and the state's role in children's education and healthcare. Although not as prominent in other Western nations, there are tentative signs of a similar conservative backlash emerging in countries like the UK, Australia, Italy, and especially Eastern Europe (Poland, Hungary, etc.). While most of this is fanned by older, less educated, and more economically marginalized sections of the population (i.e., greater insecurity inevitably results in a stronger desire for *in-group* morality), younger cohorts (while significantly more liberal) accept a much tighter degree of societal constraints than the free-wheeling Boomers would have ever contemplated.

Corporations also understand that societies are on the move and try to avoid being caught on the wrong side of popular angst and history. The same corporations that in the 1990s–2000s were proudly proclaiming maximization of returns for shareholders as their primary and only objective while insisting that free markets determine executive compensation packages (which between 1965 and 2015 rose from 50 to as high as 300 times average wages), and that the state should minimize interference with markets and mergers and acquisitions (under the private sector knows best rubric) are making a meaningful U-turn. The emphasis is already shifting toward a much broader and all-encompassing definition of stakeholders. The new US Business Roundtable mission statement, unveiled in 2019, stated, "While each of our companies serves its own corporate purpose, we share fundamental commitment to *all stakeholders*. Americans deserve an economy that allows each person to succeed through hard work and to lead a life of meaning and dignity." This is a dramatic change when compared to the statement of objectives that the same business lobbying group enunciated in the early 1990s: "The principal objective of a business enterprise is to generate *economic returns to its owners*." It is illustrative that the *Harvard Business Review*'s (HBR) collection of most important articles of its first one hundred years did not include what is arguably the single most influential paper to come out from HBR. Michael Jensen's[8] paper (1976) launched the corporate revolution by forcefully arguing that the primary responsibility of managers is to reward shareholders (or in Jensen's terms, "reconciliation of agency and ownership dilemma"). Almost anyone who studied for an MBA in 1980s–90s would have spent considerable time on this paper. Clearly, his ideas are today as unpopular as they were outstandingly influential in the Boomers' era.

The same uncertainty is permeating other topics from executive compensation plans and corporate diversity and inclusion to climate and ESG policies. Today almost every corporation is asking a question: "How far do people want us to go?" While trade-offs will be hard to navigate, it seems likely that corporate's view of their responsibilities will continue migrating closer toward standards of the 1950s–70s, rather than the "greed is good" and free-wheeling mantra of 1990s–2000s. Although the most complex transition lies ahead for the US and Anglo-Saxon corporations (as neoliberal ideas penetrated these societies to a far greater extent), everyone will need to adapt to shifting sands of history.

•   •   •

The generation that lived through the 1950s would have undoubtedly recognized most of these symptoms (from Sputnik moments to nuclear threat, and from the fear of communist subversion to upholding tribal views of one's country's values) and most likely would have shrugged off these constraints as an acceptable price to pay for a more coherent and protective, even if more stifling, society. It is likely that the Millennials and Gen Z cohorts would wholeheartedly agree.

Friedrich Engels, during one of the 19th century upheavals, is reputed to have said, "Bourgeois society stands at the crossroads, either transition to socialism or regress into barbarism."[9] One can debate what Engels meant by socialism; however, he was clearly right that capitalism was undergoing a profound transformation. Even before his death in 1895, he already witnessed many changes reducing depravation and poverty that he documented in English factories of the 1840s–50s and transitioning into new types of economic and societal relations that had only a tangential relationship to the first iteration of capitalism. Similarly, as one of the better-known modern left-wing intellectuals expressed it: "The image I have of the end of capitalism—an end that I believe is already under way—is one of a social system in chronic disrepair, for reasons of its own, and regardless of a viable alternative. While we do not know when and how exactly capitalism will disappear and what will succeed it, what matters is that no force on hand that could be expected to reverse the three downward trends in economic growth, social equality, and financial stability and end their mutual reinforcement."[10] Again, it is perfectly true that today's systems are also under considerable stress, and changes are afoot. *The only question is what type of system will replace the latest iteration of capitalism.*

As I described in my first book, whatever is coming down the pike might "look far more like an enlightened version of communism than conventional capitalism."[11] My task is not to scare readers but to sound a call to arms. *How do we survive through this painful transition while protecting as many of our freedoms as possible,* rather than descending into a world of dictatorships and various 20th century perversions of communism? After all, it is unlikely that Karl Marx would have recognized his vision of a new society in the despotic and kleptocratic regimes of Cuba, North Korea, the former Soviet Union, or even today's China. To Marx, communism was meant to be a society of such a high productivity that it would generate an abundance of goods and services to satisfy everyone's needs without the compulsion of labor, or as Marx phrased it, "From each according to his ability, to each according to his needs."[12] For many readers who might be repulsed by the possibility, or even the suggestion, of a communist future, these sentiments by Marx are not that far removed from Keynes's view in the 1930s that the ultimate challenge facing humanity is one of living well in an environment where technology and compound interest delivers such a high level of productivity that most people no longer need to toil to secure daily necessities.[13] Even Peter Drucker argued in the early 1990s that, "every few hundred years in Western history, there occurs a sharp transformation. It is creating a post-capitalist society where...the basic economic resource is no longer capital, natural resources, or labor."[14]

Are we facing a world of a select few managers organizing some structures and itinerant workers and freelancers moving in and out of temporary assignments with limited (if any) rights, protection, and security?[15] Would it be one that Yanis Varoufakis described as "technocratic feudalism"[16] with several major global technology platforms dominating the world and through algorithms determining our preferences and our values? Might it be the dark society that Peter Frase described as "abundance mixed with rentism" or "scarcity with exterminism"?[17] As governments become more dominant, the question of whether state planning and centralized allocation of resources can do a better job while alleviating some of the worst outcomes is clearly coming to the fore. As Jack Ma, the founder of Alibaba, put it, "Over the past 100 years, we have come to believe that the market economy is the best system...but in the next three decades, because of access to all kinds of data, we may be able to find the 'invisible hand' of the market." It seems like a dream come true for the likes of Vladimir Putin, Xi Jinping, or any other authoritarian leader, with neither innovation, entrepreneurship nor societal freedoms any longer being key prerequisites for success. This line of reasoning threatens not only to break the link between freedom and productivity but also to lead us to societies that might resemble George Orwell's *1984* or Robert Constanza's[18] *Mad Max*.

Instead of the above dystopian choices, I think conventional capitalism might simply slip into what can be best described as an "enlightened version of communism," defined in the original sense of the term, as a society of such a high productivity that it dispenses with the need to toil to earn a living. This would be an ideal outcome, leading to an environment of exceptionally high productivity that coexists with reasonably robust (though somewhat degraded and constrained) personal and economic freedoms. Luckily, as described in Chapter Eleven, this outcome is likely to be far more in tune with the views of today's younger generations.

My first book asked, "As we hurtle toward that uncertain future, we must decide whether our cherished individual freedoms are still necessary for the success and prosperity…Humanity is at a major turning point, and how we respond to the merger of technology and financialization will decide our future. Will it be capitalism, communism, feudalism, or despotism?"[19] Today, this question is even more pertinent, with ChatGPT and other recent breakthroughs pushing technological frontiers forward while polarization has become meaningfully more disruptive and both migratory and geopolitical tensions are now far worse than they were in 2019–20. In the years ahead, all of these issues are bound to become even more pronounced and extreme. One can observe numerous changes already moving us toward a more restrictive world by ejecting most of traditional industrial-age capitalism, as we try to reconcile the Information Age with the prevailing capital, social, and labor market norms. Whether it is the functioning of money and capital or the nature of employee-employer relations and the role of labor markets, freedom of speech and debate, everything is up for grabs.

•　　•　　•

In June 1933, the *Financial Times* heaped a great deal of praise on Benito Mussolini, with its Italian spread featuring the following headline: "The Renaissance of Italy: Fascism's Gift of Order and Progress." It described changes as follows: "The country has been remodeled, rather than remade, under the vigorous architecture of its illustrious Prime Minister, Segnor Mussolini."[20] After decades of confusion, trains were running on time, investment was growing, and persistent frictions between labor and capital were a thing of the past. Later, similar praise was in the offing for Adolf Hitler and his "remodeling" of Germany, with Hitler named the Man of the Year by *Time* magazine in its February 1939 edition. The following year, Joseph Stalin was similarly honored. Today, thirst for a strongman is evident in almost every nation, and similar arguments of "stability," "making the system work," reducing uncertainty and volatility while enhancing "national pride," are fueling another bout of an "authoritarian reflex."

As a German philosopher Georg Hegel once said, "The only thing that we learn from history is that we learn nothing from history." Harsh, but true. Memories fade, and we no longer feel the pain of preceding generations, while today's concerns overwhelm any sense of history or long-term consequences. We do not feel the pain of people who had to go through decades of extreme suffering in the wake of the first Industrial Revolution (with a label "Luddite" morphing into a pejorative description of someone who is against progress rather than of someone who suffers). Instead, we just remember glorious outcomes—ultimately everything was great. The same memory lapses explain the sharp turn that Baby Boomers took in the 1980s–90s in dismantling the world of the 1950s–60s (forgetting the painful lessons of the Long and the Great Depressions of the 19th and early part of the 20th centuries as well as lessons of the Great War and Second World War). It similarly points to today's younger cohorts who are once again remolding societies, politics, and economies, with the pace of change intensifying over coming years.

An unresolved question is how disruptive these will be, and whether younger generations will guide us toward a "world on fire" of the 1940s, with violent and unpredictable upheavals at local and global levels (from civil wars to wider conflagrations), or whether they will somehow manage to land at a far less disruptive, but more restrictive, 1950s–60s. This remains an open question, and only one thing seems clear: The next decade promises to be one of the most consequential, hardest, and the most treacherous ever to navigate. As Thomas Fuller, an English theologian, wrote in 1650, "The night is the darkest before the dawn." Complex compromises (not perfection) are needed. There are multiple alternative paths that are opening up and competing against each other—nationally, globally, and individually. Which path will we take?

As this book discusses, some choices are clearly far better than others, but as the fear gauge continues to climb, it is not yet clear whether this will awaken the best or the worst of our nature. However, what is certain is that the state is the only guardrail with sufficient credibility and the strength to help us avoid the worst outcomes.

Epilogue

"The only thing we have to fear is fear itself."
Franklin D. Roosevelt, First Inaugural Address, 1933

I n 1939, visitors to the New York Fair were welcomed by Gershwin's "Dawn of a New Day," an upbeat tune that promised the dawn of a new and more exciting world. It was played mere months before the unfolding of the greatest ever devastation inflicted by humanity on humanity, with unspeakable cruelty masquerading as legitimate grievances.

As discussed throughout this book, our current environment resembles the 1930s more than any other period in modern history. The same pressures that shaped the 1930s and led to the "world on fire" of the 1940s, are evident in abundance today—from financial crises and "secular stagnation" to low productivity and extreme inequalities, from the rise of new powers to demographics. But a lack of global consensus on what constitutes the "right" economic, social, and political models is arguably the most important commonality (something that we also share with the late 1960s to early 1980s). At such times of disorientation and rising physical and economic insecurities, the thin veneer of civilization tends to fall off and raw primitive emotions resurface, with people reaching out for extremes, in the process triggering an "authoritarian reflex" or willingness to sponsor a strongman to solve their mounting problems.

In the 1930s, there were three options on the menu: a more constrained democracy, communism, or fascism. All three involved a much greater and deeper than hitherto role of the state in economic, political, and social spheres as the only solution to the intractable problems facing societies. Communism was offering the most extreme answer of total elimination of private property and political rights in exchange for stability and equality (e.g., Soviet Union). The fascist answer was more modulated: one keeps one's property, but the private sector was completely and unreservedly subjected to the state, with messy democratic politics extinguished in exchange for economic stability and some degree of fairness (e.g., Nazi Germany, Fascist Italy and Spain, Imperial Japan). However, the wisdom of FDR and the New Deal was to find the middle ground. Some freedoms were lost (and hence, consistent complaints at the time about the "government's overreach"); however, most freedoms and democracy were preserved, and the state never fully extinguished private property rights or initiative, while still defanging the extremes. In the absence of the New Deal, it is quite possible that the US might have moved toward a fascist or communist end of the spectrum. In the answer to the question that Carl Becker posed in 1941—"Can the possessors be sufficiently dispossessed and the dispossessed be sufficiently reinstated without resort to violence, revolution, and the temporary or permanent dictatorship"[1]—FDR offered the most optimal, and ultimately successful, answer. It was not perfection or purity but highly complex compromises that were called for.

Although labels change and we no longer talk as much about communists or fascists, basic principles remain the same. Democracy is not a natural state of human existence and must be constantly nurtured by lowering inequalities, which unless checked, invariably tend to get worse. Unlike triumphant beliefs in liberal democracy (being the ultimate state of the evolution of human societies) that was so prevalent following the collapse of the Soviet Union in the early 1990s,[2] the last 15 years have seen a return of history and that of more conventional *kyklos* (or cycle) theories that were far less fashionable during the era of neoliberalism from the early 1980s until the Global Financial Crisis (2010). In economics, for example, most economic cycle theories that were the bedrock of academia in the 1910s–50s, had died out in the 1970s when equilibrium frameworks became dominant (which ruled out bad things like unemployment, asset bubbles, or recessions), and the cyclical approach was not resurrected until fairly recently, despite the obvious example of Japan which has been experiencing a "secular stagnation" since the early 1990s.

While there are more recent variations of ancient wisdom (such as Neil Howe's generational theory, Kondratieff waves, Peter Turchin's secular elites cycles, Ronald Inglehart's economic and physical security frameworks, etc.), in my view, no one summarized cycles better than Polybius,[3] a Greek-Roman historian who believed that political systems rotate through three basic forms of government: democracy, aristocracy, and monarchy, with three degenerate phases of each of these forms: ochlocracy, oligarchy, and tyranny. In other words, over a long sweep of history, monarchy frequently degenerates into tyranny, which is then overthrown by the leading citizens who create an aristocratic rule, which in turn degenerates into an oligarchy (rule by the few) that is eventually overthrown by people who create democracy. However, as democracy becomes corrupt,[4] it degenerates into ochlocracy, restarting a brand-new cycle. If Polybius were alive today, he probably would classify current political systems across most Western nations as being in a state of *Ochlocracy* (power of the masses), when a healthy democracy degenerates with disoriented and angry masses falling prey to opportunistic populists and demagogues, potentially leading to what we today call Caesarism, or rule by one individual, with most of the state and political functions emptied of their original intent and power. To Polybius, the ideal outcome is a compromise (balance or mix) between these forces (i.e., democracy, monarchy, and aristocracy) which he (erroneously) believed the Roman Republic of the 1st century BCE had achieved through exactly such a division of power. This is something that the founders of the US Constitution took seriously, resulting in what looks chaotic but in reality, is a design-driven separation of executive, legislative (in turn subdivided into popular and aristocratic branches), and judicial power. As the Roman Republic discovered, it makes such a compromise durable but not unbreakable, with the Republic already sunsetting when Polybius was finishing his histories.

Modern theories have not dispensed with the broad cyclical outlook of Polybius, Aristotle, and Plato but rather tried to identify the underlying economic, demographic, technological, and environmental drivers of these cycles, with each adding a new brick to our knowledge. As discussed throughout this book (and in my first book), the current pressures are an outgrowth of deep Financialization and the highly disruptive Information Age—what I describe as a Fujiwara effect.

While technological revolution is a natural human impulse, the speed at which technologies evolve and propagate critically depends on the cost and availability of capital, with Financialization turbocharging the Information Age. The toxic intersection between these two powerful forces is today compounded by environmental degradation, a consequence of neoliberal policies that for more than three decades prioritized growth and wealth creation, irrespective of externalities. The same neoliberal philosophies "normalized" inequalities while constraining the ability of the state to respond to climate change, excessive financialization, and growing inequities. Since the early 1980s, the idea of individual freedom, individual responsibility, and the rule of free markets was so deeply ingrained that it became a societal consensus permeating almost all economic and social policies.

As demographic experts highlight, this philosophy was in tune with Baby Boomers' views that were shaped not by the disasters of the 1910–1940s but rather by two glorious decades from the late 1940s until the late 1960s to early 1970s, which featured some of the fastest ever productivity growth rates, middle-class creation, decline in inequalities, and expansion of educational, cultural, and healthcare opportunities. It was a time of plenty. Accordingly, young Baby Boomers could never understand or appreciate their parents' and grandparents' preoccupation with guardrails nor the trust they had in the government to contain the chaos that during their lives threaten to engulf them. Instead, Boomers witnessed the negative side effects of the government's overreach: strict moral and societal values as well as the deeply imbedded discrimination (sexual, race, gender) of a hierarchical system of governments and society. They wanted freedom from the government, and the prevailing norms were viewed as obstacles that they were not prepared to tolerate. While Baby Boomers and the subsequent X cohort smashed more taboos than almost any other modern generation, they have also embarked on a three-decades-long systematic dismantling of many government and state functions, creating a world that was more entrepreneurial but less equal, more tolerant but less fair. They bequeathed to subsequent generations economic, political, geopolitical, and social polarizations; environmental degradation; and significantly weakened institutions of state.

Today, there is no longer a globally accepted consensus. Neoliberal views have been discredited in the eyes of both younger and older generations, and alternatives are, therefore, starting to widely proliferate. As a new consensus has not yet fully formed, a long period of instability and confusion beckons, not dissimilar to the 1930s when people were reaching out toward political extremes and economic models. As described in Chapter Eleven, most surveys highlight that the younger cohorts have radically different views from their parents and grandparents and are far more closely aligned with the generations that dominated the late 1940s until the early 1970s. It is likely that the electoral and political weight of Millennials and Gen Z will be impossible to ignore in as little as five years, and certainly by the early 2030s when they will be the majority of adults in most nations, becoming the single most important political block. What philosophy will underpin their outlook?

•   •   •

If one were to distill the likely future that these younger generations will promote, it would be: *"Neoliberalism is the past; state and its expanding influence is the future. Freedom of open debate is the past; in-group morality is the future."* While many will undoubtedly bemoan the loss of some of the Boomers' freedoms, at the end of the day, *constraining neoliberalism and redefining personal and economic freedoms is likely to be the only way of rebuilding a societal consensus, reducing polarization pressures, and managing geopolitics.* These compromises will be propelled by younger cohorts, against an initially stiff Boomers' resistance. But, over time, changes will be both profound and inevitable.

The next decade promises to be the most critical period in this transition from today's capitalism and work-based culture, which still dominates

Western societies, toward a yet-to-be-defined alternative system. By 1941, the number of democracies shrunk to barely a dozen countries and the world looked grim, violent, and despotic. Today, we are already down to less than thirty fully-fledged democracies, and more than 70 percent of people globally are living in various forms of totalitarianism, compared to less than 50 percent a decade ago. The period of the peace dividend (from the collapse of the Soviet Union in 1991 until the Global Financial Crisis) is also well and truly behind us, with a rising tide of terrorist acts, incidences of death in state conflicts, and more frequent breakouts of both conventional and unconventional wars. At the same time, societal polarization and inequalities are widening, while a powerful mix of technology and financialization is disintermediating both capital and labor, placing most of our "givens" into question (e.g., "one man one vote" systems, the nature of political and social relations, and even what is meant to be human).

A wide range of outcomes are on the menu, including a highly plausible possibility of a protracted "cold war" that might escalate to much deadlier "hot wars," with the transition aggravated and facilitated by "hungry wars" of climate change and a swelling tide of immigration of a greater magnitude than the world has experienced since the Barbarian invasions of the 3rd–5th centuries and the Mongol and Turkish waves of the 13th–15th centuries. It is also virtually guaranteed that we shall witness the highest (since the 1930s) incidents of domestic electoral swings as the moderate middle collapses and disoriented electorates en masse migrate from one extreme to another, inflicting significant and occasionally irreparable damage to modern institutions of state. More nations will no longer qualify as fully-fledged democracies as the foundations of politics and societies erode, while the proportion of global population residing in "anocracies" (i.e., countries that have some nominal trappings of democracy, but which are largely empty of meaning) and in outright autocracies will continue to rise. Shockingly, as in the 1930s, it might even include some of today's most developed economies and established democracies. Most Western governments will be scrambling to contain the damage by spreading their influence and tightening control over an ever-wider terrain while aiming to preserve as much of our freedoms as possible.

•   •   •

However, over the long-term, one can be much more optimistic. The future promises to be one of abundance rather than scarcity. As the last five hundred years of turbulent transitions—from the medieval feudalism to mercantile capitalism, and then through the first and second Industrial Revolutions—abundantly show, the Information Revolution would ultimately also lead to higher incomes, better health outcomes and longevity, and perhaps even greater happiness. Eventually (probably sometime in the 2040s), productivity growth rates will likely explode to 4–5 percent per annum or higher (compared to around 1 percent currently), blunting extremes and establishing new societal norms.

The only question is what happens between now and then. As FDR proclaimed on a cold morning in March 1933, "The money changers have fled from their high seats in the temple of our civilization. We may now restore that temple to the ancient truths. The measure of restoration lies in the extent to which we apply social values more noble than mere monetary profit."[5] This was as pure a repudiation of neoliberalism as one is likely to find anywhere, uttered, as it were, in the darkest days of the 1930s' Great Depression. In his 1941 inauguration address, FDR enumerated four key freedoms that are as pertinent today: "freedom of speech and expression," "freedom to worship God," "freedom from want," and "freedom from fear." FDR's clear message was that hungry, angry, and fearful people are not free.[6] Today's environment is nowhere near as bleak, but the choices facing us are just as stark. Are we up to the task? The price of failure could be the replay of the 1940s world on fire.

Figures

BIBLIOGRAPHY

Abramowitz, Alan, *The Great Alignment: Race, Party, Transformation, and the Rise of Donald Trump* (New Haven: Yale University Press, 2019).

Acemoglu, Daron, and James Robinson, *Why Nations Fail* (New York: Crown Publishers, 2013).

Acemoglu, Daron and Pascual Restrepo, "Robots and Jobs," *NBER Working Paper, 23285*, March 2017.

Acemoglu, Daron, and James Robinson, *The Narrow Corridor: States, Societies and the Fate of Liberty* (New York: Penguin Press, 2019).

Acemoglu, Daron and Pascual Restrepo, "The Revolution need not be Automated," *Project Syndicate*, March 29, 2019.

Acemoglu, Daron et al., "War, Socialism and the Rise of Fascism: an Empirical Exploration," *NBER* Working Paper 27854, September 2020.

Acemoglu, Daron, "Harms of AI," *The Oxford Handbook of AI Governance*, 2021.

Acemoglu Daron, "Are We ready for AI creative Destruction?" *Project Syndicate*, April 9, 2024.

Acemoglu, Daron and James Robinson, *Economic Origins of Dictatorship and Democracy* (Cambridge: Cambridge University, 2006).

Agarwal, Ruchir, "Industrial Policy and the Growth Strategy Trilemma," *IMF*, 31 March, 2023.

Alinaghi, Nazlia and Robert Reed, "Taxes and Economic Growth Rates in OECD Countries," *Public Finance Review*, 49 (10) July 2020.

Allen, Frederick Lewis, *Since Yesterday: The 1930s America* (Open Road Integrated Media, 1939).

Allison, Graham, *Destined for War: Can America and China escape Thucydides' Trap* (New York: Houghton Mifflin Harcourt, 2017).

Andolfatto, David, "Assessing the Impact of Central Bank Digital Currency on Private Banks," *Fed St Louis*, December 2019.

Anderson, Terry, H, *The Sixties* (New York: Routledge, 2018).

Andreessen, Mark, "The Techno-Optimist Manifesto."

Andrews, Helen, *Boomers: The Man and Women who promised Freedom and delivered Disaster* (New York: Sentinel, 2021).

Andrew, John A., *The Other Side of the Sixties: Young Americans for Freedom and the Rise of Conservative Politics* (New Brunswick: Rutgers University Press, 1997).

Arendt, Hannah, *The Origins of Totalitarianism* (New York: HBJ, 1979, first published in 1948).

Atwood, William, "How America Feels as We Enter the Soaring Sixties," *Look*, January 5, 1960.

Auten, Gerald and David Splinter, "Income Inequality in the United States: Using Tax Data to Measure Long-Term Trends," *Journal of Political Economy* (forthcoming).

Ball, Christopher, et al., "Exposure to Opposite Views on Social Media Can Strengthen Polarization," *PNAS*, August 2018.

Batalova, Jeanne, "Top Statistics on Global Migration and Migrants," *Migration Policy Institute*, July 21, 2022.

Becker, Carl L, "The Dilemma of Modern Democracy," *The Virginia Quarterly Review* 17, no.1 (Winter 1941), pp. 11–27.

Bell, Daniel, *The End of Ideology: On Exhaustion of Political Ideas in the Fifties* (Cambridge: Harvard University Press, 2000; first published by Free Press in 1960).

Betts, Paul, *Ruin and Renewal: Civilizing Europe After World War II* (New York: Basic Books, 2020).

Blanchard, Olivier, "European unemployment: The Evolution of Facts and Ideas," *NBER*, Working Paper 11750, November 2005.

Blanchet, Thomas, Emmanuel Saez and Gabriel Zucman, "Real Time Inequality," *NBER*, Working Paper 30229, November 2022.

Blom Philipp, *The Vertigo Years: Europe 1900-1914* (New York: Basic Books, 2008).

Blom, Philipp, *Fracture: Life & Culture in the West, 1918-1938* (New York: Basic Books, 2015).

Bookstaber, Richard, *The End of Theory* (Princeton: Princeton University Press, 2017).

Borstelmann, Tom, *The 1970s: A New Global History from Civil Rights to Economic Inequality* (Princeton: Princeton University Press, 2012).

Bothmer, von Bernard, *Framing the Sixties* (Amherst: University of Massachusetts Press, 2010).

Bracha, Arnat and Mary Burke, "How Big is the Gig," *Labor Economics*, 2021

Bregman, Rutger, *Utopia for Realists: Universal Basic Income* (New York: Little Brown Company, 2017).

Bremner, Robert H, "Families, Children and State" in Bremner, Robert H and Reichard, Gary W., eds., *Reshaping America: Society and Institutions* (Columbus: Ohio State University Press, 1982).

Brandon, Piers, *The Dark Valley* (New York: Vintage Books, 2002).

Brennan, Mary C., *Turning Right in the Sixties: The Conservative Capture of the GOP* (Chapel Hill: University of North Carolina Press, 1995).

Brown, Wendy, *In the Ruins of Neoliberalism* (New York: Columbia University Press, 2019).

Brunnermeier, Marcus et al., "The Digitization of Money," *NBER*, August 2019.

Brynjolfsson, Erik and Andrew McAfee, *The Second Machine Age* (New York: W.W. Norton, 2014).

Brynjolfsson, Erik, "The Turing Trap: The Promise & Teril of Human-Like Artificial Intelligence," *Creative Commons Contribution*, 2022.

Brzezinski, Zbigniew, *The Grand Chessboard: American Primacy and its Geostrategic Imperatives* (New York: Basic Books, 1997).

Brzezinski, Zbigniew, *Strategic Vision: America and the Crisis of Global Power* (New York: Basic Books, 2012).

Bush, Vannevar, "Science: The Endless Frontier: A Report to the President of the United States by Office of the Scientific Research and Development," *US Government Printing Office*, July 1945.

Calomiris, Charles and Stephen Haber, *Fragile by Design: The Political Origins of Banking Crises and Scarce Credit* (Princeton: Princeton University Press, 2014).

Carlson, Elwood, *The Lucky Few: Between the Greatest Generation and Baby Boomers*, (New York: Springer, 2008).

Carothers, Thomas and Andrew O'Donohue, eds., *Democracies Divided: The Global Challenge of Political Polarization* (Washington: The Brookings Institution, 2019).

Carstens, Agustin, "Money in the Digital Age: What Role for Central Banks," *BIS*, February 2018.

Carstens, Agustin, "The Future of Money and Payment System," *BIS*, August 2019.

Cazzaniga, Mauro et al., "Gen-AI: Artificial Intelligence and the Future of Work," *IMF*, January 2024.

Cheng, Thomas K, "Sherman vs Goliath? Tackling Conglomerate Dominance Problem in Emerging and Small Economies: Hong Kong as a Case Study," *Northwestern Journal of International Law and Business*, vol.37, issue 1, Winter 2017.

Chiu, Jonathan, "Bank Market Power and Central Bank Digital Currency," *Bank of Canada*, June 2020.

Chui, Michael et al., "The Economic Potential of generative AI," *McKinsey & Company*, June 2023.

Cohen, Geoffrey, "Party Over Policy: Dominating Impact of Group Influence on Political Beliefs," *Journal of Personality and Social Psychology*, 2003, vol.85, no.5, 808–822.

Coleman, James S, *The Adolescent Society: The Social Life of the Teenager and its Impact on Education* (New York: Free Press, 1961).

Collier, Paul, *The Future of Capitalism: Facing the New Anxieties* (London: Allen Lane, 2018).

Conway, Martin, *Western Europe's Democratic Age, 1945-1968* (Princeton: Princeton University Press, 2020).

Constanza, Robert, "Four Visions of the Century Ahead: Will it be Star Trek, Ecotopia, Big Government or Mad Max," *The Futurist*, February 2019, pp.23–28.

Coontz, Stephanie, *The Way We Never Were: American Families and Nostalgia Trap* (New York: Basic Books, 1992).

Corrado, Carol Jonathan Haskel et al., "Intangible Capital and Modern Economies," *Journal of Economic Perspectives*, Vol. 36, no.3, Summer 2022, pp.3–28.

Cowen, Tyler, "AI's Greatest Danger? The Humans Who Use It," *Bloomberg*, January 25, 2024.

Cowen, Tyler, *The Complacent Class: The Self-Defeating Quest for the American Dream* (New York: St. Martin's Place, 2017).

Craft, Nicholas, and Gianni Toniolo, *Economic Growth in Europe Since 1945* (Cambridge: Cambridge University Press, 1995).

Crozier, Michael, Samuel P. Huntington, Joji Watanuki, *The Crisis of Democracy*, Published on the Governability of Democracies to the Trilateral Commission, (New York University Press, 1975).

Dam van, Andrew, "Why are Americans getting shorter?" *Washington Post*, December 15, 2023.

Davies, William, *Nervous States: Democracy and The Decline of Reason* (New York: W.W. Norton & Company, 2018).

Deneen, Patrick, *Regime Change: Toward a Postliberal Future* (Sentinel, 2023).

DeLong, Bradford, *Slouching Towards Utopia: An Economic History of the Twentieth Century* (New York: Basic Books, 2022).

Dikotter, Frank, *How to be a Dictator: The Cult of Personality in the Twentieth Century* (New York: Bloomsbury, 2019).

Dobbs, Richard, James Manyika and Jonathan Woetzel, *No Ordinary Disruption* (New York: BBS Public Affairs, 2015).

Dobbs, Richard, James Manyika and Jonathan Woetzel, "The Four Global Forces Breaking All the Trends," *McKinsey Special Collection, Trends and Global Forces*, April 2015.

Douthat, Ross, *The Decadent Society: How We Became the Victims of Our Own Success* (New York: Avid readers Press, 2020).

Drucker, Peter, *Post Capitalist Society* (New York: HarperCollins, 1993).

Drum, Kevin, "Welcome to the Digital Revolution," *Foreign Affairs*, July/August 2018.

Economy, Elizabeth, *The World According to China* (London, Polity Press, 2022).

Economy, Elizabeth, "China's Alternative Order," *Foreign Affairs*, May/June 2024.

Eichengreen, Barry and Albert Ritschi, "Understanding West German Economic Growth in the 1950s," *LSE, Working Paper No 113/08*, December 2008.

Eloundou, Tyna, Sam Manning, Pamela Mishkin and Daniel Rock, "GPTs are GPTs: An Early Look at the Labor Market Impact Potential of Large Language Models," *Open AI and the University of Pennsylvania*, March 23, 2023.

Epstein, David, *The Range: Why Generalists Triumph in a Specialized World* (New York: Riverhead Books, 2019).

Esping-Andersen, Gosta, *The Three Worlds of Welfare Capitalism* (Cambridge: Polity, 1990).

Farber, David, *The Age of Great Dreams: America in the 1960s* (New York: Hill and Wang, 1994).

Farrell, Henry, and Abraham Newman, "The New Economic Security State," *Foreign Affairs*, November/December 2023, pp.106–122.

Federico, Giovanni, and Antonio Tena-Junguito, "World Trade, 1800-1938: A New Data Set," *EHES Working Papers in Economic History*, no. 93, European Historical Economics Society, January 2016.

Federico, Giovanni, and Antonio Tena-Junguito, "World Trade, 1800-2015," *Vox EU*, February 7, 2016.

Ferguson, Niall, "Kissinger and the True Meaning of Détente," *Foreign Affairs*, March/April 2024.

Fildes, Nic, "'Made in Australia' Drive Aims to Shift Economy from 'World's Quarry' Label," *Financial Times*, April 4, 2024.

Foer, Franklin, *World Without Mind* (New York: Penguin Press, 2017).

Ford, Martin, *The Rise of Robots* (New York: Basic Books, 2015).

Forlini, John D, *The 1930s: Road from the Past Portal to the Future*, 2013.

Foroohar, Rana, "A New Technology Boom is at Hands," *Financial Times*, 26 March, 2023.

Frase, Peter, *Four Futures: Life After Capitalism* (New York: Verso, 2016).

Freeman, Richard, "Who Owns the Robots Rules the World," *IZA World of Labor*, 2015:5.

Frey, Carl and Michael Osborne, "The Future of Employment: How Susceptible are Jobs to Computerization," *Department of Engineering Science, University of Oxford*, Summer 2013.

Frey, Carl Benedict, *The Technology Gap: Capital, Labor and Power in the Age of Automation* (Princeton: Princeton University Press, 2019).

Fried, Richard M, "1950-1960" in Whitfield, Stephen J ed., *A Companion to 20th Century America* (Malden: Blackwell Publishing, 2004).

Friedman, Milton and Rose Friedman, *Free to Choose: A Personal Statement* (Harvest Book, 1990, first published in 1979).

Fukuyama, Francis, *The End of History and the Last Man* (New York: Avon Books, 1992).

Fukuyama, Francis, *The Origins of Political Order* (New York: Farrar, Strauss and Giroux, 2011).

Fukuyama, Francis, *Political Order and Political Decay* (New York: Farrar, Strauss and Giroux, 2014).

Fukuyama, Francis, *Identity* (New York, Strauss & Giroux, 2018).

Fullbrook, Edward and Jamie Morgan ed., *Modern Monetary Theory and its Critics* (Bristol: World Economics Association, 2019).

Galbraith, John Kenneth, *The Affluent Society* (Boston: Mariner Book, first published in 1958, reprinted in 1998).

Gale, William and Andrew Samwick, "Effects of Income Tax changes on Economic Growth," *Brookings*, 2014.

Gale, William, John Sabelhous and Samuel Thorpe, "Measuring Income Inequality: A Primer on the Debate," *Brookings*, December 21, 2023.

Galor, Oded, *The Journey of Humanity: A New History of Wealth and Inequality with Implications for Our Future* (New York: Penguin Random House, 2022).

Garcia-Herrero, Alicia and Alessio Terzi, "China's Economy Cannot Export Its Problems Away," *Project Syndicate*, May 31, 2024.

Garton, Timothy, *Homelands, A Personal History of Europe* (New Haven: Yale University Press, 2023).

Gazzaley, Adam and Larry Rosen, *The Distracted Mind* (Cambridge: MIT Press, 2016).

Gechert, Sebastian and Philipp Heimberger, "Do Corporate Tax Cuts boost Economic Growth?" *European Economic Review*, 2022.

Gerstle, Gary, *The Rise and Fall of the Neoliberal Order* (Oxford: Oxford University Press, 2022).

Gilder, George, *Knowledge and Power* (Washington: Regnery Publishing, 2013).

Gilder, George, *Life after Capitalism* (Washington: Regnery Gateway, 2023).

Gitlin, Todd, *The Sixties: Years of Hope Days of Rage* (New York: Bantam Book, 1993).

Goffman, Ken and Dan Jay, *The Counterculture Through the Ages* (New York: Villard, 2004).

Goldin, Claudia and Robert Margo, "The Great Compression: the Wage Structure in the United States at Mid-Century," *NBER*, 1991.

Goodstadt, Leo F., *A City Mismanaged: Hong Kong's Struggle for Survival* (Hong Kong: HKU Press, 2018).

Gordon, Robert, *The Rise and Fall of American Growth* (Princeton, Princeton University Press, 2016). Gorz, Andre, *Reclaiming Work* (Cambridge: Polity Press, 1999).

Goudsouzian, Aram, *The Men and the Moment: The Election of 1968 and the Rise of Partisan Politics in America* (Chapel Hill, The University of North Carolina Press, 2019).

Graeber, David, *Bullshit Jobs* (London: Allen Lane, 2018).

Gray, Mary L, and Siddharth Suri *Ghost Work* (Boston: Houghton Mifflin Harcourt, 2019).

Gray, John, *The New Leviathans* (New York: Farrar, Straus and Giroux, 2023).

Hackett Fischer, David, *The Great Wave: Price Revolutions and the Rhythm of History* (Oxford: Oxford University Press, 1996).

Haidt, Jonathan, *The Righteous Mind: Why Good People are Divided by Politics and Religion* (New York: Pantheon Press, 2012).

Halberstam, David, *The Fifties* (New York: Open Road, 1993).

Halberstam, David, *The Powers That Be* (New York: Open Road, 1979).

Hanappi, Gerhard, "From Integrated Capitalism to Disintegrating Capitalism. Scenarios of a Third World War", *MPRA*, January 7, 2019.

Harari, Yuval, *Homo Deus* (New York: Harper Collins, 2017).

Harari, Yuval, *21 Lessons for 21st Century* (New York: Spiegel & Grau, 2019).

Hardt, Michael, *The Subversive Seventies* (Oxford, Oxford University Press, 2023).

Harvey, David, *A Brief History of Neoliberalism* (Oxford, Oxford University Press, 2005).

Harvey, David, *Marx, Capital and the Madness of Economic Reason* (London: Profile Books, 2019).

Haskel, Jonathan and Stian Westlake, *Capitalism without Capital* (Princeton: Princeton University Press, 2018).

Haskel, Jonathan and Stian Westlake, *Restarting the Future: How to Fix the Intangible Economy* (Princeton, Princeton University Press, 2022).

Hayek, von, Friderich, *The Road to Serfdom* (Abridged version, London: Institute of Economic Affairs, 2005, originally published in 1944).

Hayek, von, Friedrich, *Law, Legislation and Liberty, volume 1: Rules and Order* (Chicago: University of Chicago Press, 1973).

Hayek, von, Friedrich, *Law, Legislation and Liberty, volume 2: The Mirage of Social Justice* (Chicago: University of Chicago Press, 1976).

Hayek, von, Friedrich, *The Fatal Conceit: The errors of Socialism* (Chicago: University of Chicago Press, 1988).

Hazony, Yoram, *The Virtue of Nationalism* (New York: Basic Books, 2018).

Henderson, Rebecca, *Reimagining Capitalism: In A World on Fire* (New York: Public Affairs, 2020).

Hetschko, Clemens, Andreas Knabe and Ronnie Schob, "Changing Identity: Retiring from Unemployment," *SOE Papers, DIW*, 399, July 2011.

Hope, David, and Julian Limburg, "The Economic Consequences of Major Tax Cuts for the Rich", *Socio-Economic Review*, 2022, vol.20, no.2, pp.539–559.

Horowitz, Sarah, "Freelance in the US Labor Force," *BLS*, 2015

Howe, Neil, *The Fourth Turning Point is Here* (New York, Simon & Schuster, 2023).

Huntington, Samuel, "Paradigms of American Politics: Beyond the One, the Two, and the Many," *Political Science Quarterly*, vol.89, no.1 (March 1974), pp.1–26.

Huntington, Samuel, *The Clash of Civilizations and The Remaking of World Order* (New York: Simon & Schuster, 1996).

Huntington, Samuel, *Who Are We?* (New York: Free Press, 2004).

Ibrahim, Zuraidah and Jeffie Lam, *Rebel City: Hong Kong's Year of Water and Fire*, (Hong Kong and Singapore: South China Post Publishers, World Scientific Publishing, 2020).

Inglehart, Ronald, *Cultural Evolution – People's Motivations are Changing and Reshaping the World* (Cambridge, Cambridge University Press, 2018).

Iversen, Torben and David Soskice, *Democracy and Prosperity: Reinventing Capitalism through Turbulent Century* (Princeton: Princeton University Press, 2019).

Iyengar and Westwood, "Fear and Loathing: New Evidence on Group polarization," *Midwest Political Science Association*, 2014.

Jensen, Michael and William Meckling, "Theory of the Firm: Managerial Behavior, Agency Costs and Ownership Structure," *Journal of Financial Economics*, 1976, vol.3, no.4, pp.305–360.

Judt, Tony, *Postwar: History of Europe since 1945* (New York: Penguin Books, 2005).

Kahan, Dan, Ellen Peters, Erica Dawson, and Paul Slovic, "Motivated Numeracy and Enlightened Self- Government," *Behavioral Public Policy*, 2017.

Kaletsky, Anatole, *Capitalism 4.0: The Birth of the New Economy in the Aftermath of Crisis* (New York: BBS Public Affairs, 2010).

Kaplan Robert D., *The Revenge of Geography: What the Map Tells us About Coming Conflicts and the Battle Against Fate* (New York: Random House, 2012).

Kaplan, Robert D., *The Loom of Time: Between Empire and Anarchy, From the Mediterranean to China* (New York: Random House, 2023).

Karabarbounis, Loukas, "Perspectives on the Labor Share," *Journal of Economic Perspectives*, vol.38, no. 2, Spring 2021, pp.107–136.

Karma, Rogé, "Why America Abandoned the Greatest Economy in History," *The Atlantic*, November 25, 2023.

Kavanagh, Jennifer, and Michael Rich, *Truth Decay* (Santa Monica: Rand Corporation, 2018).

Kee, Robert, *1939: The World We Left Behind*, (Lume Books, 2019, first edition by Fairrealm Books, 1984).

Keen, Andrew, *How to Fix the Future* (New York: Atlantic Monthly Press, 2016).

Kehring, Mattias and Nicholas Vincent, "The Micro-level Anatomy of the Labor Share Decline," *NBER*, November 2018.

Kelton, Stephanie, *Deficit Myth*, (Public Affairs, 2020).

Kendall-Taylor, Andrea, Natasha Lindstaedt and Erica Frantz, *Democracies and Authoritarian Regimes* (Oxford, Oxford University Press, 2019).

Kendell-Taylor, Andrea and Richard Fontaine, "The Axis of Upheaval," *Foreign Affairs*, May/June 2024, pp.50–63.

Kennan, George, "Long Telegram, February 22, 1946," *The Wilson Center Digital Archive*.

Kennan, George, *Russia and the West under Lenin and Stalin* (Boston: Little Brown and Company, 1960).

Kennedy, Paul M., *The Rise of the Anglo-German Antagonism, 1860-1914* (New York: Humanity Books, 1980).

Kesternish, Iris et al., "The Effects of World War II on Economic and Health Outcomes across Europe", *Review of Economics and Statistics*, 2014, Mar 1; 96 (1): 103–118.

Keynes, John Maynard, *The Economic Consequences of Peace* (New York: Harcourt, Brace and Howe, 1920).

Keynes, John Maynard, "Economic Possibilities for Our Grandchildren," in *Essays in Persuasion* (London: MacMillan Press, 1931).

Keynes, John Maynard, *The General Theory of Employment, Interest and Money* (Pesserino Editore, first published in 1936).

King, Gary, Ori Rosen, Martin Tanner, and Alexander Wagner, "Ordinary Economic Behavior in the Extraordinary Election of Adolph Hitler," *The Journal of Economic History*, vol. 68, December 2008.

King, Mervyn, *The End of Alchemy: Money, Banking and the Future of Global Economy* (New York: W.W. Norton & Company, 2016).

Kirkpatrick, Rob, *1969: The Year Everything Changed* (New York: Skyhorse Publishing, 2011).

Klein, Ezra, *Why We're Polarized*, (New York: Avid Reader Press, 2020).

Kotkin, Stephen, "The Five Futures of Russia, and How America Can Prepare for Whatever Comes Next," *Foreign Affairs*, May/June 2024.

Kristof, Nicholas, "The Rise of China," *Foreign Affairs*, December 1, 1993.

Kuhn, Moritz, Moritz Schurlarick, and Ulrike Steins, "Income and Wealth Inequality in America, 1949- 2016," *CEPR*, June 2018.

Kurz, Mordecai, *The Market Power of Technology: Understanding the Second Gilded Age*, (New York: Columbia University Press, 2023).

Kurz, Mordecai, "How Capitalism Became a Threat to Democracy," *Project Syndicate*, May 15, 2024.

Kurzweil, Ray, *The Age of Spiritual Machines* (New York: Penguin Press, 1999).

Lacey, James ed., *Great Strategic Rivalries: From the Classical World to the Cold War*, (Oxford: Oxford University Press, 2016).

Lang, Michael, *The Road to Woodstock* (Harper Collins e-books, 2009).

Lasch, Christopher, *The Culture of Narcissism: An American Life in the Age of Diminishing Expectations* (New York: W.W. Norton & Company, 1979).

Lazerow, Jama, *1960-1974*, in Stephen Whitfield ed., *A Companion to 20th Century America* (Oxford: Blackwell Publishing, 2004).

Lee, Kai-Fu, *AI Super-Powers: China, Silicon Valley and the New World Order* (New York: first Mariner Books, 2021).

Leontief, Wassily, "Technological Advance, Economic Growth, and the Distribution of Income," *Population and Development Review* 9:3, 1983.

Lenin, Vladimir, 'What is to Be Done," *Marxists.org*

Levitsky, Steven and Daniel Ziblatt, *How Democracies Die* (New York, Crown Publishing, 2018).

Lindbergh, Anne Morrow, *The Wave of the Future* (New York: Harcourt, Brace & Company, 1940).

Linik, Stefan, "How Might 21st century De-Globalization Unfold? Some Historical Reflection," *New Global Studies* 12, no.3 (2018).

Linker, Damon, "Get to Know the Influential Conservative Intellectuals Who Help explain G.O.P. Extremism," *New York Times*, November 4, 2023.

Lowe, Keith, *Savage Continent: Europe in the Aftermath of World War II* (New York: St Martin's Press, 2012).

Lowe Keith, *The Fear and the Freedom: How The Second World War Changed US*, (New York: St Martin's Press, 2017).

Luce, Edward, "Wall Street's Bargain with Trump," *Financial Times*, January 24, 2024.

Luxemburg, Rosa, "The Crisis of German Social Democracy," *The Junius Pamphlet*, 1915.

Ma, Debin, "China's Long March Back to Stagnation," *Project Syndicate*, January 12, 2024.

MacKenzie, Findlay and Lewis Mumford, ed., *Planned Society: Yesterday, Today and Tomorrow* (New York, Prentice Hill, 1937).

MacMillan, Margaret, "How Wars Don't End – Ukraine, Russia and the Lessons of World War I," *Foreign Affairs*, June 122, 2023.

Magnus, George, "China's Quixotic Quest to Innovate," *Foreign Affairs*, May 29, 2024.

Manyika, James and Michael Spence, "Can Artificial Intelligence Reverse the Productivity Slowdown?" *Foreign Affairs*, November/December 2023, pp.70–87.

Martens, Karel and Jose Montiel Olea, "Marginal Tax Rate and Income," *NBER*, September 2017.

Marwick, Arthur, *The Sixties: Cultural Revolution in Britain, France, Italy and the United States, 1958- 1974* (London: Bloomsbury, 1998).

Marx, Karl, *Communist Manifesto*, 1848; Marxists.org, 2010.

Marx, Karl, "Critique of the Gotha Program," 1875, *www.marxists.org*.

Mason, Lilliana, *Uncivil Agreement* (Chicago: university of Chicago Press, 2018).

Mason, Paul, *Post Capitalism* (London: Penguin, 2015).

Mauro, James, *Twilight at the World of Tomorrow: Genius, Madness, Murder, and the 1939 World's Fair on the Brink of War*, (New York: Ballantine Books, 2010).

Mauro, Paolo, Rafael Romeu, Ariel Binder, and Assad Zaman, "A Modern History of Fiscal Prudence and Profligacy," *IMF Working Paper* no. 13/5.

Mazzucato, Mariana, *The Entrepreneurial State: Debunking Public vs Private Sector Myths* (Public Affairs, 2015).

Mazzucato, Mariana, *The Value of Everything: Making and Taking in the Global Economy* (New York: Public Affairs, 2020).

Mazzucato, Mariana, *Mission Economy: A Moonshot Guide to Changing Capitalism* (New York: Allen Lane, 2021).

Mazzucato, Mariana and David Eaves, "Central Banks in a Cashless World," *Project Syndicate*, April 26, 2024.

McAfee, Andrew and Erik Brynjolfsson, *Machine Platform Crowd: Harnessing Our Digital Future*, (New York: W.W. Norton, 2017).

McCloskey, Donald ed., *Measurement and Meaning in Economics* (New York: Elgar, 2001).

McCormick, Anne O'Hare, "Europe's Five Black Years," *New York Times Magazine*, September 3, 1944, p.42.

McCoy, Jennifer, and Murat Somer, "Toward a Theory of Pernicious Polarization," *Annals of the American Academy of Political and Social Science*, 2019.

Micklethwait, John and Adrian Wooldridge, *The Fourth Revolution: The Global Race to Reinvent the State* (New York: The Penguin Press, 2014).

Mokyr, Joel, Chris Vickers, and Nicholas Ziebarth, "The History of Technological Anxiety and the Future of Economic Growth: Is This Time Different," *The Journal of Economic Perspective*, vol.29, no.3 (summer 2015), pp.31–50.

Moretta, John Anthony, *The Hippies: A 1960s History* (North Carolina: McFarland & Company, 2017). Mumford, Lewis, *The City in History* (New York: Harcourt, 1961).

Newport, Carl, *A World Without Email: Reimagining Work in an Age of Communication Overload,* (New York: Portfolio/Penguin, 2021).

Oppenheimer, Andres, *The Robots are Coming* (New York: Vintage Books, 2019).

Pace, Erik, "Flashy 60s Radical Dies," *New York Times*, November 30, 1994.

Packer, George, *The Unwinding: An Inner History of New America* (New York: Farrar, Strauss and Giroux, 2013).

Packer, George, "Decline and Fall: How American Society Unraveled," *The Guardian*, June 19, 2013.

Parijs van, Philippe and Yannick Vanderborght, *Basic Income* (Cambridge, Harvard University Press, 2017).

Parikh, Tej, "Erik Brynolfsson: This Could be the Best Decade in History – or the Worst," *Financial Times*, January 31, 2024.

Pei, Minxin, *China's Crony Capitalism* (Cambridge: Harvard University, 2016).

Perez, Carlota, *Technological Revolutions and Financial Capital*, (Cheltenham, Edward Elgar, 2002).

Phillips, Leigh and Michael Rozworski, *The People's Republic of Walmart: How the World's Biggest Corporations are laying the Foundation for Socialism* (London: Verso, 2019).

Piketty, Thomas, and Emmanuel Saez, "Income Inequality in the United States, 1913-1998," *The Quarterly Journal of Economics*, 2003, 118(1); pp.1–39.

Piketty, Thomas, Emmanuel Saez, and Stephanie Stancheva, "Optimum Taxation on Top Labor Incomes," *NBER*, 2011.

Piketty, Thomas, *Capital in the Twenty First Century* (Cambridge: The Belknap Press of Harvard University, 2014).

Piketty, Thomas, and Li Yang, "Income and Wealth Inequality in Hong Kong, 1981–2020: The Rise of Pluto-Communism?" *World Inequality Lab, Working Paper 2021/18*, June 2021.

Piketty, Thomas, *Brief History of Equality* (Cambridge: The Belknap Press of Harvard University, 2022).

Platt, Gill, "Is Cambrian Explosion Coming for Robotics," *Journal of Economic Perspectives*, vol.29, no.3, Summer 2015, pp.51–60.

Plokhy, Serhii, *Lost kingdom: The Quest for Empire and the Making of the Russian Nation* (New York: Basic Books, 2017).

Plokhy, Serhii, *The Russo-Ukrainian War* (New York: W.W. Norton, 2023).

Polanyi, Karl, *The Great Transformation: The Political and Economic Origins of Our Time* (Boston: Beacon Press, 2001, first published in 1944).

Polybius, *The Complete Histories* (Digireads.com Publishing, 2014).

Posner, Eric, "The Future of Work in the AI Era," *Project Syndicate*, April 11, 2024.

Putin, Vladimir, "On the Historical Unity of Russians and Ukrainians," *Presidential Library of Russian Federation*, July 12, 2021.

Reiljan, Andres "Fear and Loathing Across Party Lines in Europe," *European Journal of Political Research*, 59 (2), pp.376–396.

Reinhart, Carmen and Kenneth Rogoff, *This Time Is Different* (Princeton: Princeton University Press, 2010).

Rifkin, Jeremy, *The Zero Marginal Cost Society: The Internet of Things, the Collaborative Commons, and the Eclipse of Capitalism* (New York: Macmillan, 2014).

Ringer, Robert, *Looking Out for Number One* (New York: Funk & Wagnalls, 1977).

Rodrik, Dani, "Sense and Nonsense in the Globalization Debate," *Foreign Affairs*, Summer, 1997.

Rodrik, Dani, *The Globalization Paradox* (Oxford: Oxford University Press, 2011).

Rodrik, Dani, "Premature Deindustrialization," *NBER*, Working Paper 20935, February 2015.

Rodrik, Dani, Reka Juhasz, and Nathan Lake, "Economists Reconsider Industrial Policy," *Project Syndicate*, April 4, 2023.

Romeo, Nick, *The Alternative: How to Build Just Economy* (New York: Public Affairs, 2024).

Rothman, David, "ChatGPT is about to Revolutionize the Economy. We Need to Decide What That Look Like," *MIT*, March 25, 2023.

Sandbu, Martin, "We are Closer to Taxing the Super-Rich," *Financial Times*, May 20, 2024.

Sanger, David, *New Cold War: China's Rise, Russia's Invasion and America's Struggle to Defend the West* (New York: Crown, 2024).

Savage, Susannah, "Can Africa one day Help Feed the World's Growing Population," *Financial Times*, April 3, 2024.

Schlesinger, Artur M., *The Vital Center: The Politics of Freedom* (Transaction Publishers, 1998; originally published by Riverside Press in 1949).

Schmitt, Carl, *The Crisis of Parliamentary Democracy* (MIT Press, 1988, First Edition published in 1923).

Schuman, Michael, "China is Losing the Chip War," *Atlantic*, June 6, 2024.

Shaxson, Nicholas, *The Finance Curse: How Global Finance Is Making Us All Poorer* (London: Bodley Head, 2018).

Shell, Ellen, *The Job: Work and Its Future in a Time of Radical Change* (New York: Currency, 2018).

Shvets, Viktor, *The Great Rupture: Three Empires, Four Turning Points and the Future of Humanity* (Boyle & Dalton, 2020).

Silva, Frederico Ferreira da and Simon Maye, "Affective Polarization in Comparative and Longitudinal Perspective," *Public Opinion Quarterly*, vol.87, issue 1, Spring 2013, pp.219–231.

Slobodian, Quinn, *Globalists: The End of Empire and the Birth of Neoliberalism* (Cambridge: Harvard University Press, 2018).

Slobodian, Quinn, *Crack-up Capitalism: Market Radicals and the Dream of a World Without Democracy* (New York: Metropolitan Books, 2023).

Solzhenitsyn, Aleksandr, *Rebuilding Russia: Reflections and Tentative Proposals* (New York: Vintage, 1991).

Slezkine, Yuri, *The House of Government: A Saga of Russian Revolution* (Princeton: Princeton University Press, 2017).

Spigel, Lynn and Mchael Curtin, *The Revolution Wasn't Televised: Sixties Television and Social Conflict* (New York: Routledge, 1997).

Standing, Guys, *Basic Income and How We Can Make it Happen* (Pelican Books, 2017).

Stiglitz, Joseph, *The Price of Inequality: How Today's Divided Society Endangers Our Future* (London: Allen Lane, 2012).

Stiglitz, Joseph, *People, Power and Profits: Progressive Capitalism for an Age of Discontent* (New York: Allen Lane, 2019).

Stiglitz, Joseph, *The Road to Freedom: Economics and the Good Society* (New York: W.W. Norton & Company, 2024).

Strain, Christopher B, *The Long Sixties: America, 1955–1973* (Malden: John Wiley & Sons, 2017).

Strauss, William and Neil Howe, *The Fourth Turning Point* (New York: Three Rivers Press, 1997).

Streek, Wolfgang, "How will Capitalism End?" *New Left Review* 87, May/June 2014.

Stucke, Maurice, and Ariel Ezrachi, "The Rise, Fall and Rebirth of the US Antitrust Movement," *HBR*, December 2017.

Suleyman, Mustafa, *The Coming Wave* (New York: Crown, 2023).

Tejfel, Henri, "Experiments in Intergroup Discrimination," 1970.

Thiel, Peter, *Zero to One* (New York: Penguin, 2014).

Thurman, Howard, *The Mood of Christmas* (Friends United Press, 1985).

Tufekci, Zenep, "Failing the Third Machine Age: When Robots Came for Grandma," *Medium.com*, 2014.

Turchin, Peter, *War and Peace and WAR: The Rise and Fall of Empires* (Plume, 2007).

Turchin, Peter, *End of Times: Elites, Counter-Elites and the Path of Political Disintegration* (New York: Pinguin Press, 2023).

Turner, Adair, *Between Debt and the Devil* (Princeton: Princeton University Press, 2016).

Tyson, Laura, and Michael Spence, "Exploring the Effect of Technology on income and Wealth Inequality," in Boushey, Heather, Bradford DeLong, and Michael Steinbaum, eds., *After Piketty* (Cambridge, Harvard University Press, 2017).

Varoufakis, Yanis, *And the Weak Suffer What They Must*, (London: Bodley Head, 2016).

Varoufakis, Yanis, *Technofeudalism: What killed Capitalism* (London: Melville House, 2024).

Vatter, Harold G, *The US Economy in the 1950s: An Economic History* (Chicago: University of Chicago Press, 1963).

Veen van der, Robert and Philippe van Parijs, "A Capitalist Road to Communism," *Theory and Society*, v. 15:5, 1986, pp. 635–655.

Vivalt, Eva, Rhodes Elizabeth, et.al., "The Employment Effects of a Guaranteed Income; Experimental Evidence from Two US States," *NBER Working Paper* 32719, July 2024.

Volcker, Paul, "The Political Economy of the Dollar," *FRBNY Quarterly Review*, Winter 1978–79.

Wallis, John Joseph, "The Concept of Systemic Corruption in American History," *NBER*, March 2006, pp.23-60.

Walter, Barbara, *How Civil Wars Start* (New York: Crown, 2022).

Warsh, David, *Knowledge and the Wealth of Nations* (New York: W.W. Norton, 2006).

Wolin, Sheldon, *Fugitive Democracy and Other Essays* (Princeton: Princeton University Press, 2001). Wasserstrom, Jeffrey, *Vigil: Hong Kong on the Brink* (New York: Columbia Global reports, 2020).

Waxman, Chaim ed., *The End of Ideology Debate* (New York: Funk & Wagnalls, 1968).

Weil, David, *The Fissured Workplace* (Cambridge: Harvard University Press, 2014).

Westad, Odd Arne, "Sleepwalking Toward War," *Foreign Affairs*, June 13, 2024.

Wolf, Martin, *The Crisis of Democratic Capitalism*, (New York: Penguin Press, 2023).

Wolfe Tom, *Radical Chic & Mau-Mauing the Flak Catchers* (New York: Farrar, Strauss and Giroux, 1970).

Wong, Chun Han "China's Xi is Resurrecting Mao's Continuous Revolution with a Twist," *Wall Street Journal*, January 1, 2024.

Wooldridge, Adrian, "How 'Shareholder Value' Became a US Mantra," *Bloomberg Opinion*, April 9, 2024.

Yankelovich, Daniel, *The New Morality: A Profile of American Youth in the 70s* (New York: McGraw Hill, 1974).

Yankelovich, Daniel, *The New Rules: Searching for Self-Fulfillment in a World Turned Upside Down* (New York: Random House, 1981).

Zahra, Tara, *Against the World: Anti-Globalism and Mass Politics Between the World Wars* (London, W.W. Norton, 2023).

Zakaria, Fareed, "How to Beat the Backlash that Threatens the Liberal Revolution," *Washington Post*, March 22, 2024.

Zubov, Shoshana, *The Age of Surveillance Capitalism: The Fight for A Human Future At the New Frontier of Power* (New York: Profile Books, 2019).

Zweig, Stefan, *The World of Yesterday* (New York, Plunkett Press, 2011, first published by Viking Press, 1943).

ENDNOTES

PROLOGUE

1. Howard Thurman, *The Mood of Christmas* (Friends United Press, 1985).
2. Fair's marketers used the pretext of showcasing fascism, convincing Mussolini that Americans didn't view fascism as anything meaningfully different from FDR's New Deal.
3. James Mauro, *Twilight at the World of Tomorrow: Genius, Madness, Murder, and the 1939 World's Fair on the Brink of War* (New York: Ballantine Books, 2010); John D, Forlini, *The 1930s: Road from the Past Portal to the Future*, 2013, pp.555–557.
4. Forlini (2013), p.557.
5. Frederick Lewis Allen, *Since Yesterday: The 1930s America* (Open Road Integrated Media, 1939), p.157.
6. Philipp Blom, *Fracture: Life and Culture in the West, 1918–1938* (New York: Basic Books, 2015), p.466.
7. Hoover can be described as one of the first "modern" US conservatives. He wrote more than two dozen books, harshly criticizing FDR's New Deal, as promoting a version of either communism or fascism and destroying his perception of the American exceptionalism and liberty. He was also against US involvement in the Second World War, as well as massive assistance that the US was providing to the Soviet Union in its fight against Nazi Germany.
8. During the Great War, more than 1.3 million Frenchmen were killed and around 1.1 million were severely wounded or maimed, representing more than 20 percent of available Frenchmen. In the case of Germany, those killed amounted to around 10 percent of German men, and if one includes veterans who were at least partially incapacitated, the number of casualties rises to approximately 15 to 20 percent.
9. Robert Kee, *1939 The World We Left Behind* (Lume Books, 2019, first edition by Fairrealm Books, 1984), p.15.
10. Rogé Karma, "Why America Abandoned the Greatest Economy in History," *Atlantic*, November 25, 2023.
11. George Packer, *The Unwinding: An Inner History of the New America* (New York: Farrar, Strauss and Giroux, 2013).
12. Ronald Inglehart, *Cultural Evolution: People's Motivations are Changing and Reshaping the World* (Cambridge, Cambridge University Press, 2018).
13. Lilliana Mason, *Uncivil Agreement* (Chicago: University of Chicago Press, 2018).
14. Viktor Shvets, *The Great Rupture: Three Empires, Four Turning Points and the Future of Humanity* (Boyle & Dalton, 2020), pp.131–144.
15. Mustafa Suleyman, *The Coming Wave* (New York: Crown, 2023), p.77.
16. Richard Dobbs, James Manyika, and Jonathan Woetzel, "The Four Global Forces Breaking All the Trends," *McKinsey Special Collection: Trends and Global Forces*, April 2015.

17. Neil Howe is arguably the best-known advocate of generational analysis. Neil Howe, *The Fourth Turning Point is Here* (New York, Simon & Schuster, 2023).
18. The GI generation is usually classified as those born between either 1901 or 1910 and 1928. The Silent Generation are those born between 1928 and 1945. Baby Boomers were cohorts born between 1946 and 1964, followed by X generation or those born between 1965 and 1980.
19. Howe (2023), p.4.
20. Philipp Blom (2015), p.455.
21. Anatole Kaletsky, *Capitalism 4.0: The Birth of the New Economy in the Aftermath of Crisis* (New York: BBS Public Affairs, 2010).
22. Niall Ferguson, "Kissinger and the True Meaning of Détente," *Foreign Affairs*, March/April 2024.
23. Carl L. Becker, "The Dilemma of Modern Democracy," *The Virginia Quarterly Review,* 17, no.1 (Winter 1941), pp.11–27.
24. Mariana Mazzucato, *The Value of Everything: Making and Taking in the Global Economy* (New York: Public Affairs, 2020).
25. This refers to intense debates between Marxists and Socialists (such as Otto Neurath) and the Austrian liberal school (such as Ludwig von Mises) about the ability to guide economies through central planning tools. No need for an "invisible hand." Refer Shvets (2020), p.27.
26. Lewis Mumford, "Forward" in Findlay MacKenzie and Lewis Mumford eds., *Planned Society: Yesterday, Today, Tomorrow* (New York: Prentice Hall, 1937), p.vi. This volume included contributions of luminaries across the global political spectrum, with all arguing for some degree of economic and societal planning.
27. Arthur M. Schlesinger, Jr., *The Vital Center: The Politics of Freedom* (Transaction Publishers, 1997; first published by The Riverside Press, 1949).
28. Polybius, *The Complete Histories* (Digireads.com Publishing, 2014), p.1.
29. Shvets (2020), p.33.

CHAPTER 1

1. John Anthony Moretta, *The Hippies: A 1960s History* (North Carolina: McFarland & Company, 2017), p.7.
2. Ibid, p.14.
3. David Halberstam, *The Fifties* (New York: Open Road, 1993), p.9.
4. Todd Gitlin, *The Sixties: Years of Hope Days of Rage* (New York: Bantam Book, 1993), p.58.
5. There were never more than ten thousand Beatniks with perhaps only a few hundred who left written history or poems, with Allen Ginsberg and Jack Kerouac being arguably the best-known representatives.
6. Halberstam (1993), p.9.
7. See discussion of European experience: Martin Conway, *Western Europe's Democratic Age, 1945-1968* (Princeton: Princeton University Press, 2020); Tony Judt, *Postwar: History of Europe since 1945* (New York: Penguin Books, 2005); Paul Betts, *Ruin and Renewal: Civilizing Europe After World War II* (New York: Basic Books, 2020).

8. Gitlin (1997), p.27.
9. William Strauss and Neil Howe, *The Fourth Turning* (New York: Three Rivers Press, 1997), p.145.
10. John Kenneth Galbraith, *The Affluent Society* (Boston: Mariner Book, first published in 1958, reprinted in 1998).
11. Gitlin (1997), p.28.
12. Terry H Anderson, *The Sixties* (New York: Routledge, 2018), p.6.
13. Halberstam (1993), p.11.
14. New starts dropped from 1million per annum prior to the Great Depression to 100,000 in 1944-45.
15. Halberstam (1993), p.112.
16. Ibid, p.113.
17. Anderson (2018), p.1.
18. Lewis Mumford, *The City in History* (New York: Harcourt, 1961).
19. Gitlin (1997), p.35.
20. Gitlin (1993), p.31.
21. Judt (2005), pp.16–17.
22. For example, the number of children at the age of 10 that were by 1945 reporting "father absent" rose to 22 percent in Germany, 27 percent in Austria, 16 percent in France and 17 percent in Poland. Also, the number of children reporting to be hungry, rose from 5 percent in 1939 to 12 percent in Austria, from 6 percent to 21 percent in Germany, from 1 percent to 12 percent in France, and from 3 to 12 percent in Italy. Refer Iris Kesternich et al., "The Effects of World War II on Economic and Health Outcomes across Europe," *Review of Economics and Statistics*, Mar 1, 2014; 96 (1): 103–118.
23. As Prokop Drtina, Justice Minister of Czechoslovakia, declared in 1945, "There are no good Germans, only bad and even worse ones....and the whole German nation is responsible for Hitler, Himmler, Henlein and Frank, and the whole nation must bear the punishment for the committed crimes." Quoted by Keith Lowe, *Savage Continent: Europe in the Aftermath of World War II* (New York: St Martin's Press, 2012), p.139.
24. Betts (2020), pp.75–126.
25. Judt (2005), p.29.
26. Nicholas Craft and Gianni Toniolo, *Economic Growth in Europe Since 1945* (Cambridge: Cambridge University Press, 1995), p.4.
27. Refer Lowe (2012), pp.3–11.
28. Anne O'Hare McCormick, "Europe's Five Black Years," *New York Times Magazine*, September 3, 1944, p.42.
29. United Nations Statistical Year Books (1949–1965).
30. Judt (2005), p.331.
31. Ibid, p.352.
32. Barry Eichengreen and Albert Ritschi, "Understanding West German Economic Growth in the 1950s," *LSE, Working Paper No 113/08*, December 2008.
33. Craft (1995), p.10.
34. UN Demographic Database; World Bank.
35. IMF Government Data Base, 2023.
36. Brad DeLong described this period as "an economic El Dorado that rhymes with

the previous years of economic El Dorado, 1870-1914," Bradford DeLong, *Slouching Towards Utopia: An Economic History of the Twentieth Century* (New York: Basic Books, 2022), p.427.

37. See Daniel Bell, *The End of Ideology: On exhaustion of Political Ideas in the Fifties* (Cambridge: Harvard University Press, 2000; first published by Free Press in 1960); Chaim Waxman ed., *The End of Ideology Debate* (New York: Funk & Wagnalls, 1968).

38. Conway (2020), p.8.

39. Francis Fukuyama, *The End of History* (New York: Avon Books, 1992).

40. William Atwood, "How America Feels As We Enter the Soaring Sixties," *Look*, January 5, 1960.

41. Gitlin (1993), pp.35–36.

42. Ibid, p.34.

43. Anderson (2018), pp.2–3.

44. Ibid, p.5.

45. Ibid, p.5.

46. According to one of the observers at the time, a legion of co-eds was far more determined on getting their man than the FBI.

47. Robert H Bremner, "Families, Children and State" in Robert H Bremner and Gary W Reichard, *Reshaping America: Society and Institutions* (Columbus: Ohio State University Press, 1982), p.6.

48. Anderson (2018), p.6.

49. Australian Women's Weekly, December 21, 1960.

50. Anderson (2008), p.6.

51. Stephanie Coontz, *The Way We Never Were: American Families and the Nostalgia Trap* (New York: Basic Books, 1992).

52. Ibid, p.34.

53. Gitlin (1987), p.32.

54. Anderson (1992), pp.3–5.

55. When Lucy Ball was becoming visibly pregnant, censors prohibited use of the word "pregnancy." Instead, they invented a new term— "expectant mother" and as Lucy Ball described it, CBS lined up a panel of a priest, minister, and rabbi to review all pregnancy scripts. She said a that it looked like a revival meeting. Similarly, during Elvis Presley's first appearances on *The Ed Sullivan Show*, he was filmed from the waist up. See discussion in Halberstam (1993), pp.159–163.

56. Halberstam (1993), p.118.

57. Richard M Fried, "1950-1960" in Stephen J Whitfield ed., *A Companion to 20th Century America* (Malden: Blackwell Publishing, 2004).

58. In June 1960, John F. Kennedy, senator from Massachusetts and the future president, told a delegation of African diplomats, "It is the American tradition to stand up for one's rights—even if the new way to stand up...is to sit down," quoted by Anderson (2008), p.23.

CHAPTER 2

1. Examples include: Bernard von Bothmer, *Framing the Sixties* (Amherst: University of Massachusetts Press, 2010); Rob Kirkpatrick, *1969: The Year Everything Changed* (New York: Skyhorse Publishing, 2011); Todd Gitlin, *The Sixties: Years of Hope Days of Rage* (New York, Bantam Book, 1993); Michael Lang, *The Road to Woodstock* (Harper Collins e-books, 2009); Arthur Marwick, *The Sixties: Cultural Revolution in Britain, France, Italy and the United States, 1958-1974* (London: Bloomsbury, 1998); Jama Lazerow, *1960-1974*, in Stephen Whitfield ed. *A Companion to 20th Century America* (Oxford: Blackwell Publishing, 2004); Christopher B. Strain, *The Long Sixties: America, 1955-1973* (Malden: John Wiley & Sons, 2017); Terry H. Anderson, *The Sixties* (New York: Routledge, 2018); John A. Andrew, *The Other Side of the Sixties: Young Americans for Freedom and the Rise of Conservative Politics* (New Brunswick: Rutgers University Press, 1997); Mary C. Brennan, *Turning Right in the Sixties: The Conservative Capture of the GOP* (Chapel Hill: University of North Carolina Press, 1995).
2. Jama Lazerow (2004), chapter 6.
3. Tom Borstelmann, *The 1970s: A New Global History from Civil Rights to Economic Inequality* (Princeton: Princeton University Press, 2012), p.1.
4. Anderson (2018), p.52.
5. Strain (2017), p.14.
6. Anderson (2018), p.10.
7. James S. Coleman, *The Adolescent Society* (New York: Free Press, 1961), p.11.
8. Judt (2005), p.347.
9. Gitlin (1993), p.19.
10. Strain (2017), p.20.
11. Even in the case of Vietnam, for every drafted person, there were at least seven who were either deferred or excused in some form. That's why the Vietnam War was known as "the rich man's war and a poor man's fight."
12. Anderson (2018), p.66.
13. Ibid, p.9.
14. Jennifer Kavanagh and Michael Rich, *Truth Decay* (Santa Monica: Rand Corporation, 2018).
15. Shvets (2020).
16. ONS, "Labor Disputes in the UK."
17. Described in Michael Hardt, *The Subversive Seventies* (Oxford: Oxford University Press, 2023), pp.88–89.
18. Anatole Kaletsky, *Capitalism 4.0: The Birth of the New Economy in the Aftermath of Crisis* (New York: BBS Public Affairs, 2010).
19. George Packer, "Decline and Fall: How American Society Unraveled," *Guardian*, June 19, 2013.

CHAPTER 3

1. Borstelmann (2012), p.12.
2. Christopher Lasch, *The Culture of Narcissism: American Life in an Age of Diminishing Expectations* (New York: W.W. Norton, 1979).
3. Ibid., p.123.

4. Daniel Yankelovich, *New Rules: Searching for Self-Fulfillment in a World Turned Upside Down* (New York: Random House, 1981) p.xiv.
5. Ibid., p.xv.
6. Ibid., p.5.
7. The first iteration was the classical capitalism that lasted until dislocations of the 1930s, which was then followed by the much tighter degree of state control of Capitalism 2.0 through 1940–70s.
8. Steven Gaines, "Jerry Rubin, His Penis and Me: A Very Short Story," *Observer*, November 28, 2014.
9. Eric Pace, "Flashy 60s Radical Dies," *New York Times*, November 30, 1994.
10. Moretta (2017), p.354.
11. Arwa Mahdawi, "Why All the Burning Man Schadenfreude? Where do I start…," *The Guardian*, 5 September 2023.
12. Helen Andrews, *Boomers: The Men and Women who promised Freedom and delivered Disaster* (New York: Sentinel, 2021), p.23.
13. Moretta (2017), p.355.
14. Andrews (2021), p.xi.
15. Yankelovich (1981), p.81.
16. Robert Ringer, *Looking Out for Number One* (New York: Funk & Wagnalls, 1977), p.x.
17. Anderson (2018), p.26.
18. Daniel Yankelovich, *The New Morality: A Profile of American Youth in the 70s* (New York: McGraw Hill, 1974), p.3.
19. Michel Crozier, Samuel P. Huntington, Joji Watanuki, *The Crisis of Democracy: On the Governability of Democracies to the Trilateral Commission* (New York University Press, 1975).
20. Packer (2013).

CHAPTER 4
1. Friedrich von Hayek, *Law, Legislation and Liberty, volume 2: The Mirage of Social Justice* (Chicago: University of Chicago Press, 1976), p.68.
2. John Maynard Keynes, *The General Theory of Employment, Interest and Money* (Pesserino Editore, first published in 1936), p.378.
3. See discussion in Quinn Slobodian, *Globalists: The End of Empire and the Birth of Neoliberalism* (Cambridge: Harvard University Press, 2018); Wendy Brown, *In the Ruins of Neoliberalism* (New York: Columbia University Press, 2019); Bradford DeLong, *Slouching Towards Utopia: An Economic History of the Twentieth Century* (New York, Basic Books, 2022); Gary Gerstle, *The Rise and Fall of the Neoliberal Order* (Oxford: Oxford University Press, 2022); David Harvey, *A Brief History of Neoliberalism* (Oxford, Oxford University Press, 2005).
4. Quinn Slobodian, *Crack Up Capitalism: Market Radicals and the Dream of a World Without Democracy* (New York: Metropolitan Books, 2023), p.8.
5. Ibid, p.8.
6. Lulu Garcia-Navarro, "Inside the Heritage Foundation's Plans for Institutionalized Trumpism," *New York Times*, January 21, 2024.
7. Slobodian (2023), p.9.

8. Brown (2019), p.29.
9. Marc Andreessen, "The Techno-Optimist Manifesto."
10. Patrick Deene, *Regime Change* (Sentinel, 2023); Yoram Hazony, *The Virtue of Nationalism* (New York: Basic Books, 2018).
11. Maurice Stucke and Ariel Ezrachi, "The Rise, Fall and Rebirth of the US Antitrust Movement," *HBR*, December 2017.
12. Business in America, "Too Much of a Good Thing," *Economist*, March 6, 2016.
13. Paul Collier, *The Future of Capitalism: Facing the New Anxieties* (London: Allen Lane, 2018), p.79.
14. US share buybacks regularly reach US$1 trillion per annum or about 3–4 percent of the US market capitalization is effectively liquidated when compared to around 1 percent two decades ago. Globally, share buybacks and dividends are consuming around US$2.5–US$3.0 trillion per annum, more than the total corporate capital expenditure.
15. Shvets (2020), pp.147–149.
16. Ibid, pp.145–156.
17. Brown (2019), p.34.
18. Von Hayek, *The Fatal Conceit*, p.118.
19. Blom (2015), p.467.
20. When questioned by reporters what checks and balances on the unconstrained presidential authority, does he (Kevin Roberts, the Head of the Heritage Foundation) envisage, the answer was the elected Congress. When it was pointed out to him that there is no evidence that in a highly partisan environment, Congress offers any meaningful checks, he could only say, "Admittedly. I mean, I readily concede that. In fact, I have friends in Congress who are tired of hearing me say that—you guys have to have more courage about this, including if President Trump is re-elected," *New York Times*, January 21, 2024. In other words, Roberts was willing to persist with the idea of a unitary presidential power, even though he accepts that in real life there are currently limited checks on such authority. Roberts is also the coordinator of the conservative *Program 2025*, which among other things, advocates mass purge of bureaucracy, elimination of various departments and commissions, replacement of civil servants with political appointees, concentration of the power in the presidency, de-prioritization of climate change policies, major cuts and overhaul of Medicaid, reduction in welfare and transfer benefits, extreme restrictions on abortion and far greater injection of religion into civic and educational systems.
21. In an almost parallel universe fashion, top Hong Kong officials repeatedly reject concerns that censorship is restricting creative freedom. From movies to Cantopop, Hong Kong's artistic contribution has been in steep decline when compared to the golden age of 1970s–90s. Refer Chan Ho, "Why Hong Kong's Cinema Has Gone Quiet," *Financial Times*, February 14, 2024.
22. The top three to four of Hong Kong's developers control in excess of 70 percent of the market.
23. SoCo.org.hk, Cage Homes and Old Private Housing Project; data for 2019.
24. From National Statistical Offices for 2020-22. Pak You, "Living large: Hong Kong Moves Out of Pint-Sized Nano Flats", *Nikkei*, September 8, 2022.
25. Chan Ho, "The Painful slump in Hong Kong Property," *Financial Times*, May 7, 2024.

26. Thomas K Cheng, "Sherman vs. Goliath? Tackling Conglomerate Dominance Problem in Emerging and Small Economies—Hong Kong as a Case Study," *Northwestern Journal of International Law and Business*, vol.37, issue 1, Winter, 2017.

27. Thomas Piketty and Li Yang, "Income and Wealth Inequality in Hong Kong, 1981-2020: The Rise of Pluto-Communism?" *World Inequality Lab, Working Paper 2021/18*, June 2021.

28. Jeffrey Wasserstrom, *Vigil: Hong Kong on the Brink* (New York: Columbia Global Reports, 2020), p.42.

29. Quoted in Slobodian (2023), p.34.

30. Just witness conservative calls to make post-Brexit Britain into a European version of Singapore.

31. Cheuk Ting Hung, "Income Inequality in Hong Kong and Singapore," August 2018, downloaded, August 2023.

32. Slobodian (2023), p.170.

33. This is why *Economist* magazine (January 12, 2024), recently compared today's Dubai to the Medici era of the 15th century Florence. Ultimately, the era that gave us marvels of the Renaissance did not survive for more than three generations of the Medici family.

34. Joseph E. Stiglitz, *The Road to Freedom: Economics and the Good Society* (New York: W. W. Norton & Company, 2024), p.215.

35. Milton Friedman and Rose Friedman, *Free to Choose: A Personal Statement* (Harvest Book, 1990, first published in 1979).

36. MacKenzie and Mumford eds. (1937), p.v.

37. Karl Polanyi, *The Great Transformation: The Political and Economic Origins of Our Time* (Boston: Beacon Press, 2001, first published in 1944).

38. Thomas Piketty, *Capital in the Twenty First Century* (Cambridge: Belknap Press of Harvard University, 2014).

39. Friedrich von Hayek, *The Road to Serfdom* (Abridged version, London: Institute of Economic Affairs, 2005, originally published in 1944).

40. Sheldon Wolin, *Fugitive Democracy and Other Essays* (Princeton: Princeton University Press, 2001).

CHAPTER 5

1. Andrews (2021), p.xiv.

2. DeLong (2022), p.465.

3. External Wealth of Nations Data Base, January 2024.

4. Jeanne Batalova, "Top Statistics on Global Migration and Migrants," *Migration Policy Institute*, July 21, 2022.

5. According to the WTO there are now over 65,000 cases outstanding, more than triple the level in 2008.

6. Dani Rodrik, "Sense and Nonsense in the Globalization Debate," *Foreign Affairs*, Summer 1997.

7. Peter Drucker, *Post Capitalist Society* (New York: HarperCollins, 1993), p.209.

8. Stefan Linik, "How Might 21st century De-Globalization Unfold? Some Historical Reflection," *New Global Studies* 12, no.3 (2018): 347.

9. Larry Summers re-ignited interest in the concept first propagated by Alvin Hansen in

the late 1930s who tried to explain inability of the US economy to recover after the Great Depression.

10. Adair Turner, *Between Debt and the Devil* (Princeton: Princeton University Press, 2016), p.29. Turner is the former head of the UK Financial Service Authority.

11. Charles Calomiris and Stephen Haber, *Fragile by Design: The Political Origins of Banking Crises and Scarce Credit* (Princeton: Princeton University Press, 2014), p.28.

12. There is a great deal of debate about after-tax and fiscal transfer allocation to different tax groups with Thomas Piketty, Emmanuel Saez, and Gabriel Zukman (PCZ) estimating that the top 1 percent share rose between 1960 and 2019 from 9 percent toward 15–20 percent. However, from a different methodology, Gerald Auten and David Splinter are suggesting a less robust increase from 8 percent to 9 to 10 percent. Others (such as William Gale, John Sabelhaus and Samuel Thorpe) tend to be in between but closer to PCZ. Most differences relate to the allocation of fiscal deficits as well as business revenues and expenses, and the extent of tax avoidance. However, the same issues do not exist to the same degree in assessing wealth distribution, with all databases showing a strong rise in wealth inequalities.

13. "The 2023 Crony-Capitalism Index," *Economist*, May 2, 2023.

14. "Inequality Inc," *Oxfam*, January 2024.

15. Joseph, Stiglitz *The Price of Inequality: How Today's Divided Society Endangers our Future* (London: Allen Lane, 2012).

16. Loukas Karabarbounis, "Perspectives on the Labor Share," *Journal of Economic Perspectives*, vol.38, Number 2, Spring 2021, pp.107–136.

17. See discussion in Bremner (1982), pp.3–30.

18. Robin Fields, "What to Know About Roiling Debate Over US Mortality Rates," *ProPublica*, April 5, 2024.

19. The latest National Health Surveys indicate that the average white American has been getting shorter when compared to the average European, with most of the blame attributed to the poor diet of the average American child and the inability of poorer sections of the population to frequently consult healthcare providers (due to unaffordable costs).

20. There are far too many studies to enumerate, and the field has become incredibly politicized. These are some of the more recent studies. Karel Martens, Jose Montiel Olea, "Marginal Tax Rate and Income," *NBER*, 2017; Mattias Kehring and Nicholas Vincent, "The Micro-level Anatomy of the Labor Share decline," *NBER*, 2018; Nazlia Alinaghi and Robert Reed, "Taxes and Economic Growth Rates in OECD countries," *OECD*, July 2020; William Gale and Andrew Samwick, "Effects of Income Tax Changes on Economic Growth," *Brookings*, 2014; Thomas Piketty, Emmanuel Saez and Stephanie Stancheva, "Optimum Taxation on Top Labor Incomes," *NBER*, 2011; Claudia Goldin and Robert Margo, "The Great Compression: The Wage Structure in the United States at Mid-Century," *NBER*, 1991; Sebastian Gechert and Philipp Heimberger, "Do Corporate Tax Cuts boost Economic Growth?" *European Economic Review*, 2022.

21. Paolo Mauro, Rafael Romeu, Ariel Binder, and Assad Zaman, "A Modern History of Fiscal Prudence and Profligacy," *IMF Working Paper* No 13/5.

22. David Hope and Julian Limburg, "The Economic Consequences of Major Tax Cuts for

the Rich," *Socio-Economic Review*, 2022, vol.20, no.2, pp.539–559. The study assessed the impact of tax cuts on the rich in 18 OECD countries between 1965 and 2015.
23. Shvets (2020), pp.195–214.
24. Refer discussion of these issues in Shvets (2020), pp.145–148.
25. Andrew Clark and Jill Treanor, "Greenspan: I Was Wrong About the Economy," *Guardian*, October 23, 2008.

CHAPTER 6
1. Ronald Inglehart, *Cultural Evolution: People's Motivations are Changing and Reshaping the World* (Cambridge, Cambridge University Press, 2018), p.8.
2. Kevin Drum, "Review of Brad DeLong's "Slouching Towards Utopia," September 2022.
3. Dave Gilson, "The CIA's Secret Psychological Profiles of Dictators and World Leaders," *Mother Jones*, February 11, 2015; Seth Davin Norrholm, "The Psychology of Dictators: Power, Fear and Anxiety," *Anxiety.org*, October 21, 2023; David Hume, "What Dictators have in Common," *History*, Winter 2019. Frank Dikotter, *How to Be a Dictator: The Cult of Personality in the Twentieth Century* (New York: Bloomsbury, 2019).
4. Hitler on the occasion of his 50th birthday (1939), argued that "In a few years I will be physically, perhaps mentally, too, no longer up to it," and, therefore stated that all war plans must be brought forward. Similarly, a Russian foreign minister (Sergey Lavrov) once reputedly told one of the oligarchs that Vladimir Putin only has three advisors – "Ivan the Terrible, Peter the Great and Catherine the Great" to explain Putin's preoccupation with his place in history.
5. Neil Howe, *The Fourth Turning Point is Here* (New York, Simon & Schuster, 2023).
6. See Steven Levitsky and Daniel Ziblatt, *How Democracies Die* (New York, Crown Publishing, 2018); Andrea Kendall-Taylor, Natasha Lindstaedt, and Erica Frantz, *Democracies and Authoritarian Regimes* (Oxford, Oxford University Press, 2019).
7. Quinnipiac University Poll, June 21, 2023.
8. Lilliana Mason, *Uncivil Agreement: How Politics Became Our Identity* (Chicago: University of Chicago, 2018), p.18.
9. Jennifer McCoy and Murat Somer, "Toward a Theory of Pernicious Polarization," *Annals of the American Academy of Political and Social Science*, 2019.
10. For example, Thomas Carothers and Andrew O'Donohue, ed., *Democracies Divided: The Global Challenge of Political Polarization* (Washington: The Brookings Institution, 2019); Alan Abramowitz, *The Great Alignment: Race, Party, Transformation and the Rise of Donald Trump* (New Haven: Yale University Press, 2019); Ezra Klein, *Why We're Polarized*, (New York: Avid Reader Press, 2020).
11. Christopher Ball et al, "Exposure to Opposite Views on Social Media Can Strengthen Polarization", *PNAS*, August 2018; Dan Kahan, Ellen Peters, Erica Dawson, and Paul Slovic, "Motivated Numeracy and Enlightened Self-Government," *Behavioral Public Policy*, 2017.
12. Henri Tejfel, "Experiments in Intergroup Discrimination," 1970.
13. Geoffrey Cohen, "Party Over Policy: Dominating Impact of Group Influence on Political Beliefs," *Journal of Personality and Social Psychology*, 2003, vol.85, no.5, 808-822; Iyengar and Westwood, "Fear and Loathing: New Evidence on Group

polarization," *Midwest Political Science Association*, 2014.

14. Quoted in William Davies, *Nervous States: Democracy and The Decline of Reason* (New York: W.W. Norton & Company, 2018), p.27.
15. Packer (2013), p.17.
16. Andres Reiljan, "Fear and Loathing Across Party Lines in Europe," *European Journal of Political Research*, 59 (2), pp.376–396.
17. Frederico Ferreira da Silva and Simon Maye, "Affective Polarization in Comparative and Longitudinal Perspective," *Public Opinion Quarterly*, vol. 87, issue 1, Spring 2013, pp.219–231.
18. "Government at a Glance 2023," *OECD*.

CHAPTER 7

1. Kevin Drum, "Welcome to Digital Revolution," *Foreign Affairs*, July/August 2018.
2. Some notable examples include: Yuval Harari, *Homo Deus* (New York: Harper Collins, 2017); Yuval Harari, *21 Lessons for the 21st Century* (New York: Spiegel & Grau, 2019); Andrew McAfee and Erik Brynjolfsson, *Machine Platform, Crowd: Harnessing Our Digital Future*, (New York: W.W. Norton, 2017); Erik Brynjolfsson and Andrew McAfee, *The Second Machine Age* (New York: W.W. Norton, 2014); Martin Ford, *The Rise of Robots* (New York: Basic Books, 2015); Franklin Foer, *World Without Mind* (New York: Penguin Press, 2017); Peter Frase, *Four Futures: Life After Capitalism* (New York: Verso, 2016); Carl Benedict Frey, *The Technology Trap: Capital, Labor and Power in the Age of Automation* (Princeton: Princeton University Press, 2019); David Graeber, *Bullshit Jobs* (London: Allen Lane, 2018); Robert Gordon, *The Rise and Fall of American Growth* (Princeton, Princeton University Press, 2016); Andre Gorz, *Reclaiming Work* (Cambridge: Polity Press, 1999); Ray Kurzweil, *The Age of Spiritual Machines* (New York: Penguin Press, 1999); Richard Dobbs, James Manyika, and Jonathan Woetzel, *No Ordinary Disruption* (New York: BBS Public Affairs, 2015); Mervyn King, *The End of Alchemy: Money, Banking and the Future of Global Economy* (New York: W.W. Norton & Company, 2016); Nicholas Shaxson, *The Finance Curse: How Global Finance Is Making Us All Poorer* (London: Bodley Head, 2018); Jonathan Haskel and Stian Westlake, *Capitalism without Capital* (Princeton: Princeton University Press, 2018); Kai-Fu Lee, *AI Super-Powers: China, Silicon Valley, and the New World Order* (New York: Farrar, Strauss and Giroux, 2018); Paul Collier, *The Future of Capitalism: Facing the New Anxieties* (London: Allen Lane, 2018); Mustafa Suleyman, *The Coming Wave* (New York: Crown, 2023); Mordecai Kurz, *The Market Power of Technology: Understanding the Second Gilded Age*, (New York: Columbia University Press, 2023).
3. Shvets (2020), p.18.
4. Richard Dobbs, James Manyika, and Jonathan Woetzel, "The Four Global Forces Breaking All the Trends," *McKinsey Special Collection, Trends and Global Forces*, April 2015.
5. Erik Brynjolfsson, "The Turing Trap: The Promise and Peril of Human-Like Artificial Intelligence," 2022.
6. Joel Mokyr, Chris Vickers, and Nicholas Ziebarth, "The History of Technological Anxiety and the Future of Economic Growth: Is This Time Different," *Journal of Economic Perspective*, vol.29, no.3 (Summer 2015), pp.31–50.

7. Laura Tyson, and Michael Spence, "Exploring the Effect of Technology on Income and Wealth Inequality," in Heather Boushey, Bradford DeLong, and Michael Steinbaum, eds., *After Piketty* (Cambridge, Harvard University Press, 2017), p.166.

8. Yuval Harari (2018), XV.

9. NY Times Editorial, March 2023.

10. Daron Acemoglu, "Harms of AI," August 2021.

11. 2022 Expert Survey on Progress of AI, August 2022.

12. The larger number of parameters significantly improves model's ability to generate coherent output.

13. For example, International Energy Agency, estimated that in 2023, AI and cryptos have already consumed 460 TWh of electricity globally (or 2%), and it estimates that by 2026 that number could double. On the current path, AI alone by early 2030s, could be consuming up to 5% of global electricity. Hence, a need for energy consumption technology breakthroughs. *IEA*, Electricity 2024: Analysis and Forecast to 2026.

14. Bill Gates characterized recent developments of AI as being as fundamental as the creation of microprocessor, the personal computer, the Internet, and mobile phones.

15. Henry Mance, "AI Keeps Going Wrong. What If It Can't Be Fixed?" *Financial Times*, April 6, 2024.

16. Allen & Overy (one of the world's largest legal firms) announced preliminary steps of rolling out AI contract negotiation tool, as David Wakeling (A&O partner) was quoted in the *Financial Times* (Dec 21, 2023), the firm's goal was to "disrupt the legal market before someone disrupts us."

17. Sulieman Mustafa, *The Coming Wave* (New York: Crown, 2023), p.77.

18. Gill Platt, "Is Cambrian Explosion Coming for Robotics," *Journal of Economic Perspectives*, vol.29, no.3, Summer 2015, pp.51–60.

19. IFR (International Federation of Robotics), September 2023.

20. Refer Rana Foroohar, "A New Technology Boom is at hands," *Financial Times*, March 26, 2023; Martin Ford (2015); Andrew McAfee and Erik Brynjolfsson (2016).

21. Andre Gorz, *Reclaiming Work* (Cambridge: Polity Press, 1999), p.1.

22. Richard Dobbs, James Manyika, and Jonathan Woetzel, *No Ordinary Disruption* (New York: BBS Public Affairs, 2015), p.8.

23. Andrew Keen, *How to Fix the Future* (New York: Atlantic Monthly Press, 2018), p.4.

24. In a prophetic article in 1983, the Nobel Prize-winning economist Wassily Leontief observed, "One might say the process by which progressive introduction of new computerized, automated, and robotized equipment can be expected to reduce the role of labor is similar to the process by which the introduction of tractors and other machinery first reduced and then eliminated horses and other draft animals in agriculture," "Technological Advance, Economic Growth, and the Distribution of Income," *Population and Development Review* 9:3, 1983, p.405.

25. Brynjolfsson (2022).

26. Acemoglu (2021).

27. Tyne Eloundou, Sam Manning et al, "GPTs: An Early Look at the Labor Market Impact Potential of Large Language Models," *Open AI and the University of Pennsylvania*, March 2023.

28. Delphine Strauss, "High-flying City workers set to be most affected by AI," *Financial Times*, November 30, 2023.

29. Mauro Cazzaniga et al., "Gen-AI: Artificial Intelligence and the Future of Work," *IMF*, January 2024.

30. McKinsey Global Institute, "Automation, Employment and Productivity," January 2017.

31. Michael Chui et al., "The Economic Potential of Generative AI", *McKinsey & Company*, June 2023.

32. Daron Acemoglu and Pascual Restrepo, "The Revolution Need Not be Automated," *Project Syndicate*, March 29, 2019; Daron Acemoglu and Pascual Restrepo, "Robots and Jobs," *NBER Working Paper, 23285*, March 2017.

33. Carl Frey and Michael Osborne, "The Future of Employment: How Susceptible are Jobs to Computerization," *Department of Engineering Science, University of Oxford*, Summer 2013.

34. Described by Ellen Shell, *The Job: Work and Its Future in a Time of Radical Change* (New York: Currency, 2018), p.61.

35. "The Gig Economy," *Daily Beast*, 2019; Sarah Horowitz, "Freelance in the US labor force," *BLS*, 2015; Arnat Bracha and Mary Burke, "How Big is the Gig," *Labor Economics*, 2021; Adam Ozimek, "Freelance Forwards," *Upwork*, 2021.

36. Tej Parikh, "Erik Brynjolfsson: This could be the best decade in history – or the worst," *Financial Times*, January 31, 2024.

37. Zenep Tufekci, "Failing the Third Machine Age: When Robots Came for Grandma," *Medium.com*, 2014; Samuel Bowles, Arjun Jaydev, "One Nation Under Guard," *New York Times, February* 5, 2014.

38. "A Scent of Musk," *The Economist*, July 20, 2019.

39. Graeber, David, *Bullshit Jobs* (London: Allen Lane, 2018).

40. Eric Posner, "The Future of Work in the AI era," *Project Syndicate*, April 11, 2024.

41. Clemens Hetschko, Andreas Knabe and Ronnie Schob, "Changing Identity: Retiring from Unemployment," *SOE Papers, DIW*, 399, July 2011.

42. See a typical line of argument of a shortage of labor and deteriorating demographics in: "Welcome to a Golden Age for Workers," *Economist*, November 8, 2023.

43. Shvets (2020), pp.161–169.

44. Carol Corrado, Jonathan Haskel et al., "Intangible Capital and Modern Economies," *Journal of Economic Perspectives*, vol.36, no.3, Summer 2022, pp.3–28.

45. Haskel and Westlake (2018); Haskel and Westlake (2022).

46. Carlota Perez, *Technological Revolutions and Financial Capital* (Cheltenham, Edward Elgar, 2002).

47. Tyler Cowen, "AI's Greatest Danger? The Humans Who Use It," *Bloomberg*, January 25, 2024.

48. Richard Freeman, "Who Owns the Robots Rules the World," *IZA World of Labor*, 2015:5.

49. Andrew McAfee and Erik Brynjolfsson (2017), p.95.

50. See discussion of such glorious outcomes in Bradford DeLong (2023).

51. According to McCloskey, cotton productivity was galloping in the late 18th century at a 2.6 percent clip but woolens at only 0.9 percent, and as the transport revolution picked up speed, its productivity started to grow as quickly as cotton (or over 2

percent). Donald McCloskey, ed., *Measurement and Meaning in Economics* (New York: Elgar, 2001), pp.249–250. A similar argument is made regarding the proliferation of social media and the Internet in recent decades. Do these new inventions increase productivity? Answer: not for a long time. Carl Newport, *A World Without Email: Reimagining Work in an Age of Communication Overload* (New York: Portfolio/Penguin, 2021). See Shvets (2020), Appendices V and VI.

CHAPTER 8

1.   Tara Zahra, *Against the World: Anti-Globalism and Mass Politics between the World Wars* (London: W.W. Norton & Company, 2023), p.xiv.
2.   Stefan Zweig, *The World of Yesterday* (New York, Plunkett Press, 2011, first published by Viking Press, 1943), p.300.
3.   John Maynard Keynes, *The Economic Consequences of Peace*, (New York: Harcourt, Brace and Howe, 1920), p.6.
4.   Ibid, p.6.
5.   Giovanni Federico and Antonio Tena-Junguito, "World Trade, 1800-1938: A New Data Set," *EHES Working Papers in Economic History, no.93*, European Historical Economics Society, January 2016; Giovanni Federico and Antonio Tena-Junguito, "World Trade, 1800-2015," *Vox EU*, February 7, 2016.
6.   2024 Edelman Global Trust Barometer.
7.   Damon Linker, "Get to Know the Influential Conservative Intellectuals Who Help Explain G.O.P. Extremism," *New York Times*, November 4, 2023.
8.   Daron Acemoglu et al., "War, Socialism and the Rise of Fascism—an Empirical Exploration," *NBER* Working Paper 27854, September 2020.
9.   Gary King, Ori Rosen, Martin Tanner, and Alexander Wagner, "Ordinary Economic Behavior in the Extraordinary Election of Adolf Hitler," *The Journal of Economic History*, vol.68, December 2008.
10. Allen (1939), p.187.
11. Zahra (2023), p.122. According to their agenda: "Every Klansman knows how there is a conspiracy of alien races and religions to overwhelm and destroy America by hordes of invaders who are hostile to our every thought and purpose and unassimilable to our society…we must get rid of the undesirable aliens, of the foreign criminals, degenerates, paupers and unfit of all kinds who are an open sore on our body politic, a social cancer, one of the worst evils from which the nation suffers" (H.W. Evans, "The Klan's Next Duty: Send Home Every Unfit Alien," *Kourier Magazine*, 2, no.3 (February 1926). It had its echo in Donald Trump's more recent speeches where he questioned why the US should have so many immigrants from what he described as "shithole countries" in Africa rather than places like Norway (AP, January 12, 2018) or called Mexican immigrants as gangsters and rapists.
12. Levitsky and Ziblatt (2019).
13. Quoted in Henry Farrell and Abraham Newman, "The New Economic Security State," *Foreign Affairs*, November/December 2023, p.106.
14. Zbigniew Brzezinski, *The Grand Chessboard: American Primacy and its Geostrategic Imperatives* (New York: Basic Books, 1997), p.55.
15. Elizabeth C. Economy, *The World According to China* (London, Polity Press, 2022), p.5.

16. Thomas Piketty, *A Brief History of Equality* (Cambridge: The Belknap Press, 2022), pp.230-232.

17. In the latest direction for foreign policy (December 2023), Xi Jinping urged its diplomats to "resolutely safeguard national sovereignty, security and development interests, with an attitude of readiness to fight and a firm will to defy strong powers… envoys must enrich their minds with the party's innovative theories, sharpen their eyes to distinguish right from wrong, and always maintain the correct political direction… put discipline and rules first and build a diplomatic iron army loyal to the party, brave in taking responsibilities, daring to fight and being good at fighting," *SCMP*, December 30, 2023.

18. Exceptionally well described in Economy (2022).

19. Odd Arne Westad, "Sleepwalking Toward War," *Foreign Affairs*, June 13, 2024.

20. Westad (2024).

21. Key Xi Quotes at China's Communist Party Congress, *Reuters*, October 16, 2022

22. Aleksandr Solzhenitsyn, *Rebuilding Russia: Reflections and Tentative Proposals* (New York: Vintage, 1991).

23. Vladimir Putin, "On the Historical Unity of Russians and Ukrainians," *Presidential Library of Russian Federation*, July 12, 2021.

24. Margaret MacMillan, "How Wars Don't End: Ukraine, Russia and the Lessons of World War I," *Foreign Affairs*, June 2023.

25. Shvets (2020), pp.41–52.

26. Serhii Plokhy, *Lost Kingdom: The Quest for Empire and the Making of the Russian Nation*, (New York: Basic Books, 2017), p.ix.

27. Guy Faulconbridge, "Putin Blasts West, Says World Faces Most Dangerous Decade since World War II," *Reuters*, October 27, 2022.

CHAPTER 9

1. James Lacey, ed., *Great Strategic Rivalries: From the Classical World to the Cold War*, (Oxford: Oxford University Press, 2016), p.4.; Graham Allison, *Destined for War: Can America and China Escape Thucydides' Trap* (New York: Houghton Mifflin Harcourt, 2017).

2. George Kennan, "Long Telegram, February 22, 1946," *The Wilson Center Digital Archive*. For a more comprehensive discussion refer George Kennan, *Russia and the West Under Lenin and Stalin* (Boston: Little Brown and Company, 1960).

3. Argentina's new president (Javier Milei) is already reconsidering Argentine's participation, months after being accepted into BRICS.

4. Refer Uppsala Conflict Database and the Peace Research Institute Oslo.

5. According to the Institute for Strategic Studies in 2023, there were 183 ongoing conflicts around the world, the highest level since 1990.

6. Vladimir Lenin, 'What is to Be Done," *Marxists.org*.

7. Ideas of "continuous revolution" with never ending corruption trials, disappearance of bureaucrats, sudden replacement of senior ministers, sacking of army generals as well as regular disappearances of business executives (to cooperate with authorities) generates a great deal of fear and confusion. CCP does not believe that China has institutional deficiencies causing proliferation of corruption and nepotism. Rather, these

are viewed through the eyes of moral and character failures that need to be regularly and continuously rectified. Whereas in 2013, around 180,000 party members and bureaucrats were disciplined for infractions, these rose to 600,000 per annum between 2018 and 2022. Chun Han Wong, "China's Xi' is Resurrecting Mao's Continuous Revolution with a Twist," *Wall Street Journal,* January 1, 2024.

8. Yuri Slezkine, *The House of Government: A Saga of Russian Revolution* (Princeton: Princeton University Press, 2017).
9. Shvets (2020), chapters 5 and 12.
10. David Harvey, *Marx, Capital, and the Madness of Economic Reason* (London: Profile Books, 2019), pp.178–179.
11. Tom Hancock, "China Ministry Blasts Local Officials for 'Blind' EV Investments," *Bloomberg,* January 19, 2024.
12. Demetri Sevastopulo and Edward White, "US Says It will Act if China Dumps Goods on Global Markets," *Financial Times,* February 19, 2024.
13. Alicia Garcia-Herrero and Alessio Terzi, "China's Economy Cannot Export Its Problems Away," *Project Syndicate,* May 31, 2024.
14. George Magnus, "China's Quixotic Quest to Innovate," *Foreign Affairs,* May 29, 2024.
15. Also, one of the few Russian-sourced battalions in the Ukrainian Army fighting the Russian invasion is also largely manned by people from Siberia. Vasilisa Stepanenko, "The Siberian Battalion: Meet the Russian nationals fighting against Putin in Ukraine's army," *Independent,* December 16, 2023.
16. Shvets (2020), p.232.
17. Stephen Kotkin, "The Five Futures of Russia, and How America Can Prepare for Whatever Comes Next," *Foreign Affairs,* May/June 2024.
18. Barbara Walter, *How Civil Wars Start* (New York: Crown, 2022).
19. On a variety of criteria (such as GNI, mortality etc.), the UN currently classifies 46 countries in the least developed category (including 33 in Africa). However, there are another 31 countries that are classified in a low-income bracket (mostly below US$3,000 per capita or less than one-tenth of developed economies).
20. Refer Shvets (2020).
21. According to the UN, infant mortality (under the age of five) has dropped in the least developed nations from truly Malthusian levels of 300 per thousand in 1950 to around 80 by 2015, and in slightly more developed economies, it was down from 236 per thousand to around 40. But female fertility in the least and less developed countries remained high at more than four children per woman and closer to 5–6 in the poorest nations and failed states.
22. Shvets (2020), p.337.
23. Dani Rodrik, "Premature Deindustrialization," *NBER,* Working Paper 20935, February 2015.
24. Daron Acemoglu and James Robinson, *Economic Origins of Dictatorship and Democracy* (Cambridge: Cambridge University Press, 2006).
25. UNHCR, July 11, 2023.
26. As MacMillan (2023) rightly highlighted, "Leaders are rarely mere machines tabulating the costs and benefits of war."

CHAPTER 10

1. Peter Frase (216), p.8.
2. For example, traveling through Soviet Union in 1932, Arthur Koestler, British author and journalist, wrote: "If history herself were a fellow traveler, she could not have arranged a cleverer timing of events than this coincidence of the gravest crisis of the Western world with the initial phase of Russia's industrial revolution. The contrast… was so striking that it led to the equally obvious conclusion: They are the future—we, the past," quoted in Piers Brendon, *The Dark Valley: Panorama of the 1930s* (New York: Vintage Books, 2000), p.250.
3. Anne Morrow Lindbergh, *The Wave of the Future* (New York: Harcourt, Brace & Company, 1940).
4. Carl L. Becker, "The Dilemma of Modern Democracy," *The Virginia Quarterly Review* 17, no.1 (Winter 1941), p.11.
5. Ibid, p.15.
6. Ibid, p.16.
7. Carl Schmitt, *The Crisis of Parliamentary Democracy* (MIT Press, 1988, First Edition published in 1923).
8. Becker (1941), p.17.
9. Mason (2018).
10. Shvets (2020), p.177.
11. Harari (2018), Introduction, p.xv.
12. This is an incredibly wide and complex field that includes economists, political scientists, and budget planners. Some of the better works are Rutger Bregman, *Utopia for Realists: Universal Basic Income* (New York: Little Brown Company, 2017); Guy Standing, *Basic Income and How We Can Make it Happen* (Pelican Books, 2017); Philippe van Parijs and Yannick Vanderborght, *Basic Income*, (Cambridge, Harvard University Press, 2017); Robert van der Veen and Philippe van Parijs, "A Capitalist Road to Communism," *Theory and Society*, v.15:5, 1986, pp.635-655.
13. Gosta Esping-Andersen, *The Three Worlds of Welfare Capitalism* (Cambridge: Polity, 1990).
14. See for example, "Basic Income as a Policy option," *OECD*, 2017.
15. Martin Sandbu, "We are Closer to Taxing the Super-Rich," *Financial Times*, May 20, 2024.
16. For example, there are already bills tabled in a number of US states (such as Arizona, Iowa, and South Dakota) that aim to ban basic income guarantees and any other form of "unearned income."
17. Witness how the latest book by Stephanie Kelton, *Deficit Myth* (Public Affairs, 2020) has quickly progressed to the New York Times best seller list.
18. "America Is Living on Borrowed Money," *New York Times Editorial*, July 6, 2023.
19. Carmen Reinhart and Kenneth Rogoff, *This Time Is Different* (Princeton: Princeton University Press, 2010).
20. Address by Jerome Powell at the Jackson Hole, August 2023.
21. Paul Krugman put succinctly in his article in the *New York Times*: "We now know that the economic expansion of 2003–07 was driven by a bubble. You can say the same about the later part of the 1990s expansion; and can say the same about the later years of the Reagan expansion….so how can you reconcile repeated bubbles with an economy

showing no inflation? Larry Summers' answer is that we may be in an economy that needs bubbles to achieve something near full employment—that in the absence of asset bubbles, the economy has a negative equilibrium rate of interest. And this has not just been since the financial crisis; it has been true since the 1980s," Paul Krugman, *New York Times*, November 16, 2013.

22. Susannah Savage, "Can Africa One Day Help Feed the World's Growing Population," *Financial Times*, April 3, 2024.

23. According to FAO (UN Food and Agriculture Association), Africa on average uses 24kg of fertilizer per hectare on land—only a fifth of global average.

24. The White House, "Building Resilient Supply Chains, Revitalizing American Manufacturing, and Fostering Broad-Based Growth," June 2021.

25. For example, "Harnessing Lightening – How Chinese Military is Adopting Artificial Intelligence," *Center for Security and Emerging Technologies*, October 2021.

26. Dani Rodrik, Reka Juhasz and Nathan Lake, "Economists Reconsider Industrial Policy," *Project Syndicate*, April 4, 2023; Martin Wolf, "How Not to Do Industrial Policy," *Financial Times*, June 18, 2024.

27. Nic Fildes, "'Made in Australia' Drive Aims to Shift Economy from 'World's Quarry' Label," *Financial Times*, April 4, 2024.

28. "IMF Warns of 'Tepid Twenties' as Global Growth Inches Higher," *Bloomberg News*, April 11, 2024.

29. Ruchir Agarwal, "Industrial Policy and the Growth Strategy Trilemma," *IMF*, 31 March, 2023.

30. "Expanding Frontiers: Fiscal Policies for Innovation and Technology Diffusion," *IMF*, April 2024.

31. Vannevar Bush, "Science: The Endless Frontier: A Report to the President of the United States by the Office of Scientific Research and Development," US Government Printing Office, July 1945, p.19.

32. Mariana Mazzucato, *The Entrepreneurial State: Debunking Public vs Private Sector Myths* (Public Affairs, 2015).

33. "Chinese Science: The Great Experiment," *Economist*, January 12, 2019.

34. Michael Schuman, "China is Losing the Chip War," *Atlantic*, June 6, 2024.

35. Shvets (2020). p.182.

36. David Epstein, *The Range: Why Generalists Triumph in a Specialized World* (New York: Riverhead Books, 2019), pp.43–50.

37. Quoted in Andres Oppenheimer, *The Robots are Coming* (New York: Vintage Books, 2019), p.261.

38. Franklin Foer, *World Without Mind* (New York: Penguin Press, 2017); Andrew Keen, *How to Fix the Future* (New York: Atlantic Monthly Press, 2016).

39. 2024 Edelman Trust Barometer.

40. Richard Freeman, "Who Owns the Robots Rules the World," *IZA World of Labor*, 2015:5.

41. For example, Nick Romeo, *The Alternative: How to Build Just Economy* (New York: Public Affairs, 2024).

CHAPTER 11

1. Quoted in Neil Howe (2023), p.xi.
2. In a 2015 survey of Millennials, the US Congressional Office estimated that generational traits scored the highest at 53%, significantly ahead of other factors, such as income, and social class, or race.
3. "The Millennial Generation," *US Congressional Institute*, 2015.
4. "On the Cusp of Adulthood and Facing Uncertain Future," *Pew*, May 2020.
5. "Majorities of Adults See Decline of Union Membership as Bad for the US and Working people," *Pew*, March 12, 2024.
6. "Millennial Dialogue on Europe," *Foundation for European Progressive Studies*, 2018.
7. Deloitte, 2023 Gen Z and Millennial Survey.
8. Pew, May 2020.
9. Pew, 2019.
10. World Value Surveys (2010–14 wave).
11. Gallup, September 14, 2023.
12. Quoted in Howe (2013), p.8.
13. Indeed, as the US General Social Survey (1974–2021) illustrated, Millennials, as they age, are not becoming more socially conservative when compared to the ageing Baby Boomers and X generations at the same stage in their life. Refer John Burn-Murdoch, "Millennials Are Shattering the Oldest Rule in Politics," *Financial Times*, December 30, 2022.
14. Howe (2023), p.4.

CHAPTER 12

1. Drucker (1993), p.168.
2. John Gray, *The New Leviathans* (New York: Farrar, Straus and Giroux, 2023), p.4.
3. No man has done more to both defend the Bretton Woods system and replace it than Paul Volcker after he became convinced that the system as it existed in the 1950s–60s could no longer be salvaged. He was instrumental in what he described as "controlled disintegration of the world economy" by reconciling the conflicting desire for globalization with the strong political and popular need to control local and national destinies (Paul Volcker, "The Political Economy of the Dollar," *FRBNY Quarterly Review*, Winter 1978–79).
4. There is a growing field of study of issues as diverse as the disappearance of bank deposits and their replacement by CBDCs, the impact on lending and liquidity, and the ability of Central Banks to respond to economic fluctuations. David Andolfatto, "Assessing the Impact of Central Bank Digital Currency on Private Banks," *Fed St Louis*, December 2019; Jonathan Chiu, "Bank Market Power and Central Bank Digital Currency," *Bank of Canada*, June 2020; Villaverde, Sanchez et al., "Central Bank Currency: Central Bank for All," *Bank of Canada*, November 2020; Marcus Brunnermeier et al., "The Digitization of Money," *NBER*, August 2019; Agustin Carstens, "The Future of Money and Payment System," *BIS*, August 2019; Agustin Carstens, "Money in the Digital Age: What Role for Central Banks," *BIS*, February 2018; Marcus Brunnermeier, Harold James, and Landau, "The Digital Money," *BIS*, August 2019.
5. This point was wonderfully articulated in 1949 by Arthur Schlesinger, *The Vital Center* (originally published by The Riverside Press, 1949, republished by Transaction Publishers, 1997).

6. Jennifer Bendery, "GOP Sen. John Kennedy Freaks Out When Reminded He Used to be A Democrat," *HuffPost*, February 9, 2024.
7. Beverley Cage, "McCarthyism Was Never Defeated. Trumpism Won't be Either," *Washington Post*, December 4, 2020.
8. Michael Jensen and William Meckling, "Theory of the Firm: Managerial Behavior, Agency Costs and Ownership Structure," *Journal of Financial Economics*, 1976, vol.3, no.4, pp.305–360.
9. Rosa Luxemburg, "The Crisis of German Social Democracy," *The Junius Pamphlet*, 1915, p.6.
10. Streek (2015), p.47.
11. Shvets (2020), p.33.
12. Karl Marx, "Critique of the Gotha Program," 1875, www.marxists.org.
13. John Maynard Keynes, "Economic Possibilities for Our Grandchildren," in *Essays in Persuasion* (London: MacMillan Press, 1931).
14. Drucker (1993), pp.4–6.
15. Wonderfully described by David Weil in *Fissured Workplace: Why Work Became So Bad For So Many* (Cambridge: Harvard University, 2014); Mary L. Gray and Siddharth Suri, *Ghost Work* (Boston: Houghton Mifflin Harcourt, 2019); and David Graber, *Bullshit Jobs* (London: Allen Lane, 2018).
16. Yanis, Varoufakis, *Technofeudalism: What killed Capitalism* (London: Melville House, 2024).
17. Frase (2016), p.8.
18. Robert Constanza, "Four Visions of the Century Ahead: Will it be Star Trek, Ecotopia, Big Government or Mad Max," *The Futurist*, February 2019, pp.23–28.
19. Shvets (2020).
20. Edward Luce, "Wall Street's Bargain with Trump," *Financial Times*, January 24, 2024.

EPILOGUE
1. Becker (1941), p.16.
2. For example, Francis Fukuyama, *The End of History* (New York: Avon Books, 1992).
3. Polybius, *The Complete Histories* (Digireads.com Publishing, 2014).
4. On the importance of corruption see, John Joseph Wallis, "The Concept of Systemic Corruption in American History," *NBER*, March 2006, pp.23–60.
5. First Inaugural Address of Franklin D. Roosevelt, Saturday, March 4, 1933.
6. Refer to extensive discussion in Stiglitz (2024), p.xiii.

About the Author

Viktor Shvets is a Global Strategist at Macquarie Capital. He is the author of *The Great Rupture: Three Empires, Four Turning Points and the Future of Humanity*, published in 2020. In his almost four-decades-long investment banking career, he worked in Sydney, Melbourne, Hong Kong, London, New York, and Moscow at a number of global investment banks, such as Citibank, Baring Securities, Deutsche Bank, DLJ, and Lehman Brothers. Over the years, he has been a highly rated equity analyst across various disciplines and is recognized as one of the more innovative market strategists, working on the intersection between finance, technology, politics and history. He is a prolific writer on key global trends and is a frequent commentator on CNBC, Bloomberg and other media outlets. Viktor was born in Kyiv, which at the time was the capital of the Soviet Ukraine. He attended Kyiv University of Trade before immigrating to Australia, where he completed Bachelor of Economics degree from the University of Sydney and Master of Commerce degree from the University of New South Wales. He is married with two sons and currently resides in New York.

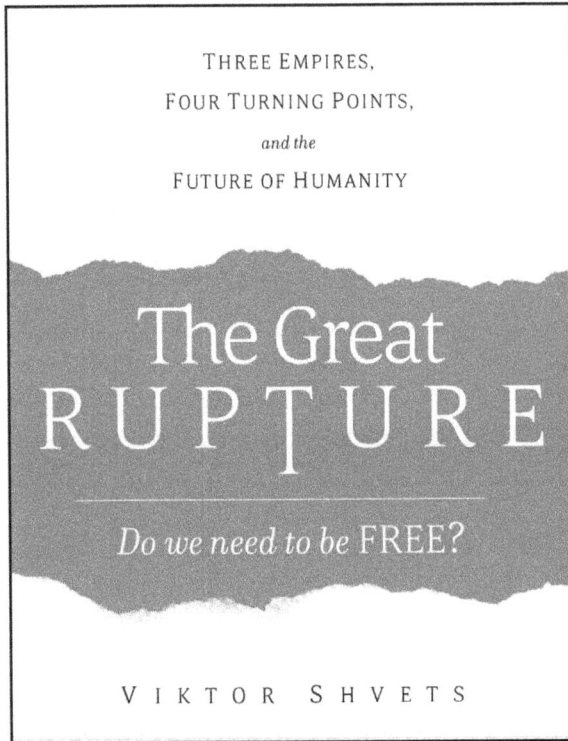

.